THE ODER-NEISSE LINE

Recent Titles in
Contributions to the Study of World History

By the Sword and the Cross: The Historical Revolution of the Catholic World Monarchy in Spain and the New World, 1492–1825
Charles A. Truxillo

Passion, Politics, and Philosophie: Rediscovering J.-P. Brissot
Leonore Loft

Sanctions and Honorary Whites: Diplomatic Policies and Economic Realities in Relations Between Japan and South Africa
Masako Osada

Personal Policy Making: Canada's Role in the Adoption of the Palestine Partition Resolution
Eliezer Tauber

One King, One Law, Three Faiths: Religion and the Rise of Absolutism in Seventeenth-Century Metz
Patricia Behre Miskimin

South Sea Maidens: Western Fantasy and Sexual Politics in the South Pacific
Michael Sturma

A History of the French Anarchist Movement, 1917–1945
David Berry

Security and Progress: Lord Salisbury at the India Office
Paul R. Brumpton

Exploring Nationalisms of China: Themes and Conflicts
C. X. George Wei and Xiaoyuan Liu, editors

Tolerance, Suspicion, and Hostility: Changing U.S. Attitudes toward the Japanese Communist Movement, 1944–1947
Henry Oinas-Kukkonen

Churchill's Guests: Britain and the Belgian Exiles during World War II
Robert W. Allen

Securing American Independence: John Jay and the French Alliance
Frank W. Brecher

THE ODER-NEISSE LINE

The United States, Poland, and Germany in the Cold War

Debra J. Allen

Contributions to the Study of World History, Number 103

Westport, Connecticut
London

Library of Congress Cataloging-in-Publication Data

Allen, Debra J., 1957–
The Oder-Neisse line : the United States, Poland, and Germany in the Cold War / Debra J. Allen.
p. cm.—(Contributions to the study of world history, ISSN 0885–9159 ; no. 103)
Includes bibliographical references and index.
ISBN 0–313–32359–3 (alk. paper)
1. Oder-Neisse Line (Germany and Poland). 2. United States—Foreign relations—Poland. 3. Poland—Foreign relations—United States. 4. United States—Foreign relations—1945–1989. 5. Cold War. I. Title. II. Series.
DK4600.O3385 A44 2003
327.730438′09′045—dc21 2002028758

British Library Cataloguing in Publication Data is available.

Library of Congress Catalog Card Number: 2002028758
ISBN: 0–313–32359–3
ISSN: 0885–9159

First published in 2003

Praeger Publishers, 88 Post Road West, Westport, CT 06881
An imprint of Greenwood Publishing Group, Inc.
www.praeger.com

Printed in the United States of America

The paper used in this book complies with the Permanent Paper Standard issued by the National Information Standards Organization (Z39.48–1984).

10 9 8 7 6 5 4 3 2 1

This book is dedicated to the memory of my sister
who kept me focused on this project.

Contents

Introduction

Poland's geographic and political situation in 1939 allowed the German and Soviet armies a relatively easy victory over the twenty-year-old Polish Republic, which emerged from the war suffering tremendous destruction of land and people. The Poland of 1945 had shorter, more defensible borders that had been shifted approximately 150 miles westward as a result of decisions made at wartime conferences. The eastern border with the Soviet Union had been agreed upon at the Yalta Conference and approximated the same line established in the 1939 Molotov–Ribbentrop Pact prior to the invasion. The western border lay along a line following the Oder and Neisse Rivers that was instituted by Allied agreement at the Potsdam Conference in July and August 1945. Varying interpretations of this agreement regarding Poland's western border soon surfaced, however. The Potsdam Accord stated that Poland's administration of the area was provisional and that Germany's borders would be finalized at a peace conference, leaving open the possibility that Poland's western border could be changed in Germany's favor. The Accord, however, also acknowledged the transfer of Germans from the area that would total in the millions, thereby suggesting that Polish control of the land east of the Oder–Neisse would be permanent. These apparent contradictions served to heighten the growing tensions between the United States and the Soviet Union as the Polish government came under the control of Soviet-trained communists, and the United States tried to formulate policies to deal with the situation. As East and West drew further apart in the decades following World War II, hope for a mutually satisfactory settlement of the border issue seemed to evaporate. Although the Polish and German governments signed a treaty in 1970 acknowledging the border, the United States withheld formal recognition of the Oder–Neisse until the revolutionary changes of 1989 and 1990, when the World War II Allies formally approved a peace treaty with Germany within its existing borders.

This study offers a reexamination of the relationship between Washington and Warsaw in the postwar years by focusing on the controversy surrounding U.S. recognition of the Oder–Neisse Line, and analyzes the perceptions of states and individuals regarding an issue that was tangled in the web of Cold War politics. This examination of U.S. policy on the border reveals that the issue added to the tensions between Washington and Moscow, negatively affected relations between the United States and Poland, and was a point of contention between the United States and West Germany. In addition, it provides evidence of the interaction of domestic, ethnic politics and foreign policy in the United States and sheds light on the bureaucratic nature of U.S. foreign policy making in the forty-five years of the Cold War.

The issue is studied chronologically to emphasize the conflicting pressures confronting each postwar presidential administration as well as the varying perceptions of the border issue held by State Department, military, intelligence, and National Security officials. Almost immediately after the war, Poland was noted as a "test case" for American policies in East Central Europe. This unenviable position resulted from a combination of factors, including U.S. relations with the Soviet Union and American perceptions of the Soviet Union's goals and strengths, Poland's geographic position, and the Polish people's centuries-long hatred and distrust of Russia and Germany, which were intensified by their wartime experiences, Warsaw's periodic distancing from Moscow's control of its domestic policies, and the existence of a large and vocal Polish immigrant community in the United States.[1] These factors made it extremely difficult for the State Department to handle an issue as controversial as one involving the potential adjustment of territory and people in a way that satisfied all, or sometimes any, of the interested parties. At the root of the difficulties between Washington and Warsaw was the tense relationship between the United States and the Soviet Union stemming from ideological, economic, and traditional differences. American policymakers were fully aware that Washington's refusal to recognize the line could and did play to Moscow's advantage. For a decade following the war, the Soviets could and certainly did claim that they were the sole defenders of Poland's territorial integrity. Many high-level American policymakers in the 1940s and 1950s, however, refused publicly to recognize the Oder–Neisse Line since they anticipated that Moscow would force the Poles to return part of the territory to the Germans. These American officials did not want to be precipitous either in approving Polish control of the area or in supporting German claims to the land only to have the Soviets force a change in the situation that would leave the United States looking and sounding powerless on the European continent.

This uncertainty resulted partly from the Potsdam Agreement, which had left open many questions but made clear that, as one of the Allied victors, the United States would play a major role in European affairs after World War II. The United States entered into an ancient cycle of suspicion and hatred among Poland, Germany, and the Soviet Union. Poland's violent history is shown in the wars of conquest for the land between the Elbe and Oder Rivers by Germanic and Slavic tribes that gave way to battles between the Teutonic Knights, Piast and Jagiellonian Catholic Poles, and Mongols. When the Polish state was created and gained power, the rulers of Germany and Russia felt threatened and collaborated to destroy it. When they had succeeded, they fought each other for control of the continent.[2] In the eighteenth century Poland's neighbors succeeded in dividing the country among the rulers of Prussia, Austria, and Russia. Although Polish nationalism remained vibrant, the Polish state ceased to exist until the German and Russian defeat in World War I, when the creation of an independent Poland was listed as one of Wilson's Fourteen Points and as part of the Treaty of Versailles. The American Senate's rejection of the League of Nations as part of the Treaty of Versailles, however, meant that the United States was not bound to intervene in Polish affairs. The newly created Polish and German Republics were unable to overcome internal and external difficulties in the 1920s and 1930s, and in 1939 Nazi Germany and Soviet Russia jointly agreed to destroy Poland again. As American leaders entered World War II, they were determined not to make what they perceived as the same mistakes made after World War I. Thus, wartime meetings, conferences, and declarations firmly tied the United States to Europe's postwar situation, including its ethnic and ideological hatreds and territorial, political, and economic uncertainties.

As the Polish government in Warsaw came increasingly under the control of Moscow-trained communists, Washington grew more reluctant to acquiesce to the demands and desires of that government largely out of the belief that to do so would be tantamount to appeasing the Soviet Union. American policymakers could not, however, simply ignore Poland because they were not fully convinced that Poland was always securely in the Soviet orbit and because they were repeatedly made aware of a large and vocal Polish American constituency. U.S. officials were constantly assessing the strength of the bond between Warsaw and Moscow since there were no "natural" ties between the Poles and Russians beyond their Slavic ancestry; American diplomats were aware of traditional Polish–Russian hostility that had been intensified by wartime events such as the Katyn Massacre and the Warsaw Uprising. The State Department knew that the Red Army and the secret police in Poland allowed little or no dissent from Moscow's view of communism's role in society and in the world order; but American officials often received mixed signals about the strength or recklessness of Polish nationalism, which might lead the Poles to reject their communist government if the United States openly supported Poland. The establishment of Poland's border along the Oder and Neisse Rivers only added to this uncertain mix.

In formal discussions Polish representatives argued that the Potsdam Agreement had confirmed the area as belonging to Poland; in private discussions, however, some of these same representatives occasionally urged

Washington's recognition of the Oder–Neisse Line in order to loosen Moscow's stranglehold over Warsaw. Such pleas suggested that the artificial bond between Moscow and Warsaw could be broken if it meant a guarantee of Poland's national security by the West's recognition of the Oder–Neisse Line. In addition to receiving such hints about possible changes in Poland's situation, American policymakers, because of Washington's insistence on an active, internationalist foreign policy, could not just dismiss Poland as a smaller power that suffered at the whim of the big powers like Germany and Russia. In addition, friendship ties between Poles and Americans were long-standing and based on common, though somewhat vague, goals of freedom, democracy, and self-determination. During the war these ideals were expressed in the Atlantic Charter and the Yalta Agreement's Declaration on Liberated Europe. In spite of these ties, Washington also had to confront the reality of the situation. The Soviets desired a buffer zone of friendly states between the Soviet Union and Germany, most importantly in Poland. The United States had few material interests in the area, and Washington recognized that the American people, in spite of popular rhetoric about freedom and self-determination, would not willingly fight a war to save East Central Europe from Soviet domination. Thus, even as the dominant superpower after the war, the United States felt its maneuverability limited.

Washington's reluctance to take a proactive role in the border issue meant that the United States often found itself reacting to Polish and Soviet initiatives. U.S. representatives in Poland closely watched press reports, analyzed official pronouncements, and tried to talk with Poles in an attempt to determine Warsaw's position on the border issue and the strength of the belief that Moscow would support that position. They soon learned that the border question was one of the few issues in which the Polish people supported the government, basically out of a fear of German aggression and revanchism. While American officials knew that the Warsaw government played on this fear to strengthen its hold on the people, they also knew that the Poles' distrust of Germany was genuine.

This fear further limited Washington's maneuverability once Germany became pivotal to U.S. and Soviet foreign policy in Europe. Rehabilitation soon replaced punishment as the goal of both the United States and the Soviet Union for their "client" German states. Although Poland shared no border with West Germany, Washington's refusal to recognize the East German regime meant that the United States looked to Bonn for the direction of German foreign policy. Neither the United States nor the Soviet Union would agree to treaty terms for a united Germany since they feared that, if reunification were allowed, control of East or West Germany would be lost and the power equilibrium on the continent drastically shifted. The U.S. government felt that it needed West Germany as a vital part of the Western defense system against potential Soviet aggression. Therefore, American policymakers did not want to alienate the Bonn government by publicly supporting Poland's claim to the Oder–Neisse Line.

Also, considering the heightened tensions between the Soviet Union and the United States, few in Washington wanted to support a communist government in Warsaw over a Western-type democratic government in Bonn.

One element underlying Washington's uncertainty about the border issue was a lack of clarity about the strength of nationalism, both among the Poles, as discussed earlier, and among the German "expellees," those removed from the area controlled by Poland according to the Potsdam Accord. Washington remained reluctant to push Bonn to strive for an accord with Warsaw out of concern that such pressure would drive West Germany into a pro-Soviet or neutral position. At the same time, Washington did not want to be forced into promoting publicly the 1937 German borders claimed by West German leaders, incorporating lands provisionally administered by Poland according to the Potsdam Agreement. American representatives in West Germany, therefore, carefully monitored the activities of the expellees. As these expellees organized into a political party and gained strength in mainstream West German parties, the State Department speculated about the West German government's ability to withstand this nationalist pressure to try to regain the land east of the Oder and Neisse Rivers. There was a suspicion almost always present in Washington that Bonn and Moscow might forge some kind of deal over the border, perhaps in exchange for a united, neutralized Germany that in American eyes was tantamount to a Sovietized Germany. Rumors persisted throughout the late 1940s and into the 1950s that a deal was being struck—either in the form of joint control of the area or the outright removal of the land from Poland's control by the Soviet Union. Some of the high-level policymakers in the State Department after World War II had served in foreign service posts in Berlin and Moscow when the Nazi–Soviet Pact of 1939 was made public. Even though these men did not perceive the Federal Republic in the same light as the Third Reich, there was an ever-present concern in the State Department that to promote the cause of reunification, West German leaders might make some type of deal with the Soviets.

As the United States and West Germany drew apart in the 1960s largely over Bonn's dissatisfaction with Washington's perceived acceptance of the status quo in Europe, including the division of Germany, the Oder–Neisse border issue again gained prominence as an increasing number of voices in West Germany and the United States promoted Western recognition of the line as an important step toward improved East–West relations. Washington let Bonn take the lead in easing tensions with Warsaw; in 1970 Bonn signed treaties with Moscow and Warsaw accepting the Oder–Neisse Line as the established border. The United States expressed satisfaction with these treaties and in 1975 signed the Helsinki Accord recognizing Europe's postwar borders. Washington continued to maintain, however, that, as one of the Four Power Allies, the United States had final say in determining Germany's borders. This ambiguous situation continued until 1989, when the overthrow of the communist governments in Central Europe cleared the way for the wartime

Allies to establish a unified Germany and to settle outstanding matters such as Germany's borders. In September 1990 the Allies signed away their remaining rights to control Germany; two months later Germany and Poland formally signed a treaty guaranteeing the Oder–Neisse border.

Throughout these years Washington felt that it could not formally recognize the line prior to a peace conference since formal recognition would contradict the stance that the United States had adamantly held since 1945, might anger an important European ally, and would offer the Soviets justification for abrogating provisions of the Potsdam agreement which they found irksome. On the other hand, Washington felt that it could not continue to promote a plan that would have returned part of the western lands to Germany since to do so would threaten the goodwill existing between the Polish people and the United States and could cause domestic difficulties. Washington perceived these Allied differences and East–West tensions during the Cold War as limiting American maneuverability on the border issue. Further complicating the matter were divisions within the foreign policy bureaucracy about the proper solution to the border problem. A basic difference persisted for decades in the views presented by officials in the Warsaw Embassy, American representatives in Bonn, and high-level officials in the State Department. American officials in Poland generally supported Western recognition of the border, probably because of their closeness to the situation, which allowed them to perceive the importance of this territory to Poland and to the Polish people who maintained a strongly pro-American attitude in the postwar years. Although the American officials in Warsaw constantly reported on the Polish view of the border issue and reiterated the strength of Polish friendship for the United States, Washington continued to view U.S.–Polish relations as secondary to U.S.–Soviet relations. Thus, the desires of the Polish people for Western support had less importance in Washington than how any U.S. action might be perceived in Moscow, largely because of Cold War perceptions that divided the world into "us against them."

Another division was evident in the thinking of State Department officials in Washington. Numerous internal memoranda by various high-level officials suggested proposals for U.S. action on the border, sometimes in Germany's favor and sometimes in Poland's. Various offices in the State Department followed up these suggestions by investigating their viability for presentation at international conferences such as the 1947 Council of Foreign Ministers meetings and the 1960 summit. That nothing came of these proposals again shows how the border issue was subsumed by relations between the two superpowers. In 1947 American representatives chose not push the issue when confronted with Soviet objections; the 1960 summit was canceled after Moscow relayed news of the capture of a U-2 spy plane.

This divergence of views within the State Department was matched by divisions in Congress that played an important role in the American foreign policy process beyond its constitutionally mandated role, by serving as a link between the foreign policy establishment and the public. Although various members of the State Department periodically objected to such "interference," the department recognized such a role and took pains to respond to congressmen's requests for information on the border in both written correspondence and in committee hearings. In the U.S. Congress members who were of Polish ancestry, who had large Polish American constituencies, or who simply had an interest in the border issue advocated on the floor of the House or Senate or in committee hearings that the United States recognize the border. While these actions often received favorable publicity in the ethnic (and sometimes in the mainstream) press, these congressmen did not have the support of the full House or Senate to push through proposals for changing America's position on the border.

For the Executive Office to continue advocating a revision of the border in Germany's favor, it would have to be willing to risk alienating these members of Congress and their Polish American constituents, who represented a potentially large voting bloc. For the members and leaders of the Polish American Congress, the largest Polish American organization, the goal was to gain American recognition of the Oder–Neisse Line in order to loosen the tie between Moscow and Warsaw and to keep viable Poland's economy, strengthened by the addition of the industrial, mineral, and agricultural benefits of the western territories. They argued also that Poland should have some type of compensation from Germany for the suffering inflicted during the war. If Germany's weakness meant Poland's strength, they believed, that was all the better, especially in light of West Germany's rapid recovery, which was aided by the United States.

The Polish American community was almost unanimous on this point after 1945, irrespective of political allegiance. This unanimity resulted in some peculiar and ironic alignments where anti-Soviet Polish Americans and Polish exiles offered some of the same reasons and justifications for maintaining the border on the Oder–Neisse Line as were offered by the small, but vocal, left-wing Polish American community and by representatives of the Warsaw regime. Although neither the Democrats nor Republicans placed the border issue on their national platforms as requested by the Polish American Congress, presidential and congressional candidates were unwilling to risk the loss of "the Polish vote" by continually promoting a revision of the border in Germany's favor.[3] In light of the geopolitical, economic, and ideological situation of East Central Europe, neither did a majority of these national candidates publicly promote recognition of the line and risk losing the support of West Germany. While Polish Americans did not succeed in their effort to persuade Washington to recognize the line prior to a peace conference, their efforts combined with the requests of the Polish government to keep the issue alive and forced both the executive and legislative branches of the government to deal with it repeatedly in the decades after World War II. This focusing of the border issue thus represented the attainment of one of the primary goals of such ethnic lobbying groups.

On the domestic level, the Oder–Neisse issue offers insight into the American foreign policy process by showing how the White House and State Department tried to handle a controversial and complex issue that involved a great deal of interaction between the Washington foreign policy establishment and elements of the public. By tracing the border issue over time and by examining the treatment accorded the various Polish American groups, Polish exiles, members of the U.S. Congress, and American foreign policy scholars, we have a clearer understanding of the pressures that the White House and State Department faced domestically in formulating, prioritizing, and implementing foreign policy.

Although American policy toward the Oder-Neisse line did not deviate from the stance established at Potsdam in 1945, the way that Washington handled the issue did change. Washington's refusal to change its border policy resulted from U.S. reluctance to be caught in the embarrassing and perhaps dangerous position of promoting a settlement of the border issue only to have the Germans, Poles, or Soviets countermand that position with force or through negotiations. The State Department could not just ignore the Oder–Neisse Line issue, however, as it faced a number of competing pressures in trying to deal with the problem within the parameters established in the Potsdam Agreement, always keeping in mind that the question of Poland's western border had a great impact on international relations as well as potential domestic political repercussions.

That American foreign policy makers failed to develop a satisfactory solution to the border problem suggests that there were a number of obstacles to finding such a solution. The overriding element was the Cold War mentality that obstructed Washington from officially promoting innovative policy positions that could be misconstrued as acquiescence to the Soviet Union's position. In spite of the various proposals presented within the State Department for dealing with the border issue, Washington decision makers expressed concern that the Soviet Union would either perceive American acceptance of the border as appeasement or would charge that American recognition of the line prior to a peace conference violated the provisions of the Potsdam Agreement and would then try to justify its rejection of other provisions dealing with Germany and Berlin. The numerous hints, suggestions, and outright statements from Polish officials that U.S. recognition of the border would give Warsaw leverage with Moscow could not outweigh this factor for American policymakers.

By adhering strictly to the letter rather than the spirit of the Potsdam Protocol, American policymakers could publicly claim that their hands were tied until the Allies reached agreement on Germany. Poles and Soviets used this inactivity to their advantage by expelling the Germans, settling the area with Poles, and developing the region, thereby strengthening their claims to the area as vital to Poland's survival. In addition, by the 1960s they could and did echo the German claim of *Heimatrecht*, that the millions of Poles in the western territories had a right to their homeland, their place of birth.

Other factors contributing to the State Department's seeming inertia on the border were fresh memories of the horrors of World War II and the chaos of the postwar situation in which Washington tried to determine who were America's friends and enemies, often based on conflicting reports from the field. American policymakers differentiated between the unfriendly Warsaw regime and the pro-American Polish people and thus justified, for example, economic aid to Poland as helping the population only until such aid appeared to be propping up the oppressive government at the expense of the people. When West Germany became an ally and friend, however, Bonn politicians could claim that a true friend and ally would support West Germans' "right" to return to the "lost provinces" in order to fulfill the ideal of self-determination, even though those politicians privately acknowledged the loss of the area to Poland. This determination of West Germany as America's friend allowed Bonn politicians further to limit American maneuverability on the border question by claiming that the protest votes of millions of expellees were at stake. While the State Department could not appear to push West Germany into an unpopular political action such as accepting the Oder–Neisse Line as the boundary, neither could it support West Germany's claim to Germany's 1937 borders and risk reviving the spirit of Lebensraum. Bonn was able to stalemate Washington's action by maintaining the specter of an "expellee vote" long after the expellees had been assimilated into mainstream politics and society largely by citing the protests of the few vocal leaders of the expellee organizations.

However, Washington itself was not above using this practice of trying to draw attention away from a controversial issue by focusing on popular programs. For example, in the 1950s the question of economic aid to Poland, Johnson's "bridge-building" program in the 1960s, and the Solidarity movement of the 1980s allowed Washington to downplay its official policy of nonrecognition of the Oder–Neisse border and focus instead on matters that appealed to Polish Americans and to the population at large with claims of sustaining humanitarianism and human rights. The final factor affecting the handling of the issue domestically was the existence of a large, vocal Polish American community with potential voting strength in key electoral states. While members of Congress, usually Polish Americans, could publicly proclaim themselves in favor of various Polish American organizations' proposals supporting U.S. recognition of the line, presidential candidates seeking a "national base of support" refused to adhere to what might be considered an "ethnic" demand. This left State Department officials trying to placate members of these Polish American organizations with assurances that Poland's welfare would be taken into account when the United States finalized decisions on Germany's borders. Such assurances were taken as just more rhetoric in light of Washington's support for the reconstruction and remilitarization of West Germany.

Thus, in formulating and acting on its policy toward the Oder–Neisse Line, Washington was concerned with its uncertain relations with Poland, West Germany, and the Soviet Union as well as with a large group of Polish Americans who represented substantial voting strength. It is crucial to remember that the State Department had to address myriad concerns with Poland over the forty-five years of the Cold War. This study concentrates on only one of those issues and peels away the layers of diplomatic action to show how American diplomats, statesmen, congressmen, and Polish American organizations dealt with the boundary issue over time in order to face the changing international and domestic political situation.

NOTES

1. John C. Campbell, *American Policy toward Communist Eastern Europe: The Choices Ahead* (Minneapolis: University of Minnesota Press, 1965), 9. Yugoslavia was also considered an exception to U.S. policy in Eastern Europe after Tito's split with Moscow.

2. John Wheeler-Bennett, foreword to Gerald Freund, *Unholy Alliance: Russian–German Relations from the Treaty of Brest–Litovsk to the Treaty of Berlin* (London: Chatto and Windus, 1957); W. W. Kulski, *Germany and Poland: From War to Peaceful Relations* (Syracuse, NY: Syracuse University Press, 1976), introduction; Piotr Wandycz, *The United States and Poland* (Cambridge: Harvard University Press, 1980), Chapter 1; Norman Davies, *Heart of Europe: A Short History of Poland* (Oxford: Oxford University Press, 1986).

3. The voting strength of the Polish American community is open to debate. See Stephen Garrett, *From Potsdam to Poland: American Policy toward Eastern Europe* (New York: Praeger, 1986); Bennett Kovrig, *The Myth of Liberation: East-Central Europe in U.S. Diplomacy and Politics since 1941* (Baltimore: Johns Hopkins University Press, 1973); Louis L. Gerson, *The Hyphenate in Recent American Politics and Diplomacy* (Lawrence: University of Kansas Press, 1964).

1 The Border Issue at the Wartime Conferences

The attack on Poland by German and Soviet troops in September 1939 after the conclusion of the Molotov–Ribbentrop Pact resulted in the destruction of the Polish Republic initiated at Versailles in 1919. The victors signed a friendship treaty on 28 September 1939 dividing Poland's lands and people. More than half of prewar Poland, including the predominantly Polish area of Białystok and the city of Lwów, was put under Soviet control. Of the 13 million inhabitants of this area, 5 million were ethnic Poles, most of whom were transported to the German-controlled areas or to Soviet labor camps. The Germans annexed the land and people of western Poland into the "General Government" and moved swiftly to apply a "thin German veneer" to the area that was less than 6 percent native German by renaming towns and cities and by forcing Baltic Germans to settle the area.[1]

As the German and Soviet invasions began, the Polish government fled to Romania, France, and finally England, trying to govern the country while in exile. When the United States and the Soviet Union joined with Great Britain in the "Grand Alliance," the London-based Polish Government-in-Exile reluctantly agreed to establish diplomatic relations with Moscow as a necessary evil to defeat the common enemy, Germany. This tense relationship ended in 1943, when the Soviet Union chose to interpret the Polish government's call for an investigation into the Katyn massacre as an accusation of Soviet culpability and severed relations with the Polish government in London. The diplomatic situation among the Allies was further complicated when in 1944 the Soviets helped establish in Lublin a rival Polish government comprising communists who disagreed with many of the postwar goals of the London government. Poland's postwar borders and the composition of the new Polish government thus provided two of the most difficult and interrelated diplomatic questions for the Allies as they tried to defeat the Axis and to negotiate a postwar world order during World War II. President Roosevelt, while publicly emphasizing traditional ties of American–Polish friendship and goodwill, told British Foreign

Secretary Anthony Eden in March 1943 that the Big Three would decide Poland's fate and that he "did not intend to bargain with the Poles."[2] While the president did not want to see the Alliance weakened because of these matters, he found that could not just ignore the Polish issue because the Polish government in London kept pressing him to deal with the question of Poland's postwar territory.[3] General Wladysław Sikorski, prime minister of Poland, personally submitted a memorandum to Roosevelt in December 1942 outlining his vision of postwar Poland. Sikorski and other representatives of the London government, after the general's death in 1943, favored the prewar border in the east and a western border that incorporated German land including East Prussia, part of Silesia, and part of Western Pomerania.[4] Roosevelt refused to commit the United States to a specified Polish border; he responded vaguely to the Poles that the United States favored an independent Poland.[5] By the spring of 1943, however, he had come to accept the idea of an eastern border along the Curzon Line, which ran slightly east of the line established by the Molotov--Ribbentrop Pact, and a western border that would incorporate East Prussia and Silesia from Germany.[6] Although Roosevelt viewed these concessions as necessary to hold the Alliance together, neither he nor his advisers publicly announced the territorial changes that they favored since doing so would open the administration to domestic criticism.

They were also silent on this issue whenever possible in international negotiations. President Roosevelt and Secretary of State Hull wished to avoid discussion of controversial questions about Poland in talks with the Soviets out of the desperate need to keep the Grand Alliance together.[7] Sikorski and other representatives of the London Polish government continued talks with the Allies, mostly concerning Poland's eastern border. Roosevelt wanted the British to take the initiative in negotiating Polish–Soviet relations, but told his foreign policy advisers that he would appeal to Stalin when they met in the fall of 1943 to accept the Curzon Line in the east with the return to Poland of the oil-rich area around Lwów.[8] At the Moscow Conference of Foreign Ministers in October 1943, the Polish question was handled in a "somewhat perfunctory way that the Russians could only interpret as indicative of little real interest on the part of the United States and Britain in Polish affairs."[9] Secretary Hull wrote later that he had no intention at the Moscow Conference of opening the boundary issue, a "Pandora's box of infinite trouble."[10] The secretary failed to appreciate the Polish government's concern over the West's seeming lack of interest in Polish affairs and was dismayed by the antagonism expressed in the Polish American press after his return.[11]

The Polish ambassador to the United States, Jan Ciechanowski, gave Hull a memorandum explaining that the Polish government, if it expected to maintain authority, could not give up its eastern territories even if Poland received compensation in the west. Hull continued to display a lack of finesse when he delivered this information to the president along with the news that the Department of State was trying to convince the Poles "that they should take a calmer outlook and not prejudice their case by undue public agitation regarding our policies."[12] In spite of such attempts to "calm" the Poles, the first formal Allied discussion at the Tehran Conference in December 1943 saw the Polish government "in a panic over what Roosevelt might do."[13] This panic proved justified.

THE TEHRAN CONFERENCE

Although the official record of the Tehran Conference is rather limited, evidence shows that this conference laid the groundwork for Poland's future loss of territory to the Soviet Union and the acquisition of land from Germany.[14] Churchill raised the Polish issue when he told Stalin at a dinner meeting on 28 November 1943 that he would like to discuss the Polish problem so that he could take a proposal back to the Polish government in London. After Roosevelt retired for the evening, Churchill and Stalin began a discussion that was to have a profound impact on Poland's future. The prime minister told Stalin that he would like to see a quid pro quo where Poles would cede eastern lands to the Soviets and receive compensatory land in the west from the Germans.[15] Demonstrating with three matchsticks, Churchill stated that he envisioned Poland moving westward, "like soldiers taking two steps left close."[16] In a meeting with Stalin on 1 December 1943, Roosevelt told Stalin that, while he personally agreed with him on the need to restore Poland and that he would like to see the eastern border moved west and the western border moved westward as far as the Oder River, he was unable to commit himself publicly because of the domestic political constraints of his position. The president noted that he had to consider a constituency of 6 – 7 million Americans of Polish descent. Stalin assured the president that he understood the situation, and he and Churchill, with Roosevelt's silent acquiescence, proceeded to settle Poland's territorial fate.[17]

At a tripartite meeting a few hours later, Churchill suggested that Poland, in return for areas given to the Soviet Union in the east, receive "'equal compensation'" in the west, including East Prussia and a frontier on the Oder. Stalin agreed that, if the Soviets got northern East Prussia (including Tilst and Königsberg), he could accept the Curzon Line and "Churchill's formula about Poland."[18] This solution, the Soviet premier noted, would give the Soviets an ice-free port and a well-deserved piece of Germany. In return for this "most peculiar 'compromise,'" the Soviets conceded the slightly more advantageous Molotov–Ribbentrop Line.[19] Churchill agreed that he would take this proposal back to the London Poles as the best offer that they could expect.[20] Roosevelt, true to his earlier word to Stalin, said very little at this session on Poland.

The communiqué released after the conference ended on 2 December reiterated the Allies' determination to defeat Germany and to formulate an "enduring peace" through international cooperation.[21] No formal written statement on the Allied position concerning Poland's border was included, but scholars who analyzed the few records of the conference later claimed that the Soviets had good reason to assume that Roosevelt had given his consent to the Curzon Line.[22] Even Herbert Feis, the author of the "official" history of U.S. wartime diplomacy, while doubting that Roosevelt actually intended to acquiesce to any specific Polish borders, conceded, "By sidestepping the question at Tehran as he did, Roosevelt left Churchill and Stalin unhindered to continue their attempt to draw frontiers for the new Poland."[23]

For the public, the results of the conference were conjectural at best. The press reports immediately following the Tehran Conference reveal that the exact nature of the discussions between the Allied leaders remained a secret; most of the speculation concerned Poland's eastern border.[24] In a *New York Times* article of 26 December 1943, Edwin James reported on the fears in "most Polish quarters" that the Soviet Union would demand a large part of prewar Poland because, he wrote, in conferences with the Russians, Roosevelt and Churchill had "not discussed Russian frontiers."[25] An editorial in the *Christian Science Monitor* reported that the Big Three had met and agreed to act together, but "that is all they are telling."[26] A *New York Times* editorial a few days later could only have increased the fears of Polish Americans. The editor, while recognizing America's traditional ties of friendship and admiration for Poland, argued that the Soviets had a case for acquiring a large part of prewar eastern Poland to ensure secure borders.[27]

Even in Congress, the specifics of the declaration were not discussed; and leaders based their opinions on the principles that were espoused. Various senators and representatives registered approval of the Tehran Declaration's commitment to the defeat of the Axis and to continued international cooperation.[28] Representative Thomas Gordon (D-IL), one of the Polish American champions of Polish causes in the House, read into the *Congressional Record* Polish Premier Stanisław Mikołajczyk's qualified approval of the declaration. Mikołajczyk hoped that the declaration's specific references to the defeat of Germany and the discussion of territorial integrity reflected a more general recognition that true peace could be built only on universal guarantees of territorial integrity.[29]

The U.S. government held to this silent policy of noninvolvement in Poland's affairs until the Yalta Conference of February 1945, when Roosevelt, Stalin, and Churchill directly confronted two of the biggest problems of the Polish question: the postwar boundaries and the composition of the government. In the advent of this wartime conference at Yalta in February 1945, Mikołajczyk and many Polish Americans took a very vocal position on these issues. Prior to this meeting, the leaders of Poland's Government-in-Exile tried to keep the border issue before Roosevelt, who wanted to continue putting off this divisive problem in order to maintain the Allied coalition.[30] After several requests for a meeting, Roosevelt finally agreed to meet with Mikołajczyk in June 1944. This meeting again shows Roosevelt's lack of candor in dealing with the Polish issue. He told the Polish leader that Stalin might not insist on the Curzon Line if friendly relations could be established between Poland and the Soviet Union. According to Roosevelt, such friendly relations could be facilitated by Polish concessions regarding the composition of the postwar government. Without admitting that he had even unofficially conceded the Curzon Line at Tehran, Roosevelt told Mikołajczyk that there was a good chance that the Poles would be able to retain Lwów and the surrounding oil fields and in the west would get East Prussia and Silesia. In response to the Polish premier's point that Stalin had already claimed Koenigsberg in East Prussia for the Soviets, Roosevelt hedged by stating that such a claim was probably not final. Mikołajczyk agreed with the president that Poland should receive Silesia since the inhabitants were largely Polish and since the Germans had used the resources of the area to fuel their war machine in the past. He made this claim, however, without specifying exactly which line he favored in the west, stating only that Poland should not have a western border that would incorporate a large, discontented German minority.[31]

Mikołajczyk continued to try to get a Western Allied commitment to Poland's territorial integrity, but with no success. In October Churchill urged him to accept the Curzon Line in the east and to receive compensation in the west.[32] Roosevelt vaguely agreed to Churchill's proposal in a carefully worded letter to Mikołajczyk on 17 November 1944. He stated that, while the United States, "'in accordance with its traditional policy,'" could not specify territorial frontiers, it would offer no objections if "mutual agreement on this subject . . . is reached between the Polish, Soviet, and British Governments." Roosevelt also showed his willingness to leave the settlement of the issue of population transfers up to the Poles: "If the Polish Government and people desire in connection with the new frontiers of the Polish State to bring about the transfer to and from the territory of Poland of national minorities, the United States Government will raise no objections and as far as practicable will facilitate such transfer."[33]

A month later Secretary of State Edward Stettinius confirmed Roosevelt's vague assurance regarding territorial changes and population transfers when he released a press statement confirming American support for a free and independent Poland. While adhering to U.S. policy that rejected territorial agreements made during wartime, the press statement cited former Secretary of State Hull's address of 9 April 1944 that had promised that the United States would not interfere in decisions "settled by friendly conference" among the nations involved. The Poles thus had reason to believe that the United States would support an agreement that Polish and other Allied representatives had discussed about the recreation of Poland.[34]

The lack of clarity about the U.S. position on the Polish border issue was corrected in the State Department's preconference briefing book for the Yalta Conference that outlined the issues of discussion. First, the briefing book explained the focus of American policy regarding Poland's frontiers: "With respect to the Polish frontier, we should use our influence to obtain a solution of this problem which would minimize future points of friction, possible Irredentism and the number of minority groups which would have to be transferred as a part of the settlement in order that the solution would contribute to the fullest possible extent to the peace and future tranquility of Europe."[35]

Specifically, this meant that the United States should support the Curzon Line, but with Lwów and the surrounding oil fields going to the Poles. In the north the Poles should get the bulk of East Prussia; and in the west there would be only minor changes from the 1939 border, including Poland's receiving a small strip of Pomerania west of the Polish Corridor and Upper Silesia.

Second, the study warned that "we should resist the exaggerated claims now being advanced by the Provisional Government in Lublin for 'compensation' from Germany which would include the cities of Stettin and Breslau in Poland and make necessary the transfer of from eight to ten million Germans."[36] This action would have made any new Polish state dependent on the Soviet Union for protection of its borders against a discontented German population unless the West specifically granted such a guarantee, an unlikely event in the face of Roosevelt's concern about maintaining Allied unity. In any case, this was not a totally new claim from the Lublin Poles. Ambassador Harriman had notified the secretary of state in a telegram from Moscow on 19 December 1944 that a very real possibility existed that the Soviet-backed Poles would demand this territory. His warning showed great insight; he urged the secretary to register some type of protest before the United States was confronted with a fait accompli, the exact situation that developed a few months later.[37]

Third, the Yalta briefing book went on to analyze possible reasons for the Lublin government's insistence on these "exaggerated claims." The authors speculated the following:

1. Poland, which would depend completely on Moscow for protection from German irredentism after acquiring a large part of German territory and transferring 8 to 10 million Germans, might become a "full-fledged" Soviet satellite;
2. If the proposed world security organization proved impossible, it would be to the Soviet advantage to have a Polish border as far west as possible;
3. By giving as much land as possible to the Poles in the west, the loss of 43 percent of its land in the east might not be felt quite as greatly.

Because of these possibilities, the authors of the briefing book urged a preconference tentative agreement with Great Britain about Polish territorial acquisitions and strongly recommended that the United States "resist any proposals for a solution based on either the Oder or the Oder–Neisse Line."[38] The briefing book also emphasized, however, that the frontier issue was "definitely secondary" to the "major problem of establishing a viable Polish Government," and it was this priority that Roosevelt maintained throughout the conference negotiations.[39]

That American and British officials agreed on the basics of Poland's borders is evident in their discussions at Malta on 1 February 1945 prior to the Yalta meeting. The British had already agreed to the Curzon Line but recognized that the United States might push for Lwów to be returned to the Poles. In the west the conferees agreed that Poland should get part of East Prussia, Danzig, the eastern tip of Pomerania, and all of Upper Silesia.[40] They specified that this would involve the transfer of 2.5 million Germans from the area as opposed to the 8 million who would have to be transferred if they agreed to a border on the Neisse River.[41] They expressed concern that a newly formed Polish government would be unable to absorb territory up to the Oder River and agreed that there was no question of accepting a frontier on the Neisse. They were aware of the difficulties involved in a large population transfer and were determined that such a transfer should be done gradually. That the border issue was tied to the question of Poland's postwar government in the minds of the British and Americans was evident in their brief summary of the conference: "If the Russians refuse to accept any solutions, such as that outlined above, the present deadlock must continue. That would be bad, but a simple recognition of the Lublin Government would be even worse."[42]

THE YALTA CONFERENCE

Although Roosevelt's advisers and the State Department staff focused a relatively large amount of attention on the Polish border question prior to the Yalta meeting, the president "found the Polish issue irritating" and preferred to concentrate at the Yalta Conference on the Pacific War and the establishment of a United Nations organization.[43] When forced to deal with the border issue in the plenary sessions, Roosevelt preferred to speak in generalities and focus on the Allies' points of agreement rather than on their seemingly insurmountable disagreements.

As the conference got under way, the border issue was handled only peripherally at the plenary sessions until the third meeting on 6 February 1945. There Roosevelt tentatively introduced the suggestion that the Soviets concede Lwów and the surrounding oil fields to the Poles in order to make the Curzon Line even more acceptable to what he termed an already agreeable American populace.[44] Stalin rejected that concession and openly declared Soviet support for a western border on the Lausitzer (western) Neisse River. This was the first time that the Soviets had specified support for the western as opposed to the eastern (Glatzer or Kłodzka) Neisse River, a calculated change, according to one Soviet scholar, and one that would place the entire area of Silesia under Polish control and involve the transfer of a large number of Germans.[45]

At the next plenary meeting on 7 February 1945, Molotov returned to Stalin's statement when he read the Soviet proposal concerning Poland that included a border in the east along the Curzon Line and in the west along the Oder and Lausitzer Neisse Rivers. Roosevelt stated that Molotov's proposals indicated that progress had been made, but objected to the foreign minister's use of the word "émigré" to describe Poles living abroad. Apart from that, Roosevelt remained quiet during the following discussions.[46] Churchill retreated from his Tehran proposal for a frontier along the Oder and responded that, while he had always supported moving Poland's frontier to the west to compensate it for lands lost in the east, it "would be a pity to stuff the Polish goose so full of German food that it got indigestion."[47] He raised the specter of British public opinion loudly opposing the transfer of such a large number of Germans from the area up to the western Neisse. Stalin met this objection by stating that most Germans had fled the area, a fact known by State Department officials, if not by Roosevelt, to be untrue.[48] Admiral Leahy, Roosevelt's chief of staff, stated in his memoirs that at this session he "had a distinct feeling that Poland was going to be treated very badly from our point of view."[49]

By the time of the Fifth Plenary Session on the afternoon of 8 February, the U. S. representatives had prepared a proposal for the treatment of Poland's borders. This proposal accepted the Curzon Line in the east with minor modifications of five to eight kilometers. In the west, the U.S. proposal accepted the idea of compensating Poland with prewar German lands in East Prussia, Upper Silesia, and "up to the line of the Oder." The Americans maintained their previous position when they found "little justification" for extending the western border up to the Lausitzer Neisse, however. The remainder of the proposal dealt with the composition of the Polish government.[50]

In response to Roosevelt's statement that the U.S. proposals were "very close" to those presented by Molotov, the Soviet foreign minister gladly noted that, while there was agreement on the Curzon Line, he could not help but point out that the negotiators disagreed about the western border. He urged that the Polish Provisional Government be consulted about the western border, having no doubt that they would support the western Neisse.[51] Rather than wrangle over the major difficulty of trying to set the exact western border, the conferees chose to focus on their general agreement that Poland should be moved west and proceeded to other matters. The Americans were aware that the statements made on Poland were so open-ended that the Soviets could "stretch it all the way from Yalta to Washington without every technically breaking it," but Roosevelt told his chief of staff that it was the best agreement possible.[52]

After the Seventh Plenary Session began on 10 February, British Foreign Minister Anthony Eden read the report of the foreign ministers' meeting held earlier that day. Churchill pointed out that some statement about the borders needed to be made since the "whole world would wonder what had been decided on this question."[53] Roosevelt stated that the Polish government should be consulted, whereas Molotov and Stalin contended that there was no need to make a definite statement on the western frontier, although some statement about the agreed-upon eastern border was necessary. At this session Roosevelt, after receiving a note from one of his aides questioning the legality of the president's making such agreements, contended that he was restricted from making border agreements by "American Constitutions (sic) reasons"; such an agreement was the responsibility of the Senate.[54] To avoid these constitutional difficulties, Roosevelt proposed some minor word changes so that the proposal read more like a summary of opinion of the three Allies than a treatylike agreement among powerful leaders. After Churchill and Roosevelt objected to Molotov's suggestion that the phrase "with the return to Poland of her ancient frontiers in East Prussia and on the Oder" be added to the statement on the grounds that it might open a Pandora's box of other frontier changes, Stalin withdrew his adviser's suggestion.[55] No further changes were made to the proposal on Poland's borders.

The final Yalta Communiqué on Poland's borders reads:

> The three heads of Government consider that the eastern frontier of Poland should follow the Curzon Line, with digressions from it in some regions of five to eight kilometers in favor of Poland. They recognize that Poland must receive substantial accessions of territory in the north and west. They feel that the opinion of the new Polish Provisional Government of National Unity should be sought in due course on the extent of these accessions, and that the final delimitation of the western frontier of Poland should therefore await the Peace Conference.[56]

The three elements of the communiqué—the Curzon Line, recognition of Poland's need for land in the north and west, and the participation of representatives of Poland's new government in border decisions—reflect Roosevelt's preference for emphasizing points of agreement to give the appearance of Allied unity. The lack of specificity would have to be addressed at the next Allied conference, but Roosevelt and most of his aides left the Yalta Conference optimistically.

He told Congress and the press that the Polish problem had been solved, and many others generally concurred with the President's assessment. Byrnes claimed that Yalta represented new heights of Allied unity.[57] Bohlen admitted that, although there was a "sense of frustration and some bitterness" among the returning delegates concerning Poland, the "general mood was one of satisfaction."[58] Admiral Leahy, on the other hand, expressed concern that the decisions at Yalta would result in a war of revenge by the Germans.[59]

The general satisfaction expressed by these governmental officials was not, however, echoed by the public once news of the Yalta Accord became known on 12 February. Mainstream public opinion reflected more resignation than satisfaction. A Gallup poll conducted among the American population in general showed that, while 56 percent of those polled believed that the agreement on Poland was about as good as could be hoped for, only 33 percent believed that the agreement was fair to the Poles.[60] The *New York Times* on 13 February 1945 ran an editorial stating that, while a more thorough analysis of the accord was needed, it appeared at first glance that the Polish and Yugoslavian solutions offered a compromise that was the best that could be obtained in "the present troubled world." The editorial agreed with Roosevelt's view of the Polish question when it stated that, in return for Western recognition of the Curzon Line and substantial compensation for Poland from prewar Germany, Stalin had agreed, in a move "even more important than the border issue," to the formation of a Polish government with representatives from both the Lublin and London Poles.[61]

The compromises of the Yalta Agreement were anathema to most Americans of Polish descent. The Polish American Congress (PAC), which had been created in Buffalo in 1944 as an "umbrella" organization for Polish American fraternal, social, and political clubs, adopted a resolution on 9 March 1945 condemning the Yalta decision as incompatible with the principles and traditions of the United States, as a violation of international law, and as incompatible with the principles of the Atlantic Charter and the commitments of the United Nations.[62] According to the authors of the resolution, Yalta represented a fifth partition of Poland; and they rejected the idea that the acquisition of prewar German lands represented fair compensation for the loss to the Soviet Union of ancient Polish land in the east. The resolution called for a quid pro quo whereby the establishment of Poland's eastern border would depend on the establishment of a definite border in the west and concluded with an appeal to the government and public opinion to revise the decisions of the Yalta Conference "in a spirit of equity and good conscience."[63] Charles Rozmarek, president of the PAC, claimed that the Yalta Accord contradicted the "sacred pledges" of the Atlantic Charter and represented a blow to freedom. The Curzon Line, according to Rozmarek, was simply a reaffirmation of the Molotov–Ribbentrop line, and he warned of the dangers of unchecked Russian aggression.[64]

The anti-Soviet Polish American press joined in condemning the Yalta Accord, while a small, but vocal, group of pro-Soviet Polish Americans praised the result of the conference. *Dziennik Związkowy*, the newspaper of the Chicago-based Polish National Alliance (part of the PAC), contained an illustration on 5 March 1945 of a woman who represented American Polonia sitting opposite a picture of Roosevelt with a caption that read, "Bitter Disappointment."[65] *Głos Ludowy*, a Polish American newspaper in Detroit with socialist and communist affiliations, on the other hand, strongly supported the decisions at Yalta and Washington's friendly policy toward the Soviet Union.[66]

The debate in the U.S. Congress reflected the mixed public reaction to the accord. Polish American congressmen vociferously opposed the Yalta decisions, and they had the support of a number of congressmen with large ethnic constituencies that opposed such compromises with the Soviet Union.[67] Congressman John Lesinski (D-MI) of Detroit requested Roosevelt's views of the accord before he addressed Congress. Roosevelt responded inconclusively to Lesinski's letter, and on 10 March 1945 Lesinski replied that in his view Yalta represented a violation of the Atlantic Charter. A few days later, nine congressmen requested and were denied an interview with Roosevelt to discuss the Yalta decisions on Poland.[68] Polish American Representative Alvin O'Konski (R-WI) called the Yalta Accord a "success for Propaganda Minister Joseph Goebbles 'second only to that of Munich.'"[69] Republican Senator Arthur Vandenberg from Michigan, a state with a large Polish American constituency, opposed the treatment of Poland at Yalta, but recognized the impossibility of altering decisions that Roosevelt and Churchill had agreed to. He recommended that the Yalta Accord be approved with the hope that the provisional government, once established in Warsaw, could improve Poland's situation.[70]

THE POTSDAM CONFERENCE

Much of this explicit opposition to the Yalta decisions on Poland centered on the Big Three's handling of Poland's eastern border. The next and final meeting of the Allies in July and August 1945 at Potsdam, Germany, focused on Poland's western border and the treatment of Germany, two overlapping issues. In the months preceding the conference, the situation had changed drastically from that facing the conferees at Yalta. Truman had replaced Roosevelt as president, Germany had been defeated and the Allied machinery for provisional control of Germany had been set in place, and the Polish Provisional Government dominated by the Lublin communists had been established with Moscow's help and Washington's acquiescence through Harry Hopkins' discussions with Stalin in May 1945.[71] Differences among the Allies that had earlier been ignored became more and more evident. One of the most immediately obvious differences concerned Poland's western border.

The Poles, with the aid of the Soviets, had taken over the administration of what was supposed to be part of the Soviet Zone of Occupation. Department of State officials in Washington sent urgent telegrams to the U.S. Embassy in Moscow in April and May 1945, instructing Ambassador Harriman and Chargé George Kennan to request information from the Soviet Foreign Office about press and radio reports that Poland had control of much of this prewar German territory. The Soviets replied to these requests with the statement that the lands had been turned over to Poland only for administrative purposes and were still part of the Soviet Zone. Kennan was then instructed to issue a memorandum which stated that reliable reports indicated that the Warsaw government had issued decrees incorporating the area into Poland and that this incorporation was a clear violation of prior agreements concerning the control of enemy territory. The Soviets responded again with the assertion that it was a military necessity to turn over administration of the area to Poland. They justified this action by citing the Yalta Accord concerning Polish gains.[72]

In preconference briefing papers, the State Department recognized this difficult situation. A report dated 6 July 1945 stated that the United States should continue to resist the "exaggerated claims" of the Warsaw government to lands up to the Oder and Neisse Rivers and instead should agree to Polish acquisitions from the greater part of East Prussia, Upper Silesia, and a small strip of German Pomerania adjoining the Polish Corridor, a position similar to that favored by the Polish government in London.[73] Although this border represented a reduction in Polish territory, it would make Poland stronger by ensuring that most of the inhabitants would be Polish, by offering Poland a viable economy, and by reducing the problems of large population transfers. Regarding this last point, the report stated that the United States should "facilitate in so far as our aid is requested" the transfer of minorities but should not allow the forced repatriation of Poles or the "uncontrolled deportation by unilateral Polish action" of 8 to 10 million Germans. In any case, the paper warned, the United States "should only with reluctance accept the Oder Line and should resist to the utmost acceptance of the Oder–Neisse."[74]

Accompanying this report was a population study of the area compiled by State Department officials that listed the numbers of Poles and Polish-speaking people in each of the territories under consideration as well as recommendations for future control of each of the provinces in question.[75] The officials who prepared the Potsdam report suggested the same borders and the same three reasons that the Soviets might be pushing for so much territory as had been suggested in the Yalta briefing papers: Poland would be totally dependent on the Soviet Union; the Soviets would have a great advantage of having Poland's border as far to the west as possible if the United Nations organization did not prove effective; and the Soviets hoped that the acquisition of territory in the west would cushion the blow of losing 42 percent of prewar Polish land in the east.[76]

The Joint Chiefs of Staff also showed an interest in the border issue in a committee report dated 26 June 1945 that reflects the committee's awareness of the importance and potential use of the border issue as well as the difficulties involved in changing the current status: "Since the political orientation of Poland with respect to either Eastern or Western European powers cannot be foreseen, this Committee is reluctant to recommend extension of the western boundary of Poland to the Oder River. However, from the military point of view, it would appear impracticable to offer serious objections to this transfer of territory from Germany if the U.S.S.R. insists upon it. The bargaining possibilities of this issue, however, should be recognized."[77]

President Truman traveled to the conference reviewing and discussing much of this briefing material; but, as at Yalta, American planners at Potsdam perceived the Polish issue as of secondary importance. Their primary concern in Europe was the question of how to handle defeated Germany.[78] As the delegates negotiated the question of Poland's western border, it became evident that the west "was on the defensive."[79]

The first in-depth discussion of Poland's western border occurred at the Fifth Plenary Session on 21 July 1945. In this discussion, the already entrenched positions of Truman, Stalin, and Churchill became apparent. The delegates had agreed at the Second Plenary Session to use the 1937 borders of Germany as a starting point for discussion; at the Fifth Session Truman contended that the Poles seemed to be getting an occupation zone of their own.[80] This decision, he said, had been made unilaterally by the Soviets, and while he had very friendly feelings toward the Polish government, he wanted such issues as borders to be discussed by the delegates. Throughout the conference Truman objected not so much to the idea of the Poles controlling some territory as to the seeming creation of a Polish occupation zone by the Soviets without consultation with the other Allies. Although the Allies had agreed at Yalta to grant the French part of the American and British zones, no similar solution to the "Polish problem" was considered, either at Yalta or Potsdam.[81] Truman revealed one of his major concerns when he warned that Soviet actions in the disputed territory would endanger reparation solutions. When Stalin replied that the Soviet Union was "'not afraid of the reparations questions'" and would renounce them if necessary, Truman again revealed that one of his goals was to avoid the mistakes of Versailles when he stated that "the United States would get no reparations anyhow. . . . We were trying to keep from paying more, as we did before."[82]

Stalin contended that it was inaccurate to state that the Poles had been given an occupation zone, since the Yalta Agreement had settled on the Curzon Line in the east and had stated that the Poles should get territory in the north and west. Stalin proposed that the Polish government, again according to the Yalta Agreement, should consult with the Allies about its western border. According to the Soviet leader, it was not logistically feasible to follow the wishes of the United States and Great Britain regarding the territories administered by Poland since, as the Soviet army moved west across Central Europe, it had to delegate responsibility to the Poles for setting up administration of the area just liberated. Stalin stated that it would be military suicide to leave the area open to German retrenchment.[83]

Churchill stated that he had much to say about the border, but emphasized that it was a matter to be settled at a future peace conference. He suggested that they focus on the practical issue of obtaining food supplies from the area. To Stalin's question of who would work the fields and harvest the crops since the Germans had fled the area, Truman, probably with State Department estimates fresh in mind, replied that 9 million Germans were still there. Stalin maintained again that they had all fled.[84] Churchill steered the discussion back to the issue of future food sources when he asked how the Allies would supply food to the occupied German area with such a greatly reduced land area and with the addition of more than 8 million ethnic Germans who would be forced out of the area administered by Poland. After Churchill added that he would like an investigation of the situation since his reports indicated that 2.5 million Germans remained in the area, Stalin presented contradictory arguments: he admitted that population transfers would pose problems, but the "German people were principally to blame for these difficulties"; a few sentences later, he stated flatly that "no single German remained in the territory to be given Poland."[85]

The three men held firmly to their initial arguments. Truman went back to the issue of a fifth zone being created and reiterated that the question of Poland's western border was closely tied to the reparations issue since the Silesian mines from which coal was being excavated were considered German by the reparations committee. Churchill, again pointing out that a population transfer would only mean future trouble for Europe and the United Kingdom, contended that the food shortage would be such as had existed in the concentration camps. Stalin again asked how the Poles, who were now cultivating the land, could be expected to give the food to the Germans. He responded to Truman's concern about reparations by stating that, while the proposal for a border on the western Neisse would lead to difficulties for Germany, it was better in the long run for the Germans to have problems than for the Poles.[86] The session ended at this apparent impasse.

Discussion of the border issue resumed at the Sixth Plenary Session of 22 July 1945 and resulted in the invitation of representatives from the Polish government to present their views. A decision on the location of the border was not, however, easily reached. In response to Stalin's question as to why the Polish government's proposal for a border on the western Neisse was unacceptable, Churchill enumerated his objections:

1. Boundaries would be set at a peace conference;
2. It was disadvantageous to Poland to take so much German territory;
3. It would "rupture" the German economy and place too heavy a burden on the occupying powers;
4. The resulting population shift would entail "grave moral" responsibilities;
5. Data on the number of Germans involved were conflicting since British reports indicated 8 or 9 million and Soviet reports claimed none.[87]

Stalin responded to two of Churchill's objections by pointing out that Germany would have fuel from the Ruhr and Rhineland and therefore would not suffer unduly from the loss of the Silesian coalfields. He rejected the estimate of 8 or 9 million Germans left in the area since, he said, many had been drafted or had fled from the Nazi Army. He pulled back from his earlier contention that no Germans were left but stated that there were fewer than 3 million. He requested that the Polish Provisional Government report to the Council of Foreign Ministers to settle this issue when it met in September. However, Churchill at this point opposed this request. He held that it was just a further delay of an issue that they should be dealing with, since in the meantime the Poles would be solidifying their hold on the area, and the food crisis would be getting worse. He proposed instead that a provisional line be drawn along the Oder River with the area east of that being part of Poland and the area west being administered by the Poles, but as part of the Soviet Zone of occupied Germany and thus liable to Allied agreements on Germany. He believed that this was in accord with discussions that he had had with Stalin at the Tehran Conference and in subsequent conversations.[88]

Truman agreed with Stalin's counterproposal of calling forth representatives from Poland but referred again to his objection that the way that the Poles had taken control of the area constituted construction of a fifth zone and was thus in violation of prior agreements. He was not ruling out the possibility that the Poles might be given the area, but it could be done only if the delegates so agreed. He emphasized that it would have to be a unanimous, not a unilateral decision.

Tension was high after Stalin objected to the proposal that he claimed had been made by the president and Churchill at Yalta; namely, that Poland's western border should be along the Oder and eastern Neisse Rivers since this border would leave the towns of Stettin and Breslau in German hands.[89] Stalin then pointed to the line that he favored on a map and told the Westerners that the issue involved was one of frontiers and could not be ignored. Finally, Churchill withdrew his objection to having the Polish government send representatives to be heard by the foreign ministers at Potsdam. They then discussed other issues.

Invitations were issued to two or three representatives of the Polish Provisional Government; but at least eight came, including Bolesław Bierut, president; Edward Osóbka-Morawski, premier; Właydsław Gomułka, deputy prime minister and minister of western territories; and Stanisław Mikołajczyk, deputy prime minister and minister of agriculture. They met with the foreign ministers on 24 July 1945 to present their views. Bierut postulated that the new border in the east would require the surrender of 18,000 square kilometers of land but would make Poland more ethnically homogeneous and was thus justified. The proposed border in the west along the Oder and western Neisse (with Stettin included) was important for security and economic reasons. Bierut here contradicted Stalin's earlier claim that all the Germans had fled the area when he contended that the 1.5 million remaining Germans would probably be willing to leave if the area were administered by Poland. The further advantage for Poland would be that Poles would no longer have to emigrate for jobs or sell their labor in this area while others made profits.[90]

Another Polish delegate, Minister of Foreign Affairs Wincenty Rzymowski, voicing support for land concessions to the Soviets in the east for the sake of peace, felt that it was only right that Germany concede land also for the sake of peace, especially the area under question which had always provided Germany with its war-making potential. He went on to provide economic reasons that the area was important to the Poles. Mikołajczyk supported his "'colleagues'" in their belief that the Oder–Neisse Line was necessary for future peace.[91]

Later that day Truman and his advisers met briefly with the Polish delegates who had just come from a meeting with Churchill, who had "lashed out with passion" about the folly of their request for so much German land.[92]

Truman reassured them that while he wanted to see justice for Poland, he objected to the arbitrary manner in which the Soviets and Poles were handling the border issue. In response to Bierut's contention that it was necessary for the Poles to take over administration of the uninhabited territory, Truman replied that full Allied agreement was required for any territorial transfers. Bierut acknowledged the legalities of the question, but stated that millions of homeless Poles would be greatly helped by the acquisition of this territory. The meeting had to end at this unsettled point because the president had to attend the Eighth Plenary Session.[93]

The frontier issue was not discussed at the Eighth or Ninth Plenary Sessions because the Polish delegates were still meeting with British, American, and Soviet representatives. The question of Poland's frontiers came up indirectly when the delegates began discussing the problems of population transfers at their session on 25 July 1945. Stalin used the estimate brought by the Polish delegates when he informed Churchill that there were about 1.5 million Germans in Poland whom the Poles had retained to work the harvest and who would evacuate as soon as the harvest was in. When Churchill said that the Poles should not do so, Stalin replied simply that, "the Poles did not ask but did as they liked."[94] Churchill again focused on the cost to England of having Germans "thrown on them."[95] Stalin said that the Poles were just taking revenge on the Germans for centuries of suffering. Truman replied that his power to deal with matters of a peace treaty was limited by the Constitution. He added that he would, of course, support any issues with the Senate that he supported at the conference.[96] Churchill stated that he would like to discuss the boundary issue since it was at the root of the success of the conference as it was closely tied to the issues of food supplies and reparations. If the delegates permitted the situation to stand, Churchill argued, the Poles would have been granted an occupation zone but none of the obligations for sharing food supplies. He added that it might be necessary to accept Byrnes' reparations proposal that each of the occupiers would take reparations from its own zone. If Churchill meant this as a warning, it fell on deaf ears. Stalin replied coldly that industrial resources were more important than food and that the Germans could and should pay reparations. The session ended without agreement, and Churchill and Eden returned to London for an unsuccessful election.[97]

While the delegates were awaiting the new British representatives, the Poles continued to restate their arguments in meetings with U.S., Soviet, and British officials. In private meetings with American and British representatives, Mikołajczyk warned that his communist colleagues were playing a "double game." He thought that they were trying to get the Western Allies to reject the proposed western border in order to nullify the Yalta agreements and thus keep the Soviet army in possession of the territory. He also urged that recognition of the border be conditional on a pledge from Warsaw to hold free elections, a move, according to historian Richard Lukas, that the western leaders were not ready to make since it might have resulted in a conference stalemate.[98] In talks that included Molotov, Mikołajczyk presented arguments similar to those of the other Polish representatives: that Poland needed the Oder–Neisse land to absorb the Poles from east of the Curzon Line and from the overpopulated central area and that cession to Poland would obstruct Germany's military potential.[99]

There was a slight shift in the U.S. position, but not toward the condition that Mikołajczyk had privately suggested. In meetings on 25 and 26 July, Ambassador Harriman told the Poles that the United States was considering offering a proposal separating the border issue from the more immediate issue of Polish administration of the territory. This, Harriman argued, would ensure that the Poles could harvest the crops and manage the industry of the area without waiting for the legal settlement of the border issue at the peace conference.[100]

The Americans continued to link the questions of Poland's border with the reparations issue. On 29 July Truman and his advisers met with Molotov, who told them that Stalin was ill with a cold and unable to attend the scheduled meeting. At this meeting, Byrnes wanted to discuss the two outstanding questions of reparations and the Polish western border. Expressing the desire to finish the conference, he told Molotov that if the Soviets would agree to his proposal that reparations be taken by each country from its own zone, he was prepared to "go further to meet the Soviet wishes" regarding the Polish border.[101] In this discussion of German reparations, they made very little progress because the Soviets favored setting a fixed amount while Byrnes held that it was impossible to establish a fixed value at that time and suggested that they use percentage figures instead.

Byrnes fared better in his discussion of the Polish border. The proposal that Byrnes handed to Molotov gave the Poles administration of the area east of a line along the Oder and eastern Neisse Rivers with final settlement of the border issue to await a peace treaty. When Molotov pointed out that this proposal left the area between the eastern and western Neisse Rivers in German hands and thus contradicted the specific request that the Polish delegates had made to the foreign ministers, Byrnes replied that since final confirmation had to await a peace conference, it was still possible that the Poles might also receive that area. Truman reiterated his stand that there were to be four, not five, occupying powers, and in any case he felt that the proposal would be acceptable to the Soviet delegation since it represented "a very large concession on our part."[102] Molotov was skeptical but agreed to present it to Stalin.

Later that evening, Stalin invited Bierut to his quarters to discuss the American proposals. Details of this conversation are sketchy, but Mikołajczyk records that Stalin, in an effort to acknowledge the U.S. concessions on the western border issue, asked the Poles to consider accepting a line on the Queiss instead of the Lausitzer (western) Neisse (see Map 1.1).[103] The Poles had to consult their own experts before deciding that, while they could not agree to a line on the eastern Neisse, they could accept a "watershed line" between the Queiss and the western Neisse. That line, they said, would deprive them of

Map 1.1

BALTIC SEA
Danzig
(Gdańsk)
FREE CITY OF DANZIG
EAST PRUSSIA
Swinemünde
(Świnoujście)
Köslin
(Koszalin)
Stettin
(Szczecin)
Oder (Odra)
Bydgoszcz
(Bromberg)
Vistula (Wisla)
Frankfurt
Poznań
(Posen)
POLAND
Fürstenberg
Crossen
(Krosno Odrzańskie)
Lausitzer Neisse (Nysa Łużycka)
Oder (Odra)
Łódź
(Lodz)
Sagan (Żagań)
GERMANY
Queiss (Kwisa)
Bober (Bóbr)
Görlitz
Liegnitz
(Legnica)
Lauban
(Luban)
Breslau
(Wrocław)
Zittau
Brieg
(Brzeg)
Oppeln
(Opole)
Glatzer Neisse (Nysa Kłodzka)
Glatz
(Kłodzko)
Neisse
(Nysa)
Katowice
(Kattowitz)
Prague
(Praha)
Ratibor
(Racibórz)
CZECHOSLOVAKIA
Ostrava
CONSIDERATION OF THE WESTERN FRONTIER OF POLAND AT THE BERLIN CONFERENCE
1937 International Boundaries
Western Limit of Polish Administration Pending the Final Determination of Poland's Western Frontier at the Peace Settlement
28776 3-60

some water installations, but would not affect the industry of Silesia.[104] Vojtech Mastny cites a Polish source that states that at a later meeting that evening the Poles rejected any concessions and Stalin agreed to their original demands. Mastny doubts, however, whether Stalin would have held to this position of a border on the western Neisse if it had become necessary to bargain with Byrnes.[105]

On the following afternoon, Byrnes submitted to Molotov a revised proposal including three points. First, Byrnes accepted Polish administration of the area east of a line along the Oder and western Neisse Rivers until final delimitation of the border would be made at a peace conference.[106] Second, Byrnes requested Soviet acquiescence in allowing Italy to join the United Nations. Third was Soviet acceptance of an American reparations plan in which the Soviet Union's chief source for reparations was its own zone, but with additional percentages of material from the Western zones, pending British approval. This was the "package deal" that the delegates discussed at the Tenth Meeting of the Foreign Ministers on 30 July 1945 (no plenary session was held because Stalin was still ill). The border proposal, according to Byrnes, was made in a "spirit of compromise" and with the hope that they could reach agreement on it and the questions of Italy and reparations.[107]

By 31 July Stalin was feeling well enough to attend the Eleventh Plenary Session, where Byrnes emphasized that all three points had to be accepted, or none of them would be settled at the conference. According to Byrnes, he had told Molotov earlier that day that the issue would be presented as a package and that he and Truman would be leaving the next day.[108] Stalin and Molotov objected to Byrnes' tactic of tying together these different issues, but after much tripartite discussion of the U.S. proposal, all three issues were approved. The following meeting and plenary sessions focused on ironing out the exact wording of the protocol that was issued on 2 August 1945. After indicating that the delegates had conformed to the Yalta Accord by seeking the opinion of the Polish Provisional Government concerning the western border of Poland, the Potsdam Protocol on Poland states:

> The three Heads of Government agree that, pending the final determination of Poland's western frontier, the former German territories east of a line running from the Baltic Sea immediately west of Swinemunde, and thence along the Oder River to the confluence of the western Neisse River and along the western Neisse to the Czechoslovak frontier, including that portion of East Prussia not placed under the administration of the Union of Soviet Socialist Republics in accordance with the understanding reached at this conference and including the area of the former free city of Danzig, shall be under the administration of the Polish State and for such purposes should not be considered as part of the Soviet zone of occupation in Germany.[109]

On the related issue of population transfers, Article 13 of the protocol states that the German population in this area should be transferred to Germany in "an orderly and humane manner" after the Allied Control Council in Germany had time to investigate and report on the ability of the German zones to absorb this population. Until that time, the delegates requested the Polish Provisional Government to suspend further transfers.[110]

Truman and Byrnes left Berlin on 2 August 2 to begin the trip home. Byrnes records that the American delegation was probably "less sanguine" than the one that had departed from Yalta, but he believed that at Potsdam they had established a basis for continued Allied unity.[111] On the trip home, Truman worked on a report of the conference that he delivered to the nation via radio on 9 August. He began the section on Poland by pointing out that the conferees had been somewhat restricted by the agreements made previously at Yalta. He also stated that the decisions at Potsdam were provisional and awaited a peace settlement but recognized that "nearly every international agreement has in it the element of compromise. The agreement on Poland is no exception. No one nation can expect to get everything that it wants. It is a question of give and take—of being willing to meet your neighbor half-way."[112]

The president then presented reasons that the agreement had been necessary to help Poland. He used some of the same arguments that Mikołajczyk and the other Polish representatives had presented to the delegates at Potsdam when he stated that Poland needed the area to repatriate the more than 3 million Poles from the area east of the Curzon Line. The territory to be administered by Poland, he went on to say, had been populated by Germans, but "most of them have already left in the face of the invading Soviet Army."[113] He used the figure given by the Poles to estimate that approximately 1.5 million Germans still lived there. The Oder–Neisse frontier would also enable Poland to better support its population, would provide a shorter and more easily defensible frontier, and finally would provide the Poles with a more homogeneous nation. This report represents a fairly straightforward account of the events of the Potsdam Conference.

What is more informative, however, is what Truman omitted from his address to the nation. In the first draft of this speech concerning Poland's border, Truman admitted, "I must in all candor say that I did not like this provision of the Berlin agreement. I still do not like it. Until almost the end of the Conference, I declined to agree to it."[114] Also, in presenting reasons for the compromise, Truman in the first draft claimed that more than 1 million Germans still living in the region were "willing to return to Germany" and that the region had long been a base of German militarism with its zinc and coal resources, and thus, "Poland, which was the first overrun and devastated nation has a justifiable moral claim to this area."[115] These additional points of justification illustrate Truman's apologetic tone in preparing the address. This tone remained in his final address, but he offered less explanation for U.S. acceptance of the Oder–Neisse Line.

Indeed, the president's justification for the agreement and the imprecise wording of the frontier agreement combined with Byrnes' "package deal" and the optimistic—or naive—caveat on the "orderly and humane" transfer of the

Germans out of the area placed under Polish control suggest that the Americans were weary of wrangling over the Polish question and were willing to accept a less than satisfactory compromise in an area over which they had no physical control. In addition, the treatment accorded the border issue by the Americans at Potsdam established a pattern in American foreign policy planning whereby the situation in Germany—whether regarding reparations, reconstruction, or politics—tended to take precedence over Poland's predicament. This pattern became increasingly evident as Cold War tensions increased in Central Europe.

As with the previous wartime conferences, the reaction to the Potsdam Protocol was mixed. The Polish American Congress was not appeased by Truman's explanation about the necessities that the conferees had confronted. Rozmarek stated that Potsdam simply confirmed the partition of Poland.[116] The general press reaction to Truman's report and to the Potsdam Communiqué was cautious approval of the cooperation displayed among the Allies. The *Christian Science Monitor* questioned the reasoning for giving the Poles the eastern bank of the Oder since they had neither a historical nor an ethnographical claim to it but speculated that the Oder–Neisse Line might prove workable if the German population was transferred out of the area.[117] This population transfer was recognized as a "harsh solution," but the editor suggested that it might prove more humanitarian in the long run if it reduced the kind of racial tensions on which Hitler had risen to power.[118] The *New York Times* focused on a different aspect of the population transfer. Although Truman in his radio address had emphasized that the decisions on Poland's western border awaited finalization at a peace conference, an editor of the *Times* contended that the population transfers envisioned in the communiqué "leave no doubt" that the territorial solution is final.[119]

Historians of Polish–American relations have also analyzed the Potsdam Accord and have offered interpretations of American words and actions. Richard Lukas states flatly that in spite of the provision stating that the Oder–Neisse Line awaited finalization at a peace conference, "what the Allied leaders did at Potsdam constituted a de facto territorial settlement." He points especially to Byrnes' "package deal" and to the fact that the Allies approved the transfer of millions of Germans—a move that "would have been absurd, not to mention inhumane" if it was only a temporary measure.[120] Denise Conover, a biographer of Byrnes, offers clarification of the secretary's decision regarding Poland's western border. She claims that Byrnes' package deal was simply part of his negotiating style; he believed that he could make temporary agreements on the spot and save finalization of those agreements for a future peace conference, just as he had made deals with congressmen in his former legislative career.[121] Like Lukas, Piotr Wandycz focuses on the authorization of the population transfers as confirming the permanency of the Potsdam border decisions.[122]

When scholars of international law have analyzed the Potsdam Accord, they have presented conflicting interpretations. Jozef Kokot and Alfons

Klafkowski argue that authorization of the population transfers did indeed signify the permanency of the Oder–Neisse Line. In addition they point to the wording of the accord, which labels much of the Oder–Neisse area as "'former German territories.'" This wording, these and other scholars contend, clearly confirms that this area was to be permanently separated from Germany.[123] German scholars, on the other hand, argue that the Potsdam provision concerning border adjustments was a violation of the Atlantic Charter denying territorial aggrandizement as a war aim. In addition, as Wolfgang Wagner points out, the provisional nature of the Polish administration of the Oder–Neisse area is emphasized by the definite pledge given by the Western Allies to support the Soviet claim to northern East Prussia at the future peace conference.[124] The expulsion of the German population Wagner interprets as an attempt by the Western Allies to provide some control over a chaotic situation rather than as acceptance of the border as permanent.[125] Elizabeth Wiskemann, who in 1956 published an analysis of the border issue, states that Germany's defeat in 1945 resulted in Poland's de facto western border on the Oder–Neisse Line.[126] She rejects the Polish claim regarding the wording of the Potsdam Accord when she states that the use of "former German territories" was simply a result of "careless drafting." Yet she is not overly sympathetic to the expelled Germans, who she claims were "on the whole . . . singularly forgetful of what their representatives, as the Nazis after all were, had done to people of Slavonic race, and singularly unaware of the element of rough justice in the treatment they now often received."[127]

In the months following the war's end, Polish and German representatives presented arguments about the finality of Poland's borders. Other disagreements included the related questions of reparations, feeding and housing the defeated German population, and overseeing the development of postwar governments in the Allies zones of Germany and in the newly created state of the People's Republic of Poland. It was the unenviable responsibility of the State Department, the president, Congress, and American representatives in Poland and Germany to respond to this task while maintaining a political eye on interested domestic groups like the Polish American Congress in order to formulate a postwar foreign policy.

NOTES

1. Piotr S. Wandycz, *The United States and Poland* (Cambridge: Harvard University Press, 1980), 240; Oscar Halecki, *A History of Poland* (New York: Barnes and Noble, 1993), 310–311; Richard M. Watt, *Bitter Glory: Poland and its Fate 1918–1939* (New York: Simon and Schuster, 1982), 444.

2. Herbert Feis, *Churchill, Roosevelt, Stalin: The War They Waged and the Peace They Sought* (Princeton, NJ: Princeton University Press, 1967), 123. See also Robert A. Divine, *Roosevelt and World War II* (Baltimore: Johns Hopkins University Press, 1969), 60, 65–66. For a more complete review of the machanations of the border issue during the war,

see Sarah Meiklejohn Terry, *Poland's Place in Europe: General Sikorski and the Origin of the Oder–Neisse Line, 1939–1943* (Princeton, NJ: Princeton University Press, 1983); Richard Lukas, *The Strange Allies: The United States and Poland, 1941–1945* (Knoxville: University of Tennessee Press, 1978); Gotthold Rhode and Wolfgang Wagner, eds. and comps., *The Genesis of the Oder–Neisse Line: In the Diplomatic Negotiations during World War II: Sources and Documents* (Stuttgart: Brentano Verlag, 1959).

3. Richard C. Lukas, *Bitter Legacy: Polish–American Relations in the Wake of World War II* (Lexington: University of Kentucky Press, 1982), 3.

4. Terry, *Poland's Place*, 3–4; Walter M. Drzewieniecki, *The German–Polish Frontier* (Chicago: Polish Western Association of America, 1959), 54; Z. Anthony Kruszewski, *The Oder–Neisse Boundary and Poland's Modernization: The Socioeconomic and Political Impact* (New York: Praeger, 1972), 18–19 and 199–204.

5. Lukas, *Strange Allies*, 31.

6. Ibid., 34.

7. Ibid., 40; Terry, *Poland's Place*, passim.

8. Lukas, *Strange Allies*, 43.

9. Ibid., 44; Wandycz, *The United States*, 272.

10. Wandycz, *The United States*, 272; Cordell Hull, *The Memoirs of Cordell Hull*, 2 vols. (New York: MacMillan, 1948), 2: 1273.

11. Hull, *The Memoirs*, 2: 1315.

12. Ibid., 1316–1317.

13. Lukas, *Strange Allies*, 45.

14. Bohlen, Roosevelt's interpreter at Tehran, records that he was "somewhat startled" at the lack of provisions for recordkeeping at Tehran. Charles E. Bohlen, *Witness to History, 1929–1969* (New York: W. W. Norton, 1973), 136–138.

15. Lukas, *Strange Allies*, 46; Terry, *Poland's Place*, 347.

16. U.S. Department of State, *Foreign Relations of the United States, Diplomatic Papers: The Conferences at Cairo and Tehran, 1943* (Washington, DC: U. S. Government Printing Office, 1961), 512. Hereafter cited as FRUS, 1943, Tehran. Martin Gilbert, *Winston S. Churchill*, vol. 7: *Road to Victory, 1941–1945* (Boston: Houghton Mifflin, 1986), 576; Wandycz, *United States*, 276.

17. FRUS, 1943, Tehran, 594; Wandycz, *The United States*, 276.

18. FRUS, 1943, Tehran, 603; Gilbert, *Winston S. Churchill*, 588–593.

19. Wandycz, *The United States*, 277.

20. FRUS, 1943, Tehran, 596–604; Gilbert, *Winston S. Churchill*, 592.

21. FRUS, 1943, Tehran, 640–641.

22. Wandycz, *The United States*, 276; Lukas, *Strange Allies*, 47. Charles Bohlen later wrote that he was "dismayed" about Roosevelt's "implied, although unstated, acquiescence to the Churchill–Stalin agreement on Polish frontiers." Bohlen, *Witness*, 151–152.

23. Feis, *Churchill, Roosevelt, Stalin*, 285.

24. Wolfgang Wagner cites W. H. Chamberlin, who wrote in 1950 that seldom "'was so much concealed from so many by so few.'" See Rhode and Wagner, *The Genesis of the Oder–Neisse Line*, 44.

25. Edwin James, "Polish Frontiers Test Allied Statesmanship," *New York Times*, 26 December 1943, sec. 4: 3.

26. *Christian Science Monitor*, 6 December 1943, 20.

27. "To the Poles and Russians," *New York Times*, 30 December 1943, 16.

28. *Congressional Record Appendix*, 78th Cong., 1st sess., pt. 12, 89 (1945): A5538.

29. Ibid., A5424.

30. Feis, *Churchill, Roosevelt, Stalin*, 299.

31. Jan Ciechanowski, *Defeat in Victory* (Garden City, NY: Doubleday, 1947), 305–306; Lukas, *Strange Allies*, 58; *Foreign Relations of the United States Diplomatic Papers, 1945, The Conferences at Malta and Yalta* (Washington, DC: U.S. Government Printing Office, 1955), 220. Hereafter cited as FRUS, Yalta.

32. Ciechanowski, *Defeat,* 332.

33. Ibid., 341–342; FRUS, Yalta, 210.

34. FRUS., Yalta, 218–219.

35. Ibid., 230.

36. Ibid.

37. Ibid., 220–221.

38. Ibid., 230–234.

39. Briefing Book for Yalta Conference, undated, Department of State Record Group 43, Records of the International Conferences, Commissions and Expositions, Box 3, in National Archives, Washington, DC. Hereafter cited as DS/NA.

40. FRUS, Yalta, 508–509.

41. Ibid.; Edward R. Stettinius, *Roosevelt and the Russians: The Yalta Conference*, ed. Walter Johnson (New York: Doubleday, 1949), 64–65.

42. FRUS, Yalta, 509.

43. Wandycz, *The United States*, 294; Bohlen, *Witness*, 177–178 claims that it was evident at Yalta that Roosevelt did not use the briefing books "as much as he should have." Byrnes, who was with Roosevelt at Yalta, commented that, although the president did little paper work before the conference, he made a "good presentation." James F. Byrnes, *All in One Lifetime* (New York: Harper and Brothers, 1958), 256.

44. FRUS, Yalta, 667–669.

45. Vojtech Mastny, *Russia's Road to the Cold War: Diplomacy, Warfare, and the Politics of Communism, 1941–1945* (New York: Columbia University Press, 1979), 180, 247. Mastny claims that Molotov was the first to make this announcement at the Fourth Plenary Session on 7 February, but both the Bohlen and Matthews minutes in FRUS, Yalta, 669, 680 quote Stalin on 6 February; Terry, *Poland's Place*, 348–349n; Anatole C. J. Bogacki, *A Polish Paradox: International and the National Interest in Polish Communist Foreign Policy 1918–1948* (Boulder, CO: East European Monographs, 1991), 126; Kruszewski, *The Oder–Neisse Boundary*, 20.

46. FRUS, Yalta, 716.

47. Ibid., 717.

48. A detailed map showing estimated German populations of the areas under discussion accompanied the Pre-Conference Briefing Papers. See FRUS, Yalta, facing 233. In conversations between Eden, Churchill, and Stettinius on 1 February, the figure of 2.5 million Germans was given. See FRUS, Yalta, 509.

49. William D. Leahy, *I Was There: The Personal Story of the Chief of Staff to Presidents Roosevelt and Truman Based on His Notes and Diaries Made at the Time* (New

York: Whittlesey House, McGraw-Hill, 1950), 306.

50. FRUS, Yalta, 792.

51. Ibid., 776–777.

52. Leahy, *I Was There*, 316.

53. FRUS, Yalta, 898.

54. Ibid., 905.

55. Stettinius, *Roosevelt*, 270–271. See also FRUS, Yalta, 905.

56. FRUS, Yalta, 974.

57. Lukas, *Strange Allies*, 141; James F. Byrnes, *Speaking Frankly* (New York: Harper and Brothers, 1947), 45.

58. Bohlen, *Witness*, 200.

59. Leahy, *I Was There*, 323; Stettinius, *Roosevelt*, 301.

60. Lukas, *Strange Allies*, 142.

61. "For Victory and Peace," *New York Times*, 13 February 1945, 22.

62. Donald Pienkos traces the history of the Polish American Congress in "The Polish American Congress—An Appraisal," *Polish American Studies* 36, no. 2 (Autumn 1979): 5–43.

63. Polish American Congress, *Polish American Congress, Inc., 1944–1948: Selected Documents* (Chicago: Polish American Congress, 1948), 36. Hereafter cited as PAC, *Selected Documents*.

64. "Poles in U.S. Split on Big 3 Decision," *New York Times*, 14 February 1945, 12.

65. Lukas, *Strange Allies*, 143.

66. Ibid. The small, but vocal, left-wing group of Polish Americans was active in Detroit throughout the 1930s. See Margaret Collingwood Nowak, *Two Who Were There: A Biography of Stanley Nowak* (Detroit: Wayne State University Press, 1989).

67. Lukas, *Strange Allies*, 144.

68. Ibid., 144–145.

69. Lansing Warren, "Congress Splits on Crimea Parley," *New York Times*, 14 February 1945, 11.

70. Lukas, *Strange Allies*, 145.

71. See ibid., 158–160.

72. U.S. Department of State, *Foreign Relations of the United States, Diplomatic Papers. The Conference of Berlin (The Potsdam Conference), 1945*, 2 vols. (Washington, DC: U. S. Government Printing Office, 1960), 1: 743–745n. Hereafter cited as FRUS, Potsdam 1 or Potsdam 2; Herbert Feis, *Between War and Peace: The Potsdam Conference* (Princeton, NJ: Princeton University Press, 1960), 36–37; Lukas, *Bitter Legacy*, 14.

73. Kruszewski, *The Oder–Neisse Boundary*, 18–19.

74. Berlin Conference Background Information, 6 July 1945, in Berlin Conference File, vol. 2, Harry S Truman Papers, Naval Aide File, Section 20, Harry S. Truman Library. Hereafter cited as HST/L.

75. Ibid., vol. 3.

76. Ibid., vol. 2.

77. FRUS, Potsdam 1: 755.

78. Byrnes, *Speaking Frankly*, 67–68; Bohlen, *Witness*, 225–226; Lukas, *Bitter Legacy*, 9; Wandycz, *The United States*, 303.

79. Wandycz, *The United States*, 303.

80. FRUS, Potsdam 2: 89–90, 208.

81. See FRUS, Potsdam 2: 208–209; Stettinius, *Roosevelt and the Russians*, 126.

82. A U.S. Delegation Working Paper of 23 July 1945 noted that the Soviet Zone, including the Polish-occupied area, contained 45–50 percent of German wealth and contended that "Soviet and Polish claims for reparation by removals of capital equipment (including 'war booty or trophies'), current production, or stocks of goods should be met solely from the Soviet Zone." See FRUS, Potsdam 2: 209, 862.

83. FRUS, Potsdam 2: 209.

84. Ibid., 210.

85. Ibid., 211.

86. Ibid., 214.

87. Ibid., 247.

88. Ibid., 250.

89. In none of the official reports of the Yalta meeting in FRUS, Yalta, do Roosevelt and Churchill specify the Neisse River—either east or west. Both referred only to a border on the Oder.

90. FRUS, Potsdam 2: 333.

91. Ibid., 332–334, 1517–1524.

92. Feis, *Between War*, 231.

93. FRUS, Potsdam 2: 356-357; Edward J. Rozek, *Allied Wartime Diplomacy: A Pattern in Poland* (New York: John Wiley and Sons, 1958), 408–409.

94. FRUS, Potsdam 2: 383.

95. Ibid.

96. Truman read this statement from a document, apparently with a manuscript notation by Byrnes that read: "For consideration and possible use before adjournment—for the record." See FRUS, Potsdam 2: 642.

97. Ibid., 385.

98. Ibid., 1128–1129, 1140–1141; Lukas, *Bitter Legacy*, 16–19.

99. Stanisław Mikołajczyk, *The Rape of Poland: Pattern of Soviet Aggression*, (New York: McGraw Hill, 1948), 137–138.

100. Lukas, *Bitter Legacy*, 16; FRUS, Potsdam 2: 403–406, 1528–1529.

101. FRUS, Potsdam 2: 472.

102. Ibid., 472, 1150.

103. Ibid., 1539; map is from ibid., facing page 1152; Mastny, *Russia's Road*, 299.

104. FRUS, Potsdam 2: 1539.

105. Mastny, *Russia's Road*, 300.

106. Feis, *Between War*, 262; FRUS, Potsdam 2: 480.

107. FRUS, Potsdam 2: 480–492; Feis, *Between War*, 259–267.

108. Byrnes, *All in One Lifetime*, 302.

109. FRUS, Potsdam 2: 1509.

110. Ibid., 1511.

111. Byrnes, *Speaking Frankly*, 86.

112. Cyril Clemens, ed., *Truman Speaks* (Webster Groves, MO: International Mark Twain Society, 1946,), 66.

113. Ibid.

114. Report to the Nation on the Potsdam Conference, 9 August 1945, in Papers of Samuel I. Roseman, Box 4, HST/L.

115. Ibid.

116. "Pole Criticized Potsdam," *New York Times*, 11 August 1945, 6.

117. "Continuing Teamwork," *Christian Science Monitor*, 3 August 1945, 16.

118. "More Light on Potsdam," *Christian Science Monitor*, 11 August 1945, 16.

119. "The President's Report," *New York Times*, 10 August 1945, 14.

120. Lukas, *Bitter Legacy*, 18.

121. Denise O'Neal Conover, "James F. Byrnes, Germany and the Cold War, 1946" (Ph.D. diss., Washington State University, 1978), 34, 39.

122. Wandycz, *The United States*, 303-304.

123. See Jozef Kokot, *The Logic of the Oder-Neisse Frontier*, trans. Andrzej Potocki, (Poznan: Zachodnia Agencja Prasowa, 1959); Alfons Klafkowski, *The Potsdam Agreement*, trans. Aleksander Trop-Krynski, (Warsaw: Polish Scientific Publishers, 1963).

124. See Rhode and Wagner, *The Genesis of the Oder–Neisse Line*, 177–179.

125. Ibid.

126. Elizabeth Wiskemann, *Germany's Eastern Neighbours: Problems Relating to the Oder–Neisse Line and the Czech Frontier Regions* (London: Oxford University Press, 1956), 6.

127. Ibid., 112 , 114–115.

2 Interpreting the Potsdam Agreement

The months following the Potsdam Conference brought forth varying interpretations of the accord concerning Poland's western border. Poland and the Soviet Union claimed that the conference had settled the border issue that would be confirmed at the peace conference. The United States continued to emphasize the provisional nature of Poland's administration of the western lands until a peace conference settled the issue. In spite of this public stand, U.S. representatives in internal correspondence recognized that the Poles already controlled much of the area, largely with the aid of the Soviet army, and that the possibility of Poland's relinquishing those lands was slim. Thus, a pattern is generally evident in the early years of the Truman administration in which State Department officials protested or objected to Polish and Soviet actions that suggested the Oder–Neisse as a permanent border, recognized privately the ineffectiveness of these protests, and disagreed among themselves about the best course of action in such a situation.

POPULATION TRANSFERS

This pattern is apparent in the transfer of the German population from the area east of the Oder–Neisse Line. Although the Potsdam Protocol requested the suspension of population transfers until the Allied Control Council developed a plan to carry out the transfers in an "orderly and humane" manner, the removal of Germans from the Polish-administered territories continued.[1] The reason for this was apparent to American Ambassador Arthur Lane when he arrived in Warsaw to take up his assignment. He wrote to the State Department his impressions of the Poles' feelings about the Germans: "The hatred against the Germans is so great—as can readily be understood after seeing Warsaw as it is now—that feeling against other races must necessarily be blind by comparison."[2] Ambassador Lane learned from the British chargè that while the Polish government agreed to postpone the expulsions of Germans according to the Potsdam directive, the Polish vice minister for foreign affairs, Zygmunt Modzelewski, added qualifications to this agreement. Modzelewski claimed that many Germans who departed the area had not been expelled, but had left voluntarily as the Soviet army advanced west. The vice minister promised that the Polish government did not want to add to the growing confusion in the area but indicated that the Poles would continue to expel Germans from Stettin, Oppeln, and Silesia—areas vital to Poland's reconstruction.[3]

The Allied Control Council for Germany began investigating the situation involving the German minority almost immediately after it received Section Thirteen of the Potsdam Protocol. On 17 August 1945 the Soviet representatives on the council estimated that about 4.5 million Germans had been removed from East Prussia, Pomerania, and Silesia and that another 1 million more would be expelled from Poland.[4] Robert Murphy, U.S. political adviser for Germany, agreed with Soviet estimates that 4.5 million had already been expelled, but calculated that 2.5 million, rather than 1 million, Germans in Poland still awaited expulsion.[5]

Washington continued its attempts to bring order out of the chaos, authorizing Ambassador Lane to approach the Polish government about suspending the expulsions and directing him to gather data on the exact number to be expelled.[6] Since Lane was out of Warsaw, Chargè Gerald Keith discussed the suspension with Vice Minister Modzelewski, who again stated that while the Polish government was willing to comply with the request, it would be easier to repatriate Poles once the Germans had left.[7] When Ambassador Lane returned to Warsaw, he sent a telegram to Acting Secretary of State Dean Acheson detailing the diplomatic landmine that the expellee issue represented for the United States. Lane reported that he had discussed the issue of population transfers with U.S. Political Adviser Robert Murphy in Berlin on 18 September. While he agreed with Murphy that "any unnecessary harshness" by the Poles toward the Germans was to be regretted, he cautioned that the government-controlled press in Poland was very quick to accuse the British and American representatives in Poland of fascist leanings if they criticized the Poles on this matter without Soviet concurrence. Lane suggested that the Western Allies seek Soviet approval of the suspension in order to quiet the rumors circulating in Poland that the British and Americans were more concerned about the return of the Germans to Germany than about the return of Poles to Poland.[8] A few days later Lane reported that the British ambassador in Warsaw agreed with him about the inadvisability of criticizing German expulsions unless the Soviet ambassador in Poland, Viktor Lebediev, concurred. When they tried to get Soviet agreement, however, Lebediev reported that he was uninformed about expulsions but would seek information from his Foreign Office.[9]

The Allied Control Council continued to investigate and on 3 October 1945 sent a request to the Polish government to report on the number, ages, sex, and occupation of the Germans who were yet to be transferred out of Poland.[10]

In spite of these requests to suspend expulsions and report to the Control Council, American representatives in Germany soon learned that Germans were still leaving the Polish-administered territories—either voluntarily or forcibly. Political Adviser Robert Murphy explained his concerns about these continuing transfers in a letter and memo to his State Department colleague in the Office of European Affairs, H. Freeman Matthews. Murphy's correspondence echoes an almost agonizingly reflective tone with the horrors of World War II still very fresh in his mind. In the 12 October 1945 letter Murphy perhaps reflected on his earlier conversation with Lane when he acknowledged that the United States might be accused of being too soft on the Germans by even mentioning the issue of expulsions. He explained, however, that his concern was not so much for the German population as for what might happen to American principles if the situation continued. He worried, "It may become too easy for us to sacrifice those same principles in regard to our own people. There are some features of the American way of life which I know we would not want to see jettisoned." Murphy made clear to Matthews that while the American representatives in Germany did not have a complete picture of the situation because of a lack of firsthand observers in the area, reports from refugees, the Office of Strategic Services (OSS), and other U.S. officials indicated that the transfers continued. Murphy stated, "I am uncomfortable in the thought that somehow in the future we may be severely blamed for consenting to be party to an operation which we cannot ourselves control and which has caused and is causing such large scale human suffering."[11]

The memorandum accompanying the letter recorded the "distress and despair" of the refugees, mostly women and children from east of the Oder–Neisse Line, and noted the presence of the "dregs of the *Herrenvolk*," the hundreds of thousands of German prisoners of war released by the Soviets. Murphy reflected that the immorality of the deportations ordered by the Nazis was one of the main reasons for the Allied effort against Hitler and pointed to the sad irony of America's now being a party to just such deportations with the Soviet Union, which directly controlled the eastern zone where many of the homeless ended up. He stated that American medical authorities in Berlin reported an average of ten deaths per day at one of the railroad stations housing refugees and observed that, "the mind reverts instantly to Dachau and Buchenwald." He acknowledged his difference of opinion with Ambassador Lane, who held the Soviets culpable since they were in charge of Poland and could relieve the suffering. Murphy placed responsibility squarely on the Poles, whose recent suffering at the hands of Germans had "undoubtedly" made them "callous to German suffering." The political adviser recognized that the United States might be unable to stop the population transfers but urged that the U.S. government make clear its attitude that the transfers were to be carried out in an orderly and humane manner according to Potsdam. Otherwise, Murphy warned, the record would indicate that the United States had been a partner in practices that it had often condemned.[12]

As American officials predicted, the population transfers continued, and in November 1945 the Polish government created a Ministry for Regained Territories to deal with the transfers and with the question of land settlement.[13] Washington received urgent requests from American representatives in Germany for clarification of procedure concerning the expellees. Murphy telegraphed to Secretary of State Brynes in Washington warnings that he received from the Office of Military Government for Germany (OMGUS) concerning the plight of the expellees. The military government estimated that there would be between 2.5–3 million victims of malnutrition and disease in the area between the Oder and the Elbe by the spring of 1946. Rather than focus on the inhumanity to the Germans of such actions, the report called attention to the serious danger of epidemic that such dislocation could mean to all of Europe, "including our troops," and also the probability of unprecedented starvation.[14] The report estimated that 10 million people had left or would move from Poland and Czechoslovakia to the Soviet zone in Germany.[15] In response to Murphy's warnings, Byrnes, though noting the gravity of the situation, offered no practical solutions.[16]

By November 1945 the Allied Control Council had developed a plan calling for the orderly transfer of 3.5 million Germans from western Poland to begin 1 December 1945 and extend through July 1946. Under this plan 2 million would go to the Soviet zone, and the remaining 1.5 million to the British zone.[17] A few days after this program was proposed, Byrnes sent Murphy notice of the department's approval along with the text of a note that the State Department was going to send the Polish government to register its disapproval of the treatment of the German expellees. In the note, the U.S. government expressed hope that the Poles would cooperate in implementing the new, orderly program of population transfers.[18]

As before, however, when Ambassador Lane received this directive from the State Department, he decided to delay immediate action. On 4 December 1945, he wired the department his five reasons for doing so. According to Lane, his staff in Warsaw had investigated the situation in western Poland and had reported that the Germans had not suffered "any widespread harsh treatment" beyond some evictions. Lane felt that the reports of Germans being mistreated were characteristic of their "whining" after losing the war and making "the picture as black as possible." Without condoning the cruelty, he referred to the mistreatment of the Poles by the Germans as making the reciprocal treatment by the Poles at least understandable. He again cited the accusations in the Polish press against the British for being too soft on the Germans and warned that such accusations would also be leveled at the United States. In an attempt to avoid this situation, Lane preferred to present an oral statement to the Polish government regarding the "alleged mistreatment of Germans." Lane then provided further justification when he stated, "The international consequences seem to be so important in this situation as to warrant a reconsideration of the instructions given me."[19] Lane later discussed the situation with the British ambassador in Warsaw, who again agreed with his assessment.[20]

Secretary Byrnes wired his approval of Lane's course of action but directed him to explain to the Polish government that the actions of the United States did not reflect a lack of appreciation for the sufferings of the Poles at the hands of the Germans but rather were based on the desire to see the relevant articles of the Potsdam Accord carried out.[21] Lane reported to the secretary his interview with the Polish foreign minister and his aide, who reassured Lane that their government had issued instructions that the evictions be carried out humanely. The Polish diplomats somewhat blithely added that Polish citizens who felt a keen sense of vengeance against the Germans often took matters into their own hands. They also told Lane that the Germans were not being treated any worse than the Poles who were returning from the east.[22]

The organized transfers envisioned in the Allied Control Council plan could not get under way until the middle of January 1946. Journalists, relief workers, and congressmen recorded the plight of the expellees. Anne O'Hare McCormick of the *New York Times* reported on the "nightmarish conditions" of the refugees in February 1946 and in the fall of that year reportedly labeled the transfer a "'crime against humanity for which history will exact a terrible retribution.'"[23] An editorial in the *New York Times* reflected Robert Murphy's concerns about the impact of the expulsions on American principles. It stated that the expulsions of the Germans after the war called to mind the horrors of the Nazis and warned that once a country allowed such actions, it was difficult to set limits for such thoughts and activities.[24] Various congressmen spoke on the floor of the House and Senate about the findings of their investigations into the horrible living conditions of the uprooted Germans and Poles.[25]

The conditions of the expellees improved during 1946 in spite of the immensity of the problem and the vengeful attitude of many of the participants. The transfers that occurred after the Allied Control Council implemented its plan involved approximately 6 million people. While the death rate was still high, the fact that the Allies in the German zones knew how many expellees to expect and roughly when to expect them saved many more lives than if the expulsions had continued as in 1945. The major evictions were completed by 1946, although another 500,000 Germans arrived in the Soviet zone from Poland in 1947. An unknown number of Germans remained.[26]

THE ESTABLISHMENT OF CONSULATES

The expulsion of the Germans from the Polish-administered territories was only one of the concerns of American diplomats in Poland. The Polish government sought and eventually received from the United States some financial aid and goods to repair the enormous destruction that the Germans (and unofficially the Soviets) had caused.[27] Another of Ambassador Lane's concerns was to establish U.S. consulates in Poland. The Polish government granted the United States permission to establish consulates in Danzig (Gdansk), Kraków, Łódz, Poznan, and Breslau (Wrocław). Ambassador Lane had to consider which of these sites could best deal with economic matters as well as keep watch on political developments outside Warsaw. As Department of State officials pondered this question, they again revealed their contradictory thinking about the status of Poland's western territories.

Before he left for Poland, Lane had notified the department's Eastern European Division that he wanted to establish three or four consular offices in Poland, one in either Gdynia or Danzig, one in Kraków, one in Poznan, and one in Łódz.[28] After he arrived in Warsaw, the American Embassy officers informed him that each of these sites would make suitable consulates. The Eastern European Division agreed with his recommendations.[29] In the final paragraph of an 8 September 1945 telegram to the department, Lane recognized the fact that the region of Gdansk was part of the territories only provisionally administered by Poland. He noted that the consulate would serve both ports of Gdansk and Gdynia but recommended that it be established in Gdansk since that city was the district headquarters. He did not place much emphasis on the fact that the United States was proposing to open a consulate in disputed territory. He wrote that the establishment of the consulate "need not imply recognition of incorporation of Gdansk into Poland provided we make it clear in requesting provisional recognition that determination of frontiers must await decisions of [the] peace conference. Boundaries of [the] Gdansk Consular District which would presumably include that part of East Prussia now under Polish administration would have to be delimited subsequently."[30] He simply recommended that the United States hold to its official line that final determination of the border awaited a peace treaty. The United States opened a consulate in Gdansk.

The next month Lane requested permission and funds to open a consulate in Stettin (Szczecin), since it would become an important port serving the Oder River and its tributaries. In his report to the department he noted that the Soviet army occupied a large part of the area and that the Polish authorities had begun to provide essential services to the city. Lane viewed the city as an important post for reporting political activity that could not be covered by the officers in Warsaw and emphasized again the "good effect" that U.S. consulates in Poland could have on U.S.–Polish relations.[31] Acting Secretary Dean Acheson denied Lane's request, not on diplomatic grounds concerning the ambiguity of Stettin's future but because of funding difficulties. He appointed two more officers to the Warsaw office who could be temporarily detailed to Stettin and notified Lane that "consideration will be given [to the] possible establishment [of a] regular office [there]."[32]

By late 1946 the financial situation grew worse, and an inspector recommended that the consulates at Poznan and Kraków be closed and that those considered for Łódz and Szczecin not be opened. The Eastern European Division, however, rejected that idea and even proposed that the United States open an additional office in Wrocław (Breslau), a city in the western territories that had been almost totally destroyed in the war. Lane had earlier concurred with the Polish Foreign Office to postpone establishment of a consulate there because of the destruction; but by 1946 the Eastern European Division, noting the tightening travel restrictions for foreigners in Poland, was worried that if the United States did not soon establish a presence in Wrocław, the area might be cut off from future visits.[33] The author of the proposal, Llewellyn E. Thompson Jr., noted that a consulate in Wroclaw would be an important listening post for Poland as well as for the Soviet zone in Germany by providing political, economic, and military information. Again, Thompson acknowledged that Wrocław was in the Polish-administered territories almost as an afterthought. In a handwritten memorandum with Thompson's initials attached to this official report, he asked, "Do you see any political objection to our opening a Consulate at Breslau in Polish administered German territory? I do not. The British already have an office at Stettin." The reply from the deputy director of the Office of European Affairs, John Hickerson: "No objection."[34]

In his memoirs of his time in Poland, Ambassador Lane admits that although the United States did not open the consular offices in Wrocław or Szczecin, the actions of the U.S. government in making such requests did indicate "our concurrence with the Polish claim to this territory."[35] Indeed, this casual approach to opening consulates in the western territories of Poland contrasts greatly with the care and concern shown by the State Department about opening consulates in the Baltic states after 1940. There the United States took pains in its diplomatic approach to avoid any indication that it recognized Soviet sovereignty of Latvia, Lithuania, or Estonia. The United States did not reopen consulates there after the war, and the U.S. ambassador in Moscow as well as other high-ranking U.S. officials did not generally visit the Baltic states. This was seen as a way to enforce the policy of nonrecognition. Yet, in western Poland, a region whose official status awaited a peace conference, the United States quickly moved to consider opening consulates. This act of diplomacy was interpreted by many as granting de facto recognition of sovereignty to the Polish government.[36]

TENSIONS IN U.S.–POLISH RELATIONS

While U.S. officials in Warsaw and Washington were trying to coordinate efforts, rumors circulated about the situation in the western territories, adding to the State Department's difficulties of stabilizing relations with Poland. In February 1946, an American representative quoted a source of unknown reliability as stating that cities in the western territories had been set afire by Polish troops and that the German population in the area was fleeing westward. Rumors were also rife about the future status of Poland's borders.

One claimed that the United Nations had passed a resolution demanding that Lwów be returned to Poland; one alleged that the United Nations had ordered Poland to evacuate territory that had been part of the German Reich of 1937.[37]

Ambassador Lane quoted a "responsible source" claiming that Polish leaders had been told in Moscow that it might be necessary to move Poland's western border east and that the Poles would receive compensation, probably Lwów and the surrounding oil fields.[38] Another report, sent to the State Department on 28 May 1946 from the naval attaché assigned to Warsaw, confirmed some of the earlier rumors regarding Soviet activity in the Polish western territories. The attaché, having traveled through part of the Polish western territories, reported that the area around Szczecin contained few Polish settlers and that many of the farmsteads had been looted or destroyed by war activity. He talked with Poles who told him that the Soviets had removed one of the rail lines and had used the other to ship out livestock and farm equipment. The attaché himself saw evidence of the latter as he followed a Russian military convoy heading east with numerous loaded wagons and livestock.[39]

DETERMINING SOVIET INTENTIONS

Reports also came into the department from American representatives in Germany who recorded their observations of the situation involving the Polish–German border. These reports generally reflect U.S. suspicion of Soviet motives, focusing on the Soviets' apparent willingness to court western Germany with intimations of a border revision. One official, Brewster Morris, speculated that since the Soviets had developed a Soviet German republic in their zone, they would now move to "bring Western Germany into line." One way to do this would be to hold out the promise of adjusting the Oder–Neisse border.[40]

The following month Political Adviser Robert Murphy reported on a meeting that tested the reliability of this speculation regarding Soviet intentions. At a meeting with members of the Polish Military Mission in Berlin, Ernst Lemmer, the deputy chairman of the Christian Democrat Union (CDU) in Berlin and the Soviet Zone, discussed the question of the Polish–German frontier in connection with the possible formation of a Socialist Unity Party in Germany. Murphy reported that the gist of this discussion was that if the Germans agreed to establish a united workers party and form a "'progressive democracy'" with an "eastern orientation," Germany might expect Soviet support for a favorable change in the Oder–Neisse frontier. During the discussion Lemmer presented his view of an acceptable frontier, stating that while he was prepared to "'write off'" East and West Prussia and Upper Silesia, he urged that a new line be drawn east of the present border. The Poles rejected this proposal outright, stating that since the Soviets had acquired much Polish territory in the east, Poland had a lot less land than before the war—even if the Oder–Neisse border were finalized. Lemmer responded to this by pointing out that the lands gained from Germany in the west were much more fertile than those lost to the Soviets in the east, implying that the Poles needed less land. The Poles then presented their suggested border, after conceding that the existing line resulted in an underpopulated Poland and an overpopulated Germany. The proposed compromises, if they were meant in earnest, might have surprised the Polish officials' superiors in Warsaw. They demanded retention of the estuary of the Oder River, including Stettin; the Oder would still serve as the border, but the regions of Lower and Central Silesia where they lie west of the Oder would be negotiable. In response to Lemmer's question, the Poles indicated that the industrial region of Waldenberg (in Lower Silesia) was more important to the Germans than to the Poles and that this region—even up to the Neisse River—was open to discussion (see Map 2.1).[41] Murphy's speculation that the Poles had arranged this meeting, probably with Soviet backing to address rumors circulating about a potential border adjustment, reveals that he did not know the degree to which the Soviets were in control of the situation.[42]

About a month later, Murphy reported another conversation that one of his staff had had with Lemmer and Jakob Kaiser, another CDU leader. Both Germans believed that in light of recent conversations that they had held with Polish representatives, the Soviets were going to present a surprise move in their zone right before the elections. They believed that this move could be the rectification of Germany's eastern border in Germany's favor.[43] Another reported rumor in late August 1946 indicated that the Soviets had notified Warsaw that they would return part of the territory annexed from Poland if Poland agreed to return to Germany part of the western territories.[44] At the same time, though, Polish Ambassador to the United States Oskar Lange, as well as other Poles informed American officials that they had received the Soviets' "solemn assurances" of full support for the Oder–Neisse Line.[45]

THE SITUATION IN GERMANY

These conflicting rumors concerning Soviet intentions in Germany and Poland were a natural part of the postwar chaos, but they also probably represent Soviet strategy to delay a decision to support the goals of either the Germans or the Poles. When American diplomats in the field reported the rumors and speculated on Soviet intentions for the Oder–Neisse border, they were trying to fill in one piece of this diplomatic puzzle. Since another part of that puzzle involved Germany, it is important to note the broad outlines of U.S. policy for Germany in order to detail its impact on the U.S. position regarding the Oder–Neisse Line.[46] Although American officials differed in their opinion about the level and duration of control to be maintained in Germany as outlined in the Potsdam Protocol and in JCS1067, the U.S. directive governing the occupation, they basically envisioned a democratic Germany, incapable of making war and with a strong economy. Washington sought German borders

Map 2.1

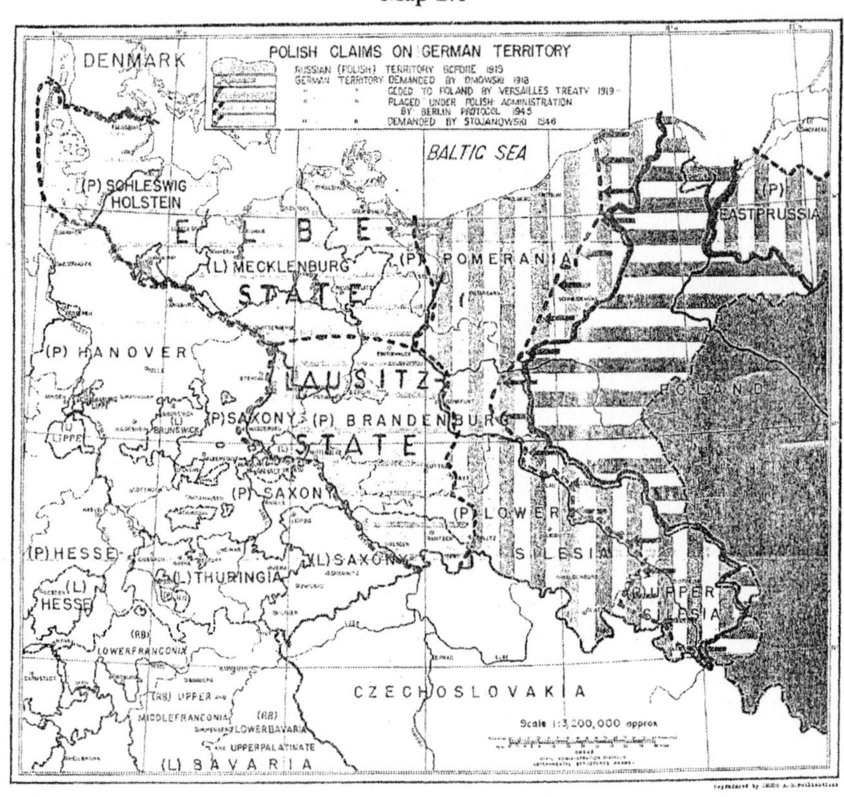
POLISH CLAIMS ON GERMAN TERRITORY
RUSSIAN (POLISH) TERRITORY BEFORE 1919
GERMAN TERRITORY DEMANDED BY DMOWSKI 1918
CEDED TO POLAND BY VERSAILLES TREATY 1919
PLACED UNDER POLISH ADMINISTRATION BY BERLIN PROTOCOL 1945
DEMANDED BY STOJANOWSKI 1946
DENMARK
BALTIC SEA
(P) SCHLESWIG HOLSTEIN
ELBE STATE
(L) MECKLENBURG
(P) POMERANIA
(P) EASTPRUSSIA
(P) HANOVER
LAUSITZ
(P) SAXONY
(P) BRANDENBURG
STATE
POLAND
(L) LIPPE
BRUNSWICK
(P) SAXONY
(P) LOWER SILESIA
(P) HESSE
(L) THURINGIA
(L) SAXONY
(L) HESSE
(P) UPPER SILESIA
(RB) LOWERFRANCONIA
(RB) UPPER AND MIDDLEFRANCONIA
(RB) LOWERBAVARIA
UPPERPALATINATE
(L) BAVARIA
CZECHOSLOVAKIA
Scale 1:3,200,000 approx

that "would clearly promote peace and recovery in Europe and in the world."[47]

In Germany's west this goal meant that the U.S. rejected the French claim to the Ruhr and Rhineland because it did not accord with ethnic or economic considerations that promoted peace, but the U.S. supported French claims for the Saar if France agreed to the principles and purposes of Potsdam. The question of Germany's eastern border proved more problematic, revealing some bureaucratic and philosophical disagreements among American officials in Central Europe. In a July 1946 summary of U.S. policy objectives in Germany, General Lucius Clay, head of OMGUS, acknowledged the transfer of the Oder–Neisse lands to Soviet and Polish control as laid out in the Potsdam Accord. Soon, however, the War Department directed Clay not to publish this policy statement since the State Department objected to the clause dealing with U.S. acceptance of the Oder–Neisse border.[48]

From Moscow in March 1946, Chargè George Kennan had cabled his analysis of the Soviet position regarding Germany. One of the major points of Kennan's analysis was that the U.S. agreement at Potsdam on the Oder–Neisse Line, in addition to satisfying Soviet strategic desires and placing Poland squarely in the Soviet orbit, had made any future cooperation between Poland and Germany impossible and had "highly complicated" Germany's future as an independent state.[49] A secret report prepared in 1946 outlining American objectives in Germany further showed that some State Department officials were having second thoughts about part of the Potsdam Agreement because of its potentially negative impact on Germany. According to this report, the United States had "reluctantly" agreed at Potsdam to the provisional occupation by Poland of territory east of the Oder and western Neisse Rivers because no other option presented itself. It noted that the devastation that Germany had caused in Poland and the Soviet Union and the establishment of a new eastern border in Poland led the Americans to believe that no "delimitation of Germany's eastern frontier would be tenable were it unacceptable to Poland and the USSR." The report qualified America's acceptance of the border as reluctant since U.S. delegates foresaw the potential for German irredentism and the problems that it would cause for Germany's economic recovery without substantially aiding Poland's recovery.[50]

Without criticizing the Potsdam Agreement directly, the report indicated that while a frontier had to be established that was still acceptable to Poland and the Soviet Union, the authors doubted Poland's ability to develop the agricultural areas provisionally placed in its control and also doubted Germany's ability to recover with its agricultural resources so severely restricted. The report favored a German eastern border that kept part of the agricultural resources of Pomerania, Brandenburg, and Lower Silesia in order to promote peace and economic recovery. In listing U.S. objectives in Germany, the authors of this report placed "final agreement on the permanent territorial composition of Germany" as the first immediate objective.[51]

SECRETARY BYRNES' STUTTGART SPEECH

Secretary of State Byrnes recognized the need to clarify publicly U.S. policy for Germany while privately addressing these growing bureaucratic tensions; he also wanted to force the Soviets to elaborate on their stance announced in a July 1946 speech by Soviet Foreign Minister Molotov. In his speech Molotov had denounced plans or attempts to agrarianize, dismember, or cede German land without approval by plebiscite; he called instead for a united, prosperous Germany.[52] Byrnes traveled to Stuttgart, Germany, in September 1946 from Paris, where he was attending a meeting of foreign ministers. At Stuttgart Byrnes delivered a speech with the encouragement of General Clay after consultation with President Truman, much of which echoed the position outlined in the secret policy paper on Germany.[53] He opened the speech with general statements about America's desire for peace and United Nations' cooperation and then outlined the U.S. desire for lasting peace in Germany. Byrnes reiterated the Potsdam provisions for a demilitarized, democratic, and neutral Germany, but with German industry repaired to an acceptable level in an economically unified Germany. He then turned to the question of Germany's boundaries and stated that at Potsdam the delegates had agreed to the Soviet desire for Königsberg and to the provisional administration by Poland of part of eastern Germany, subject to a future peace treaty. The Americans at Potsdam had been told that the Soviets and Poles already held much of this land out of military expediency.

Byrnes emphasized that at the Potsdam Conference the heads of government had not agreed to the cession to Poland of any particular area but rather had agreed to the Yalta provision that Poland would receive territory in the north and west to compensate for lands lost east of the Curzon Line. He promised that the United States would, as stated in the Yalta and Potsdam Agreements, support a revision of the western border in Poland's favor but added that the extent of the area given to Poland would be determined at a future peace conference. He reiterated U.S. support for French claims to the Saar to increase French security but noted that other than these territorial adjustments the United States would "not support any encroachment on territory which is indisputably German or any division of Germany which is not genuinely desired by the people concerned."[54] In this speech Byrnes did not alter U.S. policy on Germany as outlined at Potsdam, but the timing and emphasis of his speech resulted in an immediate response from the Polish government and led to difficulties for American officials in Poland. In addition, Polish Americans made known their dissatisfaction with the speech.

The Polish government responded with scathing rhetoric, claiming that Byrnes' speech indicated U.S. support for the revisionist campaign of "remnants of Hitler's Reich."[55] On 8 September Władysław Gomułka spoke at a meeting in Warsaw condemning the speech as reactionary for its implication that

Germany's eastern border might be changed in Germany's favor. Gomułka saw the secretary's speech as further evidence of Poland's vital need to have a strong alliance with its "true and sincere friends" in the Soviet Union.[56]

Ambassador Lane, who was unaware of the speech, responded to a request for an explanation by Acting Foreign Minister Jozef Olszewski, who had read it from the French news service. Based on the portions that Olszewski read to him, Lane assured the foreign minister that the speech could not be interpreted as a desire on the part of the United States to avoid the obligations that it had assumed at Potsdam. Olszewski told Lane that the speech would have a very unfavorable impact on Poles and would be a shock to those settlers moving into the western territories from the area east of the Curzon Line. Lane replied by emphasizing that Potsdam had given Poland only provisional control of the area and stated that if the settlers believed that their move was permanent, it was because the Polish government and press had made it out to be so.

Lane wired Secretary Byrnes that Olszewski's remarks clearly indicated the Polish government's annoyance. He informed Byrnes that he had expressed his desire to the acting foreign minister that the Polish press report the speech correctly without distortion.[57] Lane was to be disappointed in this hope. *Głos Ludu*, the newspaper of the Polish Worker's Party, contained a violent editorial calling for the Poles to denounce what it called U.S. plans for the rebirth of Germany after Poles had shed blood to regain lands in the west.[58]

The Polish Foreign Office announced its official reaction to the press a few days after Byrnes' speech. It rejected on two counts the secretary's suggestion that the Potsdam decision was not final. The first was that the agreement had specifically approved the transfer of Germans from the area; the second was that an adjustment of the border in Germany's favor would be tantamount to obligating Poland to pay Germany an indemnity since the capital and effort invested in the western territories would go to Germany.[59] Not surprisingly, Polish newspapers followed this line, emphasizing that the Oder–Neisse Line as determined at Potsdam was the final Polish frontier that Byrnes sought to change. Lane noted some obvious omissions but few outright distortions of Byrnes' speech since the press focused mainly on the alleged implications of the speech rather than the wording.[60] These press reports effectively stirred the general Polish population into violent reaction in Warsaw and Łódz.[61] Mikołajczyk's Polish Peasant Party headquarters in Warsaw was sacked and burned, and a crowd outside the U.S. ambassador's residence protested Byrnes' speech. The Polish government attempted to link the Peasant Party, already weakened by election fraud, intimidation, and terror, with America's allegedly pro-German stance.[62]

Soviet Foreign Minister Molotov responded to Byrnes' speech in a report to the Polish News Agency in Paris on 17 September 1946. Molotov claimed that Byrnes' statements regarding the Polish-administered territories caused doubts about the stability of that frontier and therefore had to be answered. He agreed that Potsdam had provisionally placed the area under

Polish administration pending a peace conference but stated that this agreement had fulfilled the Yalta Accord and was not just an "accidental [agreement], adopted under the influence of temporary considerations." He claimed that the importance of the Potsdam Agreement on Poland's borders was evident in the acceptance by the powers of the population transfers, revealing that they "never envisaged any revision of this decision in the future." So, Molotov continued, while the Potsdam protocol technically made the agreement provisional, the population transfers indicated its permanence. The border awaited only formal recognition at a peace conference since "the idea of involving millions of people in such experiments is unbelievable, quite apart from the cruelty of it, both towards the Poles and the Germans themselves."[63]

Throughout these verbal attacks and accusations, Ambassador Lane continued to support Byrnes' position as a reiteration of the Potsdam Agreement and to emphasize U.S.–Polish ties.[64] At a reception on 11 September, Ambassador Lane and Chargè Keith discussed the speech with various Polish officials, who spoke of their fears of a revival of German militarism.[65] The Americans reiterated the determination of the United States to ensure that Germany would not become another threat to its neighbors and they emphasized U.S. friendship with Poland.[66] When he traveled to Paris in October 1946, Lane discussed the speech with Department of State representatives, who told him that the intent of the speech was to "smoke out Molotov's attitude on the eve of elections in Germany."[67] In this sense Secretary Byrnes interpreted the speech as a complete victory because it forced the Soviets to express their support for Poland's retention of the Oder–Neisse area which disenchanted those Germans who looked to the Soviets as advocates.[68] Even Ambassador Lane, who did not always agree with State Department policy in Poland, admitted the effectiveness of the speech in forcing the Soviets' hand in Germany.

When he published his memoirs in 1948, Lane, however, did not fail to point out the negative impact of the speech on Mikołajczyk's political opposition in Poland.[69] When he learned of the speech, Mikołajczyk, who was in Copenhagen for a conference, immediately released a statement to the press emphasizing that retention of the territories by Poland was a question of life or death.[70] In a meeting with Lane on 27 September 1946, the Polish opposition leader discussed the Stuttgart speech and admitted that while it had hurt him politically, he did not believe that the speech reflected a viewpoint inimical to Poland's interest since it had forced the Soviets to declare their support for the Polish rather than the German communists. Mikolajczyk's support for the Oder–Neisse Line, however, was not widely reported in the Polish press; he and supporters in the Polish Peasant Party (PSL) were accused of supporting German rather than Polish claims.[71]

Although Mikołajczyk tried to keep his condemnation of the speech at a low tone, scholars of U.S.–Polish relations who later evaluated the situation did not hesitate to point out the devastating impact of the speech on the anticommunist movement in Poland. Richard Lukas finds it "incredible" that Byrnes did not take into account the potentially negative effect of the speech on U.S.–Polish relations. Lukas did not, however, ascribe any evil intentions to Byrnes when he stated, "Although he probably did not give much thought to the impact his speech would have on the Poles, Byrnes's action played into the hands of the communists, who could point with authority to their oft-repeated claim that the Soviet Union, not the United States, was Poland's only true friend."[72] Piotr Wandycz echoes Lukas' assessment when he calls the speech a "somewhat clumsy diplomatic offensive that sought to make Germany the pivot of American policy on the European continent. Its impact on American–Polish relations was bound to be unfortunate."[73] This indeed proved to be the case, as Polish Americans who closely watched the international scene pointed out to Secretary Byrnes almost immediately after the speech was made.

Charles Rozmarek, president of the Polish American Congress and Polish National Alliance, was in Paris to urge consideration of the Polish issue by the delegates to the foreign ministers conference. He handed Byrnes a memorandum on 11 September 1946, expressing dismay at the intimations of Byrnes' Stuttgart speech that made the inhabitants of Poland's western territories "the objects of international compromises and bargains" and made the territories a sort of "'Wild West'" that served Soviet expansionist interests into Western Europe.[74] In this memorandum and in a press conference the next day, Rozmarek called on the United States to recognize the Oder–Neisse Line as consistent with the Potsdam Agreement, which called these lands "'former German territories'" and which also approved the transfer of the German population.[75] "What better proof," Rozmarek asked, "could there be, that all the Three Big Powers represented at Potsdam already then considered the Oder–Niesse [*sic*] line as Poland's permanent western frontier?" He also warned that any attempts to change this position "would meet with determined disapproval and opposition" from Poles everywhere.[76]

Byrnes was not the only member of the administration to feel the wrath of the Polish American community. The vice president of the Polish American Congress, Walter Tolpa, sent Truman a letter informing him of the "deep resentment" of Polish Americans concerning Byrnes' "appeasement of Germany." Tolpa argued that the question of Poland's western border could not be decided without a revision of the eastern border and that the return to Poland of lands in the west that were historically Polish had created the conviction among the Poles that they were receiving indemnity from Germany for their years of suffering at German hands. He warned that any future deals regarding Poland, especially affecting the 4 million Poles settled in the western territories, would lead to Polish distrust of American leadership.[77] In a reply prepared by Under Secretary of State for Economic Affairs William Clayton, at the request of Truman's Secretary Matthew Connelly, Clayton explained that the U.S. held the position that while the Potsdam Agreement had specified that the final determination of the border would be made at a peace conference, Poland administered the territories until that time. He emphasized that Byrnes' speech had not indicated a departure from that position or from the belief that Poland should be compensated for the loss of land to the Soviets in the east.[78]

State divisions of the PAC also sent telegrams to Truman objecting to Byrnes' speech.[79] In addition, other Polish American groups such as the Society for the Promotion of Poland's Independence cabled the president objecting to the transfer of Poland's eastern territory to the Soviet Union and to the idea that the western territories compensated Poland for this loss. This group claimed that Poland had a historical and ethnic claim to the lands east of the Oder–Neisse border and that the new border made Poland economically and strategically strong.[80] A few weeks later, the Polish-American Labor Council of Chicago sent Truman a letter that was referred to the State Department for reply. In the letter the council protested what it saw as Byrnes' attempt to revise Germany's eastern border and thus violate Poland's historic right to the Oder–Neisse territories. The council referred to the unchanging nature of Germany's *Drang nach Osten* (drive to the east), which would only be strengthened by receiving the natural resources of Silesia.[81] Also enclosed with the letter was an analysis by the Polish-American Labor Council of U.S.–Soviet relations that called for a firm stand against the Soviets' territorial and political aggression.

In the reply, Assistant Chief of the Division of Eastern European Affairs C. Burke Elbrick reiterated the standard departmental stance that Byrnes' Stuttgart speech had not departed from the Yalta and Potsdam Agreements concerning Poland's western border, but had restated the position that Poland should be compensated for land lost to the Soviet Union. Elbrick also pointed out that Byrnes had reaffirmed U.S. interest in Poland when he stated, "'The United States will support a revision of these frontiers [i.e., northern and western frontiers] in Poland's favor. However, the extent of the area to be ceded to Poland must be determined by the final settlement agreed upon.'"[82]

A noteworthy point evident in much of this correspondence from Polish Americans concerning Poland's western territories is that they rejected the idea, expressed by the U.S. government, that the Oder–Neisse Line represented compensation for land lost to the Soviet Union in the east. Ironically, the Polish American Congress, a staunchly anticommunist organization, took the same line as the Polish and Soviet governments, which maintained that the lands east of the Oder–Neisse were historically Polish and had been taken by the Germans hundreds of years before.[83]

U.S. officials did not attempt to deal with the border on historical or ethnic grounds. The official record indicates that at the Tehran and Yalta Conferences, Stalin, Roosevelt, and Churchill generally discussed the acquisition of land by Poland in the west within the context of compensation for lands in the east to be given to the Soviet Union. Potsdam simply fulfilled parts of these earlier agreements. At Yalta Roosevelt had refused to be caught in the trap of trying to readjust ancient borders.[84] At these conferences the stated reason for Poland's new border in the west was the new border in the east.[85] In its policy statements after the war, the U.S. government held to this line. By war's end, however, the Polish American Congress and the Soviet-sponsored Polish government argued against the compensation idea. The Polish American Congress maintained that the Oder–Neisse Line was not fair compensation because the Curzon Line was illegal and because the lands were in any case historically Polish. The Polish and Soviet governments would certainly not argue against the legality of the Curzon Line. Instead, they maintained initially that Polish administration of the area was a practical necessity to deal with the postwar chaos and they later held that Poland had a historical right to its ancient lands in the west.[86]

Editorials and articles in the *New York Times* and the *Christian Science Monitor* concerning Byrnes' speech reflected the official U.S. government stance that the Oder–Neisse lands were provisionally given to Poland as compensation for lands lost to the Soviet Union.[87] Both newspapers also focused on the implications of Byrnes' speech rather than on its content. The *Christian Science Monitor* speculated that before the speech, the future peace conference that was to review the border plan had become a "mere formality" because the Poles controlled the area. Byrnes' speech, which the editor saw as a bid for Germany's favor in response to Molotov's July scheme, showed just how far the United States would go—at least rhetorically—to check the Soviets' plans for Germany.[88] The *New York Times* stated flatly that Byrnes' speech "implies that there may be a revision" [of the border] and contended that if the U.S. government simply accepted a Polish or Soviet fait accompli, it would also be guilty of violating past agreements.[89]

The Polish American press also focused on the implications for Poland of Byrnes' speech, but with a much more negative tone than that expressed in the mainstream press. Chicago's *Dziennik Związkowy* (Daily Alliance) called it a blow to the political and economic integrity of Poland and in an editorial on 9 September 1946, castigated Byrnes' position as timid, wavering, and yielding to the Germans, just as Roosevelt and Hull had yielded to the Soviets. The editor concluded with a warning that if the United States acquiesced in another violation of American ideals, the November elections would result in some changes.[90] Detroit's *Dziennik Polski* (Daily Pole) claimed that Byrnes, with Washington's approval, was recommending that Poland again become Germany's victim.[91]

The impact of Byrnes' speech continued to be felt in the days and months following. Some disagreement between the U.S. and French Embassies in Warsaw became evident when Ambassador Lane noted that Roger Garreau, French ambassador to Poland, had attended the Polish mass protest meeting on 8 September, where he "applauded the speeches hostile to the United States."[92] The State Department also reported that Garreau gave an interview to the Polish press stating that the French government believed that Poland should retain the

Oder–Neisse territory. When American representatives in Paris discussed this situation with the French Foreign Office, however, French officials replied "with some embarrassment" that Garreau "on occasion talked too much."[93] Officially, the French government refused to support a boundary line until it was discussed at a peace conference. American officials did not take this ambassadorial disagreement as evidence of a split in the Western alliance. In an evaluation of Garreau one American official wrote: "While insofar as we can determine Garreau is not a Communist, he is a Left-Centerist whose thinking and statements are frequently somewhat muddled."[94]

Of more concern to the American Embassy in Warsaw were the continued Polish media attacks against Byrnes' speech. In October Chargè Keith protested the display of a number of posters throughout Poland showing a Polish soldier in front of a map of Poland holding a gun toward a hand reaching out to Poland's western territories. The hand had a mixture of swastikas and dollar signs, and the inscription on the poster stated, "hands off our western frontier." Almost immediately the Foreign Office assured Keith that the posters would be removed, which they were.[95] A month later, however, this theme of a U.S.–Nazi Germany alliance against Poland again appeared in the Polish press. A cartoon showed Secretary Byrnes smiling in front of a flag containing swastikas and death heads where the stars and stripes of a U.S. flag would be. The caption read, "Flag of the United States of Germany (according to Byrnes' project)."[96]

American State Department officials also dealt with the repercussions of the Byrnes speech in a less public way and in a manner that suggested that the U.S. government was not prepared to put the alleged implications of the speech to the test. On 29 October 1946 representatives of the Division of Investment and Economic Affairs, the Petroleum Division, the Office of the Legal Adviser, and the Division of Eastern European Affairs met to discuss the problem of the Polish government's nationalization of property belonging to American nationals in the western territories. At the meeting it was noted that the department "in line with the principles laid down in the Secretary's speech" had instructed the embassy at Warsaw on 21 October 1946 to send a note to the Polish Foreign Office that addressed various aspects of the nationalization procedure with the following statement: "[The] US government expects that at such time as Poland acquires de jure sovereignty over German territories under Polish administration and thereby acquires [the] right to nationalize property in such territories [the] Polish Government will accord AmNats [American Nationals'] property in such territory treatment equal with AmNats property located elsewhere in Poland."[97] The Warsaw Embassy had replied that unless given specific instructions to do so, it would not send this statement to the Foreign Office since it was "undesirable to raise the question of Polish frontiers again at this time."

The representatives at the October meeting in Washington decided that while it might be technically desirable to go on record opposing Poland's right to nationalize property in the western territories, such "action might have undesirable political consequences" and might lead the Polish government to treat such property less generously than otherwise.[98] The legal adviser stated his opinion that even if no protest were filed, the legal rights of the American property owners would not be adversely affected "in the event that the properties are included in areas which may eventually be returned to Germany." The meeting participants questioned whether "the Department should pursue the full implication of the Secretary's reference to the situation in his Stuttgart speech." Chief of Eastern European Division Llewellyn Thompson received the approval of Acting Secretary Acheson, the director of the Office of European Affairs, and the under secretary of state for economic affairs not to push the U.S. position too far. It was decided not to call the attention of the Polish government to the realization that the U.S. government did not recognize Poland's right to nationalize American property in Polish-administered territories.[99]

Thus, during the early years of the Truman administration, the State Department and Military Government in Germany sifted through reports and information trying to bring some order and humanity out of the postwar chaos of Polish–German relations. American representatives tried to implement and enforce the provisions of the Potsdam Agreement with memories of Nazi Germany very fresh in their minds and with the new challenges of Soviet and Polish determination to hold on to what they had.

NOTES

1. These transfers had begun months before the war in Europe ended in May 1945. For a more thorough discussion of this topic, see Alfred M. deZayas, *Nemesis at Potsdam: The Anglo-Americans and the Expulsion of the Germans: Background, Execution, Consequences* (London: Routledge and Kegan Paul, 1977); Phillip A. Buehler, *The Oder–Neisse Line: A Reappraisal under International Law*, East European Monographs, no. 277 (New York: Columbia University Press, 1990); U.S. Congress, House, *Expellees and Refugees of German Ethnic Origin*, H. Rept. 1841 pursuant to H. Res. 238, 81st Cong., 2nds sess., 1950, 1–87. Hereafter cited as Walter Report.

2. Letter, Lane to Durby, 3 August 1945 in State Department Decimal File, Record Group 59, 711.60C/8-345. Hereafter cited as RG59 with document number.

3. Telegram, Lane to Secretary of State, 2 August 1945, in *Foreign Relations of the United States*, 1945 (Washington, DC: U.S. Government Printing Office, 1967), 2: 1266. Hereafter cited as FRUS with the year, volume, and page numbers. Much of the confusion that was reported resulted from Soviet looting as well as from German civilians who decided to return to their homes in spite of Polish claims of ownership as described in Richard Lukas, *Bitter Legacy: Polish–American Relations in the Wake of World War II* (Lexington: University of Kentucky Press, 1982), , Chapters 1, 2.

4. Telegram, Murphy to Secretary of State, 17 August 1945, in FRUS, 1945, 2: 1272.

5. Telegram, Murphy to Secretary of State, 12 September 1945, in FRUS, 1945, 2: 1274–1275. See also Telegram, Keith to Secretary of State, 15 September 1945; Telegram, Murphy to Secretary of State, 21 September 1945, in FRUS, 1945, 2: 1276–1277, 1279.

6. Telegram, Acheson to Murphy, 14 September 1945, in FRUS, 1945, 2:1276.

7. Telegram, Keith to Secretary of State, 15 September 1945, in FRUS, 1945, 2: 1276–1277.

8. Telegram, Lane to Secretary of State, 21 September 1945, in FRUS, 1945, 2: 1278–1279; officially, the contrary was true as American occupation soldiers were warned against showing too much sympathy to the German population, which had caused such suffering for the Poles and others. See *Occupation: United States Forces European Theater* (n.p.: n.d.), 19.

9. Telegram, Lane to Secretary of State, 22 September 1945, in FRUS, 1945, 2: 1280.

10. Telegram, Acheson to Steinhardt, 3 October 1945, in FRUS, 1945, 2: 1285.

11. Letter, Murphy to Matthews, 12 October 1945, in FRUS, 1945, 2: 1289.

12. Memo by Murphy, 12 October 1945, in FRUS, 1945, 2: 1290–1292.

13. Edmund Maclewski et al., *The Economic Development of Poland's Western and Northern Regions*, trans. Krystyna Cekalska (Warsaw: Panstwowe Wydawnictwo Ekonomiczne, 1961), 32. The Polish government used the terms "recovered" and "regained" to describe the Oder–Neisse territories in an attempt to emphasize that they once belonged to Poles.

14. Ibid.

15. In official, urgent correspondence the American representatives did not stipulate that the Oder–Neisse area was only provisionally under Polish administration but called the area simply "Poland." Apparently, no confusion arose from this usage, suggesting that American policymakers were operating as if the land belonged to Poland. Telegram, Murphy to Secretary of State, 23 October 1945, in FRUS, 1945, 2: 1296.

16. Telegram, Byrnes to Murphy, 26 October 1945, in FRUS, 1945, 2: 1301.

17. Telegram, Murphy to Secretary of State, 30 November 1945, in FRUS, 1945, 2: 1316.

18. Telegram, Byrnes to Murphy, 23 November 1945, in FRUS, 1945, 2: 1309–1310.

19. Lane added that when General Eisenhower had viewed the destruction of Warsaw on 21 September, he had expressed disagreement with the view that the Germans from Poland were being mistreated. Telegram, Lane to Secretary of State, 4 December 1945, in FRUS, 1945, 2: 1318–1319; Elizabeth Wiskemann in *Germany's Eastern Neighbours: Problems Relating to the Oder–Neisse Line and the Czech Frontier Regions (London: Oxford University Press, 1956),* Chapters 13-15, agrees, to a certain extent, with Lane's assessment of the situation.

20. Telegram, Lane to Secretary of State, 7 December 1945, and 12 December 1945, in FRUS, 1945, 2: 1321, 1323.

21. Telegram, Byrnes to Lane, 10 December 1945, in FRUS, 1945, 2: 1322.

22. Telegram, Lane to Secretary of State, 16 December 1945, in FRUS, 1945, 2: 1325.

23. deZayas, *Nemesis at Potsdam*, 123.

24. "Boundaries and People," *New York Times*, 16 December 1945, sec. 4, 8.

25. The 79th Congress had many such speeches. See, for example, U.S. Representative Thad Wasielewski speaking on "Some Truths about Poland," *Congressional Record Appendix,* 79th Cong., 1st sess., 91 (5 February 1945), A455–A457; Senator Eastland speaking on "American Policy towards Europe," *Congressional Record*, 79th Cong., 1st sess., 91 (4 December 1945), 11371–11372; Representative Charles Vursell speaking on "Relief for Starving People of Europe," *Congressional Record Appendix,* 79th Cong., 2nd sess., 92 (1 February 1946), A397–A398.

26. Lukas, *Bitter Legacy*, 35; de Zayas, *Nemesis at Potsdam*, 123–124; Walter Report, passim.

27. Lukas in *Bitter Legacy* analyzes the political nature of much of this economic aid, Chapter 3.

28. Memo, Lane to Davis, Tenney, and Durbrow, 29 June 1945, RG59, 125.0060C/6-2945.

29. Memo, Division of Eastern European Affairs (unsigned) to Matthews and McCarthey, 4 September 1945, RG59, 125.0060C/9-445.

30. Telegram 225, Lane to Secretary of State, 8 September 1945, RG59, 125.0060C/9-845.

31. Telegram 475, Lane to Secretary of State, 26 October 1945, RG59, 125.0060C/10-2645.

32. Telegram 603, Acheson to Lane, 1 July 1946, RG59, 125.0060C/7-146.

33. Telegram 45, Lane to Secretary of State, 7 August 1945, RG59, 125.0060C/8-745.

34. Memo, Thompson to Hickerson and Chapin, 23 November 1946, RG59, 125.0060C/11-2346.

35. Arthur Bliss Lane, *I Saw Poland Betrayed: An American Ambassador Reports to the American People* (Indianapolis: Bobbs–Merrill, 1948), 260.

36. Robert A. Vitas, *The United States and Lithuania: The Stimson Doctrine of Nonrecognition* (New York: Praeger, 1990), passim.

37. Strategic Services Unit Report on Poland, 8 February 1946, Record Group 84, Box 22, Department of State, National Archives, Suitland, Maryland. Hereafter cited as RG84 , with box number, DS/NAS.

38. Another memorandum reported the rumor that the Soviets and Poles had signed an agreement allotting more than 1 million acres of Polish western territory along the Oder–Neisse line for settlement of demobilized Soviet soldiers. Memo, Andrews to Ambassador [Lane], 20 September 1946, RG84, Box 21, DS/NAS; Telegram 268, Lane to Secretary of State, 24 August 1946, RG43, Box 83, DA/NA.

39. Naval Attache Report, 28 May 1946, RG84, Box 23, DS/NAS.

40. Memo, Gross to Hilldring, 5 April 1946, RG59, 862.00/4-646; in Airgram A-716, Murphy to Secretary of State, 23 August 1946, RG59, 862.00/8-2346, Robert Murphy cited a fairly reliable source who believed that the Soviets intended to make Eastern Germany into a Soviet Republic by 1947.

41. The Poles did not specify the eastern or western Neisse River. Message, Murphy to Secretary of State, 31 May 1946, RG84, Box 21, DS/NAS; map is an OMGUS map in RG43, Box 190, DS/NA.

42. Ibid.

43. Letter, Murphy to Secretary of State, 25 June 1946, RG59, 862.00/6-2546.

44. Telegram 4167, Caffery to Secretary of State, 22 August 1946, RG59, 860C.014/8-2246; Telegram, Murphy to Secretary of State, 31 August 1946, RG43, Box 94, DS/NA.

45. Telegram, Murphy to Secretary of State, 31 August 1946; Telegram, Lane to Secretary of State, 6 June 1946, RG43, Box 83, DS/NA; Anatole C. J. Bogacki, *A Polish Paradox: International and the National Interest in Polish Communist Foreign Policy 1918–1948* (Boulder, CO: East European Monographs, 1991), traces the handling of the issue by Polish and Soviet communists.

46. Many excellent works have analyzed U.S.–German relations after World War II. Among them are Roger Morgan, *The United States and West Germany, 1945–1973: A Study in Alliance Politics* (London: Oxford University Press, 1974); Harold Zink, *The United States in Germany, 1944–1955* (Englewood Cliffs, New Jersey: Van Nostrand, 1957); Thomas Schwartz, *America's Germany: John J. McCloy and the Federal Republic of Germany* (Cambridge: Harvard University Press, 1991); Wolfram F. Hanrieder, *Germany, America, Europe: Forty Years of German Foreign Policy* (New Haven, CT: Yale University Press, 1989).

47. Report, "The Permanent Objectives of American Policy toward Germany," 3 October 1946, in RG59, 711.62/10-346. Hereafter cited as "The Permanent Objectives." Letter, Clay to Echols, 19 July 1946, in Jean E. Smith., ed., *The Papers of General Lucius D. Clay: Germany 1945–1949,* vol. 1 (Bloomington: Indiana University, 1974), 237. Smith details the bureaucratic infighting over the administration of Germany.

48. Jean E. Smith, *Lucius D. Clay: An American Life* (New York: Henry Holt, 1990), 379, 382.

49. Summary of telegram, 8 March 1946, State Department Briefs, Naval Aide File, Box 20, HST/L.

50. "The Permanent Objectives," 4.

51. Ibid., 6, 20; the authors did not specify the approach that the United States should take or the exact border proposed.

52. U. S. Delegation Record, Council of Foreign Ministers, Second Session, Thirty-Ninth Meeting, Paris, 10 July 1946, in FRUS, 1946, 2: 869–873.

53. Memo, Hilldring for Truman, 3 September 1946, in RG59, 862.00/9-346; James F. Byrnes, *Speaking Frankly* (New York: Harper and Brothers, 1947), 187.

54. U.S. Congress, Senate, Committee on Foreign Relations, 92nd Congress, 1st sess., *Documents on Germany, 1944–1970* (Washington, DC: U.S. Government Printing Office, 1971), 59–67, hereafter cited as Senate, *Documents on Germany, 1944–1970*; Clay's biographer Jean Smith interpreted the speech as a "ringing endorsement" of Clay's policies in Germany, including American acceptance of the Oder–Neisse line; see Smith, *Lucius D. Clay,*. 386–387.

55. Ministry for Foreign Affairs of the Polish People's Republic, *Documents on the Hostile Policy of the United States Government toward People's Poland* (Warsaw: Ministry for Foreign Affairs, 1953), viii.

56. Wladyslaw Gomulka, *On the German Problem: Articles and Speeches* (Warsaw: Ksiazka i Wiedza, 1969), 4.

57. Lane, *I Saw Poland*, 260–261; Telegram 1363, Lane to Secretary of State, 6 September 1946, RG59, 862.00/9-646.

58. Telegram 1383, Lane to Secretary of State, 10 September 1946, RG59, 862.00/9-1046.

59. Edmund Stevens, "Polish Borders: Why Byrnes Plan Hit," *Christian Science Monitor*, 10 September 1946, 7. According to Stevens, even Polish civilians feared that Byrnes' speech signaled a return to the post–World War I attitude that had allowed Germany to rebuild its military capabilities.

60. Telegram 6192, Lane to Secretary of State, 18 September 1946, RG59, 760C.6215/9-1846; Letter 736, Lane to Secretary of State, 23 September 1946, RG59, 862.00/9-2346.

61. Telegram 1402, Lane to Secretary of State, 13 September 1946, RG59, 862.00/9-1346; Lane, *I Saw Poland,* 261–262.

62. *Gazeta Ludowa*, the Peasant Party newspaper, had a "firm but temperate" editorial protesting the speech as an attempt to question Poland's border in Telegram 1383, Lane to Secretary of State, 10 September 1946, RG59, 862.00/9-1046; Lane, *I Saw Poland*, 263; Piotr Wandycz, *The United States and Poland* (Cambridge: Harvard University Press, 1980), 325.

63. Polish Embassy, *Poland, Germany and European Peace: Official Documents, 1944–8* (London: Polish Embassy, 1948), 111–113. The Polish press, not surprisingly, applauded Molotov's stand. See Telegram 6192, 18 September 1946, RG59, 760C.6215/9-1846 and Telegram 6214, 19 September 1946, RG59, 760C.6215/9-1946. Wiskemann in *Germany's Eastern Neighbours*, 134, states that in this speech Molotov "pointed out what must have been in many people's minds," that acquiesence to the expulsions implied that the Oder–Neisse line was permanent.

64. Telegram 1419, Lane to Secretary of State, 16 September 1946, RG59, 711.60C/9-1646. Lane refuted Osobka-Morawski's suggestion that the speech had been given for political purposes in the upcoming U.S. election. See Telegram 1457, Lane to Secretary of State, 20 September 1959, RG59, 862.00/9-2046; Telegram, Lane to Secretary of State, 3 October 1946, in FRUS, 1946, 6: 498–500.

65. At the reception, the acting foreign minister showed Keith a clipping of an article by Katherine McLaughlin in the *New York Times,* which he interpreted as evidence of U.S. friendship toward Germany at Poland's expense. See Telegram 1391, Lane to Secretary of State, 11 September 1946, RG59, 862.00/9-1146.

66. Ibid.

67. Lane, *I Saw Poland*, 264.

68. Byrnes, *Speaking Frankly*, 192; one of Byrnes' biographers, Denise Conover, agrees that Byrnes successfully forced the issue into the open. See Denise O'Neal Conover, "James F. Byrnes, Germany and the Cold War, 1946" (Ph.D. diss.; Washington State University; 1978), 150–151.

69. Lane, *I Saw Poland*, 264–265; Telegram, Lane to Secretary of State, 27 September 1946, in FRUS, 1946, 6: 496; Lane told Byrnes in a telegram that even Poles friendly to the United States regretted the timing of the speech because of its potential to damage Mikolajczyk's chances. See Telegram, Lane to Secretary of State, 17 September 1946, in FRUS, 1946, 6: 494–495.

70. Telegram 720, Marvel to Secretary of State, 11 September 1946, RG59, 860C.014/9-1146.

71. Wandycz, *The United States,* 325; Telegram, Lane to Secretary of State, in

FRUS, 1946, 6: 496–497.

72. Lukas, *Bitter Legacy*, 60, 67.

73. Wandycz, *The United States*, 325.

74. Polish American Congress, *Polish American Congress, Inc., 1944–1948: Selected Documents* (Chicago: Polish American Congress, 1948), 94. Hereafter cited as PAC, *Selected Documents*.

75. Ibid., 94, 97.

76. Ibid.

77. Letter, Tolpa to Truman, 10 September 1946, Official File, Box 1297, HST/L.

78. Ibid.

79. Telegrams, 10, 13 September 1946, General File, Box 1922, HST/L.

80. Telegram, to Truman, 10 September 1946, RG59, 860C.014/9-1046.

81. Letter, Wieczorek to Truman, 28 September 1946, RG59, 760C.6215/9-2846.

82. Ibid.; the reply was prepared for Acting Secretary Acheson.

83. Much of the literature available on the Oder–Neisse Line is polemic and attempts to justify either Polish or German ownership of the territories based on historical ownership. See Jozef Kokot, *The Logic of the Oder–Neisse Frontier*, trans. Andrzej Potocki (Poznan: Wydawnictwo Zachodnie, 1959), passim; the journals *Polish Western Affairs and Poland and Germany*; Friedrich von Wilpert, *The OderNeisse Problem: Towards Fair Play in Central Europe* (Bonn: Atlantic Forum, 1964).

84. For a review of this attempt on the part of the Soviets, see Chapter 1.

85. Only in Mikolajczyk's notes of the Potsdam meeting is the argument recorded that the lands historically belonged to Poland. See FRUS, Potsdam 2, 1945.

86. PAC, *Selected Documents,* 108; Telegram, Kennan to Secretary of State, 17 May 1945, in FRUS, 1945: 297; Walter Drzewieniecki, *The German–Polish Frontier* (Chicago: Polish Western Association, 1959), 85.

87. "Poland's Frontiers," *New York Times*, 18 September 1946, 30; Volney D. Hurd, "Byrnes Urges Self-Rule for Germany, Raps Violation of Big 3 Economic Ties," *Christian Science Monitor*, 6 September 1946, 1.

88. "Keen Bidding," *Christian Science Monitor*, 7 September 1946, 18.

89. Bertrand Hulen, "Capital Calls Talk a Reply to Molotov Bid to Germans," *New York Times*, 7 September 1946, 1, 5; "Poland's Frontiers," *New York Times*, 18 September 1946, 30.

90. "*Byrnesa Odbudowa Niemiec Zawiera Cios Dla Polski,*" *Dziennik Związkowy*, 9 September 1946, 2; "*Byrnes Też Handluje Polską,*" *Dziennik Związkowy*, 9 September 1946, 4.

91. "*I znowu Polska Pada Ofiara,*" *Dziennik Polski*, 7 September 1946, 4.

92. Lane, *I Saw Poland*, 262.

93. Memo, MacArthur to Matthews, 23 September 1946, RG59, 760C.6215/9-2346.

94. Ibid.

95. Telegram 6737, Keith to Secretary of State, 18 October 1946, RG59, 711.60C/10-1846.

96. It was reported from a Czechoslovakian paper in *Głos Ludu* on 27 November 1946. See Letter 881, Keith to Secretary of State, 12 December 1946, RG59,

711.60C/12-1246.

97. Memo, Thompson to Matthews, Acheson, and Clayton, 30 October 1946, in FRUS, 1946, 6: 512–514.

98. Ibid.

99. Ibid.

3 The Deterioration of U.S.–Polish Relations

The Polish government in January 1947 held the general elections called for in the Yalta and Potsdam Accords, with the Polish Workers' Party and the Polish Socialist Party joining forces against Mikolajczyk's Peasant Party to win the election by fraud, intimidation, and terror. Not surprisingly, the government claimed an overwhelming victory for the so-called democratic bloc and quickly moved to consolidate its power. Representatives of the American government declared that the Yalta provision for "free and unfettered" elections had not been fulfilled but did not openly challenge the new Polish government.[1] Relations between the United States and the Polish government continued to deteriorate as the Warsaw Embassy and the State Department tried to coordinate a policy for Poland as it was being drawn closer to the Soviet government. In the ensuing years American and Polish officials had to address a number of difficult and interrelated issues involving Poland's postwar situation, including the stability of Poland's western border along the Oder–Neisse Line, one of the most volatile of these issues.[2]

DIPLOMATIC DIALOGUE ON THE BORDER ISSUE

The statements that American representatives made about the elections maintained a clear distinction between the Polish people, who were friendly toward the United States, and the Polish government, which was hostile. This position allowed the State Department to emphasize Moscow's control over Warsaw while justifying America's sympathy for, and interest in, the Polish people.[3] In spite of this carefully-worded position, Ambassador Lane asked Washington to relieve him of his duties a few days after the election. The ambassador's discouragement is evident when he writes, "For all practical purposes, my mission to Poland is ended. I believe I could do more by educating American public opinion as a private citizen than I can by remaining in Poland, where my continued presence would be considered as tacit acquiescence in the recent fraudulent elections."[4] The State Department agreed to Lane's request.

Before he left in February 1947, the ambassador continued to receive and report rumors that the Oder–Neisse Line would be moved east to favor Germany.[5] Lane called on the new Polish prime minister, Jozef Cyrankiewicz, to say farewell and to discuss the problems in Polish–American relations. Lane once again defended Byrnes' Stuttgart speech and asked Cyrankiewicz about the rumors then circulating that the Soviets intended to return part of Poland's western territories to Germany. The prime minister refused to comment on the rumor but indirectly denied the reports when he emphasized the economic importance of the territories to Poland. He also added that in losing the lands, Germany had lost the center of its imperialistic drives. Cyrankiewicz closed the interview by stating that Poland "cannot sit like a traveller with baggage packed in a railway station waiting room, once in Lwów and then in Wrocław, and where next?"[6] A few days later, Lane also called on Foreign Minister Modzelewski to say goodbye and to discuss the state of affairs. When Lane pointed out that Polish press attacks against the United States had continued in spite of his pleas, Modzelewski casually replied that such attacks were merely propaganda and promised that as soon as the question of Poland's western border was settled, "conditions would quickly be normalized."[7]

Lane's were not the only reports that showed the Polish officials' concerns with the border issue. U.S. representatives in European capitals informed Washington and the Warsaw Embassy that Polish officials were seeking support for the Oder–Neisse border. Chargè Waldemar Gallman in London reported that a Polish official had arrived there to discuss the issue with representatives of the British government, one of whom assured Gallman that they planned to do nothing more than listen to what the Poles had to say.[8] A few weeks later John Cabot, the American chargè in Belgrade, reported a conversation that he had had with the Polish Chargè Zygmunt Sten-Stoberski that was not very productive since "each of us had an axe to grind and neither wanted to have much of anything to do with the other's axe." In a cover letter accompanying the memorandum, Cabot suggested that while the conversation was not especially important, Sten-Stoberski's "obvious anxiety" about U.S. policy toward the border question "may be of some slight significance." He recounted how the Polish chargè quickly expressed his anxiety over "various indications" that the United States favored a revision of the Polish–German border. Cabot speculated parenthetically to the secretary that this might mean that the Poles were also unsure of the Soviet Union's solid support for the Oder–Neisse Line.[9]

Cabot told Sten-Stoberski that the United States had always endeavored to establish just frontiers that would not leave irredentist feelings. Thus, he said, the United States did not believe Poland's eastern border was fair and, "by the same token," believed that the western border pushed too deeply into "German ethnic territory." The Polish official replied pessimistically that the Germans would always demand more territory when they were strong enough, no matter where the frontier was set. The American chargè replied that because of this possibility the United States strongly supported the United Nations and had proposed an alliance against German aggression that the Soviets rejected.[10] The conversation then drifted into other matters, but Cabot reported that Sten-Stoberski twice more referred to the frontier issue.[11]

American representatives in Germany also reported on meetings and conversations regarding the border issue. Donald Heath, the political adviser in Berlin, informed the State Department about a meeting between Ernst Lemmer of the German CDU and General Jakub Prawin of the Polish Military Mission in Berlin. Prawin told Lemmer that since the Oder–Neisse Line had been established at Potsdam, nothing could be done about it at the upcoming Moscow meeting of the Council of Foreign Ministers. He added, however, that there was no reason that Poland and Germany could not make bilateral adjustments of the frontier. When Lemmer stressed the big problem that Germany would have feeding its population without the resources from the Oder–Neisse lands, Prawin replied that there were tremendous possibilities for developing good relations between the two states. Prawin's statements suggest that he foresaw a Polish-German border somewhere east of the Oder–Neisse Line and a trading pattern established whereby Poland provided Germany with foodstuffs, perhaps in exchange for German manufactured goods. In his analysis of the meeting, Heath contended that Prawin was "more or less" a tool of Soviet policy, but Heath thought that Prawin's hint about a border revision was noteworthy. He added that German communist views on the border were inconsistent, depending on the time and place of the public pronouncements.[12]

In spite of the Polish military commander's hints, the official correspondence from the Polish government to Washington continued to maintain that Potsdam had finally settled the border issue. There was no suggestion of a border revision in the letter that Bolesław Bierut, the new Polish president, sent to Truman on 20 February 1947. Referring to the area as Poland's "'recovered territories,'" Bierut outlined the same arguments supporting Polish retention of the land that American representatives in Europe were hearing, namely, that the Oder–Neisse border provided Poland with a basis for economic independence and security against German imperialism.[13]

This information about Poland's western border was duly received and analyzed by the Eastern European Division and was often copied to Robert Murphy, one of the American representatives preparing for the Council of Foreign Ministers meeting. Representatives of the states that had fought against Germany were invited to offer their views on relevant matters of postwar Germany to deputies of the Allied states meeting in London in January and February 1947. The representatives of the Polish government outlined in a memorandum the need for a democratic, demilitarized, and de-Nazified Germany. Until such a Germany existed, the Poles argued, the Allied Control

Council should continue to function, limiting German propaganda which favored border revision or which advocated racial superiority theories. In a meeting with the deputies on 27 January 1947, the Poles emphasized the need for security against German aggression. They claimed that the western territories were rehabilitated and that 85 percent of the more than 5 million inhabitants there were Polish. The Poles expected from the foreign ministers conference final confirmation of the Oder–Neisse Line as Poland's western border. Murphy's simple reply that the United States recognized the suffering that Poland had endured because of Germany could not have given the Poles much hope that their requests would be fulfilled.[14]

A week after this meeting, however, Murphy sent the secretary of state a memorandum of a conversation that he and Donald Heath had had with General Prawin and Ambassador Leszcycki, one of the Polish representatives to the Council of Deputies. In a cover letter, Murphy showed his awareness of the importance of the Polish border issue when he invited the secretary to pay "particular attention" to the Poles' references to that matter. During the course of the conversation, Prawin emphatically denied rumors that there had been any discussion regarding the rectification of Poland's eastern border. He was much less emphatic about the western border, however, and even hinted at a possible revision in Germany's favor. He warned, though, that the Germans were handling the issue poorly, especially the "campaign of vilification" conducted by some Germans. Prawin concluded this portion of the conversation by stating that Poland needed the territory in the west to compensate it for land lost in the east and promised that the Poles would present to the council statistics comparing the wealth of the western and eastern territories.[15]

Prawin's comment about compensation and his hints of a possible border revision directly contradicted the official line of the Polish government, which maintained that Poland had a historical right to its "recovered territories"; the government had dropped the contention that the western lands served as compensation for land lost to the Soviets in the east. Although it is possible that Warsaw had not yet made the official line known to all its representatives, it is difficult to believe that the head of the Military Mission in Berlin was not aware of the stance taken earlier by governmental representatives. This suggests either that Prawin was allowed or took more negotiating room in talks with Western representatives than the narrowly defined position held by other Polish governmental representatives or that he simply told his audience what he thought they wanted to hear. He probably recognized that American officials would acknowledge the compensation argument much more readily than the historical argument. In any case, Murphy did not comment on the discrepancy; he might have thought the justification given by the Poles for the Oder–Neisse Line less noteworthy than the mixed signals that they were sending about the border's permanence.

In addition to these hints about a possible border revision, much of the pre-Moscow Conference correspondence reveals a difference of opinion among high-level American officials about the Oder–Neisse issue and about Poland in general. The U.S. ambassador in Moscow, Walter Bedell Smith, sent Marshall his opinion of the border issue after he received word that the Polish vice premier was visiting London to present Warsaw's views to the British government. Smith wrote that while he would ordinarily defer to the opinion of two able diplomats like Arthur Bliss Lane and the British ambassador in Warsaw, he felt that he had to disagree with their contention that the Oder–Neisse Line should remain fixed. Smith saw the border issue as a clear part of the struggle for a communist or noncommunist Europe and stated flatly that the issue pitted Germany against Poland. As he saw it, Moscow had consolidated its power in Germany's eastern zone and would next move to extend its control in western Germany by forcing the Social Democrats in the western zones to cooperate with the Communist Party. The only way to counter these moves, Smith contended, was for the west to encourage the noncommunist majority in Germany, as Byrnes had done in his Stuttgart speech. Smith discounted the importance of the Poles' negative reaction to the speech, arguing like Kennan that the Soviets dominated the Poles and would probably continue to do so for a long time to come. For Ambassador Smith the position of the Poles was of little importance as long as the Germans remained oriented toward the West. Since, he wrote, there was no way to force the Soviets or Poles to relinquish the western territories if they decided to remain there, the United States should take a "firm stand on principle" for the return of part of the agricultural land to Germany in order to "cut the ground "cut from under German Communists who will of necessity follow the Kremlin line."[16]

AMERICAN OFFICIALS' VIEWS OF THE BORDER ISSUE

Ambassador Lane responded to Smith's arguments when the telegram was copied to Warsaw. Lane placed the Polish issue in a broader perspective than Smith when he argued that it was not a matter of Germany against Poland, but rather of the United States against the Soviet Union. He emphasized the importance of the struggle that American and British representatives in Poland had put up against the communists' attempts to dominate the Polish people. While he admitted that the rigged elections in January had indicated "that for [the] time being we have lost out in our fight," he was unwilling to write off the Polish population that he estimated to be "90% pro-American." He agreed with the ambassador that the Soviets and Poles could not be constrained to relinquish the western territories but interpreted this problem differently than Smith. Lane outlined the possible negative impact of any U.S. expressions of support for a border revision in Germany's favor. He contended that America's prestige in Germany would be reduced when the United States was shown to be incapable of forcing policy into action and pointed out that the Polish people, who were "almost universally" in favor of retaining the western territories as compensation for lands lost in the east, would lose faith in the Western democracies. In closing, Lane noted that he had elaborated his views in a 13 January 1947 letter to the secretary that he had copied to Moscow and London.[17]

In his January letter to Secretary of State Marshall, Lane had suggested that there were a number of reasons that the United States should not recommend at a peace conference that the western territories be returned to Germany. He cited the fact that the three major powers at Potsdam had agreed to deport the German population from the area and that the U.S. government had subsequently requested the opening of consular offices in cities in the western territories. Lane explained that the Polish people and most of his diplomatic colleagues in Warsaw interpreted such actions as indicating that the area would not be returned to Germany. He continued to differentiate between the Polish people and the Polish government when he stated that he was not concerned with the hostile attitude of the government to the American position. He warned, however, that any recommendation to revise the western border would devastate the Polish people.[18]

Lane also cited the Yalta Declaration's implication that Poland be compensated for the lost territory in the east with land in the north and west. He claimed that the Polish people would not be able to understand why Germany, a former enemy, was being treated better than Poland, a former ally. The ambassador told the secretary that he believed that the Soviets would recommend that the Poles retain the western territories and warned the secretary that if the United States recommended that Germany receive some of the land, the Polish people would believe Soviet propaganda that the Soviet Union was Poland's only friend. This, he argued, would push even the pro-American Poles firmly into the communist camp. However, the "most forcible argument" that Lane presented was also "a very practical one" when he pointed out potential diplomatic repercussions arising from the situation. Lane contended that nothing short of force would "induce" the Soviets and Poles to return land to Germany simply because the United States recommended that they do so. He added that since "certainly we are not going to war over these territories," any recommendation to return land to Germany would be perceived as an "empty" threat and would result only in pushing the Polish people "more than ever to the east." He closed by requesting a meeting with the secretary before the Moscow Conference in order to explain his position more fully.[19]

Ambassador Lane had other powerful voices aside from Ambassador Smith opposing his views, however. In a memorandum accompanying Lane's letter to Secretary Marshall, Undersecretary of State Dean Acheson rejected Lane's argument about Poland's western border. Acheson's argument, however, is somewhat confusing, and he does not address all of Lane's points. He wrote to Marshall:

Ambassador Lane states strongly that former German territories now under Polish administration should not be returned to Germany. I do not think that anyone has made this proposal. The proposal under consideration is that some of these territories to the south might be returned to Germany because otherwise Germany will not have enough agricultural production to exist and because from an economic point of view these agricultural lands are not essential to Poland.[20]

Obviously, any proposal to alter the Oder–Neisse Line in Germany's favor would give land then under Polish administration to the Germans. Perhaps Acheson was confused about the parameters of the Polish-administered territory since his statement about "territories to the south" would still include land along the Oder and Western Neisse Rivers. He was on firmer footing when he pointed out that Lane's warning about a border revision alienating the Polish people was not unique to Poland's situation. Such arguments, Acheson wrote, were made whenever border revisions were proposed. The Undersecretary felt that the attitude of the Polish people was just one of many issues to be weighed. He closed by stating with unintended irony: "I think that the matter is somewhat more complicated than Ambassador Lane's letter suggests."[21]

POLISH AMERICAN AND POLISH OFFICIALS' VIEWS

In addition to Ambassador Lane's recommendation that the United States should acknowledge the Oder–Neisse Line, Washington heard from Polish Americans and officials in the Polish government who continued to object to proposals advocating a border revision. Considering the vastly different political views of these groups, their alignment on the border issue shows one of the ironies of the postwar years. The Polish American Congress presented to Assistant Secretary Acheson a resolution adopted by the Congress calling for the revocation of the Yalta agreement and opposing revision of the Oder–Neisse Line. The Congress argued that the area was historically Polish and represented only very minor compensation for the destruction that Germany had inflicted on Poland during the war.[22] The Polish American Congress also sent Marshall a telegram on 5 March 1947 elaborating on the Polish character of the western territories and stating that since 4 million Poles had settled the area since 1945, a revision of the border in Germany's favor would mean that the Poles continued to suffer at the hands of the Germans. The Congress bluntly called any proposed revision of the line a "stupid and tragic blunder" that would strengthen the Warsaw regime and push the Polish people into Moscow's camp.[23]

The State Department also heard about the border from George Sadowski (D-MI), a Polish American congressman from Detroit. On 24 February 1947 he submitted a statement to Benjamin Cohen, State Department Counselor and one of the U.S. delegates to the Moscow Conference of Foreign Ministers. Sadowski told Cohen that he and his constituents, mostly Polish Americans, were very concerned about what he termed the "flood" of proposals sent to Congress favoring a revision of Poland's western border in order to return part of the land to Germany. He stated that Potsdam was just and correct in that it had restored Polish lands to Poland, and he argued that to return those lands to Germany would revive Prussian militarism. He related this issue to U.S. concerns for security by explaining that America's future depended largely on secure borders for Germany's neighbors. He also dealt with economic questions when he suggested that the United States could aid Poland and make a profit by supplying heavy industrial products to develop Poland's western territories. The congressman discounted the German expressions justifying the return of the land as the "same tune" sung by Germans at Versailles and noted that many German scholars had shown that Pomerania and Brandenburg were not indispensable to Germany. He closed with the hope that the delegates to Moscow would recognize the desire for peace by favoring the retention of the Oder–Neisse Line.[24]

Sadowski expanded on this memorandum when he read to the House on 28 February 1947 a statement emphasizing the need for Poland to retain the western territories. He reviewed the history of the border and labeled the Oder–Neisse Line as one of the "pillars" of peace in the future. The congressman emphasized the importance of the issue to the United States and cautioned: "To revise the Polish western frontier is to invite trouble and conflict. Even to raise the question is to create doubt and distrust among the Allies to the benefit of Germany."[25]

Representatives of the Polish government also argued against the idea of strengthening Germany by supplying it with land. This is shown in a memorandum to the State Department delivered by the Polish ambassador to the United States, Josef Winiewicz, who explained to Acheson that he had prepared it personally, and that it was not an official governmental statement.[26] The memorandum focused on the Poles' development of the area and argued that they had proved themselves capable of populating and redeveloping the land and would continue to do so for the good of Poland and Europe. On the other hand, Winiewicz argued, revising the border in Germany's favor would result in "enormous moral and material losses" for Poland as Poles were forced out of the area and Europe's economic recovery was disrupted.[27]

THE MOSCOW CONFERENCE OF FOREIGN MINISTERS

Some of the concerns expressed by Lane, Sadowski, and other American proponents of the Oder–Neisse Line were addressed by State Department officers as they prepared for the Moscow Conference, but they generally leaned toward the idea that some of the land would have to be returned to Germany to ensure adequate agricultural production in Europe. A meeting held in State Department Counselor Cohen's office on 22 and 23 January 1947 outlined an approach that the United States should take at the Moscow Conference. The delegates agreed that while it would be a tactical mistake to decide on a frontier proposal before other decisions concerning

Germany were made, they believed that it was necessary to have some concrete suggestions ready. The United States, they agreed, should favor compensation to Poland, but the final decision would be based on the well-being of the European economy and agricultural production, not just on the "national prestige" of Poland. They considered it very important to have as much information as possible regarding Polish development of the area, perhaps with the expectation that this information would confirm that the Poles had more land than they could use. The delegates directed that papers be prepared for the conference setting forth a primary U.S. proposal for the frontier as well as alternate proposals to "fall back on in bargaining with the Russians."[28]

Robert Murphy presented his proposed solution to the Oder–Neisse Line question in a telegram from London to Secretary of State Marshall, again noting Germany's recent history. When speculating on what form the eventual peace treaty with Germany would take, Murphy referred to the Treaty of Versailles' failure to establish in Weimar Germany an "enduring framework for pacific relations between victor and vanquished."[29] Since, he wrote, the border issue involved such "emotional intransigence," there seemed little chance that a treaty solution would be found acceptable to both German and Polish public opinion in the immediate future. He recognized that a treaty that failed to find a "just and enduring solution" to the problem would lead to future danger and complications, so he presented an alternative. He proposed that the Polish-administered territories be placed temporarily under the supervision of the United Nations (UN) during a "'cooling-off'" period, thereby ensuring that the agricultural resources of the region would be made available to Germany "on equitable terms." The UN administrators could also investigate the possibility of returning some of the German expellees to the area in order to alleviate the strain on Germany's overtaxed land and economy resulting from the "millions whose absorption poses an as yet unsolved problem."[30] Apparently, nothing came of this proposal; it was not one of the suggestions eventually offered for discussion at Moscow. It is nonetheless noteworthy that one of the chief American delegates to Moscow, who in conversations with Polish officials carefully refrained from even hinting that alternative solutions were being considered, suggested in an internal memorandum that something other than the outright return of part of the Oder–Neisse territories to Germany was possible. This suggests that high-level American policymakers were focused on finding a solution to Europe's postwar economic and humanitarian challenges and had not yet determined a plan of action for the border. Murphy's suggestion left open the possibility that the United States would support Poland's retention of the area.

A few weeks after Murphy wired his suggestion, however, members of his staff provided further justification for revising the border. They concluded that acceptance of the Oder–Neisse border would result in a marked disproportion of population in Poland and Germany and therefore supported the return of at least part of the land to Germany in order to obtain a tolerable standard of food consumption in that country. They addressed the question of Germany's war-making potential when they concluded that while Upper Silesia with its rich mineral and industrial resources should remain in Polish control, the remainder of the Oder–Neisse territories would not materially feed German militarism. Poland, they wrote, should be able to develop satisfactorily without all of the land that it then administered. Finally, they remarked that the Poles continued to violate the Potsdam Protocol provision for the "orderly and humane" transfer of Germans from Poland.[31]

The British government also expressed concern about the lack of a clear U.S. position on the border issue, and the British Embassy in Washington on 1 January 1947 requested clarification. A memorandum stated that the British government had reached the tentative conclusion that while "no practical alternative" existed to accepting as permanent the Polish–German frontier on the Oder–Neisse, Britain had made no final commitment. The memorandum cited Byrnes' Stuttgart speech and broadcasts on U.S. armed forces network in Germany as evidence suggesting that the United States would seek a revision of the line. The British Embassy sought to learn the intention of the U.S. delegates.[32]

Almost a month later the State Department replied in a brief memorandum with typical diplomatic rhetoric that while the United States was committed under the Potsdam Agreement to cede Königsberg and part of East Prussia to the Soviet Union as well as to compensate Poland with land, the "extent of this compensation to Poland" was "still under consideration." The memorandum made clear that the State Department was not then prepared to state a definitive U.S. position but indicated that the government was inclined to the view that "in the interest of the recovery of Europe as a whole," the area transferred to Poland should be limited to an amount that Poland could "utilize fully within a reasonable period of time."[33]

During these exchanges, preparations for the Moscow Conference continued. In order to fulfill the delegates' request for information about the situation in Poland's western territories, OMGUS in Berlin and Frankfurt and various divisions within the State Department prepared a number of reports.[34] These studies consisted of extensive statistical analyses of the area's population and industrial and agricultural potential. The military government in Germany completely agreed with the final border proposal presented by the State Department.[35] The policy paper emphasized that the United States was not committed to any specific cession of territory to Poland but was committed to make a revision in Poland's favor. The final proposal offered as the "most satisfactory" urged:

1. Cession to Poland of that part of East Prussia not assigned to the Soviet Union, as well as Danzig and German Upper Silesia (Oppeln district).
2. Establishment of the border from Upper Silesia along the 1919 border north to the

confluence of the Netze and Draga Rivers just west of Kruez, farther north to Neuwedell, then to Dramburg, west of Belgard to the Baltic Sea just east of Kolberg. (See Map 3.1.)[36]

The policy paper presented the advantages of this proposal as adding about 21,600 square miles to Poland's 1937 western and northern territory, shortening the Polish–German border, and giving Poland a 200-mile seacoast. The revised border would strengthen Poland's economy with the addition of the industrial and mineral resources of Upper Silesia and the agricultural areas of East Prussia and Eastern Pomerania. It would be sufficient, the paper argued, to meet Poland's future food and land needs. For Germany, the new border would add vital agricultural lands and the developed industrial area of Lower Silesia. This, the authors argued, would help Germany meet its "pressing requirements" for food and land and would thus be acceptable as an "equitable solution" to the democratic forces in Germany.[37]

The authors of the policy paper recommended that the secretary consider the proposal as a possible American position, but not necessarily advance it initially. If it were recommended, they wrote, Marshall should propose it for consideration based on the argument that the area needed to be utilized fully for the well-being of Europe. They also suggested that the United States recommend the creation of an investigatory commission to study the expulsion of the Germans as well as the Poles' resettlement and utilization of the area's agricultural resources.[38]

Armed with these proposals and drilled by State Department experts, Secretary Marshall headed to Moscow for the conference. He stopped in Paris to discuss with the French president and prime minister the position held by the French government; he also met with General Clay in Berlin to discuss conditions in Germany.[39] After the conference opened on 10 March, Marshall met almost daily for six weeks with French, British, and Soviet representatives.[40] The Western ministers met with Soviet intransigence at almost every session as the conference bogged down on the question of German unity; disagreement among the Western Allies on some points was also evident.

A very reliable source informed Robert Murphy in a top-secret memorandum that the Soviets were "determined to maintain a position opposed to the conceptions of the Western powers and on which it expects their resistance." The Oder–Neisse Line was one of the key issues that the Soviets would use to their advantage. Murphy was told:

> There is no doubt that the Soviet government knows exactly that these regions are not "originally Polish" but belonged to Germany for 700 years, that Poland is not in the least capable in colonizing and administrating them properly. The Soviet government knows that Germany on the other hand cannot live without her Eastern areas and because of her desperate situation will become an increasingly fertile soil for revolutionary

Map 3.1

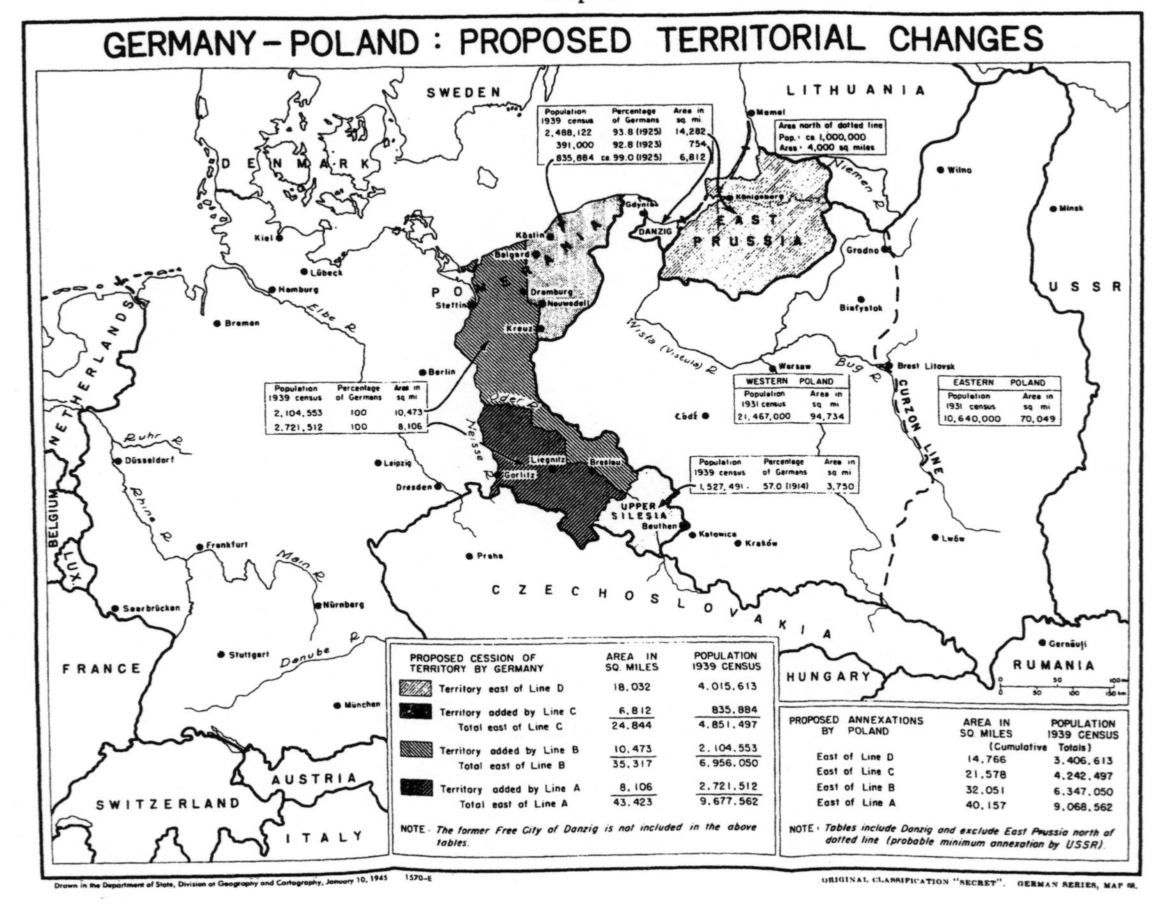
GERMANY - POLAND : PROPOSED TERRITORIAL CHANGES
SWEDEN
LITHUANIA
DENMARK
USSR
Population 1939 census | Percentage of Germans | Area in sq. mi.
2,488,122 | 93.8 (1925) | 14,282
391,000 | 92.8 (1923) | 754
835,884 | ca 99.0 (1925) | 6,812
Area north of dotted line
Pop.: ca 1,000,000
Area: 4,000 sq miles
Memel
Wilno
Minsk
Kiel
Lübeck
Hamburg
Bremen
Köslin
Belgard
Dramburg
Neuwedell
Kreuz
Stettin
Gdynia
DANZIG
Königsberg
EAST PRUSSIA
Grodno
Białystok
Niemen R
Elbe R
POMERANIA
Wisla (Vistula) R
Bug R
Warsaw
Brest Litovsk
Berlin
Population 1939 census | Percentage of Germans | Area in sq mi
2,104,553 | 100 | 10,473
2,721,512 | 100 | 8,106
WESTERN POLAND
Population 1931 census | Area in sq mi
21,467,000 | 94,734
EASTERN POLAND
Population 1931 census | Area in sq mi
10,640,000 | 70,049
CURZON LINE
Łódź
Oder R
Neisse R
Ruhr R
Düsseldorf
Leipzig
Liegnitz
Görlitz
Breslau
Population 1939 census | Percentage of Germans | Area in sq mi
1,527,491 | 57.0 (1914) | 3,750
Dresden
UPPER SILESIA
Beuthen
Katowice
Kraków
Lwów
Rhine R
Frankfurt
Main R
Praha
CZECHOSLOVAKIA
NETHERLANDS
BELGIUM
LUX.
Saarbrücken
Nürnberg
Stuttgart
Danube R
München
FRANCE
HUNGARY
RUMANIA
Cernăuţi
SWITZERLAND
AUSTRIA
ITALY
PROPOSED CESSION OF TERRITORY BY GERMANY | AREA IN SQ. MILES | POPULATION 1939 CENSUS
Territory east of Line D | 18,032 | 4,015,613
Territory added by Line C | 6,812 | 835,884
Total east of Line C | 24,844 | 4,851,497
Territory added by Line B | 10,473 | 2,104,553
Total east of Line B | 35,317 | 6,956,050
Territory added by Line A | 8,106 | 2,721,512
Total east of Line A | 43,423 | 9,677,562
NOTE: The former Free City of Danzig is not included in the above tables.
PROPOSED ANNEXATIONS BY POLAND | AREA IN SQ. MILES | POPULATION 1939 CENSUS
(Cumulative Totals)
East of Line D | 14,766 | 3,406,613
East of Line C | 21,578 | 4,242,497
East of Line B | 32,051 | 6,347,050
East of Line A | 40,157 | 9,068,562
NOTE: Tables include Danzig and exclude East Prussia north of dotted line (probable minimum annexation by USSR).
Drawn in the Department of State, Division of Geography and Cartography, January 10, 1945
1570-E
ORIGINAL CLASSIFICATION "SECRET". GERMAN SERIES, MAP 68.

communist ideologies. It is evident that this very knowledge induced the Soviet government to insist on its claims concerning the Oder–Neisse boundary. What else can support its endeavor to rule Europe more efficiently than Germans being absorbed in the communist ideology?[41]

This memorandum shows again how the Soviets viewed the border issue as a pawn to be used for political gain rather than as a question of deciding the best territorial composition of Poland or Germany. Subsequent events showed that American officials were determined to oppose this Soviet effort whenever possible.

The admonition outlined in the memorandum to Murphy was confirmed in Marshall's meeting with Britain's Ernest Bevin on 26 March 1947, where Bevin told Marshall of an interview that he had had with Stalin on 24 March. The Soviet leader, Bevin reported, had expressed disagreement with the view that Germany's population was too large and that this would lead to irredentism unless steps were taken to alleviate the strain on Germany's economy. Since this argument formed the basis of Western justification for frontier revision, there seemed little likelihood that the Soviets would agree to any proposed change.[42] On 9 April 1947 Marshall nevertheless proposed that the Polish–German border be adjusted for the reasons set forth in the Department of State policy paper, pointing out that economic and political factors had to be considered in a final settlement. He acknowledged that southern East Prussia and Upper Silesia should be Polish, but with "adequate safeguards" to ensure that the coal and other resources of the area be made available to the whole of Europe. The secretary then proposed the establishment of a boundary commission with representatives from the four council nations, Poland, and a number of other Allied states under the direction of the Council of Deputies. The commission would investigate and recommend to the foreign ministers a revision of the border that would compensate Poland for land given to the Soviet Union east of the Curzon Line and that would ensure that the raw materials and industrial resources of the area would serve the needs of Europe, especially Poland.[43]

An acrimonious and fruitless discussion followed Marshall's proposal. French Foreign Minister Bidault was more interested in Germany's western border and his precarious political position than in the Oder–Neisse Line, but he prefaced his remarks at the meeting with the statement that the provisional agreements made at Potsdam had apparently become permanent.[44] He wanted the foreign ministers to discuss general principles of boundary revision and recommended that the Council of Deputies for Germany investigate all the boundary claims against Germany and report at the next Council of Foreign Ministers meeting. British Foreign Minister Bevin leaned toward Marshall's reasons for revising the border in Germany's favor, but urged that a boundary commission study all of Germany's boundaries rather than just its eastern border. Soviet Foreign Minister Molotov stated simply that Yalta and Potsdam had settled the Polish–German boundary question. He again rejected the idea that Poland's western territories represented compensation for land lost to the Soviets in the east, because, he said, the inhabitants of the eastern territory had "wanted to join their Byelo-Russian and Ukrainian brothers."[45] Marshall, Molotov, and Bevin then proceeded to read statements made by Truman and Stalin at Potsdam and in Truman's 9 August 1945 radio address in an attempt to prove their various points. After Bidault's jibe that it was unfortunate that a French representative had not been present at Potsdam to provide a "disinterested, unbiased, and correct interpretation," the meeting adjourned.[46]

Discussion the next few days centered mainly on the French–German border. Marshall pointed out that his interest in all of Germany's borders was based on the fact that the United States had twice sent its military forces to wars started in Europe and noted that the foreign ministers were supposed to find a peaceful, lasting solution to this problem.[47] After Molotov again rejected the proposal for a four-power agreement on Germany, Marshall decided that the Soviet foreign minister's strategy was based on a "policy of delay and propaganda"; he decided to see Stalin with the hope of achieving some sort of accord on Germany.[48]

When Marshall met with Stalin on 15 April to explain his concern that the conference was not making any progress, Stalin replied noncommittally that differences were to be expected and that compromises on all questions could be made. Marshall thanked Stalin and told him that he also hoped such compromises were possible.[49] This discussion had no impact on the remaining sessions of the conference, which continued until 23 April, when at the forty-second meeting the foreign ministers agreed to refer all undecided points on the political and territorial future of Germany to the Allied Control Council for further study.[50] The Polish–German boundary was not discussed at any length in formal meetings after the 9 April free-for-all.

When Marshall returned to the United States, he broadcast a discouraging radio report on the conference on 28 April 1947, stating that the boundary issue "presents a serious disagreement and another example of complete disagreement as to the meaning of the pronouncement on this subject by the heads of the three powers." He reiterated that the United States was committed to the agreement to compensate Poland for land lost in the east and affirmed that Poland was entitled to more resources than the country had had before the war. He explained, though, that the present frontier deprived Germany of an area that before the war had provided more than a fifth of the foodstuffs on which the German people depended and that Germany would be forced to support a much larger population with much less land. He downplayed the nationalistic element of the border issue when he concluded this section of his report by stating, "Wherever the frontiers are drawn, they should not constitute barriers to trade and commerce upon which the well-being of Europe is dependent. We must look toward a future where a democratic Poland and a democratic Germany will be good neighbors."[51] Although the secretary outlined a long-range vision of European peace, he seemed to discount the nationalist fervor of both the Poles and the Germans over the border issue as well as their willingness to use the Oder–Neisse issue as a political litmus test.

The day after the radio address Lane wrote to the secretary of state that he disagreed with Marshall's views on the Polish–German border. He suggested that Marshall was unfamiliar with the Polish situation when he noted with regret that the secretary did not have an adviser familiar with Polish affairs to brief him on the matter before he had left for Moscow. He told the secretary that there were "divergent opinions" in the State Department concerning the border, and he claimed that the Soviet and Polish governments were aware of this difference of opinion. Lane requested a meeting with Marshall to discuss the issue before any public statements were made, since he was "very anxious" to support the administration's policy.[52]

Marshall agreed to a meeting that was held on 9 May 1947 in Washington. Lane told the secretary that General Eisenhower agreed with his view that since the United States had allowed the Poles to evacuate Germans, the Poles were justified in thinking that the frontier was permanent. He added that he had also discussed the matter with President Truman, who was, Lane felt, misinformed. Marshall replied that he was familiar with Lane's views but qualified Lane's statement about Truman by pointing out that the president had been forced to accept the Potsdam arrangement since, at the time of the conference, the Soviets had already held the territory. He claimed that the Soviets had deliberately twisted the meaning of the Potsdam Agreement to suit their purposes since, he said, the minutes of the meetings clearly showed that the United States. had not agreed to a definite frontier. The secretary told Lane that at Potsdam the United States had raised the issue of the orderly evacuation of the Germans, not because the Americans had agreed to the expulsions but because the Poles had already begun the deportations. Marshall contended that he was aware of the effect that U.S. border policy would have on the Polish people but stated that he did not consider the effect permanent since the United States was promoting a lasting solution that also offered a "'trading basis.'" He conveyed to Lane the "very confidential information" that the chances of changing the border were "slender," but he hoped to prevent the creation of a "tight barrier." The secretary stated that his reason for proposing a border east of the Oder–Neisse was that if Germany lost too much agricultural land, it would be forced to industrialize heavily. He pointed out the difficulty that he was having with the Soviets when he told Lane that the U.S. proposal was made in the hope of "offsetting Soviet interests in the Ruhr" by integrating Silesia into the European economy. The problem, Marshall stated, was exacerbated by Soviet rejection of a four-power agreement on Germany.

In response, Lane reiterated his belief that the U.S. proposal would lead to "lasting resentment" on the part of the Polish people. Marshall again discounted the importance of this when he replied that he understood Lane's sympathy for the Polish people since, like a theater commander during a war, Lane had been stationed in Poland and saw the situation firsthand. He suggested, though, that Lane's view was too narrow and that it was the secretary's responsibility to "deal with the picture as a whole." He closed the meeting with a warning that he would "seriously resent" Lane's taking a "public position criticizing our governmental policy." Lane assured Marshall that he had "carefully refrained" from doing so and "intimated" that he would not do so in the future.[53]

RESPONSE TO THE MOSCOW CONFERENCE

Ambassador Lane's were not the only objections to Marshall's proposal as the Polish government, the Polish people, and Polish Americans took a very public stand against the border proposals presented at the Moscow Conference that were reported extensively in the press. Marshall's statement on Germany's eastern border was released to the press in Moscow on 9 April. Not surprisingly, the Polish government almost immediately announced that it had sent an official protest to the U.S. government concerning Marshall's recommendation for the creation of a boundary commission.[54] Polish Foreign Minister Zygmunt Modzelewski presented the official view of the Polish government on 13 April. He said that his government considered the boundary issue to have been settled at Yalta and Potsdam and that any attempt to disturb the settlement of Poles in the area would only lead to increased German aggression. He condemned the secretary for addressing the needs of the Germans only and refuted Marshall's economic argument by explaining that Germany had never been self-sufficient in its food supply. Modzelewski closed by praising Molotov's stand at Moscow and claimed that Marshall's position contradicted the attitude and position of Roosevelt and Truman. He warned that the secretary's proposal would whet the German appetite for land and emphasized that the economic development of the western territories was vital to the recovery of Poland.[55]

The American chargè in Warsaw, Gerald Keith, wired his impressions of the Poles' reactions to Marshall's recommendations. Keith believed that the Polish people and government were in accord on the border issue and that the people were disappointed that the United States did not accept the matter as settled. Keith explained that Polish propaganda was making it appear that the U.S. government was anti-Polish and pro-German and that the Polish people could not understand why the United States seemed to favor Germany over long-suffering Poland. This perception, the chargè contended, resulted in confusion on the part of the Polish people, who wanted to be free of Soviet influence and control as well as to be assured against future German aggression. Keith noted the impact that governmental propaganda was having on the Polish people, who now accepted the ideas that the western territories had been part of Poland's historical lands and were necessary for Poland's survival and that the eastern lands were lost to the Soviet Union forever. In spite of the U.S. proposal for a revision of the border, Keith contended that the Poles kept "friendly sentiments" toward the United States and looked to America as their only hope for liberation.[56]

The American consul in Poznan, Howard Bowman, reported much the same reaction as Keith observed. He wrote that Marshall's statement at Moscow had caused "considerable sensation" and had resulted in a widespread press campaign questioning the wisdom of Marshall and Bevin's recommendations. Like Keith, Bowman found almost universal support for the Oder–Neisse Line, but noted that protest speeches against Marshall were much more "temperate" than the demonstrations that had followed Byrnes' Stuttgart speech.[57]

In Washington, the Polish Embassy published a booklet entitled *The New Polish–German Border: Safeguard of Peace* in February 1947 and republished it in July 1947. Addressed to the American reader, the illustrated booklet presented a fairly moderate account of the Polish view of the situation based on the Potsdam Agreement. The author, Stefan Arski, a correspondent for the Warsaw newspaper *Robotnik* (The Workman), dealt more with the confusion than the anger that Poles felt concerning the U.S. position on the border issue, especially in light of U.S. acquiescence in the expulsion of Germans from the area. He outlined the development of the area and emphasized that the western territories were vital to Poland's recovery. Although Arski did not directly address Secretary Marshall's proposals, it was probably not coincidental that the booklet was released just before and then again soon after the Moscow Conference.[58]

Once again Polish Americans ironically found themselves presenting to Washington the same argument as the Polish government concerning Marshall's proposal.[59] On 17 April 1947 Joseph Kania, president of the Polish Roman Catholic Union, one of the oldest and largest Polish American fraternal organizations, sent a telegram to President Truman protesting Marshall's recommendation to return part of Poland's western territory to Germany and to internationalize the Silesian basin. Kania argued that such a move would add to the injustice that Poland had suffered at Germany's hands. He further questioned why the United States was willing to help Turkey and Greece (with the Truman Doctrine) but unwilling to stop the annihilation of Poland by Germany, which had "clearly proved her incorrigibility."[60] A note from Matthew Connelly at the White House referring the telegram to the State Department added the information that Congressman John Dingell (D-MI) agreed entirely with Kania's views about the Oder–Neisse Line.[61]

The Polish American Congress published a resolution in April condemning Marshall's statement as "politically unfortunate" because it was "detrimental to world peace, degrading to the position of the United States, unjust in principle and presupposition, impossible of realization, illogical and impractical." The authors rejected the idea that Germany needed the land to aid in Europe's recovery by arguing that even when Germany had the land, the government had spoken of the need for Lebensraum. No matter how much land the Germans had, they always wanted more.

The authors did more than castigate Marshall's proposal, however. They claimed that it was an error to assume that the western territories compensated Poland for land lost in the east. Such an assumption, they wrote, simply acquiesced in the Soviets' territorial aggrandizement and granted them the right to fix reparations for a "condoned robbery." The resolution stated that it was wrong to capitulate to Germany's demands out of a fear of German nationalist aggression and argued for a systemic change in Europe. The authors wrote: "It is time to put an end to the conception that Germany must remain what she was. It is time for courage enough to say openly that Germany must be a third-rate nation and that the Germans, who have brought so much misery upon the world, do not deserve any consideration. . . . Instead of worrying about a strong Germany, it would be far more logical to make Poland the stronger nation, so that she could become the dominant factor in insuring peace in Europe."[62] This resolution served as a rallying point rather than a plan of action since it did not address the difficult question of how to achieve Polish self-determination in the face of Soviet determination to control Warsaw. Nor did it take into account the increasing tensions in occupied Germany.

Robert Lovett summarized the recommended Department of State response to such correspondence in an internal memorandum of August 1947, showing again the close relationship between domestic politics and foreign policy. The impetus for the memorandum was a letter from Charles Rozmarek of the Polish National Alliance. Lovett wrote that because nationality groups tended to take "strong positions on questions of international affairs," the State Department believed that "ceremonial messages by high Government officials" were apt to be "misinterpreted." He recognized, though, that for "domestic reasons" some type of reply was necessary, so he submitted an "innocuous" draft of a letter that praised the common American and Polish goals of freedom in 1776 and so on.[63] This approach was affirmed the following year, when the assistant to the chairman of the Democratic National Committee suggested that Truman send "a harmless greeting consistent with the policy of the administration" since, he said, "it would not be wise to ignore the Polish American Congress."[64]

The Polish American Congress continued to press its point with the publication of "In Defense of Poland's Western Boundary: An Economic Study," a sixteen-page booklet refuting Marshall's claim that a revision of the Oder–Neisse Line was necessary for the recovery of Europe. The authors used mainly German sources of the 1930s to show that Germany could be self-sufficient without the Polish-administered territories and that the eastern provinces of Germany had never been Germany's "breadbasket." The authors cited Nazi German officials who stated that the eastern provinces were poor and required subsidies and argued that the main reason that Germans in 1947 demanded retention of the area was for aggressive, nationalistic reasons, not because it was a vital food source. They claimed that many in the West, including Secretary Marshall, accepted this German propaganda as true and closed by asking bluntly, "Should Poland become completely unprotected and fall prey to a new German aggression?"[65]

Neither the accusation that Marshall had accepted German propaganda as a basis for his proposal nor the suggestion that he was pro-German is supported by evidence.[66] Marshall went to the Moscow Conference cautiously and well versed in the problems facing Europe.[67] He had access to numerous reports and intelligence studies prepared by OMGUS, the State Department, and the War Department that warned of the dangerous food crisis facing Germany. According to Piotr Wandycz, Marshall was "genuinely worried" that Germany would be forced to overindustrialize to make up for the lost agricultural resources, a move that could be potentially explosive.[68] Marshall left the Moscow Conference with the belief that the United States could not negotiate with the Soviets, but his proposals on the Oder–Neisse Line had not been presented in a pro-German or anti-Polish spirit.[69] Instead, his proposal was grounded in the belief that Potsdam had created a provisional situation that needed to be finalized at a peace conference for the good of all Europe. These differing perceptions of the "German problem" are reflected in the mainstream and Polish American press editorials concerning Marshall's border proposal.

Aside from the *Chicago Tribune,* which rejected the whole idea of East–West negotiations, most of the mainstream American press generally supported Marshall's stance.[70] The *New York Times* claimed that the secretary approached the border issue "delicately" but speculated that there was little chance of settling the matter at Moscow because it touched on the two broader issues of Europe's economic stability and the "good faith" of the powers in keeping agreements. The editor predicted that the Soviet Union would be embarrassed in its equivocal approach to Germany and Poland.[71] Another editorial rejected Poland's claims to its "recovered territories" by claiming that Germans had inhabited the land for centuries and by focusing of the provisional nature of the Potsdam Agreement.[72]

An editorial in the *Christian Science Monitor* stated that the Moscow Conference was not a diplomatic rout and praised Marshall for not "paper[ing] over the chasm of disagreement." The editor pointed out that the economic situation in Germany was vitally important to Americans and called for a "world-wide plan of economic support for democratic countries."[73] The *Detroit Free Press* stated flatly: "The idea of favoring Germany by short-changing Poland is nowhere entertained." The editor went on to explain that Marshall had presented his proposal in the best interests of Poland, Germany, and Europe.[74]

An opinion poll conducted by the Council of Foreign Relations in twenty-two U.S. cities in January 1947, months before the conference, showed that 41 percent of the 530 community leaders polled agreed with the position that part of the Oder–Neisse territories should eventually be returned to Germany. Contrary to the evidence presented in the editorials noted earlier, though, editors who were polled disagreed with that idea much more than did businessmen, lawyers, or educators. Even these well-informed community leaders with ties to the local Councils on Foreign Relations, however, found this question difficult to answer. Thirty-three percent of those polled were uncertain whether the land should eventually be returned to Germany, 23 percent disagreed, and 3 percent did not answer the question. The editors of the study noted: "Greater uncertainty was displayed in all categories of answers to this question than to any other."[75]

The Polish American press, on the other hand, was very certain about a solution to the problem. Newspapers as divergent as *Głos Ludowy* (People's Voice), Detroit's pro-Soviet weekly, and the anti-Soviet dailies *Dziennik Polski* (Polish Daily News) and *Dziennik Związkowy* (Alliance Daily), the Polish National Alliance publication, favored U.S. recognition of the Oder–Neisse Line and openly condemned Marshall's proposal as another betrayal of Poland. As early as January 1947, *Głos Ludowy* labeled the Oder–Neisse Line as the "acid test" to show whether Polish Americans were "genuine son[s] of Poland" or "pro-German fascist[s]." The article acknowledged that Polish American "reactionary" newspapers were calling on the Polish American Congress to organize an "energetic defence" of Poland's western border but contended that the Congress would not do so since it favored a strong Germany to fight a war against the Soviet Union.[76]

After Marshall presented the proposal at Moscow, Stanley Nowak wrote in *Głos Ludowy* that Marshall's proposal was in line with the general trend in the State Department to stop any social changes that it labeled as communist, whether they occurred in China, Greece, or Germany. Nowak claimed that the State Department's policy simply encouraged German fascism at Poland's expense. He offered American Poles two choices: either accept Marshall's reactionary policy or "support the progressive forces which will rebuild a democratic peaceful Europe, in which Poland will play an important part as a modern industrial country."[77]

Dziennik Polski called the proposal another attempt to partition Poland in order to aid the former German enemy. The editor stated that the Western world would be acting again without scruples by acquiescing in another crime against Poland just as Roosevelt had deprived Poland of its eastern lands by giving the area to the Soviet Union. The editorial chastised the Western democracies for deciding Poland's fate once again without consulting the Poles.[78]

Dziennik Związkowy also made the analogy between Marshall's proposal and the Tehran and Yalta provisions giving Lwów and Wilno to the Soviets. The editor questioned the wisdom of the proposal to place part of the western territories under international control to ensure Europe's economic stability. He pointed to the ease with which the Nazis had conquered the port of Gdansk, placed under international control after World War I, by simply ignoring the provisions of the League of Nations. Contrary to *Głos Ludowy's* accusations that the anti-Soviet newspapers were pro-German, *Dziennik Zwiazkowy* stated flatly that since Germany had caused millions of deaths, including thousands of young Americans, during World War II, it must pay a price. The editor acknowledged as debatable Marshall's argument that retention of the Oder–Neisse Line would lead to German irredentism and force the Poles to turn more to the Soviet Union. He contended that the solution was not to aid Germany by rebuilding a strong, militaristic state as after World War I since that policy would compound the errors of Tehran and Yalta and would push the Poles further into the Soviet orbit.[79]

U.S. EMBASSY OPERATIONS

After news of the Moscow Conference quieted, the U.S. Embassy in Warsaw returned to its normal operations. The new ambassador, Stanton Griffis, replaced Lane in July 1947. Coming from the business world, Griffis had no diplomatic experience before he arrived in Warsaw; his was one of Truman's "purely political appointments."[80] Griffis' naïveté contrasted sharply with Lane's background and style, but both ambassadors reached similar conclusions about U.S.–Polish relations, often differing with views expressed by State Department officers in Washington and by American officials in Germany.[81] Griffis arrived at a time when tensions were high because of continued Polish press accusations that the United States was friendly to Germany at Poland's expense.[82] He claimed that the oft-repeated charge in the Polish press that the United States wanted Germany to be the strongest, most industrialized country in Europe was a very effective "piece of Goebbelism in reverse," since, he wrote, the Poles feared and hated Germany much more than the Soviet Union.[83] After only a few weeks in Poland, Griffis noted the unanimity of feeling among Poles in supporting the Oder–Neisse Line, as well as the success of Polish propaganda in convincing the people that the United States was a "warmonger" trying to create a powerful, militaristic Germany.[84] Like Lane, Griffis was of the opinion that finalization of the Oder–Neisse Line would result in a weakening of the Soviet position in Poland since the Soviets were continually portrayed as the sole protectors of Poland's "regained territories."[85]

The ambassador's opinion about the Poles' fear of Germany was confirmed in a number of conversations that he and other Americans had with Polish officials. In September 1947 Griffis met with Polish Minister of National Defense Marshal Rola-Zymierski, who, in the course of the conversation, emphasized the Polish character of the western territories. The minister told the ambassador that in order to settle the related German question, three requirements had to be met. The first was that Germany had to be rendered incapable of aggression; the second was that Germany had to take an equal, not preeminent, place among European nations; and the third was that Germany had to reconstruct the countries that it had devastated in the war. Griffis echoed Lane's belief that the problems between Poland and Germany were "subsidiary" to the problem of U.S.–Soviet relations and emphasized Soviet intransigence on the German issue, citing the Soviets' refusal to enter into a treaty to guarantee against German aggression. Griffis and Rola-Zymierski agreed that the November foreign ministers' meeting was vitally important as East and West tried to reach an understanding about Germany.[86]

A few days later Secretary Marshall met with Polish Foreign Minister Modzelewski, who was in New York as a delegate to the United Nations, and with Polish Ambassador Winiewicz. Modzelewski prefaced his remarks about U.S.–Polish relations by stating that Poland's fate did not hinge on making a choice between the United States and the Soviet Union. Instead, Poland had had to choose between the Soviet Union and Germany, and had naturally chosen the Soviet Union. Poland, however, still "desired the closest relations with the West in all fields." After expressing the need for financial aid for Poland, Modzelewski told Marshall that the chief problem in regard to Germany was that Poland's western boundary had not yet been fixed. He claimed that U.S.–Polish relations could be greatly improved if the secretary would announce that the United States did not support a border revision since for Poland the border was not a political question but one of national survival. Marshall replied simply that he understood the minister's statement, and the conversation turned to the problem of propaganda attacks.[87]

The Polish perspective that the United States favored a quick German recovery at the expense of Poland was partially confirmed in a very telling confidential memorandum prepared on 6 October 1947 by Warsaw Embassy Information Officer Chester H. Opal. Opal's memorandum also shows how a lack of clear commitment on the border question exacerbated the confusion about the issue in various divisions within the State Department and the Military Government. After traveling to Berlin in September, Opal reported his observations of the activities and opinions of many Americans "rather high in the civilian echelon of OMGUS." He noted that while Americans in Poland referred to the Oder–Neisse territories as the "'recovered territories,'" the Americans in Germany referred to them as the "'separated territories.'" He interpreted this semantic difference as reflecting the gap in thinking between American officials in Germany and those in Poland (as well as between Poles and Germans themselves) concerning the permanence of the border. Opal related his concern with one American official who wanted to recommend to Marshall that the western territories be considered as reparations paid to the Soviet Union and who told Opal that the Poles were crueler than the Russians in expelling the Germans. This perspective, Opal believed, came directly from the

Germans themselves. The embassy officer outlined the crux of the problem: "Just as we in the Warsaw Embassy have deplored the failure of Washington to produce a definitive statement on the German problem, so American officials in Berlin believe their point of view is universally misunderstood because Washington has never 'put all the pieces of the German picture together' and held them up for the world to see."[88] He also claimed that Americans in Germany were as ignorant of the situation in Poland as Americans in Poland were of German events. Opal confirmed the fears of the Poles when he noted that American officials in Germany had developed such a "sentimental fondness" for "'Their German Problem'" that they were promoting a revival of Germany for Germany's sake rather than for the well-being of Europe. He told Crocker that he hoped that Washington had a better picture of the European situation than OMGUS held since all that came out of Berlin appeared to be "special pleading in the most restricted sense." He also reported that nobody seemed to expect much from the upcoming foreign ministers meeting in London.[89]

This pessimism about the efficacy of the foreign ministers' meeting was warranted. The Moscow Conference set the tone for future American conference proposals on the border issue, as Polish Americans on the right and left continued to urge recognition of the Oder–Neisse Line.[90] At the London Conference in November 1947, the three Western ministers agreed to accept Bevin's suggestion to create a boundary commission to study all the German borders, not just the Polish–German border.[91] Marshall reiterated that the United States supported the idea of compensation for Poland but wanted borders that would be lasting and peaceful.[92] He repeated the ideas expressed at Moscow that the agricultural and industrial resources of the Polish-administered territories must be made available to benefit all of Europe. Although the Western ministers agreed on the issue, Molotov objected to the creation of a boundary commission before the details of a peace treaty were worked out. They reached no agreement on this matter. In his 19 December 1947 report on the conference, Secretary Marshall expressed disappointment with the lack of progress made at the conference. He said that he could not reconcile Molotov's insistence on the need to prepare a peace treaty with his refusal to appoint a boundary commission, a move that the Western ministers considered a vital first step toward a peace settlement.[93] He summarized the debate at London as "but a dreary repetition of what had been said and resaid at the Moscow Conference" and concluded that no progress could be made until the chaotic situation in Europe was stabilized. This stabilization, he said, could be aided by the European Recovery Program, which had been announced in June.[94]

DISAGREEMENTS AMONG AMERICAN OFFICIALS

Throughout the closing months of 1947 and early 1948, Ambassador

Griffis continued to report on his discussions with various Poles which revealed real Polish fears of German aggression and of the alleged friendliness between the United States and western Germany at Poland's expense. Like his predecessor, Griffis disagreed with some high-level State Department officials about Poland. He continued to suggest that the Poles still had some limited autonomy from the Soviets when he stated that Poland was the "most indigestible and difficult problem to Moscow" but admitted that Warsaw was evolving into a pattern acceptable to the Soviets.[95] Griffis rejected Ambassador Smith's contention that the Kremlin's long-range plan was to incorporate Poland into the USSR on the grounds that such a move would destroy the "cordon sanitaire" that the Soviets were developing, would decrease the number of pro-Soviet votes in the United Nations, and would eliminate the propaganda advantage of claiming that the Soviets were Poland's only defender of the Oder–Neisse Line.[96]

Again like Lane, Griffis favored changes in U.S. policy that would improve relations with the Polish people and would eventually loosen Moscow's hold on Poland. On 23 February 1948 Ambassador Griffis reported a conversation in which Foreign Minister Modzelewski bluntly told him that the Polish government would ensure the cessation of the propaganda attacks on the United States if Washington officially supported the Oder–Neisse Line. Griffis considered this an "astonishing suggestion," although Lane had earlier reported a similar offer from the Poles. Griffis told Modzelewski that the border issue was intricately tied to the problems with which the Council of Foreign Ministers was dealing and he added that he personally and officially believed that the border issue would be favorably settled "when, as and if" the problems of the German treaty were solved and relations between the Great Powers were improved. After further discussing the critical Polish situation, Griffis and Modzelewski talked about the possibility of Warsaw's acting as an intermediary between Moscow and Washington in order to find a solution to the impasse between East and West. This solution would involve a revival of the American proposal for a Four-Power agreement on a demilitarized Germany and the possible settlement of the Polish border issue. In a memo to the secretary of state Griffis admitted that he did not know the impact that such a presentation by Modzelewski would have but he believed that progress could be made even if the Soviet Union failed to consider the solution since the Poles would see that the Soviets "had not been acting in good faith." Griffis stated that while he believed that the foreign minister had been speaking from the heart as a Pole and "for a moment . . . shed his Communist uniform," he acknowledged hearing a rumor that Modzelewski was soon to be replaced, possibly because of his "tendency occasionally to place Poland above the party in his thinking." Griffis asked for guidance from Marshall as to whether he should follow up on the discussion or let the idea drop since he recognized that the whole conversation could have been directed from Moscow.[97]

While the secretary expressed interest in Griffis' report and asked the ambassador if he thought that Modzelewski was speaking "spontaneously or acting under Soviet directive," he responded to Griffis' request in the negative. He told Griffis that any suggestions made by the United States to the Polish foreign minister would be reported to the Soviets and considered by them to be made on the initiative of Washington. Marshall believed that this would complicate other foreign policy negotiations and would be "interpreted as a sign of weakness" on the part of the United States. He suggested that no further approaches be made to the foreign minister at the time and thanked Griffis for his skillful handling of the matter.[98]

The following month Griffis reported that he firmly believed that the Polish government was acting independently of Moscow and that the United States would not be perceived as weak if he initiated negotiations to improve U.S.–Polish relations. He based this belief on his many talks with the Polish foreign minister and the newly appointed secretary general in the Foreign Office, Stefan Wierblowski. Griffis again requested guidance about sending a letter to the Polish government outlining the U.S. position. He submitted a draft of a letter that reiterated the advantages of a Four-Power treaty guaranteeing for forty years a demilitarized Germany. Regarding the Oder–Neisse Line the letter stated: "The settlement of the border questions being part and parcel of the German settlement should and in my personal belief would be concluded to the satisfaction of the Polish Government as a natural concomitant of any negotiations which had at their base the treaty offer."[99]

The department replied with a rather curt telegram on 6 April 1948 stating that in light of the developments in Berlin (the blockade) and elsewhere, "the proposed action might be misinterpreted and in any event [is] not now opportune."[100] This telegram shows again the State Department's unwillingness to present a clear-cut position on the border that favored the Polish view; it also fairly well silenced Griffis. He wrote in his memoirs that this was his only long and losing battle with the Department of State regarding diplomatic theory."[101] He resigned his post in the late spring of 1948 and was replaced by Waldemar Gallman.

DIPLOMATIC DISCUSSIONS ABOUT GERMANY AND POLAND

Griffis' frustration with the course of East–West relations was shared by Secretary Marshall, who decided to meet with the Western foreign ministers after formal negotiations with the Soviets failed to bring agreement on Germany. The Western Allies agreed to meet with representatives of the Benelux countries in London in early 1948 to try to reach a settlement on questions involving the western zones of Germany.[102] The agreements reached applied only to western Germany but were to provide a basis for policy toward a reunited Germany, if that came about. The six powers in London agreed to make a preliminary examination of Germany's western border but reiterated the

Potsdam provision that final delimitation of all German frontiers was to be deferred until the definitive peace treaty was signed.[103]

In spite of this emphasis that the Western powers were making no final agreements on Germany, the Soviet and Polish governments sent official notes of protest to the United States. The Polish note claimed that the London agreements violated the terms of Potsdam and failed to take into account Poland's need for security against future German aggression.[104] A few days after the note of protest was received in Washington, the foreign ministers of Eastern Europe issued a communiqué from Warsaw protesting the London Conference as an attempt to divide Germany permanently, to frustrate the conclusion of a peace treaty, and to stir up the antidemocratic and revisionist elements in Germany.[105] The ministers charged that by ignoring the German revisionist campaign to alter the Oder–Neisse Line in Germany's favor, the delegates at London had encouraged German aggression. The communiqué thus introduced another prerequisite to obtaining European security, that is, the "adoption of measures against all or any revisionist activity."[106]

Undersecretary Robert Lovett responded to the official Polish note of protest on 6 July 1948 with a note to Polish Ambassador Jozef Winiewicz. He explained that because of Soviet intransigence at the Council of Foreign Ministers meetings, the West had considered it vitally important to meet to discuss the German question. He emphasized that no decisions had been made that violated prior agreements. Although Lovett did not directly address the question of Poland's frontier, he objected to the Polish government's contention that the United States did not take full account of Poland's need for security from German aggression by pointing out that the United States had twice gone to war with Germany and was "vitally interested" in deterring further aggression.[107]

Although the Warsaw communiqué suggested a consensus among Eastern European officials, Washington and the American Embassy in Warsaw had indications of the Polish government's growing unease with the Soviet Union's reluctance to issue a firm declaration supporting the Oder–Neisse Line. There was also evidence that the Polish government was moving closer to Stalinism when Gomułka was removed as party secretary and replaced with Bolesław Bierut, and the government ordered that land be collectivized.[108] Before he left, Ambassador Griffis had reported that some Polish government officials had told him that they were deeply discouraged about U.S.–Polish relations "under Russian influence." The Poles, Griffis reported, had no idea about the Soviets' future plans.[109] In April he noted that the Polish government had stepped up its propaganda efforts, emphasizing during "Recovered Territories Week" that Poland would not be pushed back from the Oder–Neisse Line.[110]

This uneasiness between the Poles and Soviets was made apparent at a World Congress of Intellectuals as reported by the chargè in Poland Edward Crocker. The congress, probably organized by the Poles, was held in Wrocław between 25 and 28 August 1948.[111] Crocker reported that while the Poles had hoped for a Soviet "expression of approval" for the Oder–Neisse frontier, the Soviet tactics made such a declaration impossible. While, Crocker reported, the United States was the "principal target of abuse," the Polish delegates' willingness to compromise with the American and British delegates resulted in the final resolution of the Congress not specifically naming or condemning the United States.[112]

The American Embassy in Warsaw provided further evidence of the Polish government's internal difficulties and of its uneasiness with the Soviet stance. In addition, American officials received some indications that the Polish government was trying to play on the differing opinions about the Oder–Neisse Line held by officers in the Western embassies.[113] In October 1948 the British chargè in Warsaw requested clarification on the American position regarding the Polish–German border after reporting that the Polish government had suggested that British–Polish relations would be "noticeably improved" if the British expressed approval of the Oder–Neisse Line and would be prepared to support the border during German treaty negotiations. When the American Embassy officer told the chargè that American policy had "presumably" not changed from the position expressed by Byrnes and Marshall, the chargé replied that the British position was identical with the American but then pointed out two difficulties of the situation. He stated that he and his colleague were having difficulty formulating a recommendation for the British Foreign Office since the final British position on the border issue depended more on British–German relations than on British–Polish relations at the time of the peace treaty. He also claimed that there was merit in the Polish government's suggestion that it would be better to support the Oder–Neisse border publicly at the present time rather than in the future since "German mentality was still somewhat viable but would harden against [the] loss" of its eastern territories as time went on. He reiterated the belief that Polish relations with the West would "unquestionably" be improved if the West expressed support for the Oder–Neisse Line.[114] Gallman reported that the American Embassy officers had convinced the British chargè that this Polish maneuver confirmed their suspicion that the Poles were unsure of Soviet intentions regarding the border.[115]

When Ambassador Smith received a copy of this telegram, he boldly labeled British thinking on the border issue "naive and unrealistic."[116] Unlike Gallman, who seemed to be suggesting a "wait and see" attitude about the border, Smith rejected outright the suggestion that any endorsement given by the West for the Oder–Neisse Line would improve Polish relations, especially as it concerned Western relations with Germany. He stated categorically that the "Communist-dominated Polish Government" was not likely to adopt a friendly stance toward the United States as long as the United States remained "Kremlin's public enemy No. one." Instead, Smith argued, Moscow would ensure that its "Warsaw stooges" would criticize the Western governments' policies in Germany regardless of their position on the Oder–Neisse Line. Smith justified his position by stating that in addition to the already expressed need for the agricultural resources of the area, there were political and strategic reasons that the West should not recognize the line. Smith claimed: "Germany is far more important for both [the] Western powers and Soviets than Poland, and [the] struggle for power has not yet been decided there as it has in Poland. [The] Soviets undoubtedly regard [the] German-Polish frontier as their ace in [a] hole which they hope to play out some day when considered of decisive importance for [the] realization [of] German objectives."[117]

Thus, Smith argued, only the Kremlin would benefit from the Western powers' fatalistic acceptance of the Oder–Neisse Line, since the Soviets would "get credit for playing out this ace." In the meantime, Smith noted, Moscow had an excellent "whiphand" over Poland with the issue. Smith closed by reiterating a suggestion that he had made in an earlier telegram that the border issue should be kept alive because of its importance to Western objectives in Germany and because of its embarrassment to the Soviets. Smith rejected the argument that since the West could not change the situation in the satellite countries, it should simply accept it.[118]

This disagreement about Warsaw's level of autonomy from Moscow and the discussion among State Department and OMGUS officials about whether to keep the border issue in the diplomatic forefront persisted into Truman's second term in office. The Warsaw Embassy continued to monitor relations between the governments of Poland, the Soviet Union, and eastern Germany.[119] As Washington grew closer to Bonn, Polish American organizations and a group of articulate Polish American congressmen expressed increasing concern that Poland's western territories would be part of the sacrifice for a strong Western alliance.

NOTES

1. Richard Lukas, *Bitter Legacy: Polish–American Relations in the Wake of World War II* (Lexington: University of Kentucky Press, 1982), 78.

2. For more detailed information about the vital question of economic aid to Poland see ibid., 79–95; Piotr Wandycz, *The United States and Poland* (Cambridge: Harvard University Press, 1980), Chapter 6.

3. "U.S. Position on Conduct of Recent Polish Elections," *Department of State Bulletin* 16 (9 February 1947): 251; "United States Attitude toward Polish Government," *Department of State Bulletin* 16 (16 February 1947): 298.

4. Arthur Bliss Lane, *I Saw Poland Betrayed: An American Ambassador Reports to the American People* (Indianapolis: Bobbs-Merill, 1948), 290.

5. Telegram 162, Lane to Secretary of State, 30 January 1947 in State Department Decimal File, Record Group 59, 760c.6215/1-3047, hereafter cited as RG59 with document number; Telegram 289, Muccio (Berlin) to Secretary of State, 3 February 1947, RG59, 760c.6215/2-347.

6. Airgram A-111, Lane to Secretary of State, 18 February 1947, RG59, 711.60C/2-1847.

7. Telegram 313, Lane to Secretary of State, 24 February 1947, in *Foreign Relations of the United States*, 1947 (Washington, DC: U.S. Government Printing Office, 1972), 4: 421, hereafter cited as FRUS with the year, volume, and page number.

8. Telegram 610, Gallman to Secretary of State, 28 January 1947, RG59, 760C.6215/1-2847.

9. Despatch 642 with Memorandum Enclosure, Cabot to Secretary of State, 15 February 1947, RG59, 711.60C/2-1547.

10. At the 1946 Council of Foreign Ministers meeting in Paris Secretary Byrnes had proposed a 25-year guarantee of German demilitarization and disarmament, which Molotov rejected as inadequate. See *Documents on Germany, 1944–1970* (Washington, DC: U.S. Government Printing Office, 1971), 58, hereafter cited as Senate, *Documents on Germany, 1944–1970.*

11. Ibid.

12. Airgram A-132, Heath to Secretary of State, 11 March 1947, RG59, 760C.6215/3-1147.

13. Letter, Bierut to Truman, 20 February 1947, with memo from Hasett to Acting Secretary of State forwarding the letter for reply, RG59, FW711.60C/2-2047.

14. Telegram 616, Murphy (via Gallman) to Secretary of State, 28 January 1947, RG59, 740.00119 Council/1-2847.

15. Despatch 8856, Murphy to Secretary of State, 5 February 1947, RG59, 740.00119 Council/2-547; Anatole C. J. Bogacki in *A Polish Paradox: International and the National Interest in Polish Communist Foreign Policy 1918–1948* (Boulder, CO: East European Monographs, 1991), 100–101 refers to a 1943 program developed by Prawin that called for Polish control of the "'age-old Polish lands up to the Oder River and Baltic Sea joined to Poland'" but does not trace Prawin's career to his post in Berlin.

16. Telegram 273, Smith to Secretary of State, 3 February 1947, in FRUS 1947, 2: 151–152. In his memoirs Kennan stated that the Allied agreement to the Oder–Neisse Line made Poland "a military and political protectorate of the Soviet Union." See George F. Kennan, *Memoirs: 1925–1950*, Vol. 1 (Boston: Little, Brown, 1967), 215.

17. Telegram 27, Lane to American Embassy London, 10 February 1947, Department of State Record Group 43, Records of the International Conferences, Commissions and Expositions, Box 215, in National Archives, Washington, DC, hereafter cited as RG43, with the box number, DS/NA. John N. Cable offers an unflattering account of Lane in "Arthur Bliss Lane: Cold Warrior in Warsaw, 1945–47," *Polish American Studies* 30, no. 2 (Autumn 1973): 66–82. Lukas presents him in a more favorable light in *Bitter Legacy.*

18. Letter, Lane to Secretary of State, 13 January 1947, in FRUS 1947, 2: 142–145.

19. Ibid. The meeting that Lane requested was not held because Marshall left for Moscow before Lane arrived in Washington.

20. Memorandum, Acheson to Secretary of State, 25 January 1947, in FRUS, 1947, 2: 142n.

21. Ibid.

22. Polish American Congress, *Polish American Congress, Inc., 1944–1948:*

Selected Documents (Chicago: Polish American Congress, 1948), 126. Hereafter cited as PAC, *Selected Documents*.

23. Ibid., 128–129.

24. "Statement on Poland's Recovered Territories," Sadowski to Cohen, 26 February 1947, RG59, 860C.014/2-2747. An officer at the American Consulate General in Munich also reported that many of the complaints heard in Germany were similar to those made during the 1920s about Versailles. He based this on an article in the 3 March 1947 *Münchener Mittag*. See Letter, Wilkinson to Secretary of State, 11 March 1947, RG59, 760C.6215/3-1147.

25. *Congressional Record*, 80th Cong., 1st sess., 93, pt. 2 (28 February 1947): 1574–1578. In a telegram to the secretary of state on 30 April 1948 Edward Crocker, counselor at the Warsaw Embassy, expressed concern about Sadowski's views. See also Telegram 631, Crocker to Secretary of State, 30 April 1948, Group 84, Box 64, Department of State, National Archives, Suitland, Maryland. Hereafter cited as RG84 with box number, DS/NAS.

26. Memorandum of Conversation, Acheson and Winiewicz, 3 March 1947, in FRUS, 1947, 2: 185n.

27. Memorandum by Winiewicz, 3 March 1947, 860C.014/3-347, in FRUS, 1947, 2: 185–187.

28. Memorandum of Conversation, Lightner, Cohen, Hildring, et al., 24 January 1947, in FRUS, 1947, 2: 197–201.

29. Telegram 571, Murphy to Secretary of State, 27 January 1947, in FRUS, 1947, 2: 13–14.

30. Ibid.

31. Despatch 90, Murphy to Secretary of State, 20 February 1947, in FRUS, 1947, 2: 173.

32. Memorandum, British Embassy to Department of State, 31 January 1947, in FRUS, 1947, 2: 149–150.

33. Memorandum, Department of State to British Embassy, 25 February 1947, in FRUS, 1947, 2: 176.

34. Lucius Clay, *Decision in Germany* (Garden City, NY: Doubleday, 1950), 145–146; Forrest Pogue, *George C. Marshall: Statesman 1945–1949* (New York: Penguin Books, 1989), 153; "The Polish Zone of Administration in Germany," Department of State Intelligence Report, 7 January 1947, in RG43, Box 315, DS/NA.

35. Memorandum by OMGUS, Berlin, 5 March 1947, in FRUS, 1947, 2: 230; a draft of comments on the U.S. proposal stated that the United States "because of its tacit consent to Polish incorporation of the areas assigned to Polish administration and the expulsion of their German population, is not in a strong position to defend revision of the present de facto frontier in Germany's favor." The draft, however, was unsigned and undated so its origin is difficult to place. The caveat did not appear in the final proposal. See "U.S. Proposal concerning the Polish German Frontier," RG43, Box 147, DS/NA.

36. Policy Paper, undated, in FRUS, 1947, 2: 204–206; map in FRUS, Potsdam 2: 748.

37. Ibid.

38. Ibid. OMGUS Paper No. 3 offered two alternative lines that gave Poland more territory than the recommended proposal, but "without doing irreparable damage to

the German economy and to the German political scene." OMGUS also recommended the creation of an international body to regulate the area of Upper Silesia to ensure that its resources be made available to all of Europe. See "Germany's Eastern Boundaries," OMGUS Paper No. 3, 4 March 1947, in RG43, Box 190, DS/NA; "Summary of Major Comment by Military Government on State Department Papers," Tab B, in FRUS, 1947, 2: 230.

39. Congress, Senate, Committee on Foreign Relations, *Executive Sessions of the Senate Foreign Relations Committee*, 80th Cong., 1st and 2nd sess., 1:14; Charles E. Bohlen, *Witness to History 1929–1969* (New York: W. W. Norton, 1973), 258–262; Clay, *Decision in Germany*, 146; Pogue, *George C. Marshall,* 170–172.

40. Pogue, *George C. Marshall*, Chapter 12.

41. This memorandum was sent through Carmel Offie of the OMGUS Political Adviser's office in Frankfurt. In the cover letter Offie informed Murphy that the source, "my friend H. about whom I spoke to you," was "really a first-class public servant who knows Russia . . . better than any European I have ever heard of. If you want any more details about him, either Durbrow or Bohlen can tell you about him." See letter, Offie to Murphy, 12 March 1947, RG43, Box 143, DS/NA.

42. Memorandum of Conversation, Marshall and Bevin, 26 March 1947, in FRUS, 1947, 2: 289–290; Bevin's conversation with Stalin was recorded in a memorandum handed to Marshall. See "British Record of a Conversation at the Kremlin, March 24, 1947, 10:00 P.M.–11:15 P.M.," in FRUS, 1947, 2: 278–284.

43. Telegram 1274, Marshall to Acting Secretary of State, 9 April 1947, in FRUS, 1947, 2: 320–323; The Department of State, *Germany 1947–1949, The Story in Documents* (Washington, DC: U.S. Government Printing Office, 1950), 146-148. Hereafter cited as DOS, *Germany 1947–1949.*

44. Pogue, *George C. Marshall*, 176; Telegram 1274, Marshall to Acting Secretary, 9 April 1947.

45. Telegram 1274, Marshall to Acting Secretary, 9 April 1947.

46. Ibid., 322.

47. Telegram 1297, Marshall to Acting Secretary, 10 April 1947, in FRUS, 1947, 2: 323–325.

48. Pogue, *George C. Marshall*, 188; Molotov had rejected the Four Power Pact, which ensured against German aggression, which Secretary Byrnes had proposed earlier, and which Marshall favored.

49. Memorandum of Conversation, Marshall and Stalin, et al., 15 April 1947, in FRUS, 1947, 2: 337–344.

50. Pogue, *George C. Marshall*, Chapter 13; Telegram 1533, Marshall to Acting Secretary, 23 April 1947, in FRUS, 1947, 2: 383–384.

51. "Moscow Meeting of the Council of Foreign Ministers, March 10–April 24, 1947: Address by the Secretary of State," *Department of State Bulletin*, 11 May 1947, 16, pt. 2: 922. The speech was broadcast on 28 April 1947.

52. Letter, Lane to Secretary of State, 29 April 1947, in FRUS, 1947, 4: 425–426.

53. Memorandum of Conversation, Marshall, Lane, Thompson, 9 May 1947, in FRUS, 1947, 4: 427–428. As a private citizen Lane did not follow Marshall's directive. In 1947 he cochaired the Committee to Stop World Communism and in 1948 published

his memoirs of his days in Poland, *I Saw Poland Betrayed*, which was very critical of U.S. policy. In 1952 he headed the Ethnic Origins Division of the Republican Party. See Wandycz, *The United States*, 340; Lukas, *Bitter Legacy*, 133–134.

54. Telegram 537, Keith to Secretary of State, 11 April 1947, RG59, 760C.6215/4-1147. In May, Polish Premier Bierut told Chargè Keith that the Polish people were sorry that Marshall had taken such a stand on the Polish border issue and reiterated that Poland should not be made to suffer again at Germany's hands. Keith responded that Marshall's statements were based on a desire for "peace and prosperity for all peoples including Poles" and that the American people supported the secretary. See Telegram 751, Keith to Secretary of State, 14 May 1947, in FRUS, 1947, 4: 429–430.

55. Telegram 551, American Embassy Warsaw to Secretary of State, 13 April 1947, RG59, 860C.014/4-1347. The propaganda attacks on Marshall's position continued for months. In April a Polish newspaper printed a cartoon of Secretary Marshall as "Geld Marshall," the successor to the German *Feldmarshall* who defended Germany. See Despatch 1534, Keith to Secretary of State, 2 May 1947, RG59, 711.60C/5-247. In June, Keith called on the Polish foreign minister to discuss the propaganda attacks. See Telegram 971, Keith to Secretary of State, 19 June 1947, in FRUS, 1947, 4: 430–432.

56. Telegram 594, Keith to Secretary of State, 18 April 1947, RG43, Box 215, DS/NA. Keith also informed the secretary that Mikolajczyk maintained a friendly attitude toward the United States and that he recognized the "degree to which [the] issue was involved in [the] conflicting ideas of [the] U.S. and Sovs." See Telegram 598, Keith to Secretary of State, 19 April 1947, RG43, Box 215.

57. Conference Memorandum, Bowman to Keith, 16 April 1947, RG84, Box 40, DS/NAS.

58. Stefan Arski, *The New Polish-German Border: Safeguard of Peace* (n.p., 1947).

59. Various Polish American organizations sent telegrams and letters to the White House and the State Department urging recognition of the line. See Telegram, Polish Democratic Club of Rhode Island to Truman, 10 March 1947, Papers of Harry S Truman, General File, Box 1922, Harry S. Truman, hereafter cited as HST/L. Even after the Moscow Conference, the Polish Falcons of America continued to send letters. See Summary of letter, Sawicki to Truman, 1 June 1947, Papers of Harry S Truman, General File, Box 1922, HST/L.

60. Telegram, Kania to Truman, 17 April 1947, Harry S Truman Official File, Box 1297, HST/L.

61. Ibid.

62. PAC, *Selected Documents*, 131.

63. Memo, Lovett to Ross, 28 August 1947, Harry S Truman Official File, Box 1297, HST/L.

64. Memo, A.W. (at the Truman White House) to Hassett, 17 May 1948, President's Personal File 3845, HST/L.

65. Polish American Congress, "In Defense of Poland's Western Boundary: An Economic Study: Facts versus the Fiction that Poland's Recovery of Her Western Border Deprives Germany of Her 'Breadbasket'" (Chicago: Polish American Congress,

n.d.).

66. Lukas, *Bitter Legacy*, 89.

67. Congress, Senate Foreign Relations Committee, *Executive Sessions of the Senate Foreign Relations Committee*, 80th Cong., 1st and 2nd sess. (Washington, DC: U.S. Government Printing Office, 1976), 1: 14.

68. OMGUS Paper No. 3, RG43, Box 190, DS/NA; "The Polish Zone of Administration in Germany," RG43, Box 315; State Department Brief, 4 April 1947, Papers of Harry S Truman, Naval Aide Files, Box 20, HST/L; Extract from War Department Operational Summary for 14 May 1946, Memo Patterson to Truman, 11 June 1946, PSF/Subject File, Foreign Affairs File, HST/L; Wandycz, *The United States*, 332.

69. Pogue, *George C. Marshall*, 196.

70. The *Tribune* editor did not directly address the border issue but claimed in general that the Moscow Conference "mocked itself." The editor stated that there had been no diplomatic victories and that Marshall was lucky to have returned without losing his pants. See "Failure at Moscow," *Chicago Tribune*, 26 April 1947, 8.

71. "The Polish Boundary," *New York Times*, 11 April 1947, 3.

72. "Poland's Frontier," *New York Times*, 27 April 1947, IV, 8. The editorial was prompted by a letter to the editor from Boris Izanov, a Pravda correspondent who supported the Oder–Neisse Line. See "The Polish Frontier," 27 April 1947, IV, 8. The editorial prompted Stefan Arski and the editor in chief of the Polish Press Agency to write a letter to the editor, which was printed on 11 May 1947. The Poles took the editor to task for his interpretation of the Potsdam Agreement and the Allied Control Commission statement on the expulsion of Germans. See "Poland's Frontiers," *New York Times*, 11 May 1947, IV, 8.

73. "Marshall on Moscow," *Christian Science Monitor*, 20 April 1947, 16.

74. "Again Moscow Reneges," *Detroit Free Press*, 11 April 1947, 6.

75. Joseph Barber, ed., *American Policy toward Germany: A Report on the Views of Community Leaders in Twenty-Two Cities* (New York: Council on Foreign Relations, 1947), 22–23. The percentages are as follows:

	YES	UNCERTAIN	NO	NO ANSWER
Businessmen	44	33	20	3
Lawyers	43	36	19	2
Educators	31	37	26	6
Editors	37	23	40	0
Others	45	27	22	6

76. "Treachery in Time of Crisis," *Głos Ludowy* (People's Voice–*English section*), 18 January 1947, 2.

77. Stanley Nowak, "Sec. Marshall Gambles with Peace on Polish Frontiers," *Głos Ludowy (People's Voice - English Section)* 19 April 1947, 2.

78. "*I Znow Bez Pytania Polski o Przyzwolenie,*" *Dziennik Polski*, 10 April 1947, 4.

79. "*Duch Polski,*" *Dziennik Związkowy*, 11 April 1947, 4.

80. Graham H. Stuart, *American Diplomatic and Consular Practice*, 2nd ed. (New York: Appleton-Century-Crofts, 1952), 262.

81. Richard Lukas records a 31 March 1947 *New York Herald Tribune*

newsclip that before his confirmation, Griffis "astonished even the most optimistic observers in the Department of State by asserting that Poland would not become a communist nation." In Lukas, *Bitter Legacy*, 81. Griffis' memoirs presents a somewhat comical picture of his time in Warsaw. See Stanton Griffis, *Lying in State* (Garden City, NY: Doubleday, 1952), Chapter 11. Lukas writes: "Griffis, who had a sense of humor, had the strange notion that the application of humor could accomplish significant diplomatic results, despite the failures of his own attempts to be lighthearted with Polish officials." Lukas, *Bitter Legacy*, 81.

82. Lukas, *Bitter Legacy*, 81–82; Marshall instructed the embassy to inform the Polish Foreign Office that the U.S. government was "disturbed" at the distorted picture being given of America in the Polish press. See Telegram, Marshall to America Embassy Warsaw, 9 June 1947, RG59, 711.60C/6-947. The Polish ambassador to Washington gave a folder of press clippings from American newspapers to Thompson of the Division of Eastern European Affairs as a sample of anti-Polish journalism. Thompson accepted them but explained that the U.S. press did not get its stories cleared by the government before publication. See Memorandum of Conversation, Winiewicz and Thompson, 7 July 1947, in RG59, 711.60C/7-747.

83. Letter, Griffis to Lovett, 18 August 1947, in FRUS, 4: 443.

84. Telegram 1546, Griffis to Secretary of State, 24 September 1947, RG59, 711.60C/9-2447; Telegram 1463, Griffis to Secretary of State, 9 September 1947, RG59, 711.60C/9-947.

85. Letter, Griffis to Lovett, 18 August 1947, in FRUS, 1947, 4: 445.

86. Despatch 215, Griffis to Secretary of State, 23 September 1947, RG59, 711.60C/9-2347; Griffis had also met with Foreign Minister Modzelewski on 3 September. Griffis denied Polish accusations that the United States was trying to build a dominant Germany. See Telegram 1419, Griffis to Secretary of State, 3 September 1947, RG59, 711.60C/9-347.

87. Memorandum of Conversation, Marshall, Modzelewski, et al., 26 September 1947, in FRUS, 1947, 4: 446–452.

88. Memo, Opal to Crocker, 6 October 1947, RG84, Box 40, DS/NAS.

89. Ibid.

90. OMGUS and the State Department completed further studies of the German eastern border matter and recommended the same proposals as expressed at Moscow. See RG43, Box, 198, DS/NA; Ambassador Smith continued to urge Marshall to reiterate the U.S. belief in the need for "substantial rectification" of the border. See Telegram 3177, Smith to Secretary of State, 6 November 1947, in FRUS, 1947, 2: 898. Also Memo, Hassett to Department of State, 13 November 1947, forwarding Telegram from KNAPP, 13 November 1947, RG59, 711.60C/11-1247. In a letter of 22 November 1947 Rozmarek told Marshall: "By assuring Poland of her rightful western boundaries, you will not be supporting the communistic regime, a vile creation of the Yalta pact forced upon Poland, but the friendly Polish people themselves, and thus you will be helping to insure tomorrow's triumph of Christian civilization over Asiatic barbarism from the East." "*Memorandum Kongresu Polonii Am. W Sprawie Granic Polski,*" *Dziennik Związkowy*, 1947, 1. By December 1947 even *Głos Ludowy* acknowledged that the "reactionary" Polish American Congress actively supported and defended Poland's western territories. See "Marshall Is Warned on Polish Line," *Głos Ludowy* (People's

Voice– *English Section)*, 6 December 1947, 1.

91. Telegram 6219, U.S. Delegation at C.F.M. to Truman et al., 27 November 1947, in FRUS, 1947, 2: 734.

92. DOS, Germany 1947–1949, 149.

93. Ibid., 64.

94. Ibid., 63–67. The position expressed by Marshall at Moscow and London appeared in the policy statement on Germany prepared by the State Department in August 1948. See FRUS, 1948, 2: 1316.

95. Telegram unnumbered (sent to Department as #270), Griffis to American Embassy London, 20 February 1948, RG43, Box 267.

96. Ibid.

97. Telegram 272, Griffis to Secretary of State, 23 February 1948, RG59, 711.60C/2-2348; Griffis, *Lying in State*, 169–170.

98. A 7 March 1948 telegram from Griffis added weight to the idea that Modzelewski had acted independently. Griffis reported that Winiewicz had rejected his idea for the same reason as Marshall—that to suggest renewed negotiations would be interpreted by the Soviets as a sign of weakness. Griffis found it difficult to "accept fully this phrase either from the Department or from the Poles." See Telegram 343, Griffis to Secretary of State, RG59, 711.60C/3-748.

99. Telegram 454, Griffis to Secretary of State, 26 March 1948, RG59, 711.60C/3-2648.

100. Telegram 210, Lovett to American Embassy Warsaw, 6 April 1948, RG59, 711.60C/3-2648.

101. Griffis, *Lying in State*, 169–170.

102. The western leaders approved the economic union of the Saar area with France; the Ruhr would remain with Germany. See Wolfram F. Hanrieder, *West German Foreign Policy 1949–1963: International Pressure and Domestic Response* (Stanford, CA: Stanford University Press, 1967), 26–27.

103. DOS, *Germany 1947–1949*, 82.

104. See *Poland, Germany, and European Peace,* 38. The Polish ambassador in Washington handed the note to the assistant secretary of state for political affairs on 18 June 1948. See Memorandum of Conversation, Armour, Winiewicz, and Elbrick, 18 June 1948, in FRUS, 1948, 2: 368–370.

105. Beate Ruhm von Oppen, ed., *Documents on Germany under Occupation 1945–1954* (London: Oxford University Press, 1955), 300–307. Polish Embassy, *Poland, Germany and European Peace*, 17.

106. Ruhm von Oppen, *Documents on Germany*, 305.

107. DOS, *Germany 1947–1949*, 87–88; the Poles sent a second note of protest, which rejected Lovett's explanation. See *Poland, Germany and European Peace*, 41.

108. On 24 September 1948 the chargè in Warsaw reported that the Polish people were "perplexed and bewildered" by the Polish government's adherence to the Cominform and the leading role played by the Soviet Union in Poland's domestic and foreign policy. See Letter, Chargè to Department of State, 24 September 1948, RG59, 760C.6215/9-2448; Neal Ascherson, *The Struggles for Poland* (New York: Random House, 1987), 150–151.

109. Telegram 413, Griffis to Secretary of State, 19 March 1948, RG59, 711.60C/3-1948. Howard Bowman of the American Consulate in Gdansk reported that reliable sources indicated that 460 large estates in the western territories formerly owned by Germans were occupied by the Soviet army and were completely isolated. Local residents believed that there were German slave laborers on the farms and that the farms were being used for some type of military purpose. See Despatch, Bowman to American Embassy Warsaw, 6 March 1948, RG84, Box 63, DS/NAS.

110. Memo, Griffis to Secretary of State, 15 April 1948, RG59, 860C.014/4-1548. He stated again that the fear of German irredentism and military potential prompted Gomulka's belligerent speech in Wrocław during "Recovered Territories Week;" Letter, Griffis to Secretary of State, 30 March 1948, RG59, 760C.6215/3-3048. Also, various referenced telegrams summarized reasons that the Soviets hesitated to issue a declaration on the line. See Telegram 1700, Smith to Secretary of State, in FRUS, 1948, 4: 910–911; Telegram 1382, Gallman to Secretary of State, 20 October 1948, RG59, 760C.6215/10-2048.

111. Crocker stated that there was no evidence of a link between the World Congress of Intellectuals and the Cominform but in a later telegram added that the Congress showed how a "small core [of] hard-shelled Russian Communists" could "dominate [a] large group of generally well-intentioned but vaguely oriented 'do-gooders' and to pervert purpose and thoughts of majority." See Telegram 1155, Crocker to Secretary of State, 31 August 1948, in FRUS, 1948, 4: 913n.

112. Ibid.

113. Despatch 792, Ramsey to Secretary of State, 26 October 1948, RG59, 711.60C/10-2648; Airgram A-1710, Gallman to Secretary of State, 5 November 1948, RG59, 760C.6215/8-448.

114. Telegram 1382, Gallman to Secretary of State, 20 October 1948, RG59. 760C.6215/10-2048. An earlier airgram reported that Foreign Minister Modzelewski had "forcefully suggested" that the British should support the line and that Foreign Minister Bidault had promised that France would support it. The British ambassador reportedly corrected Modzelewski's contention about Bidault's statement regarding French support for the Oder–Neisse if Poland supported France's proposed border with Germany in the west. The British maintained that the border awaited finalization through a peace treaty. See Airgram A-1106, Crocker to Secretary of State, 4 August 1948, RG59, 760C.6215/8-448. The U.S. ambassador in France, Jefferson Caffery, assured Washington in October that the French Foreign Office had not been approached by either London or Warsaw about the border and that, in any case, the French government had "no thought of changing [the] point of view expressed by [the] French . . . at past CFM meetings." See Telegram 5586, Caffery to Secretary of State, 27 October 1948, RG59, 760C.6215/10-2748.

115. Ibid.

116. Telegram 2442, Smith to Secretary of State, 25 October 1948, RG59, 760C.6215/10-2548.

117. Ibid.

118. Ibid.

119. Despatch 904, Ramsey to Secretary of State, 24 November 1948, RG59, 760C.62/11-2448.

4 The Establishment of Two Germanys

As Truman's second term began, tensions between the East and the West combined with distrust and dissatisfaction among the Western Allies and their German zones. When the Polish Sejm in January 1949 abolished the Ministry for the Recovered Territories and transferred all authority for the territories to other ministries, thereby integrating the area into the "general body politic" of Poland, the German press refuted the act as contrary to Yalta and Potsdam.[1] The State Department contended daily with this type of dissension as Washington received reports from West Germany suggesting that some type of revisionist action was possible on the border question, while the Soviets hinted that they would support either Polish or German claims to the area. The State Department also continued to receive strongly worded Polish American and Polish exile expressions of dissatisfaction with the U.S. government's refusal to recognize the border. Throughout these tense times, the State Department officially held to the provisions of the Potsdam Declaration while working behind the scenes to try to determine Polish, Soviet, and German intentions concerning the Oder–Neisse Line.

SPECULATION ABOUT GERMANY

The division of Germany was solidifying in the winter and spring of 1949 as both East and West prepared for the establishment of two German governments. When the communists in Eastern Germany held a party congress in January 1949 stressing the theme of German unity, U.S. diplomats in Central and Eastern Europe speculated about their motivations and intentions. Robert Murphy, the U.S. political adviser in Berlin, suggested that "new stimuli" had been provided to communist propaganda about the possibility of an all-German government by the public airing of differences between the Germans and the Western powers. These differences included the establishment of a West German government, the questions of Germany's borders, and general occupation questions.[2] Murphy interpreted the presence of Czech and Polish officials at the congress as evidence that the Soviets were trying to persuade the Poles and Czechs to "warm up to the Germans."[3]

In Warsaw, Ambassador Gallman agreed with Murphy that the congress was intended to establish an initial basis for a rapprochement between Eastern Germany and the other Soviet satellite states.[4] He later confirmed this when the Eastern German communists capitulated to the demands of the Polish United Workers' Party that the Oder–Neisse Line be considered final and that irredentist elements be purged from the Socialist Unity Party in Germany.[5] Gallman echoed Murphy's interpretation that the Soviets were closely integrating the economies of Poland, Eastern Germany, and Czechoslovakia in order to ease tensions over the border issue and economic matters.[6]

Chargè Foy Kohler in Moscow presented a contrary assessment of this rapprochement, claiming that it provided less flexibility for the Soviets regarding the Oder–Neisse Line. He held that the division of Germany was too complete and Soviet authority in Western Germany too weak to provide any benefit to Moscow in forcing a border revision. Kohler continued to promote a plan that would "undercut" the Soviets, urging that the U.S. reaffirm the position Secretary Marshall had presented at the 1947 Moscow Council of Foreign Ministers.[7]

Conjecture about Germany's border continued to plague diplomatic relations. To carry out one of the provisions of the 1948 London Conference, a committee of the Western Allies proposed the adjustment of Germany's western border with France and the Benelux countries. In March 1949, the Soviet government sent a note to the Western governments protesting the proposal as a violation of the Big Four agreement to settle border issues at a peace conference. The new secretary of state, Dean Acheson, drafted a reply to the Soviets with the approval of the British Foreign Office, showing his willingness to keep alive the Oder–Neisse issue as a point of contention with the Soviets. Somewhat tongue in cheek, he expressed surprise about Soviet objections to territorial changes in Germany's western border in light of the Soviet attitude and actions regarding Germany's eastern border with Poland. The secretary contended that while the eastern territories constituted an area 800 times larger than the area affected by western border changes, they "have been unilaterally treated as areas permanently ceded and have been arbitrarily incorporated" into Poland and the Soviet Union. He also repeated the charge that the expulsion of Germans from the area had violated the Potsdam provision for orderly and humane transfers. Acheson reiterated U.S. policy that Germany's border would be determined at a peace conference and contended that all frontier changes until then were to be considered provisional and subject to review by the Allied powers.[8]

While these notes were being exchanged in the spring of 1949, the State Department prepared for the sixth session of the Council of Foreign Ministers to be held in Paris in May and June, convened as one of the Soviet "requirements" for lifting the blockade of Berlin. As with the previous foreign ministers meetings, there was a great deal of discussion and correspondence before, during, and after the conference about possible Soviet intentions for Poland's western border. Discussion and debate continued within the State Department and in Congress, as well as between the Polish American community and Washington regarding U.S. policy on the Oder–Neisse Line. In April 1949, Congressman Foster Furcolo (D-MA) read into the *Congressional Record* an article written by Paul Super supporting Poland's retention of the western territories. Although, Super admitted, the Soviets controlled the area and there was little that the United States could do, he predicted that the situation would be only temporary since "Russia contains the seeds of its own dissolution." In the future, he wrote, Poland would be needed as part of a strong barrier between Russia and Germany.[9] Secretary of State Acheson also received a telegram from Charles Rozmarek, president of the Polish American Congress and Polish National Alliance, protesting any plans to "carve up western Poland in favor of Germany" since the border provided only small compensation for the tremendous damage done by the Germans in Poland.[10]

PARIS COUNCIL OF FOREIGN MINISTERS

In a hearing prior to the foreign ministers' meeting, Acheson discounted the validity of arguments against the U.S. proposition that the border should be moved east. He complained to an Executive Session of the Senate Foreign Relations Committee about nine Polish American congressmen who "just . . . [had] a fit" about that proposition. When Senator Brien McMahon (D-CT), who was aware of Polish opposition to moving the Oder–Neisse Line, asked Acheson about the congressmen's argument, Acheson told the committee that it was "wholly emotional, that the Germans were bad people and had attacked Poland . . . et cetera." He acknowledged that these Polish American congressmen saw the situation as Washington "selling them [the Poles] down the river" but did not elaborate on the point.[11] Secretary Acheson replied to a question from Senator Henry Cabot Lodge (R-MA) about whether there had been an official announcement on the U.S. policy, by explaining his predecessor's position at the 1947 Moscow Council of Foreign Ministers meeting—that Potsdam had established a provisional border and that the Poles had more agricultural land than they could use. When asked by McMahon about the extent of the unusable farmland, Acheson replied that while he did not remember the exact amount, he was sure that it was more than half of the area given to the Poles. This estimate might have surprised the American officials who had prepared the report for Marshall and would more than likely have made the Poles and Polish Americans apoplectic.[12] Even though the secretary somewhat casually dismissed the arguments of the Polish American congressmen when speaking with the Senate committee, he and various State

Department officials continued to correspond and meet with them to exchange views on U.S.–Polish relations.[13]

After the foreign ministers' conference got under way, the State Department continued to hear from senators and congressmen with constituents concerned that Poland might lose part of the western territories. Most replies by State Department officers showed their interest in keeping Congress informed about the situation. Letters were received from Senator Irving M. Ives (R-NY) in May 1949 and from Senator Henry Cabot Lodge (R-MA), and in June from Congressman Richard Wigglesworth (R-MA), and Congressman Charles R. Howell, (D-NJ). In each case, the State Department officer suggested that the congressman respond to his constituents by explaining the Yalta and Potsdam Agreements, by outlining the Allies' differing interpretations of the Potsdam Agreement, and by reiterating Secretary Marshall's position as expressed at the 1947 Council of Foreign Ministers. Finally, the congressmen were also told that the Paris agenda contained neither the border issue nor the peace treaty.[14]

The State Department also heard about the Paris meeting from Stanislaw Mikołajczyk, former head of the Peasant Party who had been forced to flee Poland in 1947. Assistant Chief of the Division of Eastern European Affairs Fred Salter reported a conversation that he had had with Mikołajczyk on 11 May 1949 at Salter's home. Mikołajczyk expressed his opinion that it would be a mistake for the West to bring up the border issue at the conference since "it would be just what the Soviets wanted to happen." The Polish émigré, who had firsthand experience with Stalin's government, feared that the Soviets would use the West's initiative as an excuse, claiming that the matter had been taken out of their hands and would then offer concessions to the Germans. Mikołajczyk contended that the West could not effect any territorial changes in any case and would thus be playing into Soviet hands.[15]

Much of this pre-conference dialogue about Poland's western border involved the larger question of Soviet intentions in Germany. In his hearing before the Senate Foreign Relations Committee, Acheson explained that even though Western Germany was closely tied to the Western powers and the West Germans were "entirely cynical" about Soviet proposals for a united Germany, there was still a theoretical possibility that the Soviets would lure the Western Germans into accepting their proposal. One way that Acheson thought Moscow could accomplish this was to return part of the Oder–Neisse territories to Germany. "We have no doubt," Acheson told the senators, "that at some time or other the Russians are going to get ready to sell the Poles down the river on the eastern [German] boundary and give the Germans a larger area to live in than they now have, in the lower part, down toward Silesia." To counter that move, Acheson said, it was vitally important that the United States keep demanding revision of the border in Germany's favor so that the Soviets would not gain any credit with the Germans when they finally moved to revise the border because it will be "quite obvious that they have been forced to do it."[16]

Acheson also reiterated Secretary Marshall's concerns about the perceived difficulties in feeding the German population with the resources then within Germany's borders but he did not add any information about the Polish government's campaign to repopulate the "recovered territories" with Poles. In any case, the news that Western Germany was not firmly in the West's camp must have come as a surprise to some of the senators this late in the process. When Senator Lodge asked Acheson if he had understood correctly that Germany could still go either east or west, the secretary admitted that that was the case, but surmised that the Soviets would have difficulty offering incentives to Germany.[17]

The concern that there might be some kind of Soviet–German deal about the border was not limited to Washington. From Warsaw, Ambassador Gallman agreed with Acheson's contention and added that the Poles were aware of the possibility of a deal and were trying to guard against it. He wrote to the U.S. delegation at Paris: "Certain factors reenforce [*sic*] our long-standing suspicion . . . that Polish Communists are not entirely convinced of Soviet . . . support on [the] border issue and that [the] present border campaign [is] aimed in large part at [the] USSR and reflected Polish distruct [*sic*] of Soviet intentions and disillusionment over [the] development [of] events in East Germany."[18] Gallman then elaborated on those factors that he perceived as indicating Polish insecurity about the border. He contended that the Polish Peasant Party's view, widely quoted in the Polish press—that the Oder–Neisse Line had to serve as a basis for a future peace treaty with Germany—indicated that the Polish government was delivering a message to Moscow rather than to the West. Otherwise, the ambassador argued, the Polish government would voice its own opinion rather than "descend to use of [the] relatively unimportant PSL as [a] medium." Gallman also suggested that the Polish Peasant Party's use of terms like "'deeply convinced'" and "'firmly believes'" indicated that the party was uncertainty about the fate of the border and was seeking "reassurance."[19]

Ambassador Gallman added that another sign of Polish insecurity about Soviet intentions was Warsaw's emphasis on the "invariability" of the border. He explained that since Secretary Marshall and British Foreign Secretary Bevin had clearly outlined the West's position in 1947, the Polish government's publicity campaign had to be intended more to convince Moscow of Warsaw's "intransigence" on the border issue than to "dissuade [the] west from an already announced policy."[20]

The final reason that Gallman gave to support his view was the lack of discussion about a rapprochement between Poland and East Germany, including the previous propaganda line that the East German Socialist Unity Party had accepted the Oder–Neisse Line as final. Gallman wrote that recent East German elections must have disillusioned the Polish communists and led them to doubt whether the Soviets and the Socialist Unity Party were firmly in control of East Germany. This must have caused them to wonder whether the Soviets would "utilize [the] border trump" as they tried to improve relations with Germany, especially East Germany.[21] The ambassador speculated that the Soviets were fully aware of the "explosive" nature of the border issue and would try to avoid any further loss of prestige with Polish communists such as might occur if they agreed to any Western proposals to adjust the border.[22]

From Moscow Foy Kohler conjectured that the Soviets at Paris might make concessions to the West on a number of German issues in the hope of later exploiting Western differences on specific German matters. He suggested that one of the secondary objectives of the Soviets would be to obtain Four-Power confirmation of the Oder–Neisse Line, enabling them to offer to rectify the border unilaterally at a later time.[23]

In preparation for the Paris meeting, the State Department and OMGUS again prepared reports on the situation in Germany. The position paper prepared by the Office of German and Austrian Affairs maintained that when the boundary issue arose at the meeting, it would be to the West's advantage to reiterate Secretary Marshall's position that Poland's western border was provisional and that Germany needed part of the area because of its dense population. The authors proposed again that a boundary commission be established to study and make recommendations for all of Germany's frontiers.[24] The position paper then offered another suggestion that would have added a new and even more complicated diplomatic twist to an already complex issue—if it had been presented: "It might be stated that although the U.S. recognizes its commitment at Potsdam to support incorporation of the northern part of East Prussia into the Soviet Union, it would welcome a proposal of the Soviet Union to yield its claim to this area in Poland's favor as compensation for an adjustment along Poland's western frontier."[25] The suggestion that the Soviets turn over the Königsberg area as a gesture of goodwill to the Poles was probably made with the intention of upping the ante by placing the added burden on the Soviets of proving their intentions to the Poles. It was apparently part of the overall plan to discomfit the Soviets in Poland or East Germany by forcing Stalin's representatives to state categorically that they either did or did not intend to recognize the Oder–Neisse Line as final.

The OMGUS study of the border problem for the 1949 Council of Foreign Ministers did not contain this suggestion that the Soviets give northern Prussia to Poland as a goodwill gesture. Instead, the study continued to focus on the problem of feeding the Germans with the severance of the eastern agricultural resources and on the overall disruption to the German economy caused by the loss of the lands east of the Oder and Neisse Rivers and by the perceived overpopulation of western Germany.[26] The authors stated that the United States and Great Britain were forced to import more than 50 percent of the food consumed in Western Germany and estimated further that even if Eastern and Western Germany were united with the border remaining on the Oder–Neisse Line, Germany would have to import more than one-third of its food.[27] They contended that the issue presented "actual economic and political danger" to Germany's western neighbors since it prevented economic and political stabilization of Europe as a whole and threatened to become another Alsace-Lorraine with "explosive aspects."[28]

Although the 1949 OMGUS study was similar to the 1947 study of Germany's border, the latter had the added element of urgency as the Germans prepared to establish new states. One of the points put forth for consideration was that in spite of Molotov's 1946 pronouncement that the Potsdam Accord had settled the border question permanently, communist propaganda in Germany continued to put out "'feelers'" suggesting that a German government sympathetic to the Soviets might be given territorial concessions in the east.[29] "Up to now," the authors argued, "these have been bait on the Soviet hook; they may, however, assume a more serious aspect under developing conditions." OMGUS recognized that no German political leaders could publicly acknowledge the loss of the territories to Poland and suggested that if they were forced to do so, the result would be a "resurgence of the attitude which Military Government has been at great pains to overcome, namely that the only mistake the Germans made in the war was to lose it."[30] The authors contended that with this issue the Soviets possessed a "powerful weapon" over the Polish government that the Kremlin would use when needed. They questioned whether an all-German government should be established before the border question was satisfactorily settled, offering the specter of a Rapallo-type agreement: "The danger of a Soviet–German deal based on a return to Germany of at least part of the lost territory will most certainly assume grave proportions in the future."[31]

As for the 1947 foreign ministers' meetings, OMGUS in 1949 presented alternative solutions to the border problem. The preferred solution, as in 1947, was to grant to Poland the industrial areas of Upper Silesia and the parts of Pomerania and parts of Lower Silesia that were predominantly Polish in ethnic composition. The remaining lands would be put under German control. The second proposal, presented as a "maximum concession," was to include substantial parts of the non-Polish agricultural areas in Lower Silesia and Pomerania to Poland. In addition, OMGUS wanted to internationalize the Silesian coal and industrial resources to make them available to all of Europe. If neither alternative was accepted, OMGUS suggested that the issue be postponed pending investigation by a Four Power Commission.[32] In spite of ongoing disagreements about other issues concerning Germany, the foreign ministers of France, Britain, and the United States agreed in a 20 May 1949 meeting to insist on the provisional nature of the Oder–Neisse Line and to recommend the creation of a boundary commission.[33] Again reflecting concerns about Soviet intentions, Robert Murphy sent a memorandum to Secretary Acheson recommending that he "put the question to the Soviets whether they still stick to the Oder–Neisse line." Murphy told Acheson of his discussion with West German authorities in Frankfurt on 8 June 1949, where that question was "uppermost in the minds all Germans irrespective of political opinion."[34]

All of this preconference discussion and speculation about Soviet intentions regarding Poland's western border proved moot. The conference stalled as the widely divergent solutions between East and West over the question of German unity became evident; nothing of importance was settled at Paris. The German–Polish border was not even discussed at great length, although Acheson alluded to the matter during meetings on 10 and 12 June, when he asked if there was "any use in putting forth new proposals on the matter in view of the Soviet attitude that the frontier was final." The Soviets refused to respond to the question.[35] The conference ended on 20 June 1949, and Secretary of State Acheson reported to the Executive Session of the House Foreign Affairs Committee on 23 June 1949.

At that meeting Acheson seemed to use diplomatic rhetoric rather than frankness in his response to a question from Congressman Thomas Gordon (D-IL) about whether there had been any discussion of the frontier. Acheson said, "No, we asked the Russians to state what their position was. We favored no position."[36] While it was true that the American delegation had not presented a proposal on the border since the issue was not on the agenda and the Soviets refused to discuss it, the studies done by OMGUS as well as Acheson's own preconference presentation to the Senate Foreign Relations Committee showed that officially the State Department continued to favor an eastward shift in the border to bring more agricultural land into Germany.

The secretary, however, openly revealed to the congressmen his willingness to use the Oder–Neisse issue to discomfit the Soviets when he elaborated on the Soviets' difficult position concerning the Polish–German border:

> This is one of the most embarrassing positions for the Russians that they have. They have got to create finally a Germany that could live. . . . "What is your attitude?" we said to the Russians. "You have said in the past that the present line . . . is final and nobody can discuss it any more and all a peace treaty can do is to ratify it. Is that your attitude?" . . . The Russians refused to answer. . . . They either have to alienate the Poles and [*sic*] alienate the Germans. We just tried to keep them on that little griddle until they were well browned all the way around.[37]

The committee was apparently satisfied with this response; the members went on to discuss other matters.

SPECULATION ON GERMAN AND SOVIET INTENTIONS

A few months later the Federal Republic of Germany and the German Democratic Republic were officially proclaimed as states.[38] The new West German Basic Law became effective on 23 May 1949, and the three Western Allies recognized the Federal Republic of Germany on 21 September 1949.[39] In eastern Germany a provisional People's Council had been established in March 1948, and a constitution was drafted in October 1948 and adopted in March

1949. A People's Congress endorsed the constitution in May 1949, but final establishment of the government was postponed until after the government of the Federal Republic was proclaimed.[40] The Cold War continued to deepen as the Soviets exploded an atomic device, the Western Allies organized the North Atlantic Treaty Organization (NATO), communists took control of mainland China, and the Western Allies began seriously discussing the possibility of rearming West Germany.

American representatives in West Germany and Poland continued to monitor the activities of the Germans and Soviets. James Riddleberger of the Office of Political Affairs noted an army intelligence report concerning the Soviet position on the Oder–Neisse Line, but a difference of opinion between the Intelligence Division and Riddleberger's office was evident. On 27 August Riddleberger forwarded an intelligence report that speculated on the vulnerability of the Soviet position. It based this contention on reports that Soviet-licensed Berlin newspapers had begun insisting that the Oder–Neisse was the "border of peace" rather than continuing their former practice of ignoring the question. The intelligence report contended that this "indicates the sensitivity of the Soviet position in the German eyes in view of Soviet intransigeance [*sic*] on this point during all past attempts to negotiate a peace treaty."[41] Although Riddleberger forwarded the army report, he sent the secretary a telegram a few days later stating that his office thought the army report "misleading." He wrote that the Soviet-licensed press had not recently changed its stance on the Oder–Neisse Line, but rather had continued to maintain that the border was the peace border. The Soviet-licensed press, Riddleberger added, also continued to use the West's position against recognizing the line as a basis for the claim that the Soviets were Poland's only protector.[42] The German press continued in this vein for the next few months. The Office of Political Affairs in Berlin reported an October editorial in the Soviet-licensed *Berliner Zeitung* that presented three reasons for recognizing the Oder–Neisse Line. The editorial stated that the line was established by Allied agreement in 1944 and contended that Poland deserved secure borders after enduring two wars of conquest and that the line was necessary for peace and a strong economy.[43]

From the American Embassy in Warsaw, Chargè Cecil Lyon agreed with Riddleberger's interpretation of Soviet motives. He reported in September that Wilhelm Pieck, president of the Socialist Unity Party in East Germany, had traveled to Warsaw to try to convince Poles who were suspicious of German intentions that to establish a rapprochement, they had to choose between "'neighborly East Germany'" and West Germany, a "'replica, if a smaller'" Third Reich. According to Lyon, the Polish press continued to hammer home the theme that East German leaders wanted good relations with Poland, whereas in West Germany only Max Reimann, the leader of the Communist Party (KPD), presented that view.[44]

This Polish press report was confirmed during one of the Federal Republic's first parliamentary debates on 20 September 1949. The Adenauer government held that the Potsdam Accord had placed the territories along the Oder and Neisse Rivers under Polish control only until a peace treaty was signed. He was widely cheered by almost all parties when he stated to the Bundestag: "Under no circumstances can we therefore be satisfied with a severance of these territories undertaken unilaterally by Soviet Russia and Poland."[45] When Max Reimann responded by stating that the Oder–Neisse Line created a "frontier of peace," the recorder of the debate noted "constant vehement boos and catcalls" and shouts to "withdraw."[46]

The establishment of a West German democracy did nothing to calm the fears of Poles and Polish Americans about German aggression. Poland sent notes of protest to Washington claiming that the creation of West Germany would lead to war through "revisionist propaganda" about the Oder–Neisse Line.[47] Relations between the United States and Poland continued to worsen as American exports to Poland remained small, and propaganda attacks continued.[48] Polish Americans took up the cause of Polish displaced persons, and the Senate Judiciary Committee held special subcommittee hearings to determine whether the 1948 Displaced Persons Act should be amended to allow the immigration of more refugees and displaced persons.[49]

CORRESPONDENCE ABOUT THE ODER–NEISSE LINE

The State Department also continued to receive correspondence from members of Congress regarding their constituents' fears of potential German aggression. John Lesinski (D-MI) sent Truman a copy of a resolution given to him by the Polish Falcons of America, a well-established national organization promoting social and educational activities. The Falcons' resolution decried the efforts of American officials in Germany who were trying to "appease these self-same German imperialists" by trying to return Polish lands to Germany in the mistaken attempt to relieve the "artificial overpopulation" of West Germany. Lesinski showed that he agreed with these sentiments when he wrote to Truman: "I trust there will be no further appeasement and that no further changes in the boundaries will be made."[50] Truman's secretary referred Lesinski's letter to the State Department, where Assistant Secretary of State Ernest Gross sent the typical reply explaining the U.S. position that Potsdam had established a provisional border. The Polish Falcons must have instigated a letter-writing campaign since Connecticut Senators Raymond E. Baldwin (R) and Brien McMahon (D) received similar resolutions in October 1949. The Department of State sent them the same replies that were sent to Lesinski.[51]

The tenth anniversary of Germany's 1939 invasion of Poland offered another occasion for Polish Americans to present their views to the White House, the State Department, and Congress. On 22 September 1949 Leon Walkowicz, chairman of the Committee to Mark the Tenth Anniversary of

Germany's Attack on Poland, sent a resolution to Clement Zablocki (D-WI) expressing the conviction that Poland had a historical right to the Oder–Neisse territories and that the land provided only small compensation for the destruction that Germany had caused Poland. The committee opposed any vestiges of German militarism and contended that the Allied agreement at the 1947 Moscow Council of Foreign Ministers to liquidate Prussia showed that German militarism was a common concern.[52] Zablocki responded to Walkowicz's letter thanking him for the resolution and agreeing that it presented "a very good resume" of the issue. Zablocki told the chairman that he would be glad to quote from the resolution.[53] Walkowicz also sent the resolution to the White House, where it was forwarded to the State Department.[54] Various divisions of the Polish Falcons of America also sent a resolution to Truman opposing any U.S. efforts to appease German imperialists by returning Polish land to Germany in order to "'relieve the artificial overpopulation of Western Germany.'" The president's secretary responded with an innocuous reply thanking the Falcons for sending the resolution.[55]

DISAGREEMENTS AMONG AMERICAN DIPLOMATS

While Polish Americans were urging Washington to recognize the line, officers in the Warsaw Embassy urged another course of action that also differed from the policy proposed by the State Department. The preparation of the 1949 Policy Paper for Poland revealed a difference of opinion between the Warsaw Embassy and Washington over the handling of the border issue. In July the secretary of state forwarded a draft copy of the policy to Warsaw for comment. Although Ambassador Gallman was then in Washington for consultation, Chargè Cecil Lyon responded on 19 September with "a few frank comments and suggestions which have occurred to those of us who have read the statement." Regarding the Oder–Neisse Line the policy paper stated: "Among the numerous irritants characterizing our current relations with Poland, none is regarded more seriously by the Polish Government than our policy respecting the Polish–German frontier, provisionally fixed by the Potsdam Agreement. . . . Our attitude toward this boundary question is that we will support a revision of Germany's eastern frontiers in favor of Poland, but the extent of the area to be ceded to Poland is for determination when the final settlement is agreed upon."[56] This position had been announced by Secretary Byrnes at Stuttgart in 1946 and clarified by Secretary Marshall at the 1947 Moscow Council of Foreign Ministers.[57] The embassy's comments about the border, however, differed greatly from the department's statement:

> As events have developed, the Western border issue is perhaps now as explosive an issue to the USSR as it is to the Western Powers. The possibility of making alterations in favor of Germany must appeal, in other words, to each of the Big Four as a trump-card

which may one day be played for decisive results vis-a-vis the German people. The pressures, however, are probably greater on the USSR than on ourselves, since the Soviets are in control of East Germany and the viability of East Germany is challenged as long as it remains separated from West Germany, Pomerania and Silesia. We believe, therefore, we would be well advised to remain quiet henceforward on the border issue and let the Soviets bear the difficult burden on seeking to satisfy both Germans and Poles of the justice of the present status. If feasible we should not interject ourselves further into the problem until the Soviets are dislodged from East Germany, unless such is demanded by policy considerations vis-a-vis West Germany or peace treaty negotiations.[58]

Although both the Warsaw Embassy and Washington recognized the volatility of the border issue and accepted as genuine Poland's fear of Germany and desire to have the Oder–Neisse Line recognized as final, they disagreed over the approach that the United States should take to force the Soviets' hand. Where the embassy wanted to remain silent on the issue to make the Soviets publicly support either Poland or Germany, the policy paper stated that U.S. officials, while supporting a frontier change "in Poland's favor," would continue to emphasize the provisional nature of Poland's western border, thus implying that some of the land might be returned to Germany.

Even within the Washington offices of the State Department differences of opinion about Poland's western border were apparent. When Herbert Feis, at the Institute for Advanced Study at Princeton, wrote to George Kennan, then counselor of the Department of State, suggesting that the United States play on Soviet vulnerability regarding the Polish–German frontier, the letter seems to have caused consternation within the State Department, even though Feis' suggestion was similar to the position proposed in the policy statement for Poland. Feis' letter was seen by a number of people, and there was evidently some question about who would reply and how the response would read. An internal memorandum attached to the letter stated that while "everybody agrees that . . . we might someday wish to do this it is undesirable now, because . . . [i]t would seriously undermine the position we are trying to build up in Poland." In addition, the writer noted, it would benefit the East German regime and would show the vulnerability of the U.S. position on the Saar along Germany's western border.[59] More than a month later Kennan sent a memorandum to Colonel Henry Byroade, director of the Bureau of German Affairs, stating, "Since I doubt that I agree with the official line on this, I wonder if you would like to have drafted a reply to Feis." A few days later Kennan wrote a brief note to Feis reiterating his disagreement with the consensus on the matter, although he did not elaborate on his point that "I am somewhat out of the current on this affair—in more ways than one." He offered to discuss the matter with Feis in person since, he wrote, "it is very difficult to discuss this complex and thorny problem by correspondence."[60] No record of a follow-up meeting was attached to this correspondence, but Kennan was probably referring to the various positions circulating the State Department about the proper course to follow regarding Germany as well as to his early disagreement with the establishment of Poland's border on the Oder–Neisse.[61]

The newly created Bureau of German Affairs nevertheless continued its attempts to coordinate U.S. policy, including the U.S. position on the German–Polish border. Officially, American policy regarding the Oder–Neisse Line held that Potsdam had only provisionally placed the area under Polish administration. This official policy was confirmed by Henry Byroade who also revealed much later the difference between official and practical policy. In a 1988 interview Byroade stated that, "as a practical matter, we recognized that that [the Oder–Neisse Line] was going to be the border for a long time."[62]

AMERICAN POLICY IN WEST GERMANY

The question of Poland's western border continued to add to the difficulties of American policy planners.[63] When the Office of Political Affairs at the High Commissioner's Office (HICOG) in Frankfurt polled various branches of HICOG about information access on East–West relations, the Oder–Neisse question was one of the issues about which HICOG officers wanted more information.[64] In a memorandum prepared for a February 1950 meeting of Acheson, Kennan, Deputy Undersecretary of State Dean Rusk, and Director of the Policy Planning Staff Paul Nitze, two "main forces" of German political life were noted. One was the desire for reunification and the recovery of the Oder–Neisse territories; the other was a more stable economic situation.[65] The authors of the memorandum acknowledged that these were both natural and understandable desires and stated optimistically that if Western policies led to solutions to these problems, the West would maintain a high level of influence in Germany. They acknowledged, however, that these problems also represented a grave danger to Western policy since only the Soviets could actually effect the return of Germany's eastern territories. The possibility of a Soviet deal with the Germans increased as prospects for American aid to, and trade with, Germany lessened. "It cannot be too strongly emphasized," the authors warned, "that, once American aid becomes nominal, the attraction to deal with the Soviets will become irresistible to the Germans if markets in the West are not available because of unilateral restrictions based upon fear of competition."[66] The memorandum acknowledged the strong anti-Soviet strain in Germany that might keep the Germans oriented toward the West as long as Germany was "not rebuffed by what she considers selfish interests." The danger was the threat, increasingly perceived by Britain and France, of German economic competition. The solution was to push even harder for Western European integration before time ran out.[67]

A memorandum prepared by Byroade in March 1950 and sent to the deputy director of the Policy Planning Staff noted, among other considerations, the "traditionally undemocratic German mentality" and the presence of the eastern refugees as threats to U.S. policy in West Germany.[68] Another paper prepared in the Office of German Political Affairs by Henry B. Cox also pointed to the German expellees and refugees who actively campaigned for reunification and the revision of the Oder–Neisse Line. Cox noted that one of the principal reasons for Adenauer's protest against the Saar agreement was the feeling that any border settlement in the west before a peace treaty would harm Germany's chances of having the Oder–Neisse lands returned. The failure of the Adenauer government to integrate the expellees fully, Cox contended, was due to the fact that the government believed that the presence of a large number of unassimilated refugees would be a powerful argument for the return of the territories sometime in the future.[69]

U.S. suspicions about Soviet plans for Germany as well as the intentions of the West Germans regarding the German–Polish border increased in the spring of 1950. In April the U.S. legation in Bern reported that one of the "'satellite source[s]'" had received information from a member of a satellite cabinet that the Soviets intended to give a "'knockout'" blow to U.S. policy in Germany by offering a peace treaty to East Germany that would include the return of some of the land along the Oder–Neisse border. The Soviets, according to the informant, felt that McCarthy's "'partisan attacks'" on the administration had distracted the U.S. government and made the political atmosphere for such a move very attractive.[70] The U.S. Embassy in Moscow recognized that such rumors of a Soviet–East German peace treaty could be "'plants'" but believed that such a move would be logical and attractive from a Soviet point of view.[71]

Concern about Adenauer and Schumacher's intentions regarding the East–West struggle in Germany was reflected in a telegram from Secretary of State Acheson on 21 April 1950. Acheson recognized that various statements made by West German political leaders could have been made for internal political reasons or to wring concessions from the West. He, however, emphatically stated that "we consider it important to disabuse them of any notion that use of [the] East–West situation to wring concessions from [the] West can be productive or helpful. . . . [W]e think it equally important for them to have no delusions about the ultimate results of any attempt on their part to use [the] East–West situation in Ger[many] as a bargaining weapon."[72] U.S. High Commissioner John McCloy agreed with Acheson's assessment and reported that he had emphasized to the West German leaders the undesirability of using this Cold War struggle for specific German gain.[73]

POLISH PROPAGANDA ABOUT THE ODER–NEISSE

In light of this speculation about Soviet and West German intentions for the Oder–Neisse border, it was not surprising that the Warsaw Embassy kept a close watch on the Polish press, which had returned to the propaganda line of promoting peaceful relations between Poland and the German Democratic

Republic. In March, the embassy transmitted excerpts of a Polish article commenting on a statement made by an East German government representative. The article, according to the second secretary of the embassy, C. H. Hall Jr., reflected again the propaganda line that Poland and East Germany could and should have friendly relations. Hall pointed out, though, that the article's author made "one interesting and perhaps revealing admission, vis: 'Let us be frank, there are plenty of people in Poland who think no true German can acquiesce in the loss of Szczecin, Wrocław or Opole.'"[74] Hall reiterated that many Poles felt insecure about the western territories as evidenced by the lack of development and settlement in the area. The Warsaw Embassy's apparent uncertainty about the level of autonomy of the Polish government was shown in Hall's statement about a Polish decision, "in so far as it was a Polish and not a Kremlin decision," to expel German citizens who still remained in Poland.[75]

A telegram from Ambassador Gallman in April 1950 reported that a reliable Polish source confirmed speculation that the Poles were growing increasingly concerned about the western territories. The source spoke of "almost fatalistic" Polish uneasiness that some move to return part of the land to East Germany was "imminent."[76] When asked why Polish fears were on the rise, the informant replied that there were "political compulsions" operating on the Soviets in East Germany. He pointed to the recent "soft pedalling" of the frontier issue in the Polish press and explained that statements by German and Polish officials were primarily directed at the Germans to "ease pressure and reduce demands on Russia." He went on to add that no Poles believed that Germany would actually give up the Oder–Neisse territories, and that many Poles expected a change in the propaganda line and in the border. The Department of State must have thought this information noteworthy as one of the readers of this telegram wrote "very interesting" across the top.[77]

The Warsaw Embassy also carefully watched and reported on a visit to Warsaw of an East German delegation headed by Walter Ulbricht. On 3 June 1950 Ambassador Gallman reported that the Polish "propaganda machine" had been informed that the visit of the East Germans would be the most important communist visit since Tito's in 1946. He added, though, that no official public pronouncement on the purpose of the visit had been made.[78] The ambassador also told the secretary that *New York Times* correspondent Edward Morrow had informed him of a speculative article that he had written suggesting that the visit of the East Germans involved some change in the Oder–Neisse Line. He based this speculation on recent administrative changes within the Polish provinces that integrated some areas more firmly in the prewar Polish pattern and left others, especially those closest to the Oder–Neisse Line, in an "anomalous position." Gallman assured the secretary that the embassy was trying to gather more exact information about those changes. He confirmed that the city of Szczecin was undergoing some construction on the eastern side of the Oder River that suggested that the Poles would keep the city. He added, though, that it was doubtful that the Soviets would have told the Poles their plans for the city or even that a decision would have been made so far in advance to allow for such construction as a sign of Polish retention of the city. He reported that the embassy regularly consulted with the British Embassy in Warsaw and that the U.S. Embassy counsellor planned a trip to Szczecin to review the situation.[79]

The Moscow Embassy added to the speculation about Soviet intentions in western Poland when Ambassador Alan G. Kirk sent information to the State Department about an article that had appeared in the March–April issue of the *Proceedings of [the] Academy of Sciences of [the] USSR*. The article emphasized the permanency of Poland's borders and accused the West of being reluctant to recognize the postwar border since it "'would complicate future imperialist adventures.'"[80] Kirk warned, however, that the article should not be taken as proof that a deal returning part of the land to the East Germans was not in the making, since the Kremlin had a practice of "abrupt policy shifts" that often "catch minor actors unawares." He recommended that if the Poles were forced to return part of the land under the guise of a "'voluntary and friendly'" agreement between East Germany and Poland, the United States should use it as counterpropaganda against the Soviet position on Trieste.[81]

A few days later Kirk again speculated about Soviet intentions in light of reports from U.S. representatives in Frankfurt and Warsaw suggesting that some kind of deal involving the city or port of Sczcecin was under discussion. Kirk believed it more likely that the Soviets would push for a guaranteed access agreement between East Germany and Poland rather than an outright border modification since recent Soviet pronouncements suggested that the Soviets were not then ready for a border change. He added, though, that the Moscow Embassy believed that "sooner rather than later" the Kremlin would be forced to make territorial concessions to Germany at Poland's expense since Soviet appeal in Germany was waning slightly. Kirk's concluding statements again reflect American diplomats' uncertainty about the level of Moscow's control over Warsaw when he writes, "From here it appears" that enough progress had been made in the Soviet subordination of Poland to enable the Soviets to force a border revision under the "facade of 'mutual understanding and friendly understanding'" between Poland and East Germany.[82]

An Intelligence Division transmission of the Socialist Unity Party publication "Why Is the Oder-Neisse Line the Peace Border?" echoes Ambassador Kirk's suspicions of Soviet and German communists' intentions. The U.S. political adviser's office in Heidelberg informed the State Department that after analyzing the publication, intelligence officers agreed that it was uncompelling and "full of omissions." They believed that this publication showed that the Soviets "and their supporters" were on the defensive regarding the border question, and they suggested that the United States could use the omissions as "suitable themes for counter-attack when such a procedure becomes desirable."[83]

A minor, but still telling, action of the Polish government to emphasize

Polish ownership of the western territories was noted in May 1950, when the Polish chargè in Washington called on Fred Salter, head of the Office of Polish, Baltic, and Czechoslovak Affairs within the Office of Eastern European Affairs, to lodge a "friendly protest" against a Commerce Department's map showing the Polish-administered territories as German land. The map appeared in a booklet that was part of the International Reference Service. The Polish chargè assured Salter that he was not bringing an official protest but wanted to point out the alleged inaccuracy to the State Department, thus emphasizing the Polish government's view that the land permanently belonged to Poland.[84]

THE EAST GERMAN–POLISH AGREEMENT

The following month Ambassador Gallman reported on the visit of the East German delegation to Poland resulting in the release of a joint communiqué on 6 June stating that Poland and East Germany agreed to demarcate within one month the "inviolable frontier of peace and friendship" established along the Oder–Neisse Line, and to regulate border crossing points, frontier traffic, and river navigation.[85] American and West German officials responded almost immediately to this communiqué. On 7 June 1950 U.S. High Commissioner John McCloy released a statement with the State Department's approval reaffirming the U.S. position as stated by former Secretaries Byrnes and Marshall that the border question would be settled at a final peace conference, as agreed upon by the Allies at Potsdam. He stated further that the matter could not be settled unilaterally or bilaterally "by representatives of a regime that has no real support of the German people" and concluded that the U.S. government did not recognize the Oder–Neisse Line or the incorporation of the land into the Polish state.[86]

In the telegram reporting his press release, McCloy told the secretary that PEPCO, the Political and Economic Projects Committee in the Office of the U.S. High Commissioner, had discussed the border matter and concurred that the time was appropriate for a "full-press policy statement" on the Oder–Neisse Line "unless [the] fear of exacerbating US–Polish relations and inviting reprisals" against the American Embassy in Warsaw was considered too great. McCloy's recommendation that the Warsaw Embassy have the final word on decisions affecting the Oder–Neisse Line reflects his awareness that the border issue was as much a Polish as a German issue and mirrored the concern of officers in the Warsaw Embassy and in Washington who favored downplaying the U.S. position on the border. The release of the Polish–East German communiqué only heightened Western speculation about Soviet intentions for the border. McCloy pointed out that the border agreement, along with others, represented another "psychological slap" at both Germanys that suggested that [the] Soviets must be clearing [the] decks for [a] sole manoeuvre which will be intended to rehabilitate [the] psychological losses entailed in sponsoring these

. . . unpopular moves."[87] Although he thought it unlikely, McCloy conceded that a separate Soviet–East German de facto peace settlement was possible.[88]

From Warsaw, Ambassador Gallman labelled the joint Polish–East German communiqué as the "most explicit revelation to date" of communist plans, especially in light of the intense speculation about some type of border rectification being imminent. Gallman contended, though, that the aim of the joint declaration was "somewhat obscured" by the use of the word "'delineation'" since it suggested that a new line would be drawn.[89] He thought that the Poles and East Germans had intended to make the Potsdam arrangement "permanent, but with certain modifications." "As such," he wrote, "it is an obvious attempt to violate the arrangement." Gallman interpreted the statement in the communiqué about forthcoming agreements regarding transportation and roads in the frontier area as suggesting that East Germany had been granted considerable concessions in Szczecin, probably including free port and transit rights similar to those granted to Hungary and Czechoslovakia in 1949. The ambassador concluded that the Polish–East German agreement was the Soviets' attempt to solve the problem of building up East Germany without "undue offense" to Poland. He predicted an intense propaganda campaign within the next month.[90]

The Moscow Embassy agreed with Gallman's view that the wording of the communiqué suggested a future border rectification. Ambassador Kirk also agreed with McCloy's contention that the recent Soviet actions in Germany represented a "slap" at Germany and that the United States should expect a Soviet move in the near future to counteract the "unfavorable repercussions" of such steps. Like McCloy, Kirk felt that a separate Soviet–East German peace treaty was possible but unlikely since such a move would crystallize the division of Germany and force the Soviets to surrender their "self-proclaimed role" as the only true advocate of German unity. He believed it more likely that the Soviets would withdraw troops from East Germany and invite the Western Allies to do the same in West Germany. The ambassador also urged the State Department to follow up McCloy's press statement with a "formal three-power protest" of the communiqué for the record.[91]

Individuals in the State Department investigated the situation. On 12 June 1950 Richard Tims of the Division of Research for Europe sent to Fred Hadsel in the Office of German Political Affairs a chronology of events in the area of Szczecin whereby Poles took control of the city. Hadsel forwarded the memorandum to the Office of German Public Affairs with the suggestion that the information showing unilateral Polish action in violation of Potsdam might be useful in a propaganda campaign about the Oder–Neisse Line.[92]

Tims also sent to the Office of German Political Affairs his analysis of the Polish–East German agreement signed on 6 June 1950. Tims noted that the agreement, which included a provision confirming the Oder–Neisse Line, a cultural convention, and a series of trade agreements, represented a major political step that transcended its immediate provisions. Tims contended that the agreement represented a "comprehensive Kremlin-dream plan" to have its two satellites play complementary roles in its overall Western European strategy.[93] The border provision Tims interpreted as the Kremlin's effort to shelve temporarily the "bait of territorial revision" to West Germany. Instead, he wrote, the Kremlin apparently decided to develop East Germany economically and politically by providing it with "resources of the orbit hinterland." In the agreement East Germany renounced claim to the Oder–Neisse lands in return for broad access to Polish markets and materials, shipping rights on the Oder River, and "presumably" free use of the Sczcecin port. The latter provision could make Szczecin economically more important to East Germany than to Poland. For Poland, the agreement removed a major obstacle to improved relations with East Germany. He added, however, that while it was mutually advantageous, the agreement could nevertheless eventually make Poland East Germany's economic junior partner. In spite of this, he contended that the Warsaw regime could be "imponderably strengthen[ed]" by the agreement because of the possibility of a tremendous increase in trade. He concluded that such agreements fitted "the Moscow pattern of economic orbit integration." This research analysis was apparently not widely circulated, but it explains very satisfactorily why the Soviets were willing to support at least temporarily Poland's territorial demands at the expense of East Germany.[94]

The pronouncement by the Poles and East Germans that they would reach an agreement on the border within a month was fulfilled. On 6 July 1950 the two sides signed in the Polish border town of Zgorzelec a treaty recognizing "the fixed and existing frontier as the inviolable frontier of peace and friendship . . . which unites the two nations." They agreed to form a commission to mark the frontier formally along the established line and to set machinery in place to ratify the border agreement.[95]

The Warsaw Embassy reported the frontier agreement to Washington and indicated that, as predicted, the Polish government was implementing a propaganda campaign. Embassy Counselor Cecil Lyon told the secretary that while this publicity made it unlikely that any territorial concessions to East Germany were being considered, it seemed probable that concessions would be made dealing with free port access and navigation, as well as with economic and trade privileges in Szczecin. He admitted that the Soviet motivation in forcing the East Germans to sign "this new and seemingly unnecessarily humiliating act" was "obscure" but recognized the agreement as a rare popular victory for the Polish government.[96]

The HICOG office in Frankfurt sent a Special Intelligence Report on the Polish Administered Territories to the Department of State on 17 August 1950. The author of the report, T. L. Squier Jr., summarized the border problem as "one of the most difficult to emerge from World War II." He noted that the Oder–Neisse Line represented major psychological, industrial, and agricultural advantages to Poland; a severe loss of prestige for East Germany;

and an important obstacle to German–Soviet collaboration in general, giving the Soviets either a carrot or stick to negotiate.[97] This report also suggested that the frequent use in the Polish–East German agreement of the phrase "'established and existing border'" made a border revision in Germany's favor unlikely at least in the near future.[98] In relating the background of the agreement, the report pointed out that while it violated the Yalta and Potsdam Accords by establishing a frontier line, it simply recognized a "situation of fact" that had existed since 1945. Squier reported that the Poles, "with Soviet assistance, and in some cases without it," had occupied the territories outlined in the Potsdam Protocol as well as the city of Szczecin on the west bank of the Oder River by settling about 6 million Poles in the area, although he doubted that the Poles had the necessary resources to utilize the full potential of the city of Szczecin. Western observers, according to Squier, believed that the extremely slow reconstruction of Szczecin by the Poles indicated that the Poles themselves did not expect to be allowed to retain control of the city.

Although the report did not fully cover the political and economic roles of the western territories, Squier reported on the importance of the area for industry, settlement, and propaganda. The major asset of the western territories to Poland, Squire contended, was the acquisition of the industries of Silesia. The area had also provided the Polish government with land to resettle Poles returning from abroad or displaced by the "territorial settlement" with the Soviet Union. "Best of all, from the government's point of view," Squier wrote, "the resettlement of half-empty territory has greatly facilitated the implementation of its land reform and collectivization schemes." He did not underestimate the propaganda value of the acquisition to the Polish government, noting that even the Catholic clergy, "at odds with the government on so many issues," agreed with the government on the border issue. Thus, Squier contended, any revision of the line would have "serious repercussions" on the Polish economy, would dislocate the population, and would damage the government's prestige to such an extent "that a major shakeup of the government and party and the imposition of much stronger controls would be necessary to maintain Moscow's grip on the country."[99]

He analyzed the reaction of the East German government to the Polish agreement as presented in the Socialist Unity Party newspaper *Neues Deutschland* on 18 June 1950 as well as in other publications. The *Neues Deutschland* article justified the line by quoting the Yalta and Potsdam Agreements and Allied leaders' pronouncements and warned any latent German revisionists that the first war of German aggression had ended with the creation of the Polish Corridor and the second with the Oder–Neisse Line. Squier stated that "the inference is clear," that the Oder–Neisse Line guaranteed lasting friendship between Poland and Germany and thus formed the cornerstone of a peaceful Europe. Thus, he continued, the attitude that one held toward the Oder–Neisse Line was second only to one's attitude toward the Soviet Union "'as the touchstone of true patriotism and genuine love of peace.'"[100]

Opponents of the Oder–Neisse Line were portrayed in such East German news articles as tools of the English and American "warmongers" whose efforts would be defeated by the pooling of the material and ideological resources of East Germany and the People's Republics. Such a view, Squier noted, presented the Oder–Neisse border as the Soviet counterpart of the Schuman plan to integrate Europe.

In spite of such propaganda, Squier contended that few East Germans, even loyal party members, greeted the Polish–East German agreement with much enthusiasm. He deduced that the border agreement must "have been dictated by overriding policy needs, to which the USSR has always sacrificed momentary considerations of public opinion." Acceptance of the line by the East German government was a necessary step in the integration of East Germany into the "Soviet orbit as a full-fledged People's Democracy."[101]

The Adenauer government issued a formal protest of the Polish–East German agreement. In a letter to McCloy, the chancellor noted that the Allies in June 1945 had said that German territory would be considered within the 1937 borders, that the land had only provisionally been placed in Poland's administration, and that the German Democratic Republic did not represent a majority of Germans.[102] The Department of State gave McCloy permission to restate the Allied position that the final border awaited a peace settlement but ordered that "for various reasons" the U.S. High Commissioner's Office should not publish the text of Adenauer's letter.[103] Instead, the high commissioners sent a copy of Adenauer's letter, accompanied by their own cover letter, to all governments with missions in Bonn or military missions in Berlin and to the occupying powers.[104]

The Polish government responded vituperatively to Adenauer's nonrecognition of the Zgorzelec agreement. The U.S. Embassy in Warsaw forwarded a "typical" editorial from the 8 October 1950 *Zycie Warszawy* that castigated the U.S., British, and French high commissioners who controlled the "Bonn Hitlerites" in searching for a cause to "stimulate chauvinistic hatred" by feeding German revisionism. The West did this, according to the editorial, out of fear of the success of the government of the German Democratic Republic and of the antiwar sentiment in West Germany that had been "earmarked as the source of cheap cannon fodder." The editorial discounted the impact of Bonn's nonrecognition policy on the permanency of the Oder–Neisse Line, equating it to the ineffectiveness of Byrnes' 1946 Stuttgart speech.[105]

The Polish–East German communiqué and the American government's press response were reported and commented on in the mainstream and Polish American newspapers. The *Christian Science Monitor* questioned Soviet wisdom in promoting the agreement. An editorial on 8 June 1950 recognized that it might prove helpful to Communist Party strength but contended that the Soviet propaganda machine would have to work very hard to justify the agreement. The editorial stated that the economic aspects of the deal would require a sacrifice from the Poles and predicted that the agreement would also sow division among the Germans.[106]

A *New York Times* editorial of 8 June dismissed the agreement as "obviously dictated by Soviet Russia" but contended that it raised "serious questions" for the West. The editor stated that the Soviets were obviously motivated by the desire to compensate Poland for robbing it of the Polish eastern territories, but the editor pointed out the double advantages accrued by the Soviets, that is, "riveting" Poland to the Soviet Union while holding out to the Germans the possibility of a future revision in return for unification. The editor agreed with American policy which refused to recognize the border as final, but predicted future difficulties for the Western powers, which "have not always been diligent in emphasizing that German unification included territories beyond the Oder–Neisse line." This agreement would force the West to take a stand.[107]

In contrast with the mainstream press, the *Polish American Journal* stated flatly that since President Truman himself had recognized Poland's right to the Oder–Neisse territories, the "opinions expressed by officials of the State Department that the question of the Oder–Niesse [*sic*] frontier is not settled does not alter the situation." The editor pointed out that it would be embarrassing to evacuate Poles from an area previously turned over to them by redrawing the border.[108]

AMERICAN REACTION TO THE ZGORZELEC AGREEMENT

The signing of the Polish–East German agreement also concerned some Americans who contacted the State Department and their congressmen. Hamilton Fish Armstrong, editor of *Foreign Affairs*, sent Acheson a telegram on 8 June 1950 suggesting that if the U.S. government issued a formal protest of the Polish annexation of German lands as claimed in the recent Polish–East German agreement, the statement should also point out that the United States did not accept Soviet annexation of Polish lands in the east. This, Armstrong wrote, would encourage Polish "nationalist resistance to Russia."[109] In a memorandum attached to a draft reply for Acheson's signature, Assistant Secretary of State for European Affairs George Perkins informed the secretary that for "political reasons, the Department's policy has been to avoid making any statements concerning the United States attitude towards the Polish–Soviet boundary."[110] The draft reply to Armstrong pointed out that the German–Polish border question involved a former enemy state and thus was considered in a different light from that of the Polish–Soviet border as laid out at Yalta and agreed upon by representatives of the Polish and Soviet governments in August 1945.[111]

When Armstrong responded to Acheson's letter a couple of months later, he continued to maintain that in light of the Polish–East German agreement, the United States could gain a "propaganda point" with Poland by emphasizing that the United States had never agreed to the extension of the Curzon Line in Poland's east, which divided Eastern Galicia and gave Lwów to the Soviets. He reiterated his belief that Polish resistance to Moscow was stronger than generally believed and contended that it would be to the West's advantage to gain Poland's friendship by supporting its claim to Lwów in case of war when the Soviet army supply lines would be cut.[112] His letter was carefully scrutinized in the European Divisions of the State Department. A reply was finally prepared for Acheson's signature, even though one officer questioned whether it was "good policy for Mr. Acheson to be engaging in correspondence such as this, even with Mr. Armstrong, on a controversial issue?"[113] The reply to Armstrong pointed out the difficulties of defining the exact Curzon Line and stated that an official State Department announcement about the Polish–Soviet border would not have the desired effect.[114]

Secretary Acheson also heard from the Polish American Congress. On 19 June 1950 Charles Rozmarek informed Acheson of the unanimous decision by the Polish American Congress Executive Board to register with the State Department its views about the Oder–Neisse Line, the Zgorzelec agreement, and U.S. policy. The PAC maintained that the recent announcement by State Department officials that the Oder–Neisse Line was not final was "inconsistent with the acknowledged policy of our government and not in the best interests of the United States." Rozmarek reiterated the view that at Potsdam Truman had recognized the Oder–Neisse and had consented to the evacuation of the Germans. The finalization clause, Rozmarek contended, "had been properly understood to be a mere formality and nothing else." He questioned the wisdom of statements to the contrary as a threat to the faith that Polish people held in the moral leadership of the United States.[115]

Charles Yost, director of the Office of Eastern European Affairs, replied to Rozmarek by quoting from the 8 June 1950 State Department statement on the Zgorzelec agreement to the effect that the border question could be settled only at a peace conference. He also informed Rozmarek that the department was still considering the "broad aspects and implications of the situation" regarding the Polish–East German agreement.[116]

Congressman Wayne Hays (D-OH) wrote to the Office of Congressional Relations in the Department of State requesting information about U.S.–Polish relations in order to reply to one of his constituents. Assistant Secretary of State Jack McFall wrote Hays that while the United States desired friendly relations with Poland, recent events in Poland, including the signing of the agreement, showed that the Polish government continued to violate the Potsdam Agreement. The United States, McFall wrote, held that Germany's boundaries would be settled at a future peace conference and therefore did not recognize the Oder–Neisse border as final.[117]

The State Department recognized that this position complicated U.S. relations with Poland. The 1950 policy statement on Poland acknowledged that the government and people of Poland feared that the United States, "in its preoccupation with Soviet aggressiveness," might allow militaristic and irredentist elements in Germany to develop, especially over the border issue. The policy statement noted that while the United States had agreed at Potsdam to the provisional establishment of the Oder–Neisse Line and to the orderly transfer of the German population from the area, Washington had subsequently emphasized the "tentative character" of the Potsdam Agreement. That position, the statement read, upset Poles and Polish Americans, almost all of whom favored the line. It also noted that while the Soviet Union officially supported the line, many Poles suspected that the Kremlin would willingly shift the border in Germany's favor if such a move furthered Soviet aims in Germany. For the time being, however, communist propaganda emphasized the permanency of the border. The immediate outlook for U.S.–Polish relations was bleak beyond keeping open ties with the Polish people: "There are disquieting indications that we have not entirely succeeded in convincing our Polish friends in the face of ceaseless anti-US propaganda by their Government, that our policy toward Germany takes adequate account of the ultimate interests of Poland and other small nations neighboring on Germany."[118] The authors of the policy statement contended that only by carefully developing U.S.–German relations through restoring a peaceful and prosperous Germany into the "family of western European nations" could Polish fears of U.S. intentions be calmed.[119]

U.S. POLICIES IN POLAND AND WEST GERMANY

This policy statement met some opposition when it was reviewed in the Offices of German Economic and Political Affairs. Officers within those departments believed that it was inaccurate to state that the United States had agreed at Potsdam to the transfer of Germans from the Polish-administered territories. They claimed that the U.S. government had agreed to the transfer of Germans from Poland, without specifying the western territories. "It is true," they wrote, "that we accepted the population transfers from the Polish controlled areas, but we have never specifically agreed to an interpretation of the agreement which included these territories in Poland." They urged that the government not "give further sanction" to the population transfers by "reading into Potsdam a commitment which we never actually made."[120] While these officers are correct in the statement that the Potsdam Agreement did not specifically state that Germans would be removed from the Polish-administered territories, the context of the statement as well as the subsequent directive from the Allied Control Council in November 1945 to remove 3.5 million Germans from Poland clearly suggested that the authors included Poland's western territories in their references to Poland. While this opposition to recognizing U.S. approval of the population transfers did not become part of U.S. policy, the memorandum showed that offices in the State Department continued to view the Oder–Neisse question differently.

From Warsaw, Ambassador Joseph Flack, who was appointed in August 1950 after serving as ambassador in Costa Rica, sent his general approval of most of the policy statement. He fully agreed that the Soviet Union was attempting to bring Poland more into the Soviet orbit, and he added that in Poland the fear of an aggressive, remilitarized Germany dominated the thoughts of many Poles. He affirmed that Soviet propaganda presenting the Soviets as the sole protectors of Poland's western border had a positive affect on many Poles because of their fear of Germany. Thus, he wrote, any Western propaganda urging a border revision in Germany's favor would be met with bitter opposition in Poland. At the same time, he added, any Soviet attempts to alter the line in Germany's favor would also be met with opposition to such a point that the Soviets would have to "exercise . . . considerable military force." Flack felt that Poland's best geographical chance was in the protection of a strong United Nations but he was aware that Soviet opposition to the UN made that possibility unfavorable in Poland.[121]

The delicate situation between Germany and Poland was recognized in a study prepared by officers in the Bureau of European Affairs, the Office of Eastern European Affairs, and the Research Division for Eastern Europe. One of the main features regarding U.S. policy toward Poland was to:

> keep constantly in mind in our policy toward Germany the permanent interests of the Polish people, recognizing that the needs of both Poland and Germany, as well as those of Europe as a whole, must be taken into account in the final settlement of the problem of the boundary between the two countries; make clear to [the] Polish people by our information media that U.S. policy is not designed to encourage the re-emergence of an aggressive, militaristic Germany, but rather the integration of German capabilities with those of other European states in the interests of a free, democratic Europe as a whole.[122]

East–West relations were not the only consideration, however. The Office of High Commissioner in November 1950 again perceived the activities of the refugee groups in West Germany as a threat to U.S. policy concerning the border. The impetus for this warning was a series of news articles that had reportedly been printed in *Der Courier*, a publication of German-speaking Canadians, contending that the United States and Great Britain had reached a secret agreement with exiled Poles about the Oder–Neisse Line. The newspaper stated that the Oder–Neisse was "only a demarcation line," that the State Department had agreed to a plebiscite among current inhabitants of the western territories to settle the final line, and that German expellees from the area would not be allowed to participate in the plebiscite.[123] McCloy informed Acheson that West German newspapers had reprinted the stories, and in his report to the secretary commented that while his office assumed there was no truth in this alleged article, he requested confirmation. McCloy noted that in light of the sensitive nature of the border issue, the "increasing political stature" of the refugee and irredentist groups, and the recent rejection by Washington and

Bonn of the Zgorzelec agreement, it was vitally important that the State Department or the High Commissioner's Office issue a denial or clarification. He wanted at least a reaffirmation that the United States continued to adhere to the Potsdam Accord or at most a "definitive enunciation" of Secretary Marshall's statement at the 1947 Moscow Council of Foreign Ministers. McCloy favored a joint U.S.–U.K. or a tripartite statement but acknowledged that such an agreement would take too much time to coordinate.[124]

A few days later Acheson informed McCloy that the newspaper reports about the Oder–Neisse Line were "entirely false." Acheson denied McCloy's request for a formal statement about the matter since the State Department wanted to avoid "giving unnecessary prestige" to German refugee groups by recognizing their assertions about U.S. policy through a public denial from Washington. He gave McCloy permission, though, to discuss the situation with the British high commissioner in Germany and suggested that if both men agreed, they could issue a casual, but firm, denial of any alleged deal over the border.[125]

In spite of the understanding between Bonn and Washington that the question of Germany's eastern border remained unsettled, various divisions within the State Department continued to doubt the Federal Republic's commitment to the Western "camp" and believed that West Germany might possibly be won over by Soviet blandishments to a position of "neutrality."[126] Added to this fear and partly stemming from it was the State Department's concern about maintaining Western allied unity regarding Germany.[127] After the Soviets sent a note in November 1950 suggesting another meeting of the Council of Foreign Ministers to discuss the German question, the Policy Planning Staff and the Office of German Affairs held numerous meetings to discuss possible approaches. One possibility presented for discussion by the Policy Planning Staff was to view the Potsdam Agreement as nullified by Soviet violations.[128] Another was to maintain that a unified Germany could be achieved only by internationally supervised elections; after such elections Germany would be permitted limited remilitarization.[129] Both suggestions met opposition.

In an insightful 29 January 1951 report dealing with the legal consequences of denouncing the Potsdam Agreement, Leonard Meeker of the Bureau of United Nations Affairs assumed that some form of Soviet retaliation would be forthcoming if the United States partially or totally denounced the Potsdam Agreement. The report pointed out that if the provisions regarding the Polish-administered territories were negated, the Soviets and Poles could claim that the de facto situation regarding the frontier was made de jure and that a peace settlement as outlined in the accord was no longer necessary.[130] Also, one of the arguments against West German remilitarization was the fear that the Federal Republic would recruit soldiers from the refugees of the eastern provinces who would then force an irredentist war on West Germany. Even though Acheson continually denied such an aim on Adenauer's part, rumors persisted.[131]

When Adenauer told Berliners on 6 October 1951 that he would never sacrifice German land, implying again that he recognized Germany's 1937 borders, McCloy requested advice from Byroade about what "attitude" he should take when questioned about the U.S. position on the Oder–Neisse Line.[132] McCloy showed his unwillingness to push the issue when he wrote, "My own thought is not . . . to give [the] Germans too much encouragement." He noted that recent elections in Bremen had reflected a strong nationalistic flavor and warned that such campaigns threatened the Western integration policy.[133]

Some of this speculation about West German intentions regarding the border apparently reached Poland. In February 1951 Ambassador Flack informed the secretary that well-informed Western diplomatic sources had news of a new campaign within the Polish army of intensive political indoctrination courses emphasizing the menace of a "'neo-Hitlerian Wehrmact and new eastward aggression.'" According to the source, one of the major themes of the campaign was the necessity to defend Poland not only along the Oder–Neisse border but also at the Elbe River to show alliance with the East Germans and Soviets.[134] The Warsaw Embassy also reported a speech by Vice Premier Hilary Minc that dealt with the development of new industries and called for new settlers to the western territories. The embassy interpreted Minc's speech and a report from an experienced Finnish minister stating that the Polish government was concerned about the desire of some Poles to move out of the western lands as evidence that Poland was uncertain about the future of the western border.[135] In May, McCloy reported that responsible officials in the Ministry of All-German Affairs had information that the Poles in southern East Prussia had stepped up pressure on the Germans still remaining there to opt for Polish citizenship.[136]

Polish Americans and Polish émigrés in the United States also expressed concern to the State Department and Congress that the United States was drawing too close to West Germany at Poland's expense. Stanley Nowak, former Michigan state senator and editor of Detroit's pro-Soviet newspaper *Głos Ludowy*, sent Acheson a memorandum in February prepared by representatives of unspecified "Polish American Democratic organizations." The memorandum sounded very similar to those presented by the nationalist Polish American Congress when it focused on the common fight for freedom among Poles and Americans and elaborated on the embodiment of freedom in the Potsdam Agreement, which had returned Polish lands to Poland. Such a move, the memorandum contended, had uprooted the militaristic element in Germany and converted the area to peacetime use. These Polish Americans expressed their concern about recent U.S. policy that aided Germany while leaving Poland to repair itself and that supported the remilitarization of Germany, which was still, they claimed, under the leadership of the "same Nazi generals" who had devastated Europe. Any attempt to revise the border, the authors of the memorandum stated, would be met by "terrific resistance" from the Polish people as well as "peace-loving peoples throughout the world."[137]

The Polish Political Council also expressed its concerns about U.S. policy in German to officers of the Eastern European Division of the State Department. Stefan Korbonski presented a memorandum to the State Department expressing uneasiness about rumors that Adenauer was going to launch a revisionist campaign to recover Germany's eastern territories. Officer in Charge of Polish, Baltic, and Czechoslovak Affairs Harold Vedeler told Korbonski that the State Department continued to hold that Poland's western border was provisional pending a peace settlement with Germany. Korbonski accepted that but emphasized his concern that Adenauer and "other German Nationalist leaders" might push for a territorial recovery campaign that would then make the Polish people even more susceptible to Soviet propaganda. He had heard a report, he told Vedeler, that Chancellor Adenauer would present a memorandum demanding the return of the 1937 German borders in a meeting with the three Western Allies on 20 May 1951. Vedeler noncommittally acknowledged that the U.S. government was concerned about making any moves that did not take Polish public opinion fully into account and told Korbonski that as far as he was aware, Adenauer's May meeting was simply to discuss arrangements for relaxing occupational control of West Germany.[138]

More than a week later, two other members of the Polish Political Council, Zbiegniew Stypulkowski and Jerzy Lerski, held an interview with Thomas Dillon of the Eastern European Division.[139] Rather than express concern about U.S. relations with West Germany, however, these two men presented a number of aggressive proposals that were out of step with Korbonski's presentation. They stated that the only way that the United States could prevent the estimated 500,000 to 800,000-man Polish army from fighting for the Soviets was to recognize the Oder–Neisse Line. This, they said, would persuade the satellite nations that the West was determined to halt German aggression. Their second point was that the United States should immediately renounce the Yalta Agreement in order to encourage the Polish people to resist Sovietization and deliver an ultimatum to the Soviets demanding the freedom of Eastern European states. If the Soviets refused, the Polish émigrés said, the United States "should attack immediately." In addition, they urged that Washington break relations with the Warsaw government and recognize a free Polish government and they recommended that the State Department "organize US public opinion" in favor of such action.[140]

Dillon reported that he replied to each of the points made, stating that the U.S. position on the Oder–Neisse Line remained unchanged and that the Polish Political Council's estimates of the strength of the Polish army seemed exaggerated. He went on to explain that in Washington's view the Yalta Agreement tried by diplomatic means to prevent "the enslavement of Eastern Europe," which was already being facilitated by the Soviet army, and speculated that without the Yalta Agreement, Poland's situation might be worse, especially since Yalta laid out territorial acquisitions for Poland in the north and west. Stypulkowski and Lerski recognized that fact, "but felt that the moral position would be better if the agreements had not been made."[141]

The idea of presenting an ultimatum to the Soviet Union was, Dillon told the Poles, "fantastic on moral and political grounds and probably on strategic grounds as well." He defended U.S. policy promoting the economic and military integration of Western Europe in order to deter a Soviet attack, a policy "often overlooked by Eastern European émigrés." Dillon defended also the presence of diplomatic missions in the captive states as necessary for information gathering and for serving as "a [limited] moderating influence" on Soviet and local government actions. Finally, he explained that the State Department was not empowered to "mobilize opinion for the starting of general war" as they had contended and suggested that both men learn more about the American legislative process by "enquiring of practical politicians of both our major political parties."[142]

In his report on the meeting, Dillon commented on the overall difficulty of dealing with émigré groups interested in U.S. foreign policy. He noted that Stypulkowski and Lerski's "unusually frank" views and "completely understandable" desire for the quick liberation of Poland led Polish émigré groups to "adopt extreme positions and to ignore the problems which face the United States as a democratic country leading a coalition of countries which are also responsive to public opinion."[143] He did not comment on American Poles in this report, but a few months later he had the chance to hear views expressed by a representative of one of the largest Polish American organizations.

Charles Burke, the Washington representative of the Polish American Congress, had an interview with Dillon and Johnson of the Eastern European Division on 8 August 1951. The impetus for Burke's visit was a *New York Herald* news report of 18 August 1951 claiming that High Commissioner John McCloy had told an East German youth group: "'The growing strength of the West and resistance to the Communist regime in the East can also be expected to bring about circumstances which would permit [the] return of Germany's lost territories in the East.'"[144] Burke told Dillon and Johnson that friends in the Polish American Congress had asked him to express their concern with such remarks. When Dillon asked Burke which Polish borders he favored, Burke replied that "'we Poles'" favored the pre-1939 eastern border and the Oder–Neisse in the west. These borders, he claimed, would produce a strong Poland at the expense of Germany and the Soviet Union and would thus eliminate the weakness in Eastern Europe that had resulted in two world wars. Burke went on to discuss the problem for Eastern Europe if the Western powers integrated German troops into a defense community, claiming that this action would eliminate any hope for an East European uprising (apparently against the Soviet government). He continued this theme when he expressed the fear that the United States was arming only for defense rather than for helping the Eastern European states to free themselves from Soviet domination. He went on with undiplomatic candor when he told Dillon and Johnson that there was "too much democracy" in the United States since the press published military secrets helpful to the enemy. He continued in this vein when he stated that rather than bowing to the American public's demand for a quick demobilization in 1945, the United States and Great Britain should have marched east to defeat the Soviets with the aid of 250,000 Polish troops. Dillon then returned to the topic of Poland's western borders and told Burke that, "as far as he was aware," U.S. policy held to Secretary Marshall's 1947 Moscow Council of Foreign Ministers statement.

Both Dillon and Burke agreed that their conversation was not for public consumption. When asked about his use of the phrase "we Poles," Burke explained that he had been born in Poland but was an American citizen who had gotten into the habit of using the phrase. This statement, as well as Burke's charge that America was too democratic, did a disservice to the leaders of the Polish American Congress who always emphasized the American character of the organization's members, as well as the fact that many Polish Americans had fought and died for democracy against fascism or authoritarianism. It thus seems doubtful that Burke was stating the official views of the Polish American Congress, although that possibility was not noted in the report prepared by Dillon and Johnson. They stated only that one of Burke's remarks about the Germans being far more unpopular in Poland than the Russians contradicted earlier statements that he had made and suggested that his visit might "foreshadow a campaign of protest" by Polish American and Polish émigré groups against McCloy's remarks.[145]

This prediction proved true. In a conversation with Thomas Dillon on 18 October 1951, Polish American Congressman Thaddeus Machrowicz (D-MI) pointed out the two issues of "great concern" to Polish Americans: the Oder–Neisse Line and the Yalta Agreements. He recognized the State Department's difficulties in both matters and, like the Warsaw Embassy, thought that the best approach to the frontier question would be to "avoid making any statements about the Polish–German border." He explained that McCloy's and Adenauer's recent statements had only "made the situation worse and stirred up antagonism among Polish-Americans and Poles in Poland." The congressman emphasized that while he had a large Polish American constituency and was vitally interested in U.S.–Polish relations, he also "wanted to do all he could to help the Administration and the State Department in these difficult times," even though this occasionally put him at odds with some Polish American community leaders. He welcomed, therefore, any information that would help him continue his support for the government's policies.

In his report of the conversation Dillon noted that he had called on Machrowicz at the congressman's invitation to discuss his 12 October 1951 letter to the secretary of state. Dillon frankly told Machrowicz that the State

Department was "acutely aware" of the situation and agreed that statements about the Oder–Neisse Line "should be avoided as far as possible." He explained the government's official position that the border settlement awaited a peace conference but acknowledged that "in the meantime the situation in Eastern Europe was so uncertain that it would be unwise to take a definite stand." This statement represents a complete reversal of official policy of two years before, when Secretary Acheson told the Senate Foreign Relations Committee that the issue should be used to embarrass the Soviets and in the 1949 policy statement on Poland that implied that the United States would support a border revision in Germany's favor.

Dillon also showed Congressman Machrowicz the text of McCloy's statement and contended that the high commissioner's remarks had been distorted. Machrowicz stated that he still felt it wise to remain silent on the issue, "although he agreed that it was vitally important to prevent communist propaganda from making headway in West Germany." The two men went on to discuss the Yalta Agreements and the Polish-Government-in-Exile. In response to Machrowicz's request for information about measures to ensure against the revival of a militaristic Germany, Dillon arranged for a State Department officer "who dealt with that problem" to meet with the congressman.[146]

Machrowicz's conciliatory views, though, did not represent those of all congressmen of Polish descent. In a letter to Assistant Secretary Jack McFall, Congressman John Dingell (D-MI) apparently referred to earlier correspondence when he had accepted "as full, frank and final" McFall's and Stanton Griffis' assurances about the State Department's "attitude" toward Poland. Dingell alluded to the differing views in the State Department when he discounted McFall's suggestion that he should talk with Harold Vedeler of the Polish, Baltic, and Czechoslovak desk since, Dingell wrote, Vedeler was not the person who had to be convinced of the necessity to "correct the basic policy of the State Department regarding past errors which contributed to the forward thrust by which Poland and other unfortunate countries became satellites in the Communist orbit." He went on to suggest a new direction for American foreign policy that ironically, for a staunch New Deal Democrat, sounded very similar to the upcoming Republican campaign rhetoric of rollback and liberation.[147] He contended that in light of Soviet breaches of faith regarding the Yalta Accord, the United States and other contractual parties should abrogate the agreement. He wanted a thorough reappraisal of the whole of U.S.–Soviet relations and favored a "new and determined attitude" toward the Soviet Union embodying "an all out diplomatic and economic offensive in containing and then restraining Communism with the final objective of driving it out and defeating it wherever it has been established as in the case of Poland against the will of the people." This would be easier, he wrote, than it appeared to "people in the State Department who assumed a defeatist attitude." Some of the tactics that the United States should use, according to Dingell, were "back firing, smuggling, bribery, gun running," and reestablishing the Polish underground. He claimed that he could provide names of people who would be willing to help destroy communism in Poland and the satellite countries but refused to "make such suggestions to anyone except on the highest policy making level."[148]

Acting Assistant Secretary Ben H. Brown replied to Dingell's letter in McFall's absence and expressed great interest in hearing the congressman's suggestions about helping the captive peoples in the Soviet satellites. He informed Dingell that a member of the Policy Planning Staff would call on him soon.[149] Unfortunately, no follow-up notes were attached to this correspondence. It nevertheless shows the unusual political alignments developing after the war as even a strong supporter of President Truman's domestic policies like John Dingell expressed dissatisfaction with the trend in U.S. relations with East Central Europe.[150]

Polish American organizations also expressed concern about McCloy's statement and the general trend of U.S. policy in Central Europe. In November, Acting Assistant Secretary Brown responded to a letter from Senator Henry Cabot Lodge (R-MA) containing the text of resolutions adopted by the Massachusetts Federation of Polish Women's Clubs which expressed unease about U.S. relations with Germany and Poland. Brown explained that in McCloy's 17 August 1951 statement to the East German youth group, the high commissioner had expressed sympathy for the German expellees but had made it clear that the United States had no plans for military action to recover the territories for Germany. Brown quoted a subsequent statement by McCloy to a group of Polish war refugees in Paris where he had said, "'My chief concern was to make it clear that whatever the merits or the demerits of that line, the United States would not support any military adventures that might seek to change it.'" He went on to express sympathy for the destruction of Poland by Germany and again promoted Western European integration as the best way to "deter encroachments [on Poland] from any quarter."[151]

Brown also explained that the U.S. position on the German–Polish border continued to hold to Secretary Marshall's statement that the border would be settled at a peace conference and would take into account the needs of the Polish, German, and European peoples as a whole. Brown explained that Poland's eastern border with the Soviet Union had been established by bilateral agreement in 1945. "It is the Department's view," Brown wrote, "that the chief issue in Eastern Europe at this time is not the actual line of the Soviet frontier, but rather Soviet domination of entire countries, regardless of the location of the Soviet frontier with those countries."[152] Brown elaborated on the difficulties surrounding the border issues when he stated that the "promise of revision . . . carries with it a strong implication of willingness to use force to bring these revisions about" and offered his belief that Senator Lodge would agree that the United States could not make such commitments about any frontiers in Europe or anywhere.[153]

Brown also responded to part of a Polish Women's Club resolution dealing with U.S. policy toward West Germany. He explained that the United States was increasing the strength of its armed forces in the Federal Republic as part of the NATO commitment to defend Western Europe against "Soviet imperialism," especially after the communist attack on South Korea. Brown elaborated on the department's fear that Germany "might easily become a second Korea, with potentially disastrous results for Europe and for the entire Western World." He assured Lodge, though, that the Brussels agreement, which had approved West German participation in the defense of Western Europe, had "limitations and safeguards" to assure against a revival of "aggressive German militarism."[154]

This correspondence with members of Congress showed again that although U.S. policy toward the Oder–Neisse Line had not officially changed from the position expressed in the Potsdam Accord about the provisional nature of the border, in actual practice the Eastern European Division of the State Department was unwilling to publicize that position since it might aggravate U.S.–Polish relations with its implication that some of the land might be returned to Germany.

In a discussion with the French and British foreign ministers in November 1951, Secretary Acheson revealed that he too had accepted the idea that the United States should not stress its position on the Oder–Neisse Line. The context for the foreign ministers' discussion was an attempt by Adenauer to force the Western Allies to support publicly West Germany's claim to the Oder–Neisse territories.[155] Acheson explained, "We cannot commit ourselves at this time. This can only be done in the peace treaty." After further discussion, the three foreign ministers agreed simply to repeat the Potsdam provision that final determination of Germany's boundaries awaited a peace settlement.[156]

As a new year approached, State Department attention remained focused on Germany. When West German rearmament and participation in the European Defense Community appeared likely, the Soviets launched a propaganda campaign to try to halt this Western integration by issuing a note on 10 March 1952 calling for a neutral Germany and the withdrawal of occupation troops. Regarding the extent of German territory, the note defined Germany's borders as those established by the Allies at Potsdam.[157] The Western powers called for the establishment of an all-German government through free elections and pointed out that the Potsdam Agreement laid out no "definitive" German frontiers but had provided that territorial questions would be settled at a peace conference.[158] Subsequent Soviet notes continued to hold to the position that Potsdam had settled Germany's borders.[159]

The Soviet notes in 1952 caused consternation within the Federal Republic of Germany.[160] When Acting U.S. High Commissioner George Hays met with Chancellor Adenauer and the French High Commissioner Francois-Poncet, Adenauer's views reflected a softer tone toward the border question than in his earlier public pronouncements, although he emphasized again that no

German government could accept the line as permanent. He said that the Western powers' reply to the Soviet note should not refer specifically to the Oder–Neisse Line and urged that "friction" be avoided until such time as the problem could be solved by the Federal Republic and a "Free Poland."[161]

The U.S. response to the Soviet note on 30 March 1952 led the Downstate New York Division of the Polish American Congress to pass a resolution concerning the exact wording of the Potsdam Accord. This resolution, which Senator Ives (R-NY) read into the *Congressional Record* was, somewhat ironically, brought to the attention of the State Department through Ludwig Oberndorf, managing editor of the *Staats-Herold*, a German American newspaper published in New York.[162] The Polish American Congress resolution expressed concern about the West's "latest interpretation of the Potsdam declaration" by focusing on the semantic differences between the words "delimitation" and "determination."[163] The resolution contended that the Potsdam Accord had set the boundary along the Oder–Neisse Line and that the border had only to be delimited or marked along the existing line. In his letter to Acheson, Oberndorf asked which word was used in the official record of Potsdam.

When Oberndorf's letter was sent to the Eastern European Division, Thomas Dillon forwarded it to John Calhoun of the Office of German Political Affairs with a memorandum pointing out that it was somewhat unique since most of the correspondence regarding Poland's western frontier was sent by "Polish or Polish-American individuals and groups." He told Calhoun that as far as he was aware, there was no special significance in using the word "determination" as opposed to "delimination" [*sic*]. He then went on to explain the general policy of the Eastern European Division when dealing with the border question. Dillon's response showed once again that officers in the division opposed using the border issue as a bargaining tool with the Soviets: "In general EE [the Eastern European Division] has held the view that little can be gained by frequent or detailed pronouncements on the Polish–German border question at this time, and our replies have generally been limited to a reiteration of the statement that the final determination of this border must await the peace settlement with Germany."[164] Dillon's memorandum to Calhoun also hinted at the division of duties within the State Department when he wrote, "Inasmuch as our present correspondent appears to be taking a point of view which is somewhat more German than Polish, you may wish to have a reply prepared in your office." Dillon requested, however, to see the reply before it was mailed to Oberndorf.[165]

The reply to Oberndorf signed by Martin Hillenbrand, officer in charge of the Division of German Government and Administration in the Office of German Political Affairs, reiterated Dillon's point that while the Potsdam Agreement used the term "delimination" [*sic*], Secretaries Byrnes and Marshall used "delimination" [*sic*] interchangeably with "determination." Hillenbrand informed Oberndorf that "no special significance" could be attached to the use of the term "determination" in the 25 March 1952 note to the Soviet Union.[166]

Although the State Department handled Oberndorf's letter with relative ease, a news article allegedly appearing in *Der Schlieser*, a West German newspaper published by Silesian refugees, caught the attention of high-level State Department officials because of its implications for Soviet policy According to reports by the Associated French Press service on 4 and 5 June 1952, *Der Schlieser* carried an interview that Stalin gave to members of the Polish Press Agency, during the course of which he had stated, "'At time of world revolution national frontiers'" are only of secondary importance. "'For the moment,'" Stalin reportedly continued, the USSR "'refuses all discussion'" on the rectification of the Oder–Neisse Line "'in favor of a capitalist Germany.'" In response to a question whether he would favor negotiating with a democratic Germany about the rectification of the Oder–Neisse Line, Stalin reportedly said, "'One can envisage discussing territorial problems only after [the] re-establishment of German unity,'" and the USSR would accept only a neutral German as a negotiating partner.[167] There was some question about the accuracy of the report, however. Ambassador Kennan sent a telegram informing the secretary that on 7 June 1952 the Soviet press agency Tass had printed an article in *Pravda Izvestia* denying that Stalin had made any such remarks about Poland's border.[168] Both the alleged article and the denial received close scrutiny by State Department officers.

In another telegram on 7 June Kennan noted that the Tass denial warranted "closest attention" since the tactic of "announcement by denial" was a "time-honored institution" of the Soviets.[169] He thought that three possible propositions about the Tass report could be accepted. He noted that such denials were never made "without some special and significant purpose," that the message contained in the denial was not aimed at the general population but at well-informed proponents and opponents of the regime, and that the method used when "the thought intended to be conveyed is one for which the Kremlin wishes particularly to evade formal responsibility but with respect to which it wants its views known and seriously taken into account." Kennan told the secretary that the Moscow Embassy had no firm information about the source of the reported interview but speculated that Tass intended three things to be conveyed. Kennan's ideas again show that he believed that the Soviets would probably revise Poland's western border sometime in the future. His first point was that Moscow currently viewed the Oder–Neisse Line as the established Polish–German border. The second was that Stalin was not committing himself on whether the Oder–Neisse would remain the border as evidenced in Moscow's recent notes to the German government in which the Soviets had not formally committed themselves on the permanency of the border despite efforts to create the contrary impression. Finally, Kennan thought the Tass report was meant to warn the satellite states to be careful of "taking the name of Stalin in vain" or of taking Kremlin policies for granted.[170]

Adding to the uncertainty of East–West relations were the rising strength and national "self-assertiveness" of the Federal Republic as noted by the new U.S. high commissioner for Germany, Walter Donnelly, in a 28 August 1952 telegram to the State Department.[171] Donnelly confirmed that while the West Germans felt "deeply frustrated" about the recovery of the eastern territories, that frustration did not mean that their desire for reunification had lessened. He also warned that even though the border issue was not of immediate or critical concern, that did not mean that "it will not plague us in [the] future."[172] He stressed the linkage between the questions of German unification, the Oder–Neisse territories, and the disposition of the Soviet satellite states and asked whether it would not be prudent, in light of U.S. policy favoring German reunification, to have a clear policy toward the satellites. The high commissioner tersely asked: "With peaceful, we hope, rollback of Soviet power do we think of Eur[opean] community, complete with Schuman Plan and EDF (European Defense Force), stopping at Oder–Neisse, at old Polish border or at prewar Soviet frontiers?"[173]

Donnelly's telegram apparently received close scrutiny in the State Department. Leon Fuller of the Policy Planning Staff sent a long memorandum to Paul Nitze, director of the Policy Planning Staff, analyzing the telegram. Fuller wrote that Donnelly's telegram reflected a "growing concern" in the high commissioner's office about the "fact that the Federal Republic is now the strongest power in Europe outside the USSR, and likely to grow stronger year by year with the full implementation of current Allied policies."[174] While, Fuller noted, West Germany provided little evidence of seeking hegemony in Europe, there was a danger that the "dynamic-evolutionary phase of development" in the Federal Republic meant that there was some uncertainty and "incalculability" about "German national behavior," both toward France and the eastern states. "How soon," Fuller speculated, "German aspirations for the return of 'irredentas' in the east may force the satellite issue to the front can not be calculated, but it may be assumed as an eventuality. It will be most immediate in the case of Poland." The growing strength of West Germany, he added, increased Poland's fears of a possible deal that would force it "to disgorge annexed German territory and confront the enhanced power of a restored and enlarged Germany." After reviewing U.S. policy favoring German reunification and "at least partial restoration" of the Oder–Neisse area as "implied" since Marshall's 1947 Moscow Council of Foreign Ministers statement, Fuller warned that while there had as yet been no great urgency to provide detailed policy planning, "the necessity may soon arise to become more explicit in our east European objectives as the restoration of Germany proceeds."[175] Rather than recommend any change in U.S. policy toward the border question, however, Fuller maintained that the United States should not openly commit itself on the border but should insist that the question of Germany's eastern frontier was still open pending a peace conference. The was the point that the United States had been prepared to advance at the 1947

Moscow and London Councils of Foreign Ministers.[176]

POLISH AMERICAN REACTION

While Fuller's proposal to emphasize the tentative nature of the border decision might have strengthened the Washington–Bonn connection, it failed to give weight to the real fears of Polish Americans about potential German aggression against Poland and thus failed to give credence to the potential domestic implications of the Oder–Neisse issue. This potential was reflected in a policy statement read on the floor of the House of Representatives on 11 June 1952 by Thaddeus Machrowicz. The statement accompanied a Polish American Congress resolution and was signed by Democratic Congressmen John D. Dingell (MI), Thomas S. Gordon (IL), Clement J. Zablocki (WI), Thaddeus M. Machrowicz (MI), John C. Kluczynski (IL), John Lesinski, (MI), and Alfred D. Sieminski (NJ). The statement emphasized the importance of maintaining a strong and free United States to oppose communist aggression. Again, ironically foreshadowing Republican campaign rhetoric later in the year, the congressmen stated their support "not only of containment of communism, but also of liberation of all nations now under subjugation and enslavement behind the iron curtain."[177] Regarding Poland's western border, the congressmen stated their opposition to any suggestion of a border revision as an injustice to Poland and as a threat to the peace and stability of Europe and showed their willingness to use the question as a political issue when they declared their intention to insist that these principles be included in the Democratic platform.[178]

The Polish American Congress resolution also presented that organization's opposition to border revision. The authors of the resolution focused their appeal to the U.S Senate to "amend the [contractual] treaty with Western Germany before ratifying it, by a clear stipulation that Germany should not be paid with the ancient Polish soil bordering on the Oder and Niesse [sic] Rivers for expected military participation in the defense plans of Western Europe." The resolution claimed that the matter not only was one of justice but reflected a lesson learned from the Yalta Agreement, "where for the sake of expediency we sacrificed principles and jeopardized the future of the world." The authors pointed to the "tragic irony" of an "enslaved" Poland and a free Germany and Japan.[179]

The Senate nevertheless quickly ratified the contractual agreements with the Federal Republic on 1 July 1952, returning almost total autonomy to the West German government. In Poland the Warsaw Embassy continued to monitor the pronouncements and actions of the Polish government and people; these statements reflected insecurity about German and Soviet intentions.[180] The Democratic Platform in 1952 did not deal specifically with Poland's borders but only "look[ed] forward to the day when the liberty of Poland . . . will be restored."[181] The Republicans condemned the "tragic blunders" of

Tehran, Yalta, and Potsdam and looked "happily forward" to the independence of the peoples of East Central Europe.[182] The Republican victory offered hope to some Polish Americans that the passive policy of containment would be replaced by the active rollback of communism and would result in Poland's freedom. As Eisenhower entered office, however, the State Department continued to receive mixed signals from Germany and the Soviet Union about the Oder–Neisse Line, and persisted in its refusal to initiate a policy formally recognizing the line.

NOTES

1. The *Hamburger Echo*, a Social Democrat Party (SPD) newspaper, opposed the action as a violation of international law. The *Niederdeutsche Zeitung*, an expellee publication, expressed bitter regret that Great Britain and the United States had allowed this action without protesting to Warsaw or invoking UN aid. Airgram A-30, Groth to Secretary of State, 19 January 1949, RG59, 760C.6215/1-1949; Airgram A-51, Groth to Secretary of State, 27 January 1949, RG59, 760C.6215/1-2749; Airgram A-30, Groth to Secretary of State, 19 January 1949, RG59, 760C.6215/1-1949; Airgram A-113, Groth to Secretary of State, 1 March 1949, RG59, 760C.6215/3-149. See also "Department of State Policy Statement," 25 June 1949, in *Foreign Relations of the United States*, 1949 (Washington, DC: U.S. Government Printing Office, 1976), 5: 506. Hereafter cited as FRUS with the year, volume, and page numbers.

2. Telegram 170, Murphy to Secretary of State, 3 February 1949, in.FRUS, 1949, 3: 505–506.

3. Ibid., 507.

4. Ibid., 507n.

5. Telegram 382, Gallman to Secretary of State, 15 March 1949, in FRUS, 1949, 3: 508.

6. Telegram 502, Gallman to Secretary of State, 31 March 1949, in FRUS 1949, 3: 513.

7. Telegram 774, Kohler to Secretary of State, 29 March 1949, in FRUS, 1949, 3: 511–512.

8. Telegram 1246, Acheson to U.S. Embassy London, 8 April 1949, RG59, in FRUS, 1949, 3: 447.

9. *Congressional Record Appendix*, 81st Cong., 1st sess., 95, pt. 13, (5 April 1949): A2010–A2011.

10. "American Poles Protest," *New York Times*, 24 May 1949, 3.

11. U.S. Congress, Senate, Committee on Foreign Relations, *Review of the World Situation, 1949–1950: Hearings Held in Executive Sessions before the Committee on Foreign Relations*, 81st Cong., 1st and 2nd sess., 1974, *On the World Situation*, 9. Hereafter cited as Congress, Senate, *Review of the World.*

12. Ibid., 9.

13. These congressmen would also force an investigation of the Katyn Forest massacre.

14. Letter, Office of Secretary of State to Ives, 8 June 1949, RG59, 860C.014/6-849.

15. Memorandum of Conversation, Mikolajczyk and Salter, 12 May 1949, RG59 760C.6215/5-1249.

16. U.S. Congress, Senate, *Review of the World*, 7.

[17] Ibid., 8.

18. Telegram 116, Gallman to Paris, 20 May 1949, Record Group 43, Records of the International Conferences, Commissions and Expositions, Box 316, in National Archives, Washington, DC. Hereafter cited as RG43 with box number.

19. Ibid.

20. Ibid. Ambassador Gallman contended that his view was affirmed in a 19 May conversation between Fish Armstrong, editor of *Foreign Affairs*, and Jakub Berman, "one of [the] two most, if not [the] most, authoritative spokesman with [the] Polish Communist Party." Berman was one of the organizers of the Polish Workers' Party and had close ties with Moscow. See Anatole C. J. Bogacki, *A Polish Paradox: International and the National Interest in Polish Communist Foreign Policy 1918–1948* (Boulder, CO: East European Monographs, 1991).

21. Ibid.

22. Ibid. *New York Times* correspondent Anne O'Hare McCormick agreed with Gallman's point: "The last thing Russia can afford at this moment is to infuriate one of them [the Soviet satellites] for the sake of Germany." See *New York Times*, 24 May 1949, 3.

23. Telegram 1154, Kohler to Secretary of State, 6 May 1949, in FRUS 1949, 3: 864–867.

24. "U.S. Position at the Council of Foreign Ministers, Annex: A Program for Germany," 9 May 1949, in FRUS 1949, 3: 908–909. An editorial note suggests that the 9 May date is an error since the base text for the annex bears the date of 15 May 1949.

25. "U.S. Position at the Council of Foreign Ministers," 15 May 1949, in FRUS, 1949, 3 :902; "Annex: A Program for Germany," 909.

26. Civil Administration Division, OMGUS, "Population Problems (Refugees, Expellees, DP's [Displaced Persons] and PWs)" CFM Paris 1949, n.d., RG 43, Box 310. The authors acknowledged that while the assimilation of the refugees was a German problem, the occupying powers had an interest in it since they retained the right to determine matters related to the refugees.

27. Civil Administration Division, Office of Military Government for Germany, "Germany's Eastern Boundaries," 15 May 1949, RG43, Box 190.

28. Ibid., 5.

29. Ibid., 2.

30. Ibid., 5.

31. Ibid., 2.

32. Ibid., 1–2.

33. "Tripartite Conversations Preliminary to the 6th Session of the CFM: Report to the Foreign Ministers," 20 May 1949, RG43, Box 310.

34. Memorandum, Murphy to Acheson, 8 June 1949, in FRUS, 1949, 3: 969.

35. "Department of State Policy Statement," 25 June 1949, in FRUS, 1949, 5: 505n.

36. U.S. Congress, House of Representatives, *United States Policy in the Far*

East, Part 2, Committee on International Relations, Selected Executive Session Hearings of the Committee, 1943-1950, 8: 239.

37. Ibid.

38. Hans W. Gatzke, *Germany and the United States: A "Special Relationship"?* (Cambridge: Harvard University Press, 1980), 161.

39. For a more detailed explanation of the U.S. role in the creation of West Germany, see ibid., 174-178; Thomas A. Schwartz, *America's Germany: John J. McCloy and the Federal Republic of Germany* (Cambridge: Harvard University Press, 1991), passim.

40. Gatzke, *Germany and the United States*, 177.

41. Telegram 124, Riddleberger to Secretary of State, 27 August 1949, RG59, 760C.6215/8-2749.

42. Telegram 1325, Riddleberger to Secretary of State, 31 August 1949, RG59, 760C.6215/8-3149.

43. Airgram A-637, Taylor to Secretary of State, 19 October 1949, RG59, 760C.6215/10-1949.

44. Airgram A-1156, Lyon to Secretary of State, 13 September 1949, RG59, 760C.62/9-1349.

45. "Policy Statement of German Federal Government-Bundestag," Germany's Parliament in Action, 20 September 1949, 26.

46. Ibid., 70.

47. "Poland in Note Also Assails West Germany; Warsaw Sees Oder-Neisse Line Undermined," *New York_Times*, 6 October 1949, 11.

48. Piotr Wandycz, *The United States and Poland* (Cambridge: Harvard University Press, 1980), 334–335.

49. Ibid., 337; U.S. Congress, Senate, *Hearing before the Subcommittee on Amendments to the Displaced Persons Act of the Committee on the Judiciary to Amend the Displaced Persons Act of 1948*, 81st Cong., 1st and 2nd sess. (Washington, DC: U.S. Government Printing Office, 1950), 89–109.

50. Letter, Lesinski to Truman, 4 August 1949, RG59, 860C.014/8-449.

51. Letter, Brown to Baldwin, 13 October 1949, RG59, 860C.014/10-1349; Letter Brown to McMahon, 13 October 1949, RG59, 860C.014.1-1349.

52. One of the few agreements reached at Moscow was the official liquidation of the Prussian state, an agreement that only confirmed an already accomplished fact. See Gatzke, *Germany and the United States*, 159.

53. Letter, Walkowicz to Zablocki, 22 September 1949, Zablocki Papers, Box 169, Marquette University, Milwaukee, Wisconsin,

54. Letter, Walkowicz to Truman, 22 September 1949, Papers of Harry S Truman, General File, Box 1922, Harry S. Truman Library, hereafter cited as HST/L.

55. Letter, 24 September 1949, Polish Falcons of America, South Bend, Indiana; Letter, Polish Falcons of America, New Jersey, 25 September 1949; Letter, Polish Falcons of America, Middleton, Connecticut, 3 October 1949; Letter, Polish Falcons of America, Saginaw, Michigan, 5 October 1949; Papers of Harry S Truman, General File, Box 1922, HST/L.

56. "Department of State Policy Statement," 25 June 1949, in FRUS, 1949, 5: 504–505.

57. Ibid.

58. Letter, Lyon to Secretary of State, 19 September 1949, RG59, 711.60C/9-1949.

59. Letter, Feis to Kennan, 24 October 1949, RG59, 760C.6215/10-2449. The memorandum was signed only with initials, possibly those of Ware Adams of the Policy Planning Staff.

60. Ibid.

61. See Schwartz, *America's Germany*, passim; George F. Kennan, *Memoirs: 1925–1950* (Boston: Little, Brown, 1967), 1: 213–215, 258–266; Kennan wrote that the Oder–Neisse would make Poland "perforce a Russian protectorate, whether its own government was Communist or not." See also George Kennan, *Russia and the West under Lenin and Stalin* (Boston: Little, Brown, 1960), 361.

62. Oral History transcript, 19, 21 September 1988, HST/L.

63. The bureau recognized the importance of keeping Congress abreast of the situation, even to the point of creating a congressional liaison. Memorandum, Cheseldine to Byroade, 21 February 1950, RG59, 611.62A/2-2150.

64. Despatch, 1100, Dayton to Department of State, 9 June 1950, RG59, 611.62A/6-950. The poll was submitted in reply to a State Department Airgram of 8 February 1950.

65. Memorandum Prepared in the Bureau of German Affairs, "Germany in the European Context," 11 February 1950, in FRUS, 1950, 4: 598.

66. Ibid., FRUS, 1950, 4: 599.

67. Ibid. The memorandum went on to expand on the urgent need of integration without elaborating further on the Oder–Neisse question.

68. Memorandum, Byroade to Butler, 9 March 1950, in FRUS, 1950, 4: 679. The memorandum also noted a number of strengths in U.S. policy, including the German fear of the Soviet Union and the presence of Allied occupation troops in Germany.

69. Paper, "German Unity and East–West Political Relations within Germany," 13 March 1950, in FRUS, 1950, 4: 610–611.

70. The Bern legation thought less plausible a report from the same source that the Soviets were planning a simultaneous move in the Far East, probably against the South Korean government. Summary of Telegram, 6 April 1950, Naval Aide File, State Department Briefs, Box 22, HST/L.

71. Telegram, 18 May 1950, Naval Aide File, State Department Briefs, Box 22, HST/L.

72. Telegram 2779, Acheson to McCloy, 21 April 1950, in FRUS, 1950, 4: 632.

73. Telegram 3912, McCloy to Acting Secretary of State, 7 May 1950, in FRUS, 1950, 4: 635–637.

74. Despatch 513, Hall to Department of State, 31 March 1950, RG59, 648.62B3/3-3150.

75. Ibid.

76. Telegram 484, Gallman to Secretary, 5 April 1950, RG59, 648.62B3/4-550.

77. The source pointed to the cessation of the publication of the weekly newspaper *Odra*, which focused on the cultural and literary contributions of the

"recovered territories" as one example of the soft-pedaling of the importance of the frontier issue. See Telegram 484, Gallman to Secretary of State, 5 April 1950, RG59, 648.62B3/4-550.

78. Telegram 766, Gallman to Secretary of State, 3 June 1950, RG59, 648.62B/6-350.

79. Ibid.

80. Telegram 1564, Kirk to Secretary of State, 5 June 1950, RG59, 648.62B3/6-550.

81. Ibid.

82. Ibid.

83. Despatch 295, Corrigan to Department of State, 6 June 1950, RG59, 648.62B3/6-650.

84. Memorandum, Salter to Files, 16 May 1950, in RG59, 748.022/5-1650.

85. Beate Ruhm von Oppen, ed., *Documents on Germany under Occupation 1945–1954* (London: Oxford University Press, 1955), 497–498.

86. Telegram 4891, McCloy to Secretary of State, 7 June 1950, RG59, 648.62B3/6-750. See also FRUS, 1950, 4: 959.

87. See "Press Release," *Department of State Bulletin,* 22 (19 June 1950):1018; see also Memo, Byroade to Webb, in FRUS, 1950, 4: 953.

88. Ibid.

89. The word is generally translated as "demarcation." See Keesing's Research Report, *Germany and Eastern Europe since 1945: From the Potsdam Agreement to Chancellor Brandt's 'Ostpolitik'* (New York: Scribners, 1973), 59.

90. Telegram 782, Gallman to Secretary of State, 7 June 1950, RG59, 748.022/6-750.

91. Telegram 1608, Kirk to Secretary of State, 9 June 1950, RG59, 648.62B3/6-950.

92. Memorandum, Tims to Hadsel, 12 June 1950, RG59, 648.62B3/6-1250.

93. Memorandum, Tims to Cox, 15 June 1950, RG59, 648.6131/6-1550.

94. Ibid.

95. Ruhm von Oppen, *Documents on Germany*, 498–499.

96. Telegram 34, Lyon to Secretary of State, 10 July 1950, RG59, 648.62B31/7-1050.

97. Despatch 506, Shute to Department of State, 17 August 1950, RG59, 762C.00/8-1750.

98. Despatch 506, Shute to Department of State, 17 August 1950, RG59, 762C.00/8-1750.

99. Ibid.

100. Ibid.

101. Ibid.

102. Telegram 2144, Hays to Secretary of State, 11 September 1950, in FRUS 1950, 4: 969.

103. Telegram 2052, Webb to HICOG-Frankfurt, 14 September 1950, RG59, 648.62B3/9-1150.

104. Telegram 2144, Hays to Secretary of State.

105. Despatch 267, LeBreton to Department of State, 11 October 1950, RG59,

648.62B31/10-1150.

106. "A German-Polish Pact," *Christian Science Monitor*, 8 June 1950, 1.

107. "German-Polish 'Agreement,'" *New York Times*, 8 June 1950, 30.

108. "Oder-Niesse [*sic*] Boundary," *Polish American Journal*, 8 July 1950, 2.

109. Telegram, Armstrong to Acheson, 8 June 1950, RG59, 648.62B3/6-850.

110. Memorandum, Perkins to Secretary, 19 June 1950, RG59, 648.62B3/6-1950.

111. Draft letter, Acheson to "Ham," 22 June 1950, RG59, 648.62B3/6-850.

112. Letter, Armstrong to "Dean," 15 August 1950, RG59, 648.62B3/8-1550.

113. The internal memorandum contained the initials "B.E." See memo, Perkins to Secretary of State, 20 September 1950, RG59, FW648.62B3/8-1550.

114. Ibid. The reply letter has the words "not sent" handwritten in the margins. An internal memorandum by Marshall Shulman attached to the draft letter suggested that a memorandum rather than a letter should be returned since it "would be less of a limitation if future circumstances should ever be such that we would want to make an issue of that part of the Polish border question."

115. Letter, Rozmarek to Acheson, 19 June 1950, RG59, 648.62B3/6-1950.

116. Letter, Yost to Rozmarek, 28 June 1950, RG59, 648.62B3/6-1950. The 8 June 1950 State Department release quoted from the Potsdam Accord, Byrnes' Stuttgart speech, and Marshall's statement at the Moscow meeting of the foreign ministers. See Department of State Bulletin, 19 June 1950, 22, no. 572, 1017.

117. Letter, Hays to Department of State, 7 October 1950, RG59, 611.48/10-750; Letter, McFall to Hays, 17 October 1950, RG59, 611.48/10-750.

118. Policy Statement, in FRUS, 1950, 4: 1040–1051.

119. Ibid.

120. Office Memorandum, Calhoun to Vedeler, 19 January 1951, RG59, 611.48/1-1951.

121. Despatch 539, Flack to Department of State, 19 March 1951, in FRUS, 1951, 4: 1492–1500.

122. Airgram A-1615, Webb to London Embassy, 10 March 1951, in FRUS, 1951, 4: 1490–1492.

123. Telegram 4539, McCloy to Secretary of State, 30 November 1950, RG59, 648.62B3/11-3050.

124. Ibid.

125. Telegram 4023, Acheson to HICOG, Frankfort, 4 December 1950, RG59, 648.62B3/12-450. On 12 February 1951 Acheson telegraphed McCloy permission to use his discretion in assuring U.S. diplomatic posts in Germany that the Anders' rumor was entirely false and permitting them to deny it when necessary. See Telegram 5532, Acheson to HICOG Frankfort, 12 February 1951, RG59, 648.62B3/2-1251.

126. See Office Memorandum, Laukhuff to Jessup, 26 December 1950, RG59, 396.1/12-2650; Office Memorandum, Kellermann to Laukhuff, 28 December 1950, RG59, 396.1/12-2850; Airgram A-2133, Acheson to HICOG Frankfort, 12 January 1951, RG59, 611.62A/1-551. Kurt Schumacher, head of the SPD, fully supported Adenauer's stand that Germany still had claim to its 1937 borders and firmly believed

that the United States would not "'sell out' Germans by accepting [the] present Eastern frontier." See Telegram, unnumbered, McCloy to Secretary of State, 16 February 1951, RG59, 396.1/2-1651; Telegram, unnumbered, McCloy to Secretary of State, 19 February 1951, RG59, 396.1/2-1451.

127. Memorandum, Watts to Jessup, Bohlen, Perkins et al., 11 January 1951, RG59, 396.1/1-1151TSF.

128. Ibid.

129. Ibid.

130. Policy Review, Byroade, 29 January 1951, RG59, 396.1/1-2751.

131. Memo, Kellermann to GER and GPA, 11 January 1951, RG59, 762.5/1-1151. Kellerman reported on a conference held at Princeton University on 10 November 1950, where this fear was repeatedly aired. Also, in a Senate Foreign Relations Committee hearing on 17 June 1952 Senator Gillette asked McCloy about a report that Adenauer had confirmed such an aim in a public speech. Airgram A-1382, 17 June 1952, Confidential U.S. State Department Central Files, Foreign Affairs, 1950-1954, Reel 2.

132. "Adenauer Demands Return of Oder–Neisse Territory," *New York Times*, 7 October 1951, 1.

133. Telegram 3016, McCloy to Secretary of State, 8 October 1951, RG59, 648.62A3/10-851.

134. Telegram 679, Flack to Secretary of State, 14 February 1951, RG59, 748.5/2-1451; Flack also reported a speech by a Polish general against American efforts to unleash "'Hitlerite bandits'" against the western frontier. See Telegram 705, Flack to Secretary of State, 24 February 1951, RG59, 748.5/2-2451.

135. Despatch 655, Bowie to Department of State, 1 June 1951, RG59, 748.13/6-151.

136. Telegram, unnumbered, McCloy to Secretary of State, 4 June 1951, RG59, 762C.00/5-3151.

137. The memorandum was sent by Leo Krzycki, Jadwiga Cegielkowska, and Stanley Nowak. See Letter, Nowak to Acheson, 14 February 1951, RG59, 611.48/2-1451.

138. Memorandum of Conversation, Korbonski, Vedeler, and Dillon, 18 May 1951, RG59, 648.62B3/5-1851.

139. Zbiegniew Stypulkowski's book *Invitation to Moscow* (London: Thames and Hudson, 1951) tells of his experiences with the Germans during the war and his imprisonment in the Soviet Union.

140. Memorandum of Conversation, Korbonski, Vedeler, and Dillon, 18 May 1951.

141. Ibid.

142. Ibid.

143. Ibid.

144. Memorandum of Conversation, Burke, Dillon, and Johnson, 28 August 1951, RG59, 748.022/8-2851.

145. Ibid.

146. Memorandum of Conversation, Machrowicz and Dillon, 18 October 1951, RG59, 611.48/10-1851.

147. Gerald Banister, "The Longest-Tenured Polish-American Congressman," *Polish American Studies* 21, 1, January–June 1964, 38–40.

148. Letter, Dingell to McFall, 13 July 1951, RG59, 611.48/7-1351.

149. Letter, Brown to Dingell, 20 July 1951, RG59, 611.48/7-1351.

150. Dingell was labeled the "dean of Congressmen of Polish descent" by the *Polish American Journal.* See "Rep. Dingell Assails Pol-Am Red Leaders," *Polish American Journal*, 18 June 1955, 3; "Dingell Wants Germany, Russia to Rebuild Poland," *Polish American Journal*, 23 July 1955, 4.

151. Letter, Brown to Lodge, 19 November 1951, RG59, 648.623/11-851.

152. Ibid.

153. Ibid.

154. Ibid.

155. McCloy explained to the foreign ministers that Adenauer had given him a draft proposal urging the inclusion of a phrase that referred to the settlement of Germany's borders "'in the spirit of the Atlantic Charter.'" See Minutes of the Tripartite Foreign Ministers Meeting at the Quai d'Orsay, November 21, 1951, in FRUS, 1951, 3, pt. 2: 1598. For a more complete explanation of this attempt see HICOM/P(51) 91, 17 November 1951, in FRUS, 1951, 3, pt. 2: 1585–1586.

156. "Minutes of the Tripartite Foreign Ministers Meeting," FRUS, 1951, 3, pt. 2: 1601.

157. U.S. Congress, Senate, *Documents on Germany, 1944–1970*, 193.

158. Ibid., 194; Wolfram F. Hanrieder, *West German Foreign Policy 1949–1963: International Pressure and Domestic Response* (Stanford, CA: Stanford University Press, 1967), 70.

159. FRUS, 1952–1954, 7, pt. 1, 169–327.

160. Adenauer's critics charged that his rejection of the Soviet proposals indicated a "careless or even cynical failure to explore a last opportunity for unification." See Hanrieder, *West German Foreign Policy,* 71.

161. Telegram 2012, Hays to Department of State, 17 March 1952, in FRUS, 1952–1954, 7, pt. 1: 355–356.

162. *Congressional Record*, 82nd Cong., 98, 2nd sess., pt. 3, (16 April 1950): 4005; Memo, Dillon to Calhoun, 13 June 1952, RG59. FW648.62B3/6-652.

163. The PAC resolution stated in part:

It would seem, therefore, that whereas the Potsdam Conference of 1945 left to the future peace treaty the final delimitation of the Polish-German frontier, the western allies' notes to Soviet Russia of 1952 leave to the said peace treaty the final determination of territorial questions. Inasmuch as no Polish occupational zone of Germany was established either by the preliminary Yalta agreement . . or by . . . Potsdam . . . and as the latter decreed the transfer of the German population from the territory east of the Oder–Neisse line—it is obvious that the Potsdam Conference definitely ceded to Poland all the land from which the German population was transferred with the western allies' approval and supervision. It, therefore, seems both logical and obvious that . . . no final determination of territorial questions was left to the peace settlement.

164. Ibid. When Dillon sent Oberndorf's letter to Calhoun, he somewhat

comically suggested that it might best be classified as "Dust Bites Redskin or more accurately, perhaps, Deutsch Bites Redskin." Dillon noted that a "somewhat fuller reply" was available as needed, but the attachment he noted outlining this reply was not included with the documents.

165. Ibid.

166. Letter, Hillenbrand to Oberndorf, 20 June 1952, in Memo, Dillon to Calhoun, 13 June 1952, RG59, FW648.62B3/6-652. The managing editor was not content, however, to accept this explanation. In a brief letter to Hillenbrand of 3 July 1952 Oberndorf thanked Hillenbrand for his answer but pointed out that both he and Hillenbrand had used the word "delimination," a word not found in any dictionary, whereas "delimitation" should have been used. He asked Hillenbrand which of the two terms was used in the Potsdam Declaration. Hillenbrand politely, but briefly, informed Oberndorf that "delimination" had been used inadvertently; the term "delimitation" should have been used. See Letters, RG59, 648.62B3/7-352.

167. Telegram 7666, Dunn to Secretary of State, 9 June 1952, RG59, 648.623/6-952; Telegram 1960, Kennan to Secretary of State, 7 June 1952, RG59, 648.623/6-752.

168. Telegram 1960, Kennan to Secretary of State, 7 June 1952, RG59, 648.623/6-752. The *New York_Times* carried reports of the French Press Agency report and the Tass denial. See "Poles Quote Stalin on Oder–Neisse Line," *New York Times*, 5 June 1952, 4; "Oder-Neisse Story Denied," 19 June 1952, 4.

169. Telegram 1964, Kennan to Secretary of State, 7 June 1949, RG59, 648.623/6-752.

170. Telegram 887, Donnelly to Department of State, 28 August 1952, in FRUS, 1952–1954, 7, pt. 1: 355-356.

171. Ibid.

172. Ibid.

173. Memorandum, Fuller to Nitze, 4 September 1952, in FRUS, 1952–1954, 7, pt. 1: 357.

174. Ibid., 357–358.

175. Ibid., 360.

176. Thaddeus Machrowicz, "Our Foreign Policy," Extension of Remarks, *Congressional Record_Appendix,* 82nd Cong., 2nd sess., 98, pt. 10 (11 June 1952): A3607–A3608.

177. Ibid.

178. Ibid.

179. Despatch 175, Steere to Department of State, 3 November 1952, RG59, 648.62/11-1452. Steere analyzed speeches given by two Polish representatives at the International Conference for Peaceful Settlement of the German Issue in Berlin as reported in the Polish Press Agency's Information Bulletins as "serving immediate Polish ends" while also aiding Soviet objectives in Germany: preventing close cooperation between Germany and the West, and "of an essentially European solution of the German problem."

180. Donald B. Johnson, comp., *National Party Platforms*, 1 (Urbana: University of Illinois Press, 1978, rev. from 1956), 476.

181. Ibid.

182. Ibid.

5 Eisenhower's First Term

Relations between the United States and Poland remained tense as the Eisenhower administration entered the White House. In early 1953 Warsaw charged that the United States violated Polish air space, and the Polish Foreign Ministry published a book containing fifty-six documents alleging that the United States conducted a foreign policy hostile to Poland's sovereignty.[1] Washington accused the Polish government of harassing American diplomats in Poland.[2] This tension between Washington and Warsaw contrasted greatly with the warm rapport of Washington and Bonn, aided by the personal and professional friendship of Eisenhower's secretary of state, John Foster Dulles, and Konrad Adenauer. In the midst of this precarious trilateral relationship lay the Oder–Neisse border issue. Washington maintained that the border would be set at an eventual peace conference, Bonn publicly supported the expellees' claims to the territory, and Warsaw maintained that the western border had been determined and was unchangeable as a "frontier of peace." Throughout this time, the State Department continued to hear rumors about possible changes in the border. These rumors, combined with the increasingly vocal demands of Polish Americans for U.S. recognition of the border, kept the Oder–Neisse Line issue in the forefront of State Department concerns during Eisenhower's first term.

DIPLOMATIC TREATMENT OF THE ODER–NEISSE ISSUE

Some American officials continued to express an awareness of the need to treat the border issue with finesse. In an exclusive press interview given in late January 1953, outgoing President Truman had proudly stated that as president he had never recognized "'Poland's grab of German territory.'" The interview had been reported in Germany by American-licensed newspapers, and in February 1953 a secret memorandum from Lewis Galantiere, an adviser to Radio Free Europe, revealed the potential volatility of this kind of statement during such tense Cold War times. Galantiere bluntly stated: "Our interest in this statement is direct and manifold. When a President of the United States speaks against the Oder–Neisse Line he plays Moscow's game and is guilty of crass counter-propaganda."[3] He charged that President Truman's statement had reinforced the Polish government's sole propaganda theme that the United States was pro-German (or pro-Nazi) and anti-Polish. This position, Galantiere argued, forced the Polish people to support the Warsaw regime and thereby strengthened Moscow, which directly contradicted the stated goals of Radio Free Europe and Voice of America to discourage popular cooperation with satellite regimes. Galantiere closed by warning that such statements, combined with "the indiscretions of the politically infantile [Ambassador] Stanton Griffis . . . could come close to putting us out of business in Poland."[4] Some members of Congress went farther than Galantiere and openly expressed support for the Oder–Neisse Line.

Polish American congressmen who had formed an informal caucus during the Truman administration as well as other members of Congress concerned about the border issue for personal or professional reasons often corresponded and met with Polish American and Polish exile groups. Much of this correspondence was read on the floor of the House or Senate to show support for causes of the Polish American community. One Polish American congressman, Clement Zablocki (D-WI), read a letter that he had received from the secretary of the Polish National Democratic Committee in March 1953 stating that the committee, "jointly with the whole Polish nation," considered the Oder–Neisse Line fixed at Potsdam and awaited only final confirmation in a peace treaty.[5]

The same month Thomas Gordon (D-IL) read into the *Congressional Record* an article from the *Polish American Journal*, a monthly English-language newspaper considered to reflect the general opinion of the Polish American community.[6] In the article an international affairs commentator claimed that Polish communists successfully used the border issue to gain the support of the Polish people. They were aided in this, he contended, by the fact that the West had not taken a positive stand on the issue.[7]

Senator William Langer (R-ND) presented to the Senate the views of the National Committee of Americans of Polish Descent (KNAPP), an extremely anti-Soviet Polish American group formed during the war. Langer read the resolutions adopted at KNAPP's 24 October 1953 meeting, boldly claiming the group's dissatisfaction with Eisenhower's lack of action in liberating the Soviet satellites and opposing the rearmament of Germany as a danger to Eastern Europe. This group also opposed any suggestions that even part of Poland's western territories might be returned to Germany.[8]

The American Embassy in Warsaw reported an incident that occurred between the Italian ambassador in Poland and the acting Polish minister for foreign affairs in May 1953 that further affirms the sensitive nature of the diplomacy surrounding the Oder–Neisse issue. Acting Foreign Minister Stefan

Wierblowski had reportedly told the Italian ambassador of his uneasiness with a statement made by Italy's foreign minister concerning the provisional nature of Poland's western border. The Italian ambassador supported his foreign minister's statement by pointing out to Wierblowski that the Potsdam Agreement had temporarily placed the area under "'Polish administration.'" Otherwise, he argued, the Potsdam Declaration would have used a term like "Polish sovereignty" to indicate that the land transfer was permanent. Wierblowski did not protest further. In his report to the State Department, U.S. Ambassador Joseph Flack suggested that Wierblowski might have merely been making a show of "personal bravado" to assert his position after a medical leave of absence, but Flack acknowledged that "Polish sensitiveness" about the Oder–Neisse issue was shared equally by the Polish government and the Polish people.[9] The American ambassador's statement shows that he was aware of the need for sensitivity in handling the controversial border issue.

Even administration members close to the President recognized the explosive nature of the issue. In its 11 December 1953 report, the National Security Council Planning Board reiterated that U.S. policy in the Soviet satellites should promote peaceful separation from Soviet control but warned that anticommunism and nationalism, two elements that served to counter Soviet domination, also divided the satellite nations themselves. The board took special note of the Polish-occupied territories, predicting that the question of control over the area would "become increasingly serious as nationalist sentiment ferments." The Planning Board also recognized that most Poles supported the Polish claim to the Oder–Neisse Line, and acknowledged the effectiveness of communist propaganda that claimed that if the Soviets and communists retreat from Poland because of Western pressure, Germany would enjoy hegemony over Poland.[10]

The impact of the border issue on diplomacy was again evident when Poland and the United States exchanged diplomatic notes in January and March 1953. In these notes the Polish government accused the United States of espionage activity, subversion of the Polish government, and aiding the "revisionist appetites of Western German militarism, directed against the territorial integrity of Poland."[11] The first secretary of the Warsaw Embassy recommended that Washington avoid a point-by-point refutation and respond instead with a "clear, brief, and dignified statement" about U.S. policy toward Poland.[12] When *Trybuna Ludu,* one of the major Warsaw newspapers, published an editorial propagandizing the Polish note, Counselor Loyd Steere of the Warsaw Embassy recommended that Washington issue an official response emphasizing America's support for Polish independence since World War I and outlining the Soviet Union's aggressive activities in Poland after 1939. Steere also suggested that the U.S. note "face up to the Yalta Agreement" by making clear the fact that the loss of Poland's eastern territories was the result of Soviet demands that, because of the wartime situation, Poland's friends could not withstand. Instead, Steere argued, the Western Allies could only soften the blow by compensating Poland for the loss with land in the north and west.[13] The secretary of state, however, did not take up the counselor's recommendation. Dulles wired the embassy that the Polish note was "such shoddy propaganda that the United States should not dignify it by replying to it."[14] Washington thus maintained its silence on the Oder–Neisse Line issue rather than engage in a rhetorical duel with Warsaw.

POLISH ÉMIGRÉ AND POLISH AMERICAN VIEWS

Not surprisingly, Polish émigrés and Polish Americans watched events in Poland closely. As they had since 1945, Polish Americans expressed concern over U.S. ties to West Germany and tried to influence foreign policy to satisfy their demands for improved relations with the Polish people. They maintained as one of their primary goals U.S. recognition of the Oder–Neisse Line. Officials in the Eisenhower administration continued to receive correspondence from Rozmarek and members of the Polish American Congress in which the organization emphasized pride in its American character while recognizing its Polish ethnicity. Polish Americans used Polish Constitution Day on 3 May as an occasion for speeches in Congress and for celebrations in Polish American communities. On 10 May 1953 the Polish Constitution Day Committee of Lowell, Massachusetts, sent Eisenhower a letter demanding action to bring about Poland's freedom. One of these demands included recognition of Poland's prewar eastern boundary and the Oder–Neisse Line in the west.[15] The Eisenhower State Department responded to such letters with the same type of indefinite reply as had the Truman administration. On 11 June Howard Cook, chief of the Division of Public Liaison, sent a reply to the Lowell organization thanking the committee for the letter but omitting any reference to the border issue. He enclosed a copy of Dulles' press release commemorating the 162nd anniversary of the Polish Constitution and affirming the "warm, friendly sympathy" of the United States for the Polish people.[16]

Other groups representing Polish nationals also sent letters and telegrams to the White House, the State Department, and the Congress urging specific actions. The Polish Government-in-Exile and representatives of various other organizations such as Mikołajczyk's National Democratic Committee, the Council of National Unity, and the Assembly of Captive European Nations (ACEN) provided Washington with information about the international Polish community.[17] The ACEN was created in New York in 1954 to promote activities that would help the Soviet satellite nations free themselves.[18]

Although these émigré organizations generally agreed that the United States was overcommitting itself in West Germany and that the United States needed a more active foreign policy in Eastern Europe, they competed among themselves for political and financial support and feuded about whether Poland's western border should be on the Oder–Neisse Line.[19] An internal memorandum from the State Department to the White House noted that largely because of this rivalry, the State Department had avoided replying to such groups above the bureau level since this would lead to jealousy.[20] The impetus for this memorandum was a letter to Eisenhower from Tadeusz Bielecki of the Polish Council of National Unity asking four specific questions about U.S. relations with Poland, including a question about the U.S. stance on the Oder–Neisse issue. A reply was drafted for the signature of Deputy Assistant Secretary in the Bureau of European Affairs Jacob Beam. Beam did not attempt to answer Bielecki's questions but simply sent a copy of Eisenhower's 26 September 1956 statement: "'There can be no permanent solution of the situation in Poland until the Polish people are given an opportunity to elect a Government of their own choosing.'"[21]

In a similar exchange Stefan Korbonski of the Polish Political Council-Working Committee in the U.S.A. (and former member of the Polish Government of National Unity) informed the State Department that Poles were closely following Adenauer's discussions in Washington in April 1953 in the hope of hearing a definite statement on the liberation policy. Korbonski argued that it was a good time for such a statement since the Soviets were battling among themselves for control after Stalin's death. He also warned, however, that if the Polish border question were opened again during U.S.–West German talks, "the ill-effect on the morale of the Poles at home and abroad would be far-reaching"; they would feel that once again Poland was "an object of international bargaining." This, he wrote, would weaken the Polish spirit of resistance that so far had kept the Soviets from totally dominating Poland and would simply feed Soviet propaganda. Harold Vedeler and Willard Allen of the State Department's Division of Eastern European Affairs, who met with the Polish émigrés, did not directly address Korbonski's concerns but simply told them that their views would be brought to the attention of the appropriate State Department officers.[22]

Although these replies to Polish exiles used typical noncommittal language similar to language in those sent to Rozmarek and the Polish American Congress, the fact that Rozmarek received replies from the acting secretary of state (and sometimes the secretary or president) rather than bureau chiefs suggests that the State Department considered the Polish American Congress more politically important than the émigré groups. The treatment accorded these groups' comments regarding international conferences reinforces this possibility. When Stefan Korbonski and Adam Niebieszczanski of the Polish Political Council requested a meeting with Eisenhower's assistant, Sherman Adams, to deliver a memorandum prior to the president's meeting with Adenauer, some protocol questions were debated. Internal memoranda dealing with the request reveal the conflict between foreign policy and domestic considerations in the Eisenhower White House. John Simmons, chief of protocol, responded to Adams' request for recommendations regarding

Korbonski's visit by stating that "from a foreign policy standpoint," the request should be denied. He noted that the council was one of three major Polish émigré groups; to receive representatives from one would open up a "heavy and burdensome" schedule of receiving representatives of other exile groups. He added that since the Department of State was coordinating the president's meeting, someone from the State Department should officially receive Korbonski and Niebieszczanski.[23]

Simmons' suggestion made an impact; on 9 July 1953, the acting chief of protocol at the Department of State informed Adams that the Polish Political Council representatives had been received by the director of the Office of Eastern European Affairs on 1 July and had delivered a letter from the Polish Political Council in London to Eisenhower. The émigré group had called for the creation of a "strong barrier" in Central Europe to check Soviet and German moves. Such a barrier, the council argued, should comprise a Polish border on the Oder–Neisse, a free Poland, and a unified Germany. The State Department representative informed the council members that U.S. policy on the liberation of Eastern Europe was firm.[24] No discussion of the German issue was noted. In avoiding this opportunity to explain its Central European policies to Polish émigré groups, the State Department was serving the political needs of the administration while doing little to try to ease suspicions about the increasingly friendly relations between Washington and Bonn.

Charles Rozmarek of the Polish American Congress expressed his concerns about possible concessions to West Germany at the Bermuda Conference. In a 27 November 1953 letter to Eisenhower and Dulles, Rozmarek wrote that he had read in the press that the leaders would discuss Germany's western border; he believed it probable that the question of the eastern border would also arise since German propaganda continued to tie together the two border questions. Without calling for specific action, he requested Eisenhower to treat the border matter justly since it was of great concern to Polish Americans and because of the injustices done to Poland by Roosevelt at Yalta. He reminded the president that the western territories had historically belonged to Poland and, by slightly exaggerating the truth, justified this claim by noting that the Polish names of cities, rivers, and mountains had survived despite attempts to Germanize the area.[25] Although the bulk of the letter dealt with Roosevelt's activities at Yalta regarding Poland's eastern border, Rozmarek emphasized the demands of the Polish American Congress for Poland's independence and territorial integrity.

When the White House referred the letter to the State Department, officials there advised that a reply be sent after the Bermuda Conference ended. This advice was followed and on 10 December 1953, Deputy Assistant Secretary for European Affairs James Bonbright sent Rozmarek a typical reply informing him that U.S. policy was directed toward the "creation of conditions under which Poland . . . can reestablish . . . independence." He then quoted a statement from the postconference communiqué regarding the Western governments' unwillingness to accept as permanent the present division of Europe and their hope that freedom could be found through peaceful means.[26]

If the thought of a meeting of the three Western powers to discuss Germany worried Rozmarek, the idea of another foreign ministers meeting among the "Big Four" in Berlin in January 1954 made him apoplectic since he believed that the West always came away from these conferences with less than the Soviets. In a letter much less guarded than his communication of the previous month, Rozmarek noted: "It is now a matter of historical record that diplomatic meetings conducted behind closed doors by three or four big powers, one of whom represents a ruthless, godless, totalitarian dictatorship dedicated to the suppression of human freedom and national independence, unavoidably end in victory for the dictator and defeat for the outwitted representatives of free nations."[27] He expressed the fear that in an attempt to "buy peace at any price," concessions would be made to the Soviets such as confirming the territorial acquisitions that they had made since World War II. Again without advising a specific course of action regarding Poland's western border, Rozmarek urged Dulles to demand the restoration of Poland's territorial integrity. He also requested a public statement about the policy of liberation as proclaimed during the presidential election campaign.[28]

The reply prepared by the State Department was typically diplomatic, quoting previous statements about U.S. policy opposing the captivity of peoples in East Central Europe. One statement in the letter was unusual, however, in that Rozmarek was informed that his letter had not only been "studied very carefully in the Department of State," but had also been taken to Berlin by the American delegation. A further indication that Rozmarek's views were held in some esteem by the State Department was the fact that Acting Secretary of State Walter B. Smith, rather than a division head, signed the responding letter.[29] The special treatment accorded Rozmarek could, of course, have been only a political move since Rozmarek was one of the most prominent Polish Americans supporting Republican candidates whereas the political allegiance of Polish exiles—if they were enfranchised Americans—was unknown. This situation might also demonstrate that the Dulles State Department distrusted Soviet intentions and promises as much as did the Polish American Congress. In any case, the West made no concessions at the Berlin Conference; like most of the previous foreign ministers meetings, this one came to nothing.

THE DEVELOPMENT OF POLAND'S WESTERN TERRITORIES

Ironic alignments resulted from the Oder–Neisse issue when Polish Americans and Polish émigrés echoed arguments made by Polish government representatives in Warsaw who continued to reiterate Poland's claim to the "Recovered Territories." One important justification given by Warsaw was that following the end of the war the area had been settled by Poles and was fully incorporated into the Polish economy. The government repeatedly claimed that the western territories were almost completely rehabilitated. In the spring of 1953 officers in the American Embassy in Warsaw investigated these claims. Loyd Steere conducted a 1,800-mile automobile tour of the western territories through Upper and Lower Silesia, Pomerania, Szczecin, Gdansk, East Prussia, and Braniewo to observe their development. He wired his impressions of the trip, concluding that Warsaw exaggerated its claims of almost complete recovery in the area.

Steere drew four conclusions from his investigation. The first was that while the Poles had been induced to settle the whole area, there was still a great deal of underpopulation in the western territories, except for the Silesian coal and industrial areas. Second, the Poles were not making a definite effort to reconstruct or replace the war damage of the area. Neither the government nor private individuals were investing sufficiently to aid the recovery of the area except in some key industrial and military installations. Third, a number of "ghost towns" existed where the main buildings were thoroughly destroyed and the few inhabitants in the smaller buildings made only minor repairs to their houses. This suggested to Steere that the residents intended to remain only a short time since few major renovation projects were undertaken. Finally, he noted that the countryside looked better than the towns with a "large share" of the arable land being cultivated. The lack of manpower, however, was evident in the types of farming methods and choice of crops, with labor-intensive crops such as potatoes and sugar beets being avoided in favor of grains. Farms with arable land were lying fallow and pasturelands proliferated. State farms were generally in better shape than individually owned farms, but even they were behind in production.

Steere speculated that the Polish occupation of the western territories was in a "holding operation," which suggested that the peasants farming the land did not believe that the move into the area was permanent. He noted that the Polish government's efforts to induce peasants to settle the western territories were not entirely successful, as many peasants seemed to be squatters rather than farmers. He concluded by informing the department that he had discussed the situation with "all the more senior members of the Diplomatic Corps with considerable experience in Poland," and they had agreed with him that the majority of Poles did not regard the western territories as permanent Polish acquisitions. Instead, Poles believed that the western border pushed too far into Germany and that an independent, unified Germany could not accept such a border. Steere did not speculate on the effect that U.S. relations with West Germany might have on the situation but noted that the Polish government's diatribes against the allegedly revisionist Adenauer government had paradoxically contributed to the Polish outlook that a negotiated settlement with West Germany would result in a new western Polish border.[30]

Evidently, some members of the Polish government began to take seriously the lack of progress in the western territories. The American Embassy noted a few occasions where Polish officials de-emphasized propagandistic claims and offered a realistic assessment of the situation. In March the Polish government announced the resettlement campaign for 1953. The embassy reported to Washington that the new campaign was on a much smaller scale than the 1952 campaign and focused on state farms. This, the embassy officer concluded, reflected Warsaw's realistic reassessment of the number of homesteads that could be prepared and the number of peasants who could be "'induced'" to settle in the western territories.[31]

In May 1953 the Polish minister of agriculture admitted in an article published by the Polish press that the results of the resettlement campaign had thus far been unsatisfactory. The second secretary of the Warsaw Embassy reported that in this article the agriculture minister had blamed the failure on the lack of concern of local authorities and on "'kulaks'" who wanted to retain a cheap labor supply for their own farms. The article noted that many peasants in the overpopulated historic provinces had never heard of the resettlement campaign, and the article emphasized the advantages that the new settlers could enjoy such as free transportation to the west, short-term tax exemption, and various governmental subsidies. The embassy officer who reported this article to Washington expressed his doubt that such incentives would overcome the apathy of the tradition-bound peasant who also questioned the security of the western territories.[32]

Such seemed to be the case as recovery of the western territories remained slow throughout the 1950s. When the Polish government's decrees making neglect or abandonment of the land severely punishable failed to coerce the peasants into higher productivity, Warsaw shifted to a program fostering "young 'pioneers'" to settle the western territories. While this program met with some success, the final results were evidently limited.[33] In July 1954 the first secretary of the British Embassy in Warsaw reported to his American colleagues that on his trip through the western and northern territories he saw few improvements in the war-damaged towns and villages.[34] Charles Wasserman, a Canadian journalist, echoed Steere's 1953 assessment after his 4,000-mile trip through Poland's west in 1957. He noted that little progress had been made in restoring the area in spite of Polish government statements to the contrary.[35] Finally, Walter Drzewieniecki, a Polish American scholar who actively supported Poland's claim to the western territories, acknowledged in his 1959 publication, *The German–Polish Frontier*, that although some progress was made after the 1956 reforms were implemented, "rehabilitation of the Western Territories is not yet complete." He claimed that this lack of progress was partly a result of the uncertainty about the border.[36]

The insecurity that these officials, journalists, and scholars noted was increased in part by some of the statements and actions of various American representatives regarding the Federal Republic of Germany. As Washington grew closer to Bonn and began to call for the remilitarization of West Germany,

Polish fears of German revisionism increased. While the new U.S. high commissioner for Germany, James Conant, did not share the same warm friendship with Adenauer as had John McCloy, diplomatic channels between Washington and Bonn remained open and friendly. The Eisenhower administration invited Adenauer to Washington for a twelve-day visit in April 1953. The issue of the Oder–Neisse Line was not among the topics that Adenauer wished to cover.[37] While the Polish–German border question made a good political issue in West Germany as candidates campaigned to appeal to the expellee vote, it was not an official issue of debate between the United States and the Federal Republic. American officials remained suspicious of the expellees' activities in trying to force Bonn to act on the border.[38] At least officially, Bonn and Washington held the same position on the matter—that the Potsdam decision provided for Polish administration of the area until a peace treaty was signed. With that basic agreement, the two sides focused on other foreign policy questions.

Eisenhower told Adenauer's aide, Herbert Blankenhorn, that U.S. policy toward Germany was based on West Germany's integration into Western Europe and on the "ultimate unification of Germany."[39] Adenauer agreed with this assessment. The chancellor's main goal was the return of full sovereignty to the Federal Republic; he thought that the best way to achieve this was through integration with the West through participation in the European Defense Community (EDC).[40] When the French National Assembly voted against ratification of the EDC, Britain's Anthony Eden proposed that West Germany contribute to the defense of Western Europe by participation in NATO. In an attempt to calm fears that Bonn intended to use its integrated military force for specific West German aims, Adenauer agreed to renounce the use of force to obtain territorial changes or reunification.[41] After much debate and discussion, the treaties approving Bonn's participation in NATO were ratified in May 1955. Western occupation of Germany ended; the U.S. high commissioner became the ambassador to Bonn. Shortly thereafter, the Soviet Union recognized the government of its East German satellite and created the Warsaw Pact to counter the perceived threat of NATO.

These positions regarding Germany's future were maintained relatively unchanged by East and West during the major foreign policy conferences of Eisenhower's first term: at Bermuda in December 1953, the Council of Foreign Ministers in Berlin in January and February 1954, and the Geneva Summit in July 1955.[42] Although Washington acknowledged the need to maintain public agreement with Bonn, the support U.S. foreign policy administrators gave to Bonn was neither unconditional nor undisputed. The State and Defense Departments disagreed over the length of time to allow for approval of the EDC treaty.[43] In an August 1953 report the National Security Council (NSC) Planning Board stated that it would be unwise to specify the borders of a united Germany in any public proposals. The board admitted that to recognize the Oder–Neisse Line as permanent would antagonize many Germans, especially the refugees. On the other hand, to claim for Germany all the territories then administered by Poland would "seriously prejudice negotiations" with the Soviets and might be interpreted by many Germans as an attempt to delay unification. The U.S. negotiators, the NSC report stated, must be ready to agree to a solution "mutually acceptable to Germany and the States immediately concerned."[44]

In September 1953, members of the State Department met to plan for the foreign ministers' conference in Berlin. When the question of German boundaries came up, Coburn Kidd of the Office of German Political Affairs admitted that little could be done at the conference without German participation. Dulles, however, stated that the U.S. delegates needed a "substantive position on boundaries" for discussion purposes, especially since it was necessary to combat the fear that West Germany would use the EDC to regain the prewar German borders.[45] Kidd claimed that in general the United States maintained the position that "Free Poland" should get part of the industrial region of Upper Silesia and that the Germans should get some of the agricultural lands of Pomerania and Brandenburg since these changes would not entail large population shifts. He added, though, that Adenauer was not hopeful of obtaining a quick solution to the border problem. Dulles replied that he had informed Secretary Marshall at the 1947 Moscow Conference that freedom of movement across borders was more important than where the boundaries were drawn, a position that de-emphasized Polish nationalist sentiments that adamantly supported Polish control and ownership of the "recovered territories."[46] The meeting participants' immediate shift to discussing guarantees of German nonaggression suggests that Secretary Dulles viewed the border issue more as a German than a Polish matter, thereby implying that a border adjustment would be made in Germany's favor, thus negating the need for Germany's use of force. The secretary also showed his willingness to support almost full German sovereignty when he emphasized that the Germans, rather than the three Western governments, were responsible for guaranteeing nonaggression. Dulles' views, of course, differed drastically from those of Rozmarek and the Polish American Congress as well as from the leaders of the Polish émigré organizations who maintained that Allied control of Germany was a matter of vital importance to Poland's national security.

THE WEST GERMAN EXPELLEES

Washington's relationship with Bonn continued to be affected by European events. American HICOG representatives in Bonn and Berlin, out of concern for a consistent public stand on the border issue by the U.S. and West German governments, constantly monitored the activities of expellee organizations whose members claimed the right to return to their former homes. These organizations had been legalized in the American zone in 1947 and by the mid-1950s had united into one of West Germany's most powerful lobbying groups. They represented one-fifth of the Federal Republic's population, had a number of representatives in the Bundestag, and were partially financed by the federal government.[47] The three major political parties in West Germany rejected Poland's claims to the Oder–Neisse territories, and Adenauer, as a politician concerned about elections, was willing to use the border issue to gain votes for the CDU in the 1953 elections.

When President Eisenhower pledged in his State of the Union address in February 1953 that the United States favored a "new, positive foreign policy" and would not recognize commitments made in secret understandings that allow "the enslavement of any people in order to purchase fancied gains for ourselves," many West Germans interpreted the statement to mean that the territorial provisions of the Yalta and Potsdam Accords would not be preserved. Shortly after this address, Chancellor Adenauer intimated at a 6 February 1953 press conference that Eisenhower's State of the Union message had suggested U.S. support for the return of the Oder–Neisse territories. High Commissioner James Conant immediately responded; he quashed any hopes that the Germans might have developed by stating that Eisenhower's statement about secret agreements did not apply to Germany. He reiterated that the border issue would be settled at a peace conference.[48]

Adenauer was not the only German trying to make political gain from Eisenhower's speech. Shortly after the State of the Union message, the chief of the Displaced Populations Division at the High Commissioner's Office in Bonn, Guy Swope, reported that the information service of the expellee organization, *Göttinger Arbeitskreis*, had issued an article from its Washington correspondent that was printed in several West German newspapers. The article contended that "'prominent Washington circles'" had taken up the Oder–Neisse Line issue and the question of the expellees' right to their homeland. Two proposals were reportedly being considered. The first was a plebiscite among expellees in West Germany to determine the number of those wishing to return to their homeland along with the subsequent computation of the number of square miles to be returned to those expellees. The second proposal was for the return of Pomerania, East Brandenburg, and Lower Silesia to the Germans; the Poles would retain Upper Silesia and East Prussia permanently.[49]

Like Adenauer, the Washington correspondent maintained that Eisenhower's State of the Union message had indicated prospective changes in U.S. foreign policy that would be more in line with the desires of the expellees. According to the correspondent, these forthcoming changes meant that the expellees had a "special responsibility" to be involved in the settlement of the frontier question, which affected all of Europe. As such they should study the first proposal very closely and reject the second since it violated Article II of the Atlantic Charter, which stated that no territorial changes would be allowed without the consent of those involved. Swope noted, however, that at the same time that this report was published, the information service of one of the most important expellee organizations, the League of Expelled Germans (Zentralverband Vertriebener Deutscher), had warned the expellees not to take Eisenhower's statements as an indication of a new foreign policy focus since such statements were largely meant to affect Moscow.[50]

Other HICOG representatives also reported on the activities and press reports of the expellees in West Germany, pointing out how far afield the average German was from U.S. policy positions. An officer in the American Consulate General in Bremen reported in March 1954 that in discussions with Germans, the expellees repeatedly asked one question, almost to the point of "obsession": why had the United States allied with the Soviet Union to defeat Germany during the war? He claimed that Germans in general reflected insecurity about Germany's place in the international scene and looked for reassurance of U.S. friendship and the admission that the U.S.–Soviet wartime alliance had been a mistake.[51] Constance Harvey, chief of the Division of External German Affairs in Bonn, reported that while expellees often voiced their disgust at the Polonization of the Oder–Neisse area, in private conversations with Americans "many such Germans" admitted that they were resigned to the loss of the territory. Nevertheless, Harvey warned, the increasingly aggressive irredentist statements by expellee leaders were bound to "arouse suspicions among Germany's neighbours."[52]

ADENAUER'S CONDOMINIUM PROPOSAL

After the CDU victory in the September 1953 elections, Adenauer tempered somewhat his public statements about expellees' rights to a homeland, although he did not disclaim the area as German; his cabinet continued to have an active minister for refugees. The difficulty of Adenauer's position was evident a few days after the election when he made statements during a press conference that had most of the expellee organizations up in arms.[53] In an exclusive interview with an Associated Press correspondent on 8 September 1953, Adenauer said that the solution to the border question had to be based on the existence of a "free Poland" and should never be a cause for war. He then added, "'One could envisage perhaps a condominium [joint rule], or perhaps some kind of regime under the United Nations.'"[54] Almost immediately, the expellee press issued statements opposing any sort of condominium proposal. Shortly thereafter the federal press service explained that the Associated Press article "'presents a completely distorted version taken out of the context and sense of the Chancellor's words.'" This official government statement, Constance Harvey contended, was prompted by the vociferous reaction of the expellees.[55] Dr. Walter Braeutigam, chief of the Eastern Section of the West German Foreign Office, expanded on the press service statement. He reaffirmed that Adenauer had not intended to suggest any aggressive moves on the part of the Federal Republic but had wanted to indicate that international lawyers in

West Germany were exploring various solutions to the border issue. The condominium proposal was, Braeutigam added, "the most awkward" of the solutions being considered.[56]

Although it might have been the "most awkward" of possible solutions to the boundary question, the idea of a German–Polish condominium continued to surface during Eisenhower's first term and was reported with varying degrees of scepticism by State Department officers. In January 1955 two separate sources noted by the State Department suggested that the Polish Government-in-Exile might consider a Polish border to the east of the Oder–Neisse. In a conversation with Cecil Lyon, director of the Office of German Affairs, Albrecht von Kessel of the West German Mission in Washington reported that the prime minister of the Polish Government-in-Exile, Stanislaw Mackiwicz, had told a reliable source that "the Poles" (apparently the exiled Poles) were willing to recognize the "old German eastern border, that is, returning East Prussia, etc.," to the Germans in return for German support of Polish claims to Lwów and Vilno. Von Kessel asked Lyon to keep the conversation confidential, probably recognizing that public announcements about a discussion concerning the potential movement of Poland's borders eastward would result in protests by Polish Americans.[57]

Such fears appeared to have been well founded when, a few days later George Lister of the Office of Eastern European Affairs sent a memo to Lyon informing him of a press conference that Mackiewicz had held in New York. As reported in *Dziennik Związkowy*, Chicago's Polish American daily newspaper, Mackiewicz responded to a question regarding his stand on Poland's western territories: "I stand on the ground of the Treaty of Riga, and the Oder–Neisse line. However, I must categorically declare that the government of Chancellor Adenauer and the German political circles are not engaged in any revisionist action. I have heard nothing of any such action. The present German policy is pacifistic." Even though Mackiewicz had not repeated any of his ideas about moving Poland's western border as Von Kessel reported and had publicly expressed his support for the Oder–Neisse Line, the reaction of the Polish American community to such unqualified faith in West Germany is reflected in the *Dziennik Związkowy* headline: "Did Mackiewicz Come to America to Defend Germans?"[58]

Cecil Lyon met again with Albert von Kessel in January 1955 to discuss the condominium proposal that the French press had recounted. A French correspondent reported that Moscow had proposed to the Polish and East German governments a plan calling for a condominium involving Pomerania, Brandenburg, and Lower Silesia if a neutral, unified Germany were created. In return, the Poles would receive the Königsberg area in East Prussia and the Lwów area in West Galicia. Von Kessel told Lyon that the German Foreign Office was not taking the proposal too seriously but had instructed him to inquire about the views of the State Department. Lyon responded that the U.S. Embassy in Paris had not yet reported such a story, but he told Von Kessel that he would discuss the matter with Livingston Merchant, the assistant secretary for European affairs. Lyon also speculated that the story might be factual since he believed that the Soviets were ready and able to use the Oder–Neisse issue more to their advantage than they had in the past. Von Kessel replied that he also believed that the Soviets might be willing to make such a deal since it followed the "Russian pattern of treatment of Poland."[59]

A few months later, the condominium rumor re-surfaced in Warsaw. Ambassador Flack reported: "For some little time a number of my colleagues have been mentioning to me from time to time with bated breath a rumor which has been current here and perhaps elsewhere in Europe, to the effect that a condominium (joint sovereignty) might be declared for a portion of eastern and western Poland. . . . As yet these rumors have not been sufficiently specific as to define the limits or boundaries of such areas of joint sovereignty."[60] He added that one of his colleagues had suggested that the French, West Germans, or Soviets had started such rumors "as a disturbing political element." He emphasized that the embassy could not confirm such rumors and speculated whether the Poles "who still retain such a strong sense of nationality" would accept the condominium solution.[61] The Berlin HICOG office was also unable to confirm the condominium rumor.[62]

MORE RUMORS ABOUT THE ODER–NEISSE TERRITORIES

In addition to this speculation about a Polish–German condominium, American representatives in Central Europe continued to hear rumors from a number of sources about possible deals concerning Polish cities being returned to East Germany. The Americans interpreted these rumors as suggesting that Moscow, rather than Warsaw, controlled the destiny of the Polish western territories and that in spite of Soviet and Polish assurances to the contrary, some type of deal returning part of the Oder–Neisse territories to Germany was possible. In March 1953 N. Spencer Barnes, chief of the Eastern Affairs Division at HICOG Berlin, analyzed press reports from Stockholm claiming that the administration of Stettin (Szczecin) would be given to the East Germans. Barnes wrote that although HICOG had no proof of such a change, it "would not be illogical" since the city was an important commercial port for East German barges, and he continually heard reports about Polish resistance against the Soviets in the area.[63] He added that such a rumor did not necessarily mean that supervision of Stettin would be given to the East Germans but suggested that the Soviets might make some move to raise the status of the "'more reliable'" East Germans. "In view of the tentative arrangements on the Oder–Neisse boundary in the Potsdam Agreement," Barnes wrote, "such developments may warrant careful observation."[64]

The following month, though, Barnes sent to the Department of State the report of a conversation that he had had with a "'reliable German source'" refuting rumors about Stettin. The source claimed that there were various signs indicating that the Poles would retain Stettin, such as the continued segregation of the Germans from the Poles and the lack of movement of Germans back into Pomerania or Silesia.[65] Such reasonable observations, however, were not enough to quash rumors about a possible deal. On 24 March 1955 Ambassador Flack reported that along with the condominium rumor, he had been hearing that the Soviets had offered East Germany the Polish cities of Wrocław and Szczecin; in return the Poles would receive Lwów and the surrounding territory. Flack could not substantiate this rumor and admitted that it "sounds fantastic and even ridiculous," especially in light of the heavily Ukrainian population of Lwów which would cause the Polish government "additional troubles" if it were returned to Poland.[66]

Other rumors also surfaced. In July 1955, shortly before the Geneva Summit, the American Embassy in Bonn reported that both the general and expellee press in West Germany were discussing the possible return of part of the Oder–Neisse territory to Germany in return for assurances of a neutralized and united Germany. According to reports, the Soviets were contemplating the return of Pomerania and Silesia to Germany in return for the "'rapid realization of an independent reunited Germany and the non-inclusion of the future West German forces into the western military pact.'"[67] Although Embassy Counselor Elim O'Shaughnessy could not confirm that the West German government took these rumors seriously, he reported that one top official in the Bundeszentrale für Heimatdienst had stated that his office believed the Soviets were ready to make "far-reaching" proposals at the Geneva Summit in order to secure the withdrawal of U.S. troops from Germany and Europe.[68]

Even within the United States rumors were afloat about a deal involving a shift of Poland's borders eastward. The Polish American Congress expressed concern regarding possible concessions made to Soviet imperialism in a memorandum sent to the State Department prior to the Geneva Summit of July 1955. The memorandum warned that the Soviets were using this "temporary display of . . . cordiality" as a "breathing spell" to prepare for the complete domination of East Central Europe. To defend against such a move, Rozmarek and the officers of the PAC who signed the memo urged the government to demand freedom for these states and to support the creation of an independent "neutral belt of nations" that would strive to maintain peace "in an effort to preserve their national existence." Poland, with an eastern border along the Riga Line and a western border along the Oder–Neisse, would constitute the most important nation within this group because of its size, location, economic potential, and "passionate love of freedom." This "free and independent" Poland would serve to separate Russia from Germany, a reminder of the danger to peace of a potential Russian–German alliance. The authors of the memorandum recognized that the creation of such a cordon sanitaire would require the use of force but contended that further "appeasement" was only an invitation to a future war with a stronger, more militarily prepared Soviet Union.

With true Wilsonian-style rhetoric the authors closed by stating: "When the U.S. shows unrelenting opposition to all that is evil, when it tries to right the wrongs committed against the victims of Yalta and when it builds a solid foundation for peace based on liberation, God will bless our land and its people and protect our children from slavery."[69]

In addition to the Polish American Congress, other Polish American and Polish exile groups continued to make known to the U.S. Congress their views regarding Poland's western border. The National Committee of Americans of Polish Descent (KNAPP) had the ear of Thaddeus Machrowicz (D-MI), who on 12 May 1955 read on the floor of the House another of the organization's resolutions that had been passed to honor Polish Constitution Day. This resolution called on Congress and the executive department to recognize the Oder–Neisse Line as Poland's western border to preserve peace and aid the economic and political stability of Europe.[70]

On 7 July 1955 Machrowicz, "because of the importance of the forthcoming Big Four conference," read a letter on the floor of the House that he had received from well-respected Polish exile General Kazimierz Sosnkowski after a conversation that the two men shared. The letter called for the restoration of independence to the countries of Central Europe and analyzed the advantages of Poland's western border on the Oder–Neisse Line that had, he claimed, been determined at Potsdam. The advantages that Sosnkowski mentioned reflected the same arguments that Poles and Polish Americans had been making since 1945, that is that Poland's economy was strengthened with the inclusion of the Silesian minerals and industry and that the line served as a barrier to Germany's *Drang nach Osten*. Sosnkowski also added that Poles were forced by Western intransigence about the line to cooperate with the Soviets and suggested that better relations between Poland and the West would result from formal recognition of the line. From an international perspective, Sosnkowski claimed that all the captive nations regarded the issue as a "test case" for Western policy and warned: "If these truths are underestimated," Soviet propaganda would thereby be strengthened.[71]

Machrowicz's Polish American colleague from Detroit, John Dingell (D-MI), also corresponded with members of the Polish American community. Like Machrowicz, Dingell made known his views about the position that Eisenhower should take at Geneva by reading to the House of Representatives his reply to a letter that he had received from the Michigan Division of the Polish American Congress inviting him to attend a meeting of representatives of organizations representing Americans of East European descent. In his letter, Dingell stated that Poland's eastern border should be restored to its prewar status and that its western border should be maintained along the Oder–Neisse Line with absolute guarantees to Poland of Silesian resources. "'I repeat,'" Dingell wrote, "'the perpetrators of World War II, both Germany and Russia, should be compelled to rebuild, restore, and replace all destruction and plunder.'" Dingell closed by stating that the Polish American Congress should go on record as favoring the creation of a "strong tier of nations" as a buffer between the "two arch conspirators," Germany and the Soviet Union.[72] This proposal for the creation of a neutral buffer zone comprising the states of East Central Europe was similar to the position taken by the Polish American Congress in its memorandum to the State Department of 6 July 1955. This suggests that Dingell, who was active in Polish American issues, was familiar with the national proposal and was going on public record supporting it. Dingell's letter was much less bellicose than the PAC memorandum; however; he did not refer to the use of force that would be necessary to implement such a plan. Any concern that the U.S. delegation to Geneva might have felt about taking such a public stand on the question of East Central Europe proved unnecessary when the Soviets blocked any such discussion at Geneva, labeling it interference in the internal affairs of sovereign states.[73]

Rumors about possible changes in the Oder–Neisse border continued after the Geneva Summit. In September 1955 Walter Stoessel of the Office of Eastern European Affairs reported to his boss, Jacob Beam, that a reliable source at RAND had heard from a prominent Polish émigré about a deal in the works. Although the source could not say exactly where the new border would be, the deal would reportedly involve part of Poland's western territories in return for the area around Lwów. Beam evidently thought this information was important. A handwritten note on the corner of the memorandum indicated that the report was "very interesting" and directed Stoessel to send copies to the Bureau of European Affairs, the Office of German Affairs, and Deputy Undersecretary Robert Murphy.[74]

In light of these continuous rumors, it is not surprising that Poles both before and after the Geneva Summit took a number of actions solidifying their hold on the western territories, as reported by American representatives in Warsaw, Berlin, and Bonn. Constance Harvey in Bonn notified the Department of State that anti-German sentiment was on the increase in Poland as evidenced by reports of terrorism against German-speaking inhabitants in Poland's western territories in January 1954. He further substantiated the State Department's view that the Soviets rather than the Poles controlled the fate of the border when he wrote: "If the Soviets intended to permit the reunification of Germany, one would expect them to take steps to consolidate their hold on the populations of the neighboring satellites. The evidence . . . indicates that the embers of anti-German feeling is [*sic*] being fanned in Poland, presumably to impress on the Germans the finality of the Oder–Neisse line."[75] He reported also that some of the Germans who were forced out of the western territories might flee to West Berlin and give eyewitness accounts of anti-German terrorism in Poland. This, Harvey warned, could result in more public pronouncements by "some of the hot-headed German nationalists whom the communists are fond of quoting."[76]

In March 1954 Harvey also notified the department that expellee and government sources in the Federal Republic reported that the Poles were transporting more Germans out of the Oder–Neisse territories into East Germany. Almost all of these Germans, Harvey noted, were unable to work either because of age or physical disability. The transports reportedly began in October 1953 and involved an unconfirmed number of people, with some reports estimating 30,000 persons, and another 18,000 families. The transfers were completed relatively secretly, and the East German press office instructed newspapers not to mention them. Future transfers were expected, apparently as a result of a deal between the Polish and East German governments.[77]

In October 1954 the HICOG office in Bonn reported that the Polish government had implemented further changes in the administrative structure of the western territories, perhaps an indication that the Poles intended to eliminate any remaining vestiges of the German character of the area.[78] The Polish government also took the opportunity to celebrate the tenth anniversary of the "'reunification of Silesia with Poland'" on 19 June 1955. The American Embassy in Bonn reported that the celebration was generally interpreted as a warning to the Federal Republic not to try to promote discussion of the Oder–Neisse Line at the Geneva Summit.[79]

Warsaw also took a more concrete step to secure its claims to the western territories. On 12 June 1955 the government decreed that full property rights were to be granted to Polish settlers who leased former German farmlands. This decree involved about 400,000 Polish farmers and would, according to Elim O'Shaughnessy, who reported it, make it more difficult for the western territories to be used as a bargaining tool.[80]

The fifth anniversary of the Zgorzelec (Görlitz) Treaty offered a press opportunity for a show of friendship between the leaders of the East German and Polish governments in July 1955. Otto Grotewohl and Boleslaw Bierut met to celebrate the "peace frontier" and to counteract, according to the HICOG officer reporting the meeting, Western publicity that the Oder–Neisse Line issue was unresolved and was a possible topic for discussion at Geneva.[81]

Secretary Dulles was apparently interested in some of these reports. In October 1955 he sent a request to the American Embassy in Warsaw to verify an Associated Press report that Poland was planning to offer 250,000 Germans who remained in the western territories the option of either adopting full Polish citizenship or emigrating to Germany. A Polish official reportedly stated: "'We cannot continue to have what amounts to stateless people in such numbers. If they want to be Poles with the full responsibility that goes with that, well and good. If they want to leave rather than be Poles, we must face that issue in each individual case.'"[82] The embassy was unable to confirm this report or to add any information about the story. Ambassador Jacobs reported that rumors had been circulating about such an option being offered but added that people with whom he had spoken were pessimistic about chances for such a policy to be implemented. This view, he felt, was reinforced by a recent press statement, "obviously made with approval [of the] Polish regime," by a visiting Belgian diplomat to the effect that no Germans lived east of the Oder–Neisse Line.[83] Such statements would indicate that the Polish government was publicly denying that there was a problem of an unassimilable ethnic minority in Poland's western territories. Therefore, the government could argue, there was no reason that Poland needed to consider a deal with either West or East Germany.

POLISH–WEST GERMAN RELATIONS

In light of the number of reports about a possible shift in Poland's borders, it was expected that the Polish government would take steps to contradict such rumors. Especially noteworthy, though, considering Moscow's apparent hold on Warsaw, was that the Poles continued such actions in the face of fairly wellsubstantiated Soviet willingness to use the Oder–Neisse Line as a bargaining tool, as the Soviets tried to halt or at least slow down the integration of the Federal Republic of Germany into the western community. These actions by the Polish government to emphasize and solidify its hold on the western territories suggest that Warsaw perceived itself as having some maneuverability within the Soviet orbit, the limits of which would be shown in the coming years.

Such actions did not, however, lead Warsaw to make recognition of the Oder–Neisse Line a precondition to establishing relations with the Federal Republic, at least not initially.[84] In this the Polish government followed the example of the Soviet Union and announced its willingness to normalize relations with West Germany in 1955, even though Moscow rejected Adenauer's contention that he had the right to seek the revision of Germany's borders.[85] In their declarations, Polish officials did not link the frontier issue with political conditions.[86] The American Embassy in Warsaw was aware, largely through press reports, that one of Warsaw's foreign policy aims was the normalization of relations with Bonn, even though the possibility reportedly "aroused some uneasiness locally. . . . that a 'deal' might be in the offing over Poland's Western Territories."[87] In any case, the Adenauer government repeatedly rejected these offers largely because of the Hallstein Doctrine's stipulation against West German recognition of any state having diplomatic relations with East Germany and because of the unsolved and related question of German reunification.[88] After the fall of 1957 the Polish government expressed less interest in establishing diplomatic relations with the Federal Republic until Bonn recognized the Oder–Neisse Line, an event that did not occur until 1970.[89] As W. W. Kulski, a scholar of German–Polish relations, claims, "The rejection of Polish offers proved later on to be a grave error of the Adenauer government. . . . The Brandt government established diplomatic relations [with Poland] but under more onerous conditions."[90]

The diplomatic feelers between Poland and West Germany combined with the post-Geneva "'relaxation'" and the rapprochement between Moscow and Bonn resulted in a somewhat softer propaganda tone on the part of the

Polish regime, according to an embassy dispatch in June 1956. Although the Polish press displayed an increased interest in the "German problem," especially remilitarization and the Western Alliance, the First Secretary of the Embassy Valdemar Johnson reported that the government had beaten the "propaganda drum," especially concerning the Oder–Neisse Line, "less often and more softly."[91] He added, however, that this easing of propaganda rhetoric did not preclude Poland from using the postwar "'traditional'" celebration of "(East) German-Polish Friendship Week" as an occasion to remind everyone "probably not leastwise the USSR" that the Oder–Neisse Line was the "inviolable" Polish border as established by treaty with East Germany.[92]

OPINIONS ON THE ODER–NEISSE ISSUE

U.S. voices, in contrast, were not so easily silenced. During Eisenhower's first term the Polish American Congress became more intentional in presenting its concerns about U.S. policy toward West Germany and Poland, by creating in 1955 an organization within the Polish American Congress to deal specifically with the Oder–Neisse Line issue. The Polish Western Association of America, headquartered in Chicago, lobbied for U.S. recognition of the line and provided information about activities and pronouncements by the U.S. and West German governments concerning Poland's western territories. For example, Adenauer's June 1956 visit to the United States prompted the Polish Western Association of America to send a duplicate letter to the chancellor and the State Department emphasizing the Polish character of the Oder–Neisse area and calling for a Polish–German stand against "the eastern wave of barbarity threatening Western culture and civilization."[93] Although this letter prompted no great policy changes, the Polish Western Association of America served as an important source of information about the situation east of the Oder–Neisse Line. Its English-language quarterly journal contained scholarly articles about Poland's history and current events affecting the western territories and published association correspondence to and from American and West German governmental representatives.

Poland's cause also continued to be promoted in Congress through the efforts of Machrowicz and Thomas Gordon (D-IL). They read into the *Congressional Record* resolutions and declarations that they received from the Polish American Congress and from the Polish Western Association of America that called for a reappraisal of U.S. policy toward Poland's western border. These organizations continued to maintain that Poland had a historical right to the land and that the U.S. position only aided the Soviets' hold on Poland.[94]

The final year of Eisenhower's first term saw Machrowicz engage in a debate with Carroll Reece (R-TN), who urged that the United States make clear that it recognized the German boundaries as they existed in 1937. This meant, of course, that Reece favored the return to Germany of land east of the Oder and

Neisse Rivers administered by Poland and the Soviet Union. On 8 February 1956 Reece spoke on the floor of the House about the expulsion of Germans from East Prussia and from the other areas beyond the Oder–Neisse Line as one of history's great tragedies. He spoke favorably of a memorandum written by a respected native of East Prussia who stated that East Prussian expellees in the Federal Republic were determined to return peacefully to their homeland. Machrowicz on 30 April 1956 refuted Reece's contention, recalling that at Potsdam the Allies agreed to place the western territories under Polish administration and recognized the right of transfer of the German population. He went on to note that the Allied Control Commission had established a plan to transfer the remaining Germans from the area in November 1945. He did not state categorically that the Poles had been given the area outright but claimed that these activities had created a de facto situation whereby the Poles controlled the Oder–Neisse territories. "The final settlement of boundaries at the Peace Conference," he said, "can therefore be envisaged as a formal recognition of the existing state of affairs." The congressman added justification to this by noting that since 1945 the Poles had repopulated and revitalized the area. He stated that to acquiesce to Reece's proposal that the United States formally recognize Germany's 1937 borders would only alienate the people of Poland, serve the needs of communist propaganda, and be a major blow to America's international prestige. He closed by reminding his audience that East Prussia, the area favored by Reece, was one of the major centers of German imperialism that had led to U.S. involvement in both world wars.[95] This rather restrained debate between the congressmen from Michigan and Tennessee continued into the next year and garnered a good deal of attention within the Polish American community.

The propaganda value of the Oder–Neisse issue was raised again in early 1956 by an unexpected source when John McCloy, former U.S. high commissioner for Germany, wrote that West Germany should renounce claims to the Oder–Neisse territories. In the foreword to a well-publicized book by Henry Roberts, *Russia and America: Dangers and Prospects*, McCloy wrote that West German demands for return of the land made it impossible for the Poles to cooperate with the West and advocated that West Germany accept the loss as a step toward reunification and in order to loosen Poland's ties with the Soviet Union. He qualified his suggestion by adding that he did not condone the Potsdam territorial decisions but felt that acceptance of the line was a way to "achieve the maximum freedom for peoples everywhere."[96] McCloy's statement was widely commented on in the German press; according to a *New York Times* correspondent, the general reaction of West Germans was "polite, if negative."[97] Although McCloy's suggestion was rejected in the Federal Republic, American journalists writing in the *New York Times* and *Christian Science Monitor* reported that the improved East–West dialogue was leading West Germans to admit in private circles that a compromise with the Poles over the Oder–Neisse issue might be possible.[98] American journalists and officials also warned, however, that the time was not right to discuss possible compromises on the border issue, largely because of the vociferous expellee groups.[99]

Such warnings were proven to show great insight when a few months later the publication of Elizabeth Wiskemann's *Germany and Its Eastern Neighbours* stirred a considerable controversy.[100] Wiskemann, a respected English scholar of European history, refuted many of the German claims to the Oder–Neisse territories when she wrote in the conclusion: "With regard to the principle of ceding territory to the Germans it should perhaps be recalled that territorial gains in the past have seemed to fortify the worst elements in that nation, while weakening those groups with a genuine feeling of human responsibility. Further, if one considers the recent record of the German minorities in eastern Europe, it is difficult to wish them back there."[101]

The American Embassy in Bonn observed and reported on the West German reaction to Wiskemann's work. Elim O'Shaughnessy recounted in August 1956 that although the book itself had initially gone largely unnoticed except by "minor refugee groups," excerpts of the book reprinted and reviewed in *New Statesman* and *Nation* "evoked sharp comment" in the West German press. Critics complained of its sponsorship by the Royal Institute of International Affairs but recognized that the views expressed in the institute's publications did not necessarily reflect those of the government.[102]

The matter did not drop with the press critiques of Wiskemann's book, however. O'Shaughnessy reported further that Herbert Kraus, a professor from the University of Göttingen, had published an article in the *Federal Bulletin* in response to Wiskemann's contention that the Oder–Neisse Line should be recognized as permanent. He rejected the idea that there was a fundamental antagonism between Germany and Poland (and Czechoslovakia) and denied that the evacuation of Germans from the Oder–Neisse area was only an acceleration of a movement already in progress. Kraus maintained that the Oder–Neisse Line violated international law and the Atlantic Charter and that the Soviet Union had already broken the promises made to its wartime allies. He concluded by chastising the Royal Institute for being connected with such a study.[103] O'Shaughnessy pointed out in his report that neither the British nor West German governments were officially advocating the policies being debated, but the controversy surrounding the publication of Wiskemann's book shows the volatility of the Oder–Neisse issue in the Federal Republic in the mid-1950s. The report could have been interpreted as confirmation that any public statements from Washington suggesting even minor policy changes concerning the Oder–Neisse Line were unwise from a diplomatic stance.

There was, in any case, very little likelihood of Washington's publicly supporting Poland's position. The establishment of Bonn–Moscow relations and the offers from Warsaw to Bonn to follow suit had very little substantive impact on U.S.–Polish relations. The so-called thaw after Stalin's death did not lead the U.S. administration to soften its stance toward the Soviet Union and its satellites.[104] In his press statement after the Geneva Summit, Dulles affirmed that the conference had "registered a certain transformation" in relations between the Soviet Union and the West that meant that the danger of war had lessened. He warned, however, that there were no quick or easy solutions to the problems existing between East and West. Regarding the Soviet satellite states, Dulles told the press that the United States had made it clear to the Soviets that the American government and people attached great importance to the right of self-determination and objected to the "revolutionary and subversive activities of international communism." The secretary admitted that while the Soviets had not given any assurances, he continued to hope that "developments will in fact tend to eliminate these causes of tension."[105]

U.S.–POLISH RELATIONS

One problem that the secretary's press statement did not anticipate, though, was that these developments in Poland and other satellite countries could be and were interpreted in different ways. This difference was brought out when the British ambassador in Warsaw, Sir Andrew Noble, urged that Britain and the United States do more to encourage the nascent "'Polish policy'" that he believed was emerging in the "post-Geneva situation" in Poland.[106] He saw this policy as an indication that Warsaw was reexamining its foreign policy to become more independent of Moscow and predicted that if the Soviet Union tried to make a deal with Germany at Poland's expense, the situation would become critical. Noble recognized that Poland would not immediately leave the Soviet orbit, but he urged that Great Britain and the United States work for a policy of rapprochement with Poland in order to show the Poles that they could more easily work with the West than with the Soviets.[107]

Dulles rejected such thinking when he sent to the American Embassy in Warsaw his analysis of American relations with Poland. The secretary wrote that the views expressed by the embassy generally corresponded with the position held by the State Department, but he added some qualifying comments.[108] One of his qualifications was that in spite of the recent "changes in Communist tactics in Poland," the department had seen no evidence to confirm the establishment of an "independent 'Polish' policy."[109] Dulles favored the promotion of "evolutionary changes" in Polish policies such that the United States should be ready to "encourage and foster any *bona fide* tendencies toward independence and national freedom from Moscow." He did not elaborate on what constituted such changes but made it clear that the United States would not make concessions based on "sham independence."[110]

In the following months Washington had to evaluate a number of changes as reported in dispatches and telegrams from the Warsaw Embassy. In May 1956 Ambassador Jacobs sent word of a meeting with Jozef Winiewicz who had "strongly belaboured" the point that great changes were taking place that Washington should recognize as warranting policy adjustments. According to Winiewicz, the Polish government sincerely wanted to improve relations with the United States but could not and should not sever friendly ties to the Soviet Union.[111] Winiewicz also protested the State Department's Polish Constitution Day statement about the "bondage of Poland," claiming that such statements only hindered the development of stronger ties between Poland and America.[112]

The American ambassador also reported a couple of weeks later on an article in *Zycie Warszawy*, one of Warsaw's leading newspapers, that labeled U.S.–Polish relations as "'not ideal but passable.'" The author castigated the United States for the usual reasons of supporting Mikolajczyk in the hope of turning Poland toward capitalism, treating Poland as part of the socialist camp rather than as a separate entity, and supporting revisionist West Germany and restrictive trade practices with Poland. He noted that Poland had responded by restricting American "bourgeois publications" and jamming Western radio broadcasts, but then admitted that Poland had committed a number of "blunders" such as discounting American technological and medical achievements. The author of the newspaper article emphasized the strong ties that existed between the USSR and Poland but optimistically stated that Washington would see that this was no reason that U.S.–Polish relations could not also be strong. He called for the removal of U.S. trade restrictions and increased cultural, scientific, and press exchanges.[113] Jacobs suggested that the article "may constitute [a] feeler" and an attempt by the Poles to "exploit [the] situation for promotion [of] 'better relations.'"[114]

The development of stronger ties with the United States was not, however, the central focus of the Polish government, which was in disarray after Khrushchev's speech to the Twentieth Party Congress denouncing Stalin's activities. Władysław Gomułka, who had earlier been released from prison after advocating a "Polish road to socialism," continued to gain popularity, and the Polish Communist Party underwent some important changes. The uprising of workers in Poznan in June 1956 caught the government by surprise, and the immediate response of Premier Cyrankiewicz was that it had been instigated by "'imperialist provocateurs.'" The State Department immediately denied such charges, and the Polish government dropped the accusation.[115] On 29 June 1956 a State Department representative told news correspondents that "all free peoples will be watching to see whether or not the Polish people will be allowed a government which will remedy the grievances which have brought them to a breaking point."[116]

The events of the "Polish October" proved these words true as world attention turned to Warsaw during mid-October 1956.[117] As Gomułka and his followers moved closer to the seat of power, anxiety heightened that the Stalinists in the Polish government would violently oppose the rise of these "reformers." When Khrushchev and other top Soviet officials arrived unannounced in Warsaw, tension reached a peak as the Soviet military was alerted to be ready for action. Gomułka refused to negotiate under this threat; Khrushchev acknowledged that a "Polish road to socialism" did not mean an end to communism or withdrawal of Polish troops from the Warsaw Pact, while the revolution in Hungary and the Suez Crisis diverted the attention of the Soviet delegates. They left Warsaw without forcing Gomułka to back down.[118]

Throughout these events Washington remained observant but cautious. In a radio address on 21 October, Dulles assured the Soviets of nonintervention when he stated that U.S. interference in the situation would result in bloodshed and could precipitate a world war.[119] As the crisis was averted and tensions eased, U.S.–Polish relations initially returned to the same footing as before the dramatic October events.[120]

The first Eisenhower administration was content to monitor the situation in Poland and Germany. American representatives in both states reported the activities and rumors involving the Oder–Neisse border, but the State Department did not act on any of these rumors. Officials of the State Department and White House responded innocuously to the lobbying efforts of Polish Americans and Polish exiles for U.S. recognition of the border. These groups received more support from Polish American members of Congress, especially Machrowicz, Gordon, and Dingell; but this support was not widespread enough to override the State Department's general wait-and-see attitude. However, as the effects of the Polish October became increasingly evident, some members of the State Department and respected foreign policy scholars began to consider the possibility of readjusting Washington's position on the border issue.

NOTES

1. Telegram 444, Flack to Secretary of State, 27 February 1953, 611.48/2-2753, RG59. Secretary Dulles sent policy guidance that the *Voice of America* treat the book as typical propaganda that distorted traditional U.S.-Polish friendship. In Telegram 148, Dulles to American Embassy Warsaw, 12 March 1953, 611.48/3-1253; Dulles to American Embassy Warsaw, 13 March 1953, in State Department Decimal File, Record Group 59, 611.48/3-1353. Hereafter cited as RG59 with document number.

2. Piotr Wandycz, *The United States and Poland* (Cambridge: Harvard University Press, 1980), 350.

3. Airgram A-72, Galantiere to Lang, 3 February 1953, in the Declassified Documents Reference System, Fische Series, 1987, No. 1148.

4. Ibid. Griffis had aided the escape of Mikolajczyk from Poland and in addition was a political appointee who some professional diplomats felt was unqualified for an ambassadorship. See Stanton Griffis, *Lying in State* (Garden City, NY: Doubleday, 1952).

5. Letter, Wojcik to Zablocki, 20 March 1953, Zablocki Papers, Box 169, Poland File.

6. Charles A. Baretski, "A Content Analysis of the *Polish American Journal* Newspaper in Reflecting the Political Attitudes, Issues and Perspectives of the Polish-American Group during the Period, 1950–1966," (Ph.D. diss., New York University, 1969).

Baretski noted that among the congressmen who subscribed to the newspaper were Thomas Gordon, John Lesinski, Clement Zablocki, and O'Konski (187).

7. *Congressional Record Appendix*, 83rd Cong., 1st sess., 99, pt. 9 (16 March 1953): A1324–1325.

8. *Congressional Record*, 83rd, 2nd sess., 100, pt. 1 (12 January 1954): 155–156.

9. Despatch 424, Flack to Department of State, 11 May 1953, 648.62B3/5-1153, RG59.

10. White House Office of Special Assistant, Box 8, NSC 174, Dwight D. Eisenhower Library, hereafter cited as DDE/L.

11. Despatch 350, American Embassy Warsaw to Department of State, 17 March 1953, RG59, 611.48/3-1753.

12. Ibid.

13. Despatch 369, Steere to Department of State, 24 March 1953, RG59, 611.48/3-2453.

14. Airgram A-82, Dulles to American Embassy Warsaw, 3 April 1953, RG59, 611.48/3-2453.

15. Letter, Polish Constitution Day Committee to Eisenhower, 10 May 1953, 748.03/5-1053, RG59.

16. Ibid.; *Department of State Bulletin*, 28, no. 725 (18 May 1953): 721.

17. Memorandum for the Record, Re: Polish Émigré Politics, 20 January 1955, 648.62A/1-1855, RG59.

18. Wandycz, *The United States*, 351.

19. Memorandum for the Record, 24 January 1955, 648.62A/1-1855, RG59; Wandycz, *The United States*, 351. Stefan Korbonski, one of the Association of Captive European Nations (ACEN) leaders, noted in his memoirs that after 1956 trouble arose among the various nationalities in the ACEN over the Poles' attitude toward West Germany and the Oder–Neisse Line. See Stefan Korbonski, *Warsaw in Exile*, trans. David J. Welch (New York: Frederick A. Praeger, 1966), 164.

20. Memorandum, Howe to Goodpaster, 16 October 1956, RG59, 611.48/10-1656.

21. Letter, Beam to Bielecki, 24 October 1956, RG59, 611.48/10-2256.

22. Letter, Korbonski to unspecified, 7 April 1953, RG59, 611.62A/4-753; Memo of Conversation, Korbonski and Vedeler, 9 April 1953, RG59, 611.62A/4-953.

23. Letter, Rhodes to Adams, 17 June 1953, Simmons to Adams, 23 June 1953, Polish Political Council–London to Eisenhower, 20 June 1953; Muir to Adams, 9 July 1953, Central Files, Official File, Box 886, DDE/L.

24. Ibid.

25. Letter, Rozmarek to The President, 27 November 1953, RG59, 396.1/11-2753. The re-Polonization of the names of cities, towns, and rivers was, in fact, a conscious effort on the part of the Polish government almost immediately after the Potsdam Conference.

26. Ibid., Bonbright to Rozmarek, 10 December 1953.

27. Letter, Rozmarek to Dulles, 18 January 1954, RG59, 396.1.BE/1-2554.

28. Ibid.

29. Ibid. Assistant Secretary of State for European Affairs Livingston

Merchant, who had received the letter from Karol Burke, Washington representative of the Polish American Congress, requested Walworth Barbour of the Office of Eastern European Affairs to prepare a reply for the secretary or acting secretary's signature.

30. Despatch 409, Steere to Department of State, 28 April 1953, RG59, 748.022/4-2853, Microfilm Series LM87, Reel 5.

31. Despatch 348, American Embassy Warsaw to Secretary of State, RG59, 848.20/3-1653, Microfilm Series LM 87, Reel 9.

32. Despatch 440, Redington to Department of State, 26 May 1953, RG59, 748.022/5-2653, Microfilm Series LM87, Reel 5.

33. Elizabeth Wiskemann, *Germany's Eastern Neighbours: Problems Relating to the Oder–Neisse Line and the Czech Frontier Regions* (London: Oxford University Press, 1956), 224–228. Wiskemann contends that the amount of land lying fallow was more the result of the government's tax plans and general inefficiency than of the peasants' unwillingness to farm it. Writing in 1954 and 1955, she admitted that the issue was confused and that statistics could be used to support various contentions.

34. Memorandum 47, Dennis to Department of State, 27 July 1954, Box 22, RG84, DS/NAS.

35. Charles Wassermann, *Europe's Forgotten Territories* (Copenhagen: R. Roussell, 1960), passim. Wassermann's book was first published in West Germany in 1957 as *Unter Polnischer Verwaltung* by Bluechert Verlag in Hamburg. In the foreword to the 1960 book, Wassermann states that conditions had not changed much since 1957.

36. Walter M. Drzewieniecki, *The German-Polish Frontier* (Chicago: Polish Western Association of America, 1959), 116, 120.

37. Telegram 4340, Bonn to Secretary of State, 24 March 1953, RG59, 611.62A/3-2453. For a thorough analysis of U.S. relations with the Federal Republic see Thomas A. Schwartz, *America's Germany: John J. McCloy and the Federal Republic of Germany* (Cambridge: Harvard University Press, 1991); Wolfram F. Hanrieder, *West German Foreign Policy 1949–1963: International Pressure and Domestic Response* (Stanford, CA: Stanford University Press, 1967); Hans W. Gatzke, *Germany and the United States: A "Special Relationship"?* (Cambrdige: Harvard University Press, 1980); Wolfram F. Hanrieder, *Germany, America, Europe: Forty Years of German Foreign Policy* (New Haven, CT: Yale University Press, 1989).

38. Hanrieder, *West Germany Foreign Policy*. 127n; see also Letter, Conant to Merchant, 25 April 1955, in *Foreign Relations of the United States*, 1955–1957 (Washington, DC: U.S. Government Printing Office, 1988), 5: 148. Hereafter cited as FRUS with the year, volume, and page number.

39. Telegram, Dulles to HICOG Bonn, 6 June 1953, Ann Whitman/International Series, Box 13, Germany 1953 (5), DDE/L.

40. Adenauer's personal view on reunification is debateable. See Schwartz, *America's Germany*; Hanrieder, *West German Foreign Policy*; Hanrieder, *Germany, America, Europe*.

41. Schwartz, *America's Germany*, 291; Wladyslaw W. Kulski, *Germany and Poland: From War to Peaceful Relations* (Syracuse, NY: Syracuse University Press, 1976), 108.

42. Memo, Fuller to Bowie, 5 January 1954, in FRUS, 1952–1954, 7, pt. 1: 733–740; for an analysis of the German question at these conferences, see Hanrieder,

West German Foreign Policy; Schwartz, *America's Germany*; Manfred Jonas, *The United States and Germany: A Diplomatic History* (Ithaca, NY: Cornell University Press, 1984); Gatzke, *Germany and the United States.*

43. Memorandum on German Policy Paper, 4 August 1953, White House Office of Special Assistant for National Security Affairs: Records 1952-61, NSC Series, Policy Papers Subseries, Box 6, DDE/L.

44. Position Paper re Germany (NSC 160/1), 17 August 1953, in White House Office of the Special Assistant for National Security Affairs, NSC Series, Policy Papers Subseries, Box 6, DDE/L.

45. This fear had been expressed when Acheson presented a review of the world situation to the Senate Foreign Relations Committee in 1950–1951.

46. Memorandum of Conversation, 396.1/7-2653 [*sic*] in FRUS, 1952–1954, 7: 634–638.

47. Kulski, *Germany and Poland*, 101; Wiskemann, *Germany's Eastern Neighbours,* 184, 207; Wiskemann analyzes the refugee organizations in Chapters 19 and 20; German domestic politics is analyzed in Karl W. Deutsch and Lewis J. Edinger, *Germany Rejoins the Powers: Mass Opinion, Interest Groups, and Elites in Contemporary German Foreign Policy* (Stanford, CA: Stanford University Press, 1959).

48. U.S. President, *Public Papers of the President of the United States* (Washington, DC: Office of the *Federal Register*, National Archives and Records Service, 1956), Dwight D. Eisenhower, 1953, 13–14. Hanson W. Baldwin, in "Eisenhower Bests Reds," *New York Times*, 4 February 1953, 4, stated that this could "be applied" to the territorial provisions of Yalta and Potsdam. The *New York Times* correspondent noted, however, that, "the force of his words is primarily psychological and moral." "Conant Pledges Bonn a Voice on Treaty Fixing," *New York_Times*, 13 February 1953, 1.

49. The area around Königsberg was to remain in Soviet control. Despatch 2528, Swope to Department of State, 24 February 1953, RG59, 648.6213/2-2453.

50. Ibid.

51. Despatch 168, American Consulate General Bremen to Department of State, 4 March 1954, RG59, 611.62A/3-454.

52. Despatch from Harvey, "The Question of the German Eastern Territories and Chancellor Adenauer's Condominium Proposal," 5 October 1953, RG84, 1953 Territorial Boundaries File, Box 19, DS/NAS. In June 1952 a public opinion poll showed that 85 percent of West Germans believed that the eastern territories belonged to Germany. About 61 percent said they were confident that Germany would recover the area, but only 24 percent advocated the use of force to recover the lost territories.

53. Ibid. Harvey suggested that Adenauer's statement "may have been intended partly to mitigate the effect abroad of the rising clamor of the refugee groups." Wiskemann claims that one of the major leaders of the expellees, Dr. Hans Lukaschek "welcomed it as indicating a move towards something like the conception of the League of Nations regime in Upper Silesia from 1922 to 1937." Wiskemann, *Germany's Eastern Neighbours*, 206.

54. "Adenauer Expects Army Pact in 1953," *New York Times*, 9 September 1953, 6.

55. Harvey, "The Question of the German," 5 October 1953, RG84, Box 19.

56. Ibid. Harvey commented that Braeutigam's remarks seemed to indicate that "serious work is proceeding on a position to be taken" on Germany's eastern territories. Wiskemann, *Germany's Eastern Neighbours*, 206ff.

57. Memorandum of Conversation, Von Kessel and Lyon, 18 January 1955, RG59, 648.62A/1-1855.

58. Memorandum for the Record, Lister to Lyon, Thurston, and Vedeler, 24 January 1955, RG59, 648.62A/1-1855.

59. Memorandum of Conversation, von Kessel and Lyon, 24 January 1955, RG59.

60. Despatch 394, Flack to Department of State, 24 March 1955, RG59, 748.022/3-2455.

61. Ibid.

62. Despatch 839, Henry to Department of State, 26 April 1955, RG59, 762C.022/4-2655.

63. Despatch 816, Barnes to Department of State, 31 March 1953, RG59, 762B.563/3-3153.

64. Ibid.

65. Despatch 841, Barnes to Department of State, 8 April 1953, RG59, 762B.563/4-853.

66. Despatch 394, Flack to Department, 748.022/3-2455.

67. Despatch 27, O'Shaughnessy to Department of State, 7 July 1955, RG59, 762.022/7-755.

68. Ibid.

69. "Memorandum Relative to the Big Four Conference in Geneva Presented to the State Department on Wednesday, July 6, 1955 by the Polish American Congress, the Spokesman for 6,000,000 Americans of Polish Descent," in Zablocki Papers, Box 169, Marquette University Library, Milwaukee, Wisconsin.

70. *Congressional Record Appendix*, 84th Cong., 1st sess., 101, pt. 15 (12 May 1955): A3263–A3264.

71. *Congressional Record Appendix*, 84th Cong., 1st sess., 101, pt. 16 (7 July 1955): A4959–A4960.

72. *Congressional Record*, 84th Cong., 1st sess., 101, pt. 8 (11 July 1955): 10271–10273.

73. "Delegation Record of the Second Plenary Session of the Geneva Conference, 18 July 1955," in FRUS, 1955–1957, 5: 370; Wandycz, *The United States*, 350. In spite of this, the Geneva Conference was seen to open the way to increased East–West understanding.

74. The handwritten note was unsigned but was probably written by Beam since the memo was directed only to him; Memo, Stoessel to Beam, 3 September 1955, RG59, 748.022/9-355.

75. Despatch 2098, Harvey to Department of State, 29 January 1954, RG59, 762C.00/1-2954. An Associated Press (AP) correspondent reported in December 1954 that Warsaw had drawn up a plan with the German Red Cross to allow the remaining Germans in Poland to leave by 1956. See "Poland to Allow Bonn to Regain 100,000 Germans," *Christian Science Monitor*, 20 December 1954, 6.

76. Ibid.

77. Despatch 2560, Harvey to Department of State, 22 March 1954, RG59, 762C.00/3-2254.

78. Despatch 819, HICOG Bonn (unsigned) to Department of State, 15 October 1954, RG59, 748.022/10-1554.

79. Despatch 39, O'Shaughnessy to Department of State, 11 July 1955, RG59, 762C.022/9-1155.

80. Ibid.

81. Telegram 9, Parkman to Secretary of State, 5 July 1955, RG59, 762C.022/7-555; Telegram 20, Parkman to Secretary of State, 7 July 1955, RG59, 762C.022/7-755.

82. Outgoing Telegram 98, Dulles to American Embassy Warsaw, 6 October 1955, RG59, 748.08/10-655.

83. Telegram 226, Jacobs to Secretary of State, 11 October 1955, RG59, 748.08/10-1155.

84. Kulski, *Germany and Poland*, 112; Kulski suggests that the "Polish initiative must have been taken in concert with Moscow, since it was taken prior to the October 1956 crisis in Polish–Soviet relations."

85. Clifton Daniel, "Moscow Rejects the Reservations Adenauer Filed," *New York Times*, 16 September 1955, 1. See also Letter, Dulles to Byrnes, 6 October 1955, RG59, 648.613/9-1655.

86. Kulski, *Germany and Poland,* 112.

87. Despatch 497, American Embassy Warsaw to Department of State, 16 June 1955, RG59, 748.022/6-1655. The U.S. official also reported that a Catholic deputy of the Sejm discounted the idea that such a deal would be made. See also Despatch 503, Johnson to Department of State, 26 June 1956, RG59, 648.62A/6-2656.

88. The so-called Hallstein Doctrine, announced by Adenauer to the Bundestag on 22 September 1955 after relations with Moscow were reestablished, claimed that the Federal Republic would punish with various means, including the severance of diplomatic relations, any third-party state that established diplomatic relations with the German Democratic Republic. When Yugoslavia put this to the test in 1957, the Federal Republic broke off relations with Belgrade.

89. Kulski, *Germany and Poland*, 112.

90. Ibid.

91. Despatch 503, Johnson to Department of State, 26 June 1956, RG59, 648.62A/6-2656.

92. Ibid.

93. "Position of the Polish Western Association of America with Reference to Polish Western Borders," letter in author's possession, June 1956.

94. *Congressional Record Appendix*, 84th Cong., 2nd sess., 102 (11 June 1956): A4673–A4674; 84th Cong., 2nd sess., 102 (2 July 1956): A5198.

95. *Congressional Record*, 84th Cong., 2nd sess., 102, pt. 6 (30 April 1956): 7304–7305.

96. Henry Roberts, *Russia and America: Dangers and Prospects* (New York: Mentor Books, 1956), xiv–xvi. The book was first published under the auspices of the

Council on Foreign Relations by Harper and Brothers.

97. M. S. Handler, "Germans Ponder M'Cloy Remarks," *New York Times*, 3 June 1956, 33.

98. Ibid.; J. Emlyn Williams, "West Germany Ponders Polish Ties," *Christian Science Monitor*, 19 May 1956, 1. Premier Cyrankiewicz in a televised interview with a United Press correspondent in Paris stated, "Even in Western Germany" people were beginning to realize the need to approach the Oder–Neisse issue realistically. Reported in Despatch 58, Symans to Department of State, 6 August 1956, RG59, 748.13/8-656.

99. Williams, "West Germany Ponders," Ambassador Conant reported on 14 October 1956 that Bundestag Vice President Carlo Schmid's Social Democratic Party (SPD) statement calling for "'mutual concessions'" from Germans and Poles to settle the border issue "brought a sharp reaction" from the Association of Expelled Germans and the union of Landsmannschaften. See Telegram 1388, Conant to Secretary of State, 14 October 1956, RG59, 762C.022/10-1056.

100. Public discussion of the Oder–Neisse issue in West Germany was also stimulated around the same time by a statement that Nikolai Bulganin made on 25 July 1956 in Katowice that Poland's western border was permanent. Adenauer responded, and von Brentano issued a public statement published in the *Hannoversche Allgemeine Zeitung* and the *Rhein-Neckar Zeitung*. See Despatch 259, O'Shaughnessy to Department of State, 10 August 1956, RG59, 762C.022/8-1056.

101. Wiskemann, *Germany's Eastern Neighbours,* 294.

102. Despatch 259, O'Shaughnessy to Department of State, 10 August 1956, RG59, 762C.022/8-1056.

103. Despatch 342, O'Shaughnessy to Department of State, 27 August 1956, RG59, 762C.022/8-2756.

104. Wandycz states that Western propaganda into Poland was actually increased at this time as the Free Europe Committee launched leaflets carried by balloons after Western radio broadcasts were jammed in the satellites. See Wandycz, *The United States*, 350, 352.

105. "Appraisal of Four-Power Conference at Geneva," *Department of State Bulletin*, 33, no. 841 (8 August 1955): 218–219.

106. Despatch 66, Oechsner to Department of State, 31 August 1955, RG59, 648.00/8-3155.

107. Ibid.

108. Instruction A-199, Dulles to American Embassy, Warsaw, 28 March 1956, RG59, 611.48/3-2856. Dulles refers to Despatch 76 of 12 September 1955, Despatch 238 of 10 January 1956, and an unnumbered report of a conversation with Noble on 30 December 1955, not in the writer's possession. Dulles' qualifying comments, though, suggest that the embassy officers who recorded the dispatches agreed to a certain extent with Noble's view of the situation.

109. Ibid. Another disagreement that Dulles had with Noble was his idea to soften *Voice of* America (VOA) and BBC broadcasts into Poland.

110. Ibid.

111. Telegram 845, Jacobs to Secretary of State, 18 May 1956, RG59, 611.48/5-1856.

112. Telegram 846, Jacobs to Secretary of State, 18 May 1956, RG59,

611.48/5-1856.

113. Telegram 891, Jacobs to Secretary of State, 30 May 1956, RG59, 611.48/5-2956.

114. Ibid.

115. Wandycz, *The United States*, 354.

116. "U.S. Concern for Welfare of Polish People: Statement by Lincoln White," *Department of State Bulletin,* 35, no. 889 (9 July 1956): 55.

117. For a thorough analysis of these events, see Zbigniew K. Brzezinski, *The Soviet Bloc: Unity and Conflict*, rev. and enl. (Cambridge: Harvard University Press, 1969), 239–268.

118. Wandycz, *The United States*, 356–357.

119. Ibid., 359.

120. On October 26 Jacobs reported a conversation between Winiewicz and Eric Johnston, an American businessman involved in film export, in which Winiewicz reiterated that Poland would remain securely in the socialist camp with a strong Soviet alliance and wanting three things from the U.S. government: to stop the balloon propaganda, normalize trade relations, and increase cultural and scientific exchanges. Telegram 538, Jacobs to Secretary of State, 26 October 1956, RG59, 611.48/10-2656. Although the question of economic aid overrode concerns about the Oder–Neisse Line issue in U.S.–Polish talks during these final months of Eisenhowers first term, negotiations between Warsaw and Moscow reportedly included Gomułka's search for a Soviet guarantee of Poland's western border. See Telegram 562, Jacobs to Secretary of State, 29 October 1956, RG59, 611.48/10-2956; Telegram 1216, Bohlen to Secretary of State, 15 November 1956, RG59, 748.11/11-1556 HBS; Telegram 1230, Bohlen to Secretary of State, 16 November 1956, RG59, 748.11/11-1656.

6 The Impact of the "Polish October"

The State Department was more actively involved with the Oder–Neisse issue during Eisenhower's second term than during his first. Washington initially enjoyed very friendly relations with Bonn but endured tense relations with Warsaw. In 1957 a plebiscite returned the Saar area to German control, and the subsequent French–German rapprochement opened the way for the European Economic Community of West European states. As Cold War tensions eased somewhat in the late 1950s, relationships began to shift. Differences between the United States and West Germany over the resolution of the German problem became evident. Bonn, with a political eye on the expellee groups, grew suspicious of Washington's intentions regarding reunification, while Warsaw, experiencing increased maneuverability in taking its own "road to socialism," developed broader contacts with the West. The State Department began vigorously pursuing the idea of urging Bonn to recognize the Oder–Neisse Line, one of the primary obstacles to the establishment of diplomatic relations between Poland and West Germany. Although this idea did not reach fruition during the Eisenhower presidency, it reflects the changing perceptions of the Polish situation held by some members of the American foreign policy community.

THE "POLISH OCTOBER"

The "Polish October" brought real changes to the Polish people in many areas. The Warsaw regime curtailed the overt activities of the secret police, abandoned collectivization, acknowledged the Catholic Church, and sought ties with the West in both cultural and economic areas.[1] In January 1957 Deputy Undersecretary of State Robert Murphy responded to an "urgent invitation" from Polish Ambassador Romuald Spasowski to meet with Deputy Foreign Minister Jozef Winiewicz to discuss issues of concern in Poland including the security of Gomułka's position, the place of the Catholic Church, and the state of the economy. Murphy noted that "their manifest eagerness to demonstrate a desire for close association between the present Polish Government and the United States was so pronounced as to be almost embarrassing."[2] In the course of their conversation with Murphy, the Poles spoke very frankly about the "extensive" and "covert" control that "the Soviets exercised . . . through Party channels" in Poland. Winiewicz told Murphy that while Gomułka had been imprisoned, he had been given no reading material except the works of Stalin, and thus when he was released from prison, he was "ignorant of practically every major event that had happened since his original incarceration." The deputy foreign minister pointed out that this was a great handicap for Gomułka but one that he was able to overcome rapidly. The Poles expressed hope that lasting progress could continue as it had since the "'October revolution,'" especially in light of the "anxieties, suspicions, and internal difficulties" hampering the Soviet leadership.[3] By the end of the meeting, Murphy concluded that both Winiewicz and Spasowski, "by implication, innuendo and reference," conveyed the idea that they were "patriotic Poles" rather than "communists at heart." Their main hope, according to Murphy, was that the Soviets would not contrive a situation that would permit them to intervene forcibly in Poland.[4] As Winiewicz tried to distance Poland from Soviet control, he focused mainly on the issue of economic aid, even though he was aware that Washington's main incentive for such aid was to loosen Moscow's hold on Warsaw. He expressed hope that Poland could exchange coal for American grains, cotton, and coal-mining equipment if the Soviet Union did not interfere. Winiewicz praised Ambassador Jacobs' handling of a difficult situation in Warsaw and offered no criticisms of U.S. policy toward Poland.[5]

WEST GERMAN OPINION ON THE BORDER ISSUE

American officials were aware that the situation in the Soviet satellite states was also of great interest to West Germany. Foreign Minister Heinrich von Brentano recognized that the satellites were beginning to experience the "stirring of the forces of freedom" but cautioned against expecting too much of the Soviet Union. His pronouncements, however, show that Washington should not have expected great changes in Bonn's position either, largely because of the political situation. In a speech before the Bundestag on 31 January 1957, the foreign minister reiterated that the Federal Republic sought to restore the borders of 1937 and have them confirmed in a peace treaty. He added, though, that the German government and people, including the expellees, recognized that the matter had to be settled through negotiations rather than by force. He contended that Germans were willing to make concessions to obtain unification but warned that concessions must "'not be in the direction of a diminution or endangering of freedom, justice or security.'"[6] When reporting the speech to Washington, the American Embassy at Bonn stated that this was the "clearest statement of the Federal Republic's position on this matter that the Embassy has seen."[7] It also showed how far apart the Federal Republic of Germany and Poland still were on the border issue.[8]

Although Bonn officially maintained the position of nonrecognition of Poland's western border, American representatives in Germany occasionally noted that German officials sometimes expressed divergent views.[9] The American consul general in Hamburg reported that on 21 January 1957 Hamburg's Mayor and Bundesrat President Dr. Kurt Sieveking delivered an address about German foreign policy with the cautionary note that his remarks should be interpreted as his personal views, not as official policy. He favored establishing diplomatic relations with Poland in order to settle outstanding problems, including the border question. Unlike von Brentano, Sieveking "strongly implied" that German concessions to Poland, including recognition of the Oder–Neisse Line, would be necessary.[10] Hamburg's representative in Bonn disavowed the mayor's address, claiming that it in no way weakened the Federal Republic's legal claim to the area.[11] U.S. Consul General Edward Meney pointed out that these protests were much stronger and more widespread than those arising from similar proposals made by McCloy and von Brentano in 1956, even though Meney thought that Sieveking's was a "careful speech." He parenthetically added that members of the Federal Government, including von Brentano, had previously "distanced" themselves from some of Sieveking's remarks about establishing diplomatic relations with Poland. Meney predicted that the border issue would continue to be an "extremely sensitive one" and claimed that Sieveking's address represented his "naiveté and lack of political consciousness" because he believed that he could address the press as a private citizen rather than as a governmental representative.[12]

West German perceptions of the border question did not go unnoticed in East Germany or Poland. Bernard Guffler at the U.S. mission in Berlin informed the secretary that the Foreign Ministry of the German Democratic Republic (GDR) had issued a statement on 5 February 1957 asserting that the border had been fixed at Potsdam and that the East German government considered the issue closed. The East German statement claimed that the Western dialogue about the border was simply an attempt to sow discord among Poland, East Germany, and the Soviet Union. The statement also denied a 29 January *New York Times* article claiming that East German officials had told Polish officials that their attitude toward the border could be affected by current developments in Poland. In commenting on the statement, Guffler contended that the most interesting aspect of it was that the East German government felt compelled to issue a statement regarding the border, suggesting that this could reflect the "sensitivity" of the East German government regarding relations with Poland as well as a desire to forestall discussion of the border issue among the East German people.

In April the first secretary of the Warsaw Embassy, Richard Johnson, informed the State Department that Foreign Minister Adam Rapacki had expressed to the Sejm a "certain degree of interest" in establishing normal relations with the Federal Republic of Germany, differentiating between the minority of Germans who wanted to "distract Polish alertness" and the majority sincerely interested in establishing relations with Poland. He called for a "more active Polish policy" in that direction.[13] The distinction that Rapacki made between the majority of West Germans who favored closer relations with the East bloc and the small number who opposed ties to Poland would be made again and again in the coming years as the question of diplomatic recognition was considered. Polish officials seemed to be challenging the West German public and politicians to confront the revanchist West Germans who obstructed the formation of better relations with the East, a challenge not accepted until the 1960s.

A DEBATE IN THE U.S. CONGRESS

The U.S. Congress also continued to address the situation in Poland, again focusing on the question of economic aid to Poland.[14] In February 1957 Thomas Gordon (D-IL) read into the *Congressional Record* a Polish American Congress resolution urging U.S. recognition of the Oder–Neisse Line to "bolster the faith of the enslaved nations," to dispel the fear of German militarism, and to recognize Poland's right to compensation from Germany.[15] Congressional discussion about the border reached a peak in a debate between Representatives Reece (R-TN) and Machrowicz (D-MI).

On 16 May 1957 Carroll Reece spoke about the Oder–Neisse Line and its impact on the Germans expelled from the area. Condemning the expulsion of the Germans as genocide and a violation of their right to self-determination, Reece repeated the claims that the lands were vital to Germany's food production and that the Polish government was not able to settle the area fully. The congressman, reviewing the history of the area, contended that the border violated international law and was the result of a unilateral Soviet act that kept Poland securely tied to the Kremlin. Reece claimed that the real test of so-called Polish independence would be to renounce claims to the territory and voluntarily withdraw from the "illegally occupied area of Germany." Only that step, he said, would free Poland from "political servitude" to Moscow. Washington, he warned, must not fall into Moscow's trap of compromising tenets of international law at the risk of violating principles of freedom and justice. He advocated a solution similar to the resolution of the Saar problem where the French agreed to the reunification of the area with Germany in return for a profitable economic treaty.[16]

Thaddeus Machrowicz responded to Reece's comments on 15 August 1957, calling them "distorted" and therefore "dangerously misleading in . . . [their] conclusions." Machrowicz pointed out that Reece had failed to focus on the barbarities of the Nazis in Poland and had misinterpreted the Allied decisions of World War II. He repeated the claim that the Allied leaders at Potsdam had established the line with the intention of making it permanent, as evidenced by their recognition of the necessity of removing the German population from the area. Machrowicz denied Reece's contention that the area was Germany's breadbasket by citing statistics about the food production in the territories while under German and Polish control. He agreed with Reece's assessment that without Germany's eastern provinces the Federal Republic had to import about 40 percent of its foodstuffs and pay for this with exports of manufactured products. Where Reece read the statistic as a warning of the competition that this represented for Western Europe and the United States, Machrowicz saw it as a natural adjustment of West Germany's booming economy and compared it favorably to Britain's food production. Machrowicz concluded by calling for Western recognition of the border in order to weaken the tie between Warsaw and Moscow and to gain the gratitude of the Soviet satellite states. He recognized the difficult situation and warned that "careless talk . . . might only nourish dangerous illusions in Germany. It could embolden the extremists among the Germans and distil the heady spirit of German nationalism which has cost the world so much."[17] Both congressmen acknowledged that the border issue tied Warsaw more securely to Moscow; their differences lay in their perceptions of the situation in the Oder–Neisse lands and in the solutions that they presented.[18]

This debate stimulated a great deal of discussion both in and out of Congress. John Lesinski (D-MI) rejected Reece's points on the floor of the House; two Polish American scholars published pamphlets responding to Reece's charges.[19] In May 1957 Thomas Gordon, as chairman of the Committee on Foreign Affairs, sent to the secretary of state a copy of House Resolution 248, written by Daniel Flood (D-PA), which dealt with "the sense of the House of Representatives with respect to the steps which should be taken by the United States to assist the people of Poland in their struggle for freedom."[20] The resolution recognized that Poles had made real gains toward freedom and independence and called on the United States to help secure further advantages by providing economic aid and relief. Regarding the border issue the resolution stated: "The United States should recognize Poland's western boundaries as established in the Potsdam agreement thereby bolstering the faith of the enslaved nations of Eastern Europe in American leadership, dispelling their fear that the revival of predatory militarism in Germany is being achieved with American help, and depriving Russia of her only claim for keeping Soviet troops in Poland."[21]

The State Department did not agree with this assessment. In a point-by-point analysis of the Resolution sent to Gordon on 4 June 1957, Assistant Secretary Robert C. Hill reiterated that U.S. policy concerning the border was based on the Yalta and Potsdam Declarations, which meant that the line awaited final confirmation at a peace conference. Hill stated that although efforts to obtain a peace agreement had so far failed, "we do not believe that the issue of the German–Polish boundary can be properly separated from the other diverse issues involved with a satisfactory peace settlement." He added that the State Department did not believe it possible to get an agreement on the border issue before a peace treaty was signed.[22] The State Department thus continued to maintain that the border was temporary pending a peace settlement and added a rider that would often be repeated during the next few years: no piecemeal settlement of problems concerning Germany should be expected. The author of the resolution, Daniel Flood (D-PA), often referred to the resolution during debates on U.S. aid to Poland, but the resolution itself did not receive much attention after it was returned from the State Department.[23]

In addition to his response to Reece, John Lesinski addressed the House of Representatives a number of times about the border issue, focusing upon Germany's relation to Poland in settling the issue. On 13 June he read an article from the News Letter of the Polish American Congress that again questioned the increasingly vocal German claims to the Oder–Neisse lands as vital to the recovery of West Germany. The author cited statistics offered by German scholars in the 1930s that refuted the "life or death" claims of those who said that the lands had to be returned to Germany.[24] The same day Lesinski read an article by Joseph Sanocki of the Polish American Congress of Hollywood, California, which appeared as the first issue of the newsletter entitled "Polish Western Territories." Sanocki also warned that a one-sided picture of the situation was being painted: German propaganda, especially from the expellee groups, was being readily accepted by the American public and government. He added that these revisionist demands came only from the expellee organizations. The German nation as a whole, he wrote, favored acceptance of the border, and he cited statements by various German leaders such as Sieveking and Martin Niemoeller that suggested that West Germany would accept the line. Like other Polish American spokesmen and Polish officials, Sanocki made a distinction between the expellee minority and the German majority when he contended that the German refugee organizations should be seen as a "conscious attempt" to disturb world peace.[25] He concluded by reiterating the number of years that Poland had owned each of the provinces in the western territories to show that the provinces were "in the hands of their rightful owners--the Poles."[26] The next week Lesinski repeated his call for Western recognition of the Oder–Neisse Line by reading into the *Record* a 22 June 1957 article from the *Polish American Journal* that used historical precedence to justify Polish ownership of the area.[27]

In the Senate, John Kennedy (D-MA) spoke extensively on 21 August 1957 about the inadequacies of U.S. policy in Poland and Eastern Europe. Although his address focused mainly on the question of economic aid to Poland, he concluded by pointing out that the Polish problem had to be considered within a wider European context, especially Poland's relations with Germany. Although he generally supported U.S. policies in Germany, he wanted Adenauer to follow up on his public expression of willingness to establish relations with Poland. Kennedy stated further that he realized that this move would raise the collateral issue of Poland's western border, which, "perhaps more than any other, serves to create gravitational pulls in Poland toward Russia." He did not want the United States to circumvent the Potsdam provision and impose a border settlement; he favored a policy whereby the United States would encourage the "many reasonable voices" in West Germany that had expressed interest in finding an accommodation. He recognized that a settlement would be difficult but pointed to the high level of prosperity in West Germany as aiding the assimilation of a great majority of the expellees.

The senator added that the United States should avoid wherever possible "minor irritants which can be magnified into national affronts." Here he cited a recent State Department action regarding the issuance of passports to those persons born in the Oder–Neisse territories that angered Poles and played into Soviet hands. He explained that until 1957 Poland was designated as the country of origin for persons born in Breslau or Stettin (he did not use the Polish names for these cities). For "whatever the reason," Kennedy said, the State Department had changed that designation to "Germany—under Polish administration."[28] What the senator did not add here was the information that he had from the State Department explaining the change. This information included a letter that Kennedy had received in May 1957 from Ludwig Oberndorf, the managing editor of a German American newspaper in New York, complaining about the fact that Americans of German descent who had been born in the Oder–Neisse lands were forced to designate Poland as their country of origin. Kennedy communicated with the Passport Office of the State Department and was told by Director Frances Knight that although it presented a difficult situation, the State Department would be more accurate by changing its designation. In the future, Knight told Kennedy, persons born in the area would have passports showing their place of birth as "'Poland (under Polish administration) formerly Germany.'"[29]

Kennedy's remarks in Congress were supported by the Polish Western Association of America, which appreciated "whatever . . . [he] might say on the problem of the present Polish Western boundary."[30] The Polish government also appreciated Kennedy's speech; as with many of the speeches of American congressmen regarding Poland, Kennedy's was reported in the Polish press. Ambassador Beam commented in a telegram to Washington that the treatment accorded the speech reflected the Polish government's "clear satisfaction in having [a] prominent senator support" its view favoring closer relations between Poland and the United States.[31]

In addition to these addresses on the floor of the House and Senate, congressmen continued to receive letters from constituents interested in the border issue. As their predecessors had done, members of Congress often sought information from the State Department before they replied. Senator

Kennedy received a letter from a businessman in Buffalo, New York, urging that the Polish border issue be presented for settlement to the United Nations through the State Department. Kennedy innocuously replied that while he hoped to see a free and united Poland, the realities of the world situation made that unlikely in the near future. The senator did not address the UN issue.[32] On 21 August Representative William Bates (R-MA) forwarded to the State Department a letter from a constituent asking about the border situation, along with a request for information about the issue. A week later Acting Assistant Secretary for Congressional Relations John S. Hoghland II replied to Bates with the standard response that Potsdam had provisionally established the border and that it would not be proper or possible to obtain agreement on the issue prior to the peace conference.[33]

U.S.–POLISH RELATIONS

The State Department promptly replied to such requests for information but remained largely unaffected by this debate and discussion in Congress about the Oder–Neisse Line. Although U.S.–Polish relations began to improve, it can be attributed at this stage more to changes in the Polish government than to the actions of Congress or Polish American organizations. The State Department prepared a summary of "Talking Points" regarding U.S.–Polish relations for an Adenauer visit in May 1957, which stated that the Gomulka regime's empowerment was considered "the most important development in Western interests . . . behind [the] Iron Curtain since Tito's exclusion from [the] Soviet bloc." The authors of this summary stated that the State Department viewed the new Polish government as a "subversive influence in the bloc" that should be handled in "such a way as to enhance its effect." America's primary goal, they continued, was to "prevent [the] restoration of a Stalinist regime in Poland and to prevent a popular uprising which might lead to Soviet military intervention," not an easy task in the best of circumstances.[34] The Warsaw government effected some immediate changes by removing "anti-Gomulka (Stalinist)" Poles from positions of authority. The Polish Embassy in Washington responded to one of the irritants in U.S.–Polish relations by informing the State Department that it was urging Warsaw to treat Polish American tourists in Poland as Americans rather than as Polish nationals or "potential repatriates."[35]

Greater improvements in U.S.–Polish relations, however, continued to be hindered by Polish perceptions of American involvement with West Germany and the bad relations between Poland and the Federal Republic. Polish officials expressed concern about rumors that German Americans vocally opposed the border.[36] After a luncheon conversation with the Polish Ambassador to the United States Romauld Spasowski, Ambassador Beam reported to Deputy Undersecretary of State Robert Murphy that Spasowski had mentioned American Catholic opposition to Polish policy. According to

Spasowski, American Catholics of German descent were organizing a campaign under Cardinal Spellman's leadership to oppose any improvement in U.S.–Polish relations in order to keep alive German aspirations for a recovery of the Oder–Neisse territories. Beam did not put much stock in the report; he told Spasowski that he was kept well informed of such events and had not heard a hint of such a campaign. The ambassador was more critical in his report to Murphy, speculating that the Poles were probably "employing the German bogey" to excuse their own actions supporting Soviet foreign policies in Europe.[37]

The Poles also expressed concern about U.S. involvement in West Germany. In September 1957 Ambassador Beam informed the secretary of state that the Polish Agricultural Minister Edward Ochab, who was rumored to be in line for the premiership, had spent most of the time during their recent conversation discussing the "German problem." Ochab said that the Poles were disturbed about the recent trends in Germany toward increased militarism and revanchism and contended that the only possible alternatives resulting from this situation would be either overt German aggression or acceptance of the present frontiers. "He regretted," according to Beam, that "West Germans seemed to feel that [they] could count on US support." Beam reported that he based his reply on the current Western policy toward German reunification and European security and the "well-known US position on [the] frontiers." He pointed out to Ochab that Adenauer was on record as favoring a peaceful solution and emphasized that U.S. sympathy for Poland had been demonstrated in two world wars and in adherence to the United Nations' charter opposing aggression.[38]

In the same telegram Beam reported a conversation with Deputy Foreign Minister Winiewicz, who had continued the "anti-Adenauer theme" while the two men discussed recent American disarmament proposals outlined by Secretary Dulles. In analyzing these conversations, Beam reported that he was somewhat puzzled by the statements and speeches against Adenauer since they were "in some respects harmful [to] Polish foreign policy." He suggested that they might represent Polish reaction to German election rhetoric and/or might serve Gomulka's domestic program, especially his efforts to repopulate the western territories and to justify to the public his support for the Soviet Union as the only power to recognize Poland's western border. Beam closed with the observation that the up-coming Polish–Yugoslav negotiations would offer interesting reflections of the situation in Central Europe, a prediction that proved true.[39]

Gomulka and Cyrankiewicz traveled in September 1957, to Belgrade where Tito, under the watchful eye of U.S. Embassy officers in Belgrade, recognized the Oder–Neisse Line as Poland's frontier.[40] The consequences of Yugoslavia's endorsement of this border were made evident in October 1957 in a complicated series of diplomatic steps. According to Oliver Marcy, American chargè in Belgrade, Bonn had instructed the West German chargè in Belgrade to inform the Yugoslavian government that Bonn viewed the Yugoslav declaration as a "'grave' matter" that greatly hindered bilateral relations.[41] A few days later Belgrade compounded the gravity of the situation by recognizing East Germany, probably at Khrushchev's urging.[42] Bonn immediately imposed the Hallstein Doctrine sanction and broke off relations with Belgrade on 19 October 1957.

Relations between Warsaw and Bonn continued to worsen when the Adenauer government repeatedly rejected Gomulka's offer to establish relations with the Federal Republic without preconditions. American officials reported that the Poles had stiffened their attitude, although the limits of Warsaw's willingness to continue negotiations were unclear. Gomulka's government raised the stakes in the fall of 1957, when Warsaw informed Bonn that it would normalize relations only after the Federal Republic recognized the Oder–Neisse frontier as Poland's border. Subsequent pronouncements by Warsaw officials, however, suggest that the government would have been satisfied with a less definite proviso about the border as long as diplomatic relations were established.[43]

Relations between Bonn and Warsaw affected the relationship between Bonn and Washington, but officially ties between these two Western capitals remained strong as the leaders continued to reiterate the strength and unity of the alliance. Privately, however, the State Department expressed caution about being drawn into supporting publicly all of Chancellor Adenauer's objectives. When Adenauer was scheduled to meet Dulles and Eisenhower in May 1957 to discuss U.S.–German relations, a memorandum from C. Burke Elbrick, assistant secretary of state for European affairs, cautioned the secretary that the American Embassy in Bonn had learned that Adenauer would attempt to get U.S. agreement to issue a "'Potomac Charter,'" a statement of policies and principles about German reunification and European security.[44] Elbrick recommended that the president not be drawn into a discussion of such a charter and not hold out much encouragement until the State Department was able to review draft proposals of the idea.[45] Eisenhower and Adenauer held an amicable discussion, and they issued a joint declaration reaffirming their common goals.[46]

The American Embassy in Bonn also reported a conversation between Joseph Jaenicke, a West German press officer, and First Secretary of the Bonn Embassy David Linebaugh, in which Jaenicke claimed that since West Germany had settled most of its problems with its Western neighbors, the government could now turn its attention to problems in the East. He stated that most officials in the Foreign Office and in the government had not "thought through" Germany's eastern problems, as evidenced by von Brentano's confession that he did not know the "answer to a question involving Poland because he had not thought about the subject." This situation, Jaenicke said, was now changing, and the "higher echelons" were putting a "good deal of thought and discussion" into an Eastern policy.[47]

The focus of such discussion, Linebaugh reported, was the status of West German–Polish relations involving broader questions such as the Oder–

Neisse Line, German reunification, and U.S.–USSR disarmament policies. Jaenicke told Linebaugh that no decisions would be made before a new cabinet was formed in November and that there was still some disagreement about procedures since some Foreign Office officials preferred first to establish relations with one of Poland's neighbors, thereby avoiding the Oder–Neisse border issue. Jaenicke expressed skepticism about that prospect since relations with Poland were of primary importance to Bonn.[48] Speculation about the Poles' willingness to "finesse or leave aside" the border issue during negotiations to establish formal relations was evident when Jaenicke noted that Gomulka's recent speech had not included border recognition as a precondition to establishing relations with West Germany. The possibility for such negotiations was slight, however, as shown by Jaenicke's closing remarks. He contended that the extensive coverage in the West German press had led the Poles to grow overconfident about the strength of their bargaining position with an "anxious" West German government. As a result, he said, Bonn would "try to cool off the subject so far as public discussion is concerned in an effort to avoid the appearance of over-anxiety."[49]

Jaenicke's discussion touches on the many "contradictions and paradoxes" of West German foreign policy outlined by Wolfram Hanrieder in his 1989 work *Germany, America, Europe: Forty Years of German Foreign Policy*. As the West German government tried to formulate a policy for East Central Europe, it had to confront the reality of being a divided state striving for full sovereignty within an integrated Western Alliance. Bonn's eastern policy, according to Hanrieder, was "at its core a policy that reflected territorial aspirations" and was thus suspect by the Eastern states. In addition, Adenauer's political temperament kept him from pursuing an Eastern policy as actively as he pursued a Western one. This proclivity resulted in the Adenauer government's "being the protector of the status quo" with Bonn trying to hold as a "trump card," the Potsdam provision that Germany's borders would be settled at a final peace conference to be used when the issue of German reunification was to be addressed.[50]

Adenauer's imprecise stance was evident in an interview on CBS television on 22 September 1957, when he reiterated the pledge not to use force in recovering the border and offered some hope that a solution would be found:

> I have always said that we shall never make any war on account of the Oder–Neisse Line. But I can well imagine a development in which this [border] question would find a solution in a unified Europe. I have always stressed the right to the homeland, to the place where one was born. . . . one day this whole area—Upper Silesia and so on—will, in my opinion, have to be within the Coal and Steel Community, and also within the Common Market, and all of the political borders which we have today will more and more lose their importance. We will have to look patiently for a solution within the course of a general development.[51]

Once again the border issue resulted in an ironic rhetorical alignment. Adenauer's professed expectation that political borders would eventually become unimportant sounded very similar to Khrushchev's and Gomułka's pronouncements that borders would wither away once communism was established. In any case, his statement about a united Europe was a noncommittal generality, like many of his remarks about the Oder–Neisse border. Adenauer was evasive when asked directly whether West Germany would accept the Oder–Neisse Line if Warsaw granted Germans the right, in the chancellor's terms, "to return to the country from where they were expelled." He replied that recognition of the German right to a homeland combined with the integration of the area into a "higher economic system of order" might "initiate a development" that would lead to a solution to the border question.[52]

Elim O'Shaughnessy, the American Embassy counselor in Bonn, told Washington that a member of the Foreign Office in charge of satellite affairs had commented that Adenauer was speaking extemporaneously and that "as far as he is aware, the Chancellor's remarks . . . have no special significance and do not reflect any studies prepared in the Foreign Office." O'Shaughnessy reminded Washington, however, that when Adenauer had caused some excitement in 1953 by proposing in a press interview the establishment of a joint Polish–German condominium or United Nations control to settle the border issue, the Foreign Office had denied the accuracy of that report but privately confirmed to the embassy that German legal experts had been studying such possibilities. The counselor seemed to be warning the State Department that in spite of what the West German Foreign Office confirmed or denied publicly about Adenauer's speech, chances were good that his remarks had some validity.[53]

POLISH FOREIGN MINISTER RAPACKI'S VIEWS EXPRESSED

While the State Department assessed reports about Adenauer's pronouncements on the border, officials were also preparing for the visit of Poland's foreign minister, Adam Rapacki, who was to speak before the United Nations General Assembly. Ambassador Beam sent a personal, but classified, letter to Secretary Dulles on 17 September 1957 urging him to receive Rapacki and suggesting possible discussion topics. The letter also contained Beam's assessment of the foreign minister; he reported that Rapacki was a "remnant of the Socialist Party" who was hindered somewhat by "his need to live down his Western-oriented past."[54] In an interesting insight into the Polish foreign policy establishment, Beam speculated that Rapacki had more influence in the government as a Politburo member than in a Foreign Office controlled by a "clique of smart careerists" who generally settled conflicting foreign policy issues in favor of the Soviets. Accompanying Rapacki would be former Polish Ambassador to Washington, Jozef Winiewicz, who "makes a show of pro-Western sentiments but is tricky," according to Beam.[55]

Regarding the content of their potential discussion on German–Polish relations, Beam urged Dulles not "even to try to explain, much less apologize for Chancellor Adenauer whom most Poles profess to distrust." Instead, Beam suggested that Dulles urge the Poles to "see for themselves what is happening in Western Germany, from which they have been so long cut off."[56] He told the secretary of his conviction that the Poles sincerely desired to establish a neutral zone in Central Europe, especially if their security against Germany was guaranteed through "a general pact in which the U.S. would take part." He suggested that Dulles ask Rapacki directly what he thought of the situation in the Soviet Union and if he could provide information about the recent Polish–Yugoslav talks.[57]

Dulles replied to Beam on 1 October 1957 that State Department officials with whom he had conferred did not think it was a good time for him to meet with Rapacki. He felt that it would look too much as if Washington were making overtures to Warsaw at a time when economic negotiations needed to be conducted quietly. A meeting with the Polish foreign minister, Dulles wrote, would "bring U.S.–Polish relations too much into the public eye."[58] A few days later, though, Assistant Secretary Elbrick sent Dulles a memorandum suggesting that since Rapacki had initiated the request for a meeting, the secretary should meet with him.[59]

Elbrick's suggestion was apparently accepted, and Dulles met with Rapacki on 16 October 1957.[60] The Bureau of European Affairs prepared reports on possible items for discussion, one of which was the border question. A memorandum to the secretary reiterated that the U.S. position on the border issue was based on the Potsdam Agreement that final delimitation awaited a peace settlement.[61] In the course of the conversation Rapacki followed up on the disarmament issue that he had raised in his speech at the United Nations, emphasizing the importance to Polish foreign policy of the German question, especially West German rearmament: "The situation in respect to Germany is the criterion by which the average Polish citizen judges foreign policy in general. Thus, the danger of German remilitarization is the most important mortgage weighing on the relations between Poland and the West."[62] Rapacki said that Poland saw the disarmament issue as part of the dangerous question of German militarization that created not only an immediate threat to Poland but also a "political threat" by encouraging "revisionist tendencies in Germany." He again differentiated between the general German public and the vocal revisionist minority when he stated that while Poles realized that the majority of Germans favored good relations with Poland, they were also aware that the problem of German rearmament and the "lack of clarity" on the part of the West regarding the Oder–Neisse Line represented a potential incentive for the revival of militarism and revisionism. He offered insight into the West German political situation when he told Dulles of his talks with German Ambassador Pfleiderer, who had said that while "no serious German politician" thinks that a change in the border possible, the refugees certainly had an influence on the German government. Rapacki said that he thought that it would be better to be truthful about the situation since that would "prevent the fostering of dangerous illusions by the Germans."[63]

Dulles responded by recognizing that the German issue was of primary importance to Poland, especially after two world wars, and candidly told Rapacki that even though Washington and Bonn had a strong relationship, the United States was clearly aware of the importance of maintaining limits on Germany. The secretary then elaborated on the less publicized aspect of containment, which Wolfram Hanrieder later termed "Washington's . . . policy of double containment"—the policy of limiting Soviet power and restraining West Germany by tying it to international organizations and treaties. Dulles told Rapacki that the only way to control Germany was to make it a "living part of a whole dominated by peaceful elements" such as through the Brussels Treaty and NATO that sought to "render them [German forces] ineffective when acting by themselves." The secretary assured the foreign minister that while this integration plan did not find favor with the Soviets or with Rapacki himself, the "aims of Poland and the United States are the same although their methods may differ." When Rapacki expressed the view that Poland would suffer if German troops controlled French troops, Dulles admitted that such might be the case if it were not for the presence of American troops in Germany, "the best guarantee of peace for Poland." Although they disagreed on this final point, the talks in general were friendly, with Rapacki expressing satisfaction with the tenor of U.S.–Polish relations and the economic assistance offered to Poland during a transitional period when Poland was moving toward greater democracy.[64]

IMPROVED U.S.–POLISH RELATIONS

Dulles' admission to the Polish foreign minister of this "double containment" policy suggests a degree of frankness that the Poles could not have imagined a few years before. In spite of the personal friendship between Dulles and Adenauer, strains between Washington and Bonn combined with the openness of the "Polish October" began to have an impact on U.S. perceptions of the situation in East Central Europe. Although this altered perception did not result in Washington's expressing acceptance of the Oder–Neisse Line, the State Department continued to try to avoid offending the Poles with constant reiterations of the Potsdam Accord and by 1959 began actively to pursue a solution to the Oder–Neisse problem.

Improved relations between Washington and Warsaw were reflected in an analysis of Polish pronouncements regarding the United States, prepared by the State Department's Division of Research for the USSR and Eastern Europe. Thomas Larson, division chief, reported to Valdemar Johnson of the Office of Eastern European Affairs that, "on the whole, <u>official</u> criticism of the United

States or its policies have [*sic*] been couched in general terms, and there has been a tendency to avoid explicit identification of the US with the policies being criticized." He noted two exceptions, however. The first was a PZPR Central Committee statement on the fortieth anniversary of the Bolshevik Revolution, suggesting that the United States had profited from World War II while the USSR had suffered. The second was a statement by General E. Kuszko, deputy chief of the political board of the Polish army, claiming that "imperialist circles" in the United States and Western Europe were fomenting revisionist claims to recover the Oder–Neisse territories. Larson's recommendations for responding to the two statements again reveal the changing treatment accorded the border issue within the State Department. Larson suggested that during the current economic talks, American representatives object to statements about wartime profiteering by reminding the Polish officials that "Americans read the papers" and were upset by such accusations. Rather than respond to Kuszko's statement about American "revisionist" activities by reiterating U.S. border policy, Larson stated: "Because of the thorny and complicated nature of the problem of former German territories now under Polish administration, it may not be desirable to bring this quotation to the attention of members of the Polish delegation."[65]

This low-key approach to the border issue did not, however, mean a policy change, as was made evident about a week later. Ambassador Beam told the Department of State on 12 November 1957 that Warsaw Embassy officers were very interested in a Polish newspaper correspondent's conversation reported in a dispatch from the American Embassy in Bonn on 7 October 1957. The Polish correspondent had stated that "the officers of the American Embassy in Warsaw felt just as he did about the Oder–Neisse Line." Beam assured the secretary that officers of the Warsaw Embassy "avoid whenever possible discussing Poland's western frontier" but explained that when confronted with the issue, they cited the "official position that this frontier is to be determined in a future peace treaty, it being hoped that by that time agreement can be reached between Poland and a reunited Germany."[66]

Beam also pointed out that the Polish press paid great attention to "leading Polish-Americans" who publicly supported the Oder–Neisse Line. He noted: "Shrewd Poles have remarked that the Polish lobby in the United States, which may be more vocal than any similar pro-German group, would prevent the U.S. Government from accepting a boundary delimitation against Poland's will, especially in the light of increased sympathy for the present regime after the events of October 1956."[67] He went on to add that neutral diplomats in Warsaw had reportedly stated that West Germany should use the border issue as a bargaining tool "to make concessions in order to enlist a more understanding Polish attitude in the matter of German reunification."[68] Beam seemed to agree with the idea that since U.S. maneuverability on the border issue was limited by Polish American interest groups, Washington should support a West German effort to settle the problem. Thus, although Washington and the American

Embassy in Warsaw privately acknowledged that the U.S. position on the border issue hindered the development of better relations with Poland, the State Department was not yet ready for direct action since the German problem continued to be the focus of discussions and reports involving U.S.–Polish relations.

SPECULATION ON POLISH–WEST GERMAN RELATIONS

The NSC Planning Board prepared a top-secret policy statement on Germany in December 1957 that emphasized the importance of Germany in America's overall European policy. The Planning Board was optimistic about prospects for political stability in West Germany but added that the United States had to continue to reiterate its desire for German reunification in order to calm Bonn's fears that Washington and Moscow would make some type of agreement, perhaps on disarmament, without settling the reunification problem. The report contended that the cooling relations between Bonn and Moscow and the increasing flexibility of Bonn's relations with Eastern European states were advantageous to U.S. interests since the expansion of West German influence in East Europe would lead to looser ties between Moscow and the satellite states.

The wait-and-see policy of the United States regarding the Oder–Neisse Line was again reflected in this policy statement that noted that officials in the Federal Republic had hinted to the Western Allies that some kind of compromise solution to the border question was desirable. The NSC maintained that it would be "unwise" for the United States to "take a position on the boundary, at least until prospects for a settlement are more promising, because to do so would incur the ill will of either the Poles or the Germans, or both."[69] This policy statement confirmed that Washington would not take the initiative in settling the border issue but would continue to monitor relations between Bonn and Warsaw.

American governmental representatives expressed concern about the possibility of a powerful Germany outside of the Western Alliance. A memorandum of the 354th meeting of the NSC on 6 February 1958 clarified U.S. policy for Germany and its potential impact on East Central Europe. To begin the discussion, Secretary Dulles pointed out the similarity between Washington and Moscow's policy with respect to Germany. He stated that "after many private conversations with Soviet leaders" he believed that neither of the powers would or could accept an independent, unified Germany in Central Europe. His reasoning suggests again the American government's fear of an uncontrolled Germany when he stated: "We simply could not contemplate reunifying Germany and then turning it loose to exercise its tremendous potentialities in Central Europe." Although he praised the energy of the Germans and their ability to recover from the wartime devastation, he maintained that "the world could not risk another repetition of unlimited power." Dulles opposed the idea of German reunification as a policy "in and by itself" and emphasized instead the vital importance of the context within which Germany reunified. He summed up this delicate position by stating that the United States could not accept Soviet terms for reunification but at the same time had to try to "keep the Germans happy" until a suitable reunification plan was accepted.

George Allen, director of the U.S. Information Agency, raised the specter of a German–Soviet deal when he stated: "We would be faced with a terrible force, if Soviet Russia and Germany joined together."[70] The president replied flatly that a neutralized Germany would be Sovietized and contended that the best way to handle the German problem was to strengthen NATO with Germany as a member. This would, he added, perhaps "encourage the satellites to throw off the Russian yoke," pointing out again Washington's perceptions of the link between Germany and the states of East Central Europe.[71] The possibility of a neutral, unified Germany was dismissed here without being considered an option, but the State Department continued to express concern about such an eventuality.

This fear of a reunified Germany was echoed by Gomułka when Ambassador Beam reported a conversation that Gomułka had with a "high Polish source" in February 1958. The Polish leader reportedly expressed bewilderment at the West's attitude toward a post-Adenauer, economically powerful Germany since, he believed, some Germans in the Ministry of Defence showed unrepentant views similar to those in Germany in the 1930s. The "Eastern provinces," the Polish leader believed, would always give the Germans a cause for war, and he did not understand the West's support for German rearmament "unless they themselves are thinking in terms of war." He believed also that the United States was "particularly irresponsible" about the German situation but thought that it originated from a lack of understanding about the true impact of Hitler's occupation of Europe. According to the source, Gomułka saw both East and West Germans as equally untrustworthy, in spite of official East German policy. Gomułka's fears of Germany were described as "almost pathological" and shared by most Poles.[72] Ambassador Beam commented that the report of Gomułka's views rang true and was reiterated by Foreign Minister Rapacki's expressions of a "personal hatred of Germans." While this was an important point to keep in mind, Beam added, it was also important to note that the Polish government continued to express a "strong interest" in establishing better economic relations with both Germanys.[73]

The question remained, however, whether West Germany was willing to recognize the Polish government. Amory Houghton of the American Embassy in Paris reported on rumors that West Germany was planning to compromise with the Poles on the border issue. He told the secretary about an informal conversation between Etienne Manac'h, assistant director for Eastern European affairs in the French Ministry of Foreign Affairs and the Polish Embassy counselor in the presence of a U.S. Embassy officer. Manac'h acknowledged the Poles' concern for the Oder–Neisse border but stated his conviction that West German officials would be prepared to recognize the line if Germany were reunified. He claimed that there were signs indicating that the Federal Republic was ready to undertake a move within the framework of the Paris Accords to agree to discount the use of force as a means to rectify the border question.[74]

Houghton went on to report that when American Embassy personnel had questioned Manac'h, he stated that he had heard of the Paris Accords scheme from a French official who had recently traveled to Bonn, where the Germans "appeared to be giving serious consideration" to the border question. The French official added that while he recognized that the borders had to be finally settled at a Four-Power conference, he thought that it would "reassure" the Poles and increase Polish pressure on the Soviets if West Germany gave "some sign" to the Poles on a confidential basis that it "did not intend [to] make trouble" over the border issue.[75]

The Poles' eagerness to establish communication with the Federal Republic was confirmed informally in May 1958, when Dr. Marian Dobrosielski, first secretary of the Polish Embassy, took the opportunity at a cocktail party to discuss Polish–German relations with Ernest Ramsaur Jr. of the Office of German Affairs. Dobrosielski told Ramsaur that Poland was eager to establish diplomatic relations with West Germany. When asked about the border problem, Dobrosielski stated that while Poland could not publicly affirm that the Oder–Neisse issue was open to discussion, he believed that once normal relations were established, the governments could address it. The American Embassy officer added, however, that Dobrosielski also stated that he did not believe that there was much room for maneuverability on this issue since the area had suffered heavy destruction which had been partially repaired with Polish money. Dobrosielski also followed the Soviet line when he stated in response to Ramsaur's statement about the eastern territories that while Wilno and Lwów were "traditional Polish cities," little else in the region was Polish, and much of the land was "largely swampland."[76] In addition to discussing the border question, Dobrosielski dealt with the Polish fear of German remilitarization and emphasized the difficult position of Poland. He "seemed to be suggesting," Ramsaur noted, "that the West should give them the benefit of the doubt and make things easier for them." Dobrosielski requested a meeting with Ramsaur to discuss the German situation, but no definite meeting date was set.[77]

The possibility of the establishment of Polish–West German diplomatic relations was discussed further when Heinrich von Brentano met with Secretary Dulles and other State Department officials in June 1958 in Washington. In response to Dulles' question, von Brentano stated that he had been thinking about the situation for some time and added that the Cabinet and Bundestag would be discussing the question soon. He saw two "especially important" difficulties, however, in the Oder–Neisse border issue and the impact of recognition on other East bloc countries. Von Brentano was hopeful that the first problem could be handled fairly easily in the same manner which the Federal Republic had used to deal with recognition of the Soviet Union; that is, to exchange letters stating that the two powers agreed to disagree on the question.[78]

The West German foreign minister was less hopeful about the second problem since Poland had established diplomatic relations with East Germany. Von Brentano feared that if the Federal Republic granted recognition to Poland, other states might believe that Bonn was being inconsistent since it had broken relations with Yugoslavia after Tito recognized East Germany. He thought that this would lead states in the Middle and Far East to recognize East Germany and might cause the other Soviet satellite governments to push for Bonn's recognition. He was afraid that this whole process would hinder what little progress had been made toward German reunification. He thought it might be helpful, however, if the Federal Republic reassured Poland that no German government would try to readjust the border by force and urged that discussions between Bonn and Washington continue as long as Washington maintained the position that Bonn's recognition of Poland would not "prejudice" chances for German reunification.[79]

The Bundestag discussion to which von Brentano referred was held in mid-June and reported to Washington by First Secretary of the Bonn Embassy Harry Schwartz. Prior to the meeting of the Foreign Affairs Committee, the chairman assigned Freiherr zu Guttenberg of the Christian Social Union (CSU) to write a report for the committee on the question of West German recognition of Poland. Guttenberg stated that West Germany should not recognize Poland "primarily because of the problem of the Oder–Neisse line." Recognizing Poland would involve some recognition of the border, which, he claimed "would be impossible" for Bonn. He discounted the suggestion (mentioned by von Brentano to Dulles) that letters be exchanged between West Germany and Poland reserving recognition of the boundaries because, he said, once a West German ambassador was established in Warsaw, he would find it "almost impossible" to avoid "direct or indirect acknowledgement of the existence of the Oder–Neisse Line as a de facto boundary." Guttenberg argued further that West German recognition of Poland would only cause the Soviets to tighten their grip on Poland, would cause the Polish people to lose faith in West German condemnation of communist governments, and would lead other states in Asia, Africa, and the West to believe that the Federal Republic was renouncing reunification and accepting the status quo—including the Oder–Neisse Line and the German Democratic Republic.

The final point of Guttenberg's report was even more pessimistic, almost fatalistic when he rejected the idea that by establishing relations with Poland, the Federal Republic could directly calm the Poles' fear of a remilitarized West Germany:

The fears of the Poles cannot be removed this way. The only way in which the Poles' fear of Germany, the Poles [*sic*] feeling that Germany some day will take action to recover the German territories now under Polish rule would be, in fact, for a settlement to be reached righting the wrong done to Germany by rectifying the Oder–Neisse line thus eliminating the reason for the German pressure for change and the underlying cause of Polish fears. Pending rectification of the frontier nothing that we Germans or anyone else could say to the Poles can remove their worry or fear that Germany will some day do something about the Eastern territories.[80]

Since the Poles based much of their reasoning for retaining the Oder–Neisse lands on the grounds that they were historically Polish territories and that they somewhat compensated Poland for the wrongs done to Poland by Germany, Guttenberg's assertion that adjusting the border in Germany's favor would right "the wrong" done to Germany showed how far apart these two positions were. Most of the committee members concurred with Guttenberg's assertion that the time was not right for West German recognition of Poland, although a few believed that establishing relations would be helpful.[81]

Around the same time as the Bundestag was discussing the seemingly impossible task of normalizing relations with Poland, Polish officials in Washington continued to press American State Department representatives to urge West Germany to initiate diplomatic recognition of Poland, often with the stated objective of loosening Moscow's hold over Warsaw, a reason directly contradicting Guttenberg's assertion. At a reception at the Polish Embassy in Washington a representative of the Polish Press Agency pleaded to Valdemar Johnson of the Office of Eastern European Affairs for "discreet efforts" on the part of the United States to help Poland gain "limited independence" from the Soviet Union, especially by urging West Germany to establish relations with Poland.[82] The next day, Ambassador Spasowski reiterated to Jameson Parker of the Office of Public Affairs the Poles' desire to "regain their freedom and their association with the West, especially the United States, if this could be done gradually and without violence." Parker reported that while Spasowski had expressed the hope that West Germany would establish relations with Poland, he was extremely doubtful that it would happen because of the problem surrounding the border.[83]

The doubts voiced by the Polish ambassador about the border were echoing those of George Kennan, one of the early participants in discussions about the Oder–Neisse Line. Kennan, who had been in Warsaw to deliver a lecture at the Institute of International Affairs, sent to Central Intelligence Agency (CIA) Director Allen Dulles a memorandum summarizing his impressions of Poland. When he sent the memorandum to the White House, Dulles noted that although he did not agree with all of Kennan's views, these "keen" observations represented the "best summary . . . on the evolving situation there."[84] Kennan was impressed by how far Poland had moved from Marxist–Leninist principles and how freely the Polish intelligentsia spoke its beliefs and feelings favoring Western concepts over Soviet influences. At the same time, however, he believed that little possibility existed for this freedom to result in Poland's successfully pulling out of the Soviet communist orbit largely because Gomulka and his "convinced communists" did not share the intellectuals' pro-West orientation.[85] Kennan also noted two other factors tying Poland to the Soviet Union: the Warsaw Pact's guarantee of Soviet troops in Poland and the issue of Poland's western border. Kennan wrote: "Having abandoned hope for the recovery of the eastern regions lost to Russia, the Poles view their own retention of the areas taken from the Germans as a matter of life and death," that if the Oder–Neisse territories were given to Germany, Poland would cease to be a viable state. He added that the Poles were "extremely nervous" about the border because they recognized that the border settlement was an "unnatural and extreme one" that the Soviets had "lured" them into in order to make Poland dependent on the Soviet Union. Kennan contended that the Poles had to come to the realization that the "depressed state" of the area indicated that they were incapable of returning it to its former "populousness and prosperity," which was a "serious argument against the perpetuation of the present arrangement."[86]

Kennan also stated that the Poles recognized that no West German political party could accept the border situation and that only formal acceptance of the Oder–Neisse Line by "all important elements of German political life" could prevent the development of a "massive demand" in Germany for border revision. Since the Poles' future was closely tied to their past, they saw protection only in the "Russian orientation." "Those people were right," Kennan argued, "who saw in the new frontier settlement, in 1945, the creation of an anomaly which would mortgage Polish independence to the Russians for many years to come," a view that Kennan would reiterate in his future writings but that presented little direction for future policy.[87] He offered scant hope for improvement when he told Dulles that in the absence of Bonn's acceptance of the Oder–Neisse Line, the best that the West could hope for would be that the freedoms that Poles enjoyed would continue so long as any threat to them would be opposed. In light of this situation, Kennan suggested that American policy should attempt to increase cultural contacts and avoid policies designed to drive a wedge between Poland and the Soviet Union or to "make trouble" between the Polish regime and the population. Finally, he favored reducing international tensions that would then allow the Poles "to play something more resembling an independent role in international affairs."[88] Thus, although Kennan continued to maintain that the initial decision to establish Poland's border on the Oder–Neisse Line was an error, he consciously offered no guidance for changing the situation. Indeed, the direction that he favored for American policy in Poland sounded very similar to the Eisenhower administration's policy of promoting "evolution, not revolution." In spite of this rather pessimistic assessment and in the face of seemingly insurmountable differences, Warsaw refused to shut the door completely on the possibility of gaining West German recognition.

This was shown in the controversy surrounding a statement that Polish Deputy Defense Minister Zarzycki made at a demonstration marking the anniversary of Germany's invasion of Poland. Ambassador Bruce reported from Bonn on 5 September 1958 that the SPD, which had been the strongest advocate of Bonn–Warsaw relations, released a statement condemning as "unacceptable" Zarzycki's declaration that as a precondition to diplomatic recognition Bonn had to accept the Oder–Neisse Line. The SPD statement endorsed the Federal Government's position on the border and warned the Polish government that official endorsement of Zarzycki's statement would complicate an already difficult situation.[89] Either Zarzycki spoke without official backing or the SPD warning had an effect on the Polish government, since Ambassador Beam in Warsaw reported on 15 September 1958 that the Polish Press Agency had inserted an editorial note in its 4 September news bulletin to the effect that Zarzycki's "unauthorized sentence" regarding the border should be deleted from his speech. Beam also noted that *Trybuna Ludu* did not include the sentence in its account of Zarzycki's speech, even though it had an editorial critical of the SPD statement.[90]

According to Ambassador Bruce, the speech was also condemned in *Diplomatische Korrespondenz*, a "semi-official publication" prepared by the West German Foreign Office. An article appearing in the 9 September 1958 issue questioned how Zarzycki's reproaches of the Federal Republic's alleged intentions toward the Poles coincided with his advocacy of normalizing relations between West Germany and Poland. The article also contended that Zarzycki was "completely unrealistic" in setting this precondition since "'German people in all parts [of] Germany are in complete agreement'" that the boundaries of a united Germany could only be settled at a peace treaty and that no "'responsible'" German government could renounce the Oder–Neisse lands. When reporting the article, Bruce noted that the desk officer who had prepared it told him that there was increasing pressure for the establishment of some type of diplomatic relations between West Germany and the East bloc states and that statements such as Zarzycki's only hindered such a development.[91] Foreign Minister Rapacki condemned the SPD's statement supporting the government's position on the Oder–Neisse line in a speech that he gave in Wrocław as reported in *Neues Deutschland*, the Communist Party newspaper in East Germany. Howard Trivers, chief of the Eastern Affairs Section of the U.S. Mission in Berlin, reported to Washington that the *Neues Deutschland* article used the opportunity to confirm the policy of friendship between Poland and East Germany as based partly on East German recognition of the Oder–Neisse border. Trivers predicted that the East German regime would continue to exploit this policy as an advantage over the Federal Republic.[92]

In spite of these official condemnations in Bonn and Warsaw, the question of Polish–West German relations continued to occupy discussions between West German and U.S. officials. An NSC policy statement on Germany in September 1958 confirmed that the government and popular opinion in West Germany favored closer relations with the East, especially Poland. The policy statement contended that West Germany's strongly expressed sympathy for Polish efforts to gain more independence from the Soviet Union "tended to offset antipathy based on the Polish annexation of former German territory." The authors of the NSC document recognized, however, that no change in the border situation could be expected in the near future because of West Germany's fear that establishing relations with the satellites would hurt chances for German reunification.[93]

On 10 September 1958 the first secretary of the Bonn Embassy noted that Foreign Office representative Count von Baudissin, although not directly involved with satellite issues, had expressed his opinion that from a reunification standpoint the establishment of relations with Poland at that time would be a mistake since it would arouse Soviet suspicions and increase the importance of Soviet troops in East Germany. He contended that even if official diplomatic recognition were granted, the Oder–Neisse Line question would make relations tense. Von Baudissin felt that it might be possible sometime in the future to improve relations if the German public could accept the renunciation of the Oder–Neisse lands and if Poland supported a reunified Germany, but he held out little hope that such renunciation would come quickly in light of the political competition for the expellee votes.[94]

The counselor of the German Embassy in Washington, Rolf Pauls, also spoke about the issue of diplomatic recognition to Edward Freers, director of the Office of Eastern European Affairs, on 26 September 1958. Pauls informed Freers that the West German government was split on the issue with Adenauer and the CDU majority favoring caution, contending that trade and other "practical aspects" of Polish–West German relations would continue despite a lack of formal recognition. Pauls also confirmed that the issue had been further complicated by Polish Deputy Defense Minister Zarzycki's statement requiring acceptance of the Oder–Neisse Line as a precondition to diplomatic recognition. Pauls predicted that neither Gomulka nor Cyrankiewicz would repudiate this precondition, especially in light of Bonn's perception that Gomulka's precarious position would lead him to follow Soviet directives more closely.[95]

Counselor Pauls' contention was confirmed by the Warsaw Embassy in a memorandum of an alleged conversation between Gomułka and "an old Polish friend." In the course of the conversation Gomułka expressed confidence about his internal position but confirmed that he planned to travel to the Soviet Union to "play down the suspicions which the Russians had been showing towards him and his country."[96] Gomułka contended that suspicion was "part and parcel" of the Soviet nature, but he wanted to allay any distrust so he could continue his internal developments. He acknowledged that he had been "personally told off by Khrushchev on the telephone, although not recently," and recognized that "they were always on the lookout for some insult" from him or the Poles.[97] Khrushchev used the occasion of Gomułka's visit to issue an ultimatum to the

Western Allies questioning the efficacy of the Potsdam Accord and threatening to turn Berlin over to the East German government within six months unless a solution to the German problem were found. He warned that West German revisionists who coveted Poland's western lands were "playing with fire."[98] In a show of solidarity, Gomułka also made several statements about the United States and the German Federal Republic that were protested by American and West German officials.[99] At a press conference on 26 November 1958, Secretary Dulles pointed out that Allied obligations in Berlin did not derive from the Potsdam Agreement and suggested that if Khrushchev carried out his warning about nullifying part of the Potsdam Accords, Poland's territorial claims would be "greatly compromise[d]."[100]

The initial American response was not, however, as belligerent as Adenauer would have liked, with Secretary Dulles speaking about the possibility of the United States accepting East Germans as "agents" of the Soviet Union. By January 1959, though, Washington stiffened its position and implemented plans for military maneuvers. In that month the Soviets sent to Washington a draft peace treaty for Germany that recognized the existence of two Germanys whose borders would be those that existed on 1 January 1959. Germany was to renounce all claims to former German territories in the east along the line stated in the Potsdam Accord. At a news conference on 13 January 1959, Secretary Dulles said that the Soviet proposal represented an attempt to "isolate and segregate" the German people, which would only lead them to become "a restive and dangerous force" as after Versailles. He reiterated that the best way to deal with Germany was to integrate it as Adenauer favored, another oblique reference to the policy of "double containment."[101] On 16 February the United States responded to the Soviet note by stating that the numerous points of disagreement could better be dealt with at a foreign ministers conference. The Soviets agreed, and a meeting was set for May 1959.[102]

While the two superpowers were exchanging notes, State Department representatives continued to monitor the impact of the situation in East Central Europe. The counselor of the Bonn Embassy reported a discussion that he had had with the Polish desk officer in the West German Foreign Office who warned that the possibility of a rapprochement with Poland was further away than ever. He claimed that Gomułka's "attacks" on the Federal Republic, especially statements regarding West Germany's alleged revanchist policies in Eastern Europe, and Khrushchev's "anti-West German tirade" had "dulled and chilled" Bonn's desire for formal relations. The West German official held out little hope for improvement as he expected the "anti-German tirades" to become louder as Gomułka moved closer to the Kremlin in an attempt to "counteract the almost certain Polish popular objection" to closer ties between Warsaw and Moscow.[103]

Polish officials tried to repair the damage. Before he returned to Poland from a United Nations session, Deputy Foreign Minister Jozef

Winiewicz and Polish Ambassador Romuald Spasowski sought a meeting with Undersecretary Christian Herter in order to express the Polish government's "firm intention" of continuing to work toward improved relations with the United States. Herter pointed out to Winiewicz that while the U.S. government recognized the difficulties of the Polish situation, he believed that Gomulka's remarks in Moscow went "beyond the necessities required by current pressures and realities." Winiewicz confirmed that Polish policy continued to favor increased economic and cultural contacts with the United States, but he emphasized that such relations had to be considered within the context of Polish–Soviet relations and "the realities of the present international situation," especially the Polish view of Germany. Herter reassured Winiewicz that the Federal Republic was firmly tied to NATO, a not-so-subtle reference to the controls limiting potential independent West German action.[104]

A couple of days later Ambassador Spasowski spoke with Deputy Assistant Secretary Foy Kohler about U.S.–Polish relations and Gomułka's anti-American remarks. Like Herter, Kohler acknowledged the geopolitical limitations of Polish foreign policy and recognized that the United States would have differences with Poland over world events. He added, however, that because of the friendly nature of U.S.–Polish relations, the United States expected Polish statesmen to refrain from making "inaccurate and hostile statements" about the United States that only hindered a better understanding of Poland by the American public and Congress. Spasowski gave the same response that Winiewicz had given Herter, that the United States should consider Gomułka's statements within the context of international realities, including Polish–Soviet relations and the Polish fear of a rearmed Germany. The two men reiterated their governments' desire to continue friendly relations, but Kohler cryptically warned that it went against Poland's self-interest to "permit its alliance with the Soviet Union to exclude other opportunities which are available to it."[105]

In an alleged attempt to "make amends for Gomułka's attacks" on the United States, Polish delegates who had visited the United States earlier in the year gave a dinner for Ambassador Beam and other American Embassy officers. Beam reported that the Poles were very friendly and expressed no criticisms of the United States but verbalized deep concern about German rearmament. Winiewicz accepted the reassurances of American representatives but told Beam that "Germany's word [was] no good in Poland" and that other guarantees were required; he predicted that the German question would be much discussed within the next few months. Beam reported to the secretary of state that he interpreted Winiewicz's statements as "raising storm signals respecting impending developments" and also as a request for U.S. "forbearance."[106]

The next day Ambassador Beam sent a telegram to Washington noting a conversation that the Swiss ambassador had had with Rapacki and another member of the Polish Foreign Ministry. The Swiss ambassador told Beam that the Poles had explained that Poland would like to see the maintenance of two Germanys, perhaps in a confederation. They also dismissed Gomułka's anti-U.S. remarks as necessary for Polish–Soviet relations and told the Swiss ambassador that whatever Gomułka might feel about the East German government, he would not "tolerate" the elimination of a communist state on Poland's western border where Poland could exert some influence. When reporting the conversation, Ambassador Beam commented that the Poles appeared to be caught in a dilemma over fears about Germany and about the worsening Berlin situation.[107]

In discussions with American representatives, Polish officials bemoaned Gomulka's closer allegiance with Moscow. The counselor of the American Embassy in Djakarta, John Henderson, notified the State Department that a Polish Embassy officer had spoken with him at a diplomatic reception and apologetically referred to "'Comrade'" Gomulka as "slipping backward, perhaps irrevocably, into the hands of Moscow."[108] The Pole expressed dismay and confusion about the situation in Poland that contrasted so greatly with the freedoms allowed during the "Polish October." When Henderson pointed out Gomulka's difficult position in light of Soviet military strength, the Polish official recognized this but said that he was "greatly worried" about the upcoming Party Congress in Poland in March, where only "hand-picked, pro-Moscow delegates" would be in attendance, and the Polish people would have no voice. He simply hoped that the United States would encourage more East–West travel since the Poles who had visited West Germany were greatly impressed by the Western economic superiority.[109]

The NSC policy statement on Poland for 1959 confirmed that the worsening relations between Poland and West Germany served to strengthen the bond between Poland and the Soviet Union and to complicate U.S.–Polish relations. The policy statement noted that Poland's solution to the German problem was the same as that offered by the Soviets: a confederation of two neutral German states with the western territories as part of Poland. The NSC statement reiterated that while American officials had tried to emphasize that it was in Poland's best interest to have the Federal Republic of Germany closely tied to NATO, they had made little progress with the Poles because of the unsettled Oder–Neisse question and the continued remilitarization of West Germany. The policy statement recognized the complexity of the border problem, its impact on U.S.–West German relations, and the "fluid nature of these relations" but could not recommend a new policy position. The NSC contended that a new position on the border: "should not be formulated until it appears that serious negotiations on a German peace settlement will take place or that other developments, not excluding U.S. initiative, indicate an impending international discussion of this issue. In that event, high-level U.S. consideration should be given to the problem immediately."[110] In light of the proposed Soviet peace treaty and its rejection by the United States, as well as hard evidence about worsening Polish–West German relations and the strength of the Polish–Soviet ties, chances for "serious negotiation on a German peace settlement" were slim. Yet, the relatively softer wording of the NSC policy statement as well as diplomatic activities in the following few months suggest that the State Department was reevaluating its position on the border issue and that the diplomatic doors between Bonn and Warsaw were still not completely closed. The American Embassy in Bonn reported on a meeting that Adenauer held with CDU Bundestag representatives that confirmed that the Federal Republic hoped to improve relations with Poland and Czechoslovakia. The expressed conditions showed that West Germany's willingness to negotiate was limited, however. Adenauer continued to reject the use of force to change the borders but reiterated West Germany's stance that borders would be determined at a peace conference and that the right to a homeland as expressed in the UN Charter had to be upheld.[111] Dispatches from the Warsaw Embassy summarizing news articles in the early months of 1959 informed Washington that while the Polish press closely followed events in West Germany, editorials were not overly critical.[112] At the same time, U.S. officials and journalists saw evidence of a renewed campaign to increase support for Polish control of the western territories. On 4 March 1959 the *New York Times* reported that Warsaw had announced new incentives for the sale of land in the west at reduced rates and with tax cuts, contending that this represented an example of the Polish unease regarding the permanence of the border in light of the West's position and of Bonn's propaganda.[113] The Warsaw Embassy also reported in March that the Polish Press Agency had released a news story about a Los Angeles group calling itself the "Circle of Friends of the Polish Western Territories" that supported the further development of the area and wanted to "spread true information."[114]

The tense situation in Germany led Henry Kissinger, director of Harvard University's Center for International Affairs, to offer his analysis of the problem. In an 8 March 1959 *New York Times Magazine* article, Kissinger emphasized the importance of maintaining Western unity in the face of the Soviet threat. Along with the suggestion for a firmer, clearer stand on Berlin and measures to create Western cohesion, he recommended the creation of a concept of a "greater Europe" by cultural and scientific exchanges open to the Soviet satellites. He added that strategic measures could also be taken to support this concept, one of which was that NATO could give Poland a "military guarantee" of the Oder–Neisse Line as Poland's border to lessen Soviet control of Poland by eliminating the bogey of German revisionism. According to Kissinger, this idea "encountered very little opposition" when he discussed it during his visit to West Germany.[115]

The possibility of any such European peace settlement was of vital interest to the Polish American Congress and led the officers of the organization to seek an interview with State Department representatives to discuss it. On 16 March 1959 Charles Rozmarek and other PAC officials, including Congressman

Roman Pucinski (D-IL) and Charles Burke, met with Foy Kohler, deputy assistant secretary for European affairs, and Valdemar Johnson of the Office of Eastern European Affairs to present a resolution on the European situation. Although very low-key and orderly, the meeting stirred a great deal of controversy when it was reported in the Polish American press. The resolution called on the United States to negate the Soviet political advantage in Poland by recognizing the Oder–Neisse Line. The lack of such recognition, Rozmarek argued, gave the Soviets the opportunity to offer West Germany a "'deal'" at Poland's expense; recognition would quiet the "vociferous" German revanchists who threatened peace. Such a deal, the resolution argued, might involve withdrawal of Germany from NATO or a new military and/or economic Soviet–German pact in return for a border adjustment. The resolution reiterated the Congress' position that the Oder–Neisse land represented recovered territory for Poland and was not considered as compensation for land given to the Soviets and that the Potsdam Accord and the Allied acceptance of the removal of Germans from the area had indicated that the border was to be permanent.[116]

In his response Kohler reiterated that the U.S. government did not favor Soviet attempts to gain acceptance of the status quo in Eastern Europe, but he pointed out that the Oder–Neisse question was a very complicated problem. He told Rozmarek that if the United States gave approval for one aspect of the Potsdam Agreement, such as formal recognition of a provisional border, the Soviets could use to their advantage that recognition to justify other activities dealing with the accord. He said that the United States had to consider the Potsdam Agreement in its "global aspects" and pointed out the importance of a Polish–German rapprochement. The representatives then went on to discuss the possibility of opening reciprocal consulates in Poznan and Chicago, although no firm indication of U.S. intentions was given.

A couple of weeks after the Polish American Congress interview, astonishing articles appeared in the Polish American press claiming that the State Department favored recognition of the Oder–Neisse Line and that American officials believed only a small, unimportant minority in West Germany favored revision.[117] Also, the Downstate New York Division of the Polish American Congress formulated a resolution to the Committee on Foreign Relations that Jacob Javits (R-NY) read on the floor of the Senate voicing gratification for the "welcome stand adopted by the Department of State" favoring recognition of the Oder–Neisse Line.[118] Following up these reports, Richard Johnson and Valdemar Johnson of the Office of Eastern European Affairs met on 7 April 1959 with representatives of the Polish American Congress, Richard Mossin of the U.S. Information Agency (USIA), and the first secretary of the Polish Embassy. Mossin told Johnson that he had been among the press corps at the interview with the PAC delegates and confirmed that Rozmarek and Pucinski had indeed told the press that Kohler supported State Department recognition of the border with a few minor changes and had stated that only a small minority in West Germany opposed revision. Mossin emphasized that since such remarks were considered "'too good to be true'" by the reporters, they had checked the statements with Rozmarek and Pucinski before filing their stories.[119] After this interview, when Johnson explained to First Secretary of the Polish Embassy Edward Kmiecik that the articles "were highly inaccurate, containing both fabricated and distorted information," Kmiecik replied that this "confirmed the Embassy's impressions" of the stories.[120] On the same day Valdemar Johnson expressed to Charles Burke, Washington representative of the PAC, the department's concern about the articles that had appeared in Polish-language newspapers in the United States and in Europe. Burke assured Johnson that he greatly regretted any difficulties that the articles caused the department and explained that after the 16 March meeting the PAC delegates had been "besieged" by Polish-language press reporters. He believed that "the extemporaneous nature of remarks made by members of the delegation and their hurried conversion by the reporters into telephoned stories probably accounted for the inaccuracies and distortions." Burke emphasized that on matters such as this the Polish American Congress usually issued very carefully phrased press releases and assured Johnson that such inaccuracies would not happen again.[121]

While these press reports were embarrassing to the State Department, they did not cause any real difficulties for policymakers. Of greater concern were reports of the Third Party Congress in Warsaw, where Gomułka was securing his position at the expense of the freedoms that Poles had gained after October 1956.[122] On 10 April 1959 Ambassador Spasowski met with Robert Murphy and Valdemar Johnson to talk about his eyewitness impressions of the Party Congress. After discussing the economic situation in Poland and the generally good U.S.–Polish relations, Spasowski referred to the strong statements made at the congress about West Germany, especially about German rearmament and the possible revision of the Oder–Neisse Line. When he pointed out that none of the Western states had recognized the border and contended that such recognition would "do a great deal to ease Polish anxieties," Murphy replied only that the United States and Germany appreciated Poland's concerns about the German situation. Spasowski then asked whether such an acknowledgment might lead to recognition by West Germany of the Oder–Neisse border, and here Murphy, rather than giving the typical departmental response that final confirmation of the border awaited a peace treaty, told Spasowski that "he would not exclude this possibility." He said that the Germans had "learned a lot from World War II" and favored reduced tensions and a "constructive approach" to the problem. After discussing the Rapacki plan briefly, the ambassador returned to the border question by asking if the United States "could officially approve" the line. Murphy again deviated from the departmental reply that the United States could not accept a "piecemeal" solution to the German problem when he told Spasowski that "he could not answer that at this time but," the recorder noted, "he assured the

Ambassador that the question was receiving most careful attention in the Department." Spasowski was "pleased to hear this."[123] Murphy and Spasowski went on to discuss the harsh statements emitted at the Party Congress regarding the United States and agreed in closing that press inquiries about the meeting should be answered in general terms about the condition of U.S.–Polish relations.[124]

This conversation gives one of the first suggestions that Washington was actively pursuing a solution to the border question as part of the larger German problem. Spasowski's conversation with Foy Kohler on the same day, however, reveals that the United States expected something in return. During lunch Spasowski raised the border question in reference to President DeGaulle's statement on 25 March 1959 that he supported German reunification within its existing borders.[125] Kohler noted that they discussed the issue "at length," while Spasowski urged him to make a firm statement on the border. Although such a declaration was not forthcoming, Kohler, using more candor than was usual in such discussions, pointed out to the ambassador that "frankly . . . this was one of the few levers we had to press for a German settlement" and that the Poles should not expect the United States to surrender the advantage without making some "real progress." He pointed also to Bonn's rejection of the use of force to adjust the border as evidence of progress on the issue. When Kohler asked Spasowski about the eastern territories given to the Soviet Union, the ambassador "made a very good and logical case for the philosophical acceptance of the eastern frontiers as a closed matter." Kohler told the ambassador that he seemed to apply logic to the eastern matter but not to the western questions.[126]

The State Department also anticipated that the border issue would be raised at the Geneva Council of Foreign Ministers from May to August 1959. The Intelligence Research Bureau of the State Department prepared a candid report on the possible Soviet positions on various aspects of the border problem. The report clearly stated that although the Potsdam Accord had maintained that Germany's borders would be determined at a peace conference, the agreement allowed a "*de facto* extension" of Poland's borders westward. Since that time, the intelligence report claimed, the Soviets had acted with "sensitivity and vigor" and sometimes "belligerently" on border matters, presenting various positions like the one of January 1959 that favored the borders as they existed on 1 January 1959. The intelligence officers pointed out that this would approve the inclusion of Szczecin as Polish, a matter not definitely covered in the Potsdam Agreement. The report confirmed that recent "low-level, unauthorized reports" indicated that the Soviets were considering a border adjustment in East Germany's favor, but the authors considered unlikely "changes of any significance" since the complications affecting Poland and interbloc relations were too great. The authors cited a speech by Khrushchev in Leipzig proposing that present borders remain until the bloc countries reached full communist status at which time borders would become inconsequential and would probably disappear.[127] The border issue proved not, however, to be a high-priority item on the agenda of the Geneva meeting. Although the conference was supposed to address all aspects of the German issue, Berlin was the highlight. The Herter Plan, the Western response to Khrushchev's Berlin ultimatum, had been worked out with West German representatives, including a distrustful Adenauer, prior to the conference. It attempted to link reunification with disarmament and European security. As with previous gatherings of the foreign ministers, nothing much came of this meeting, but Khrushchev's six-month ultimatum passed quietly.[128]

When Ambassador Spasowski met with Foy Kohler on 22 May 1959 to discuss the Geneva meeting, he received more potentially encouraging words about the Oder–Neisse Line issue. The conversation turned to the border question after Spasowski referred to a 17 May 1959 *New York Times* article concerning West Germany's position on the issue.[129] The article by Sydney Gruson claimed that the West German government planned to present a statement reaffirming its position that the border issue would be settled only at a peace conference, largely in response to the January 1959 Soviet note claiming that the 1 January 1959 German borders should be considered final. Gruson openly declared that while the West was not inclined to change Germany's border, the current position was maintained for "bargaining purposes." He went on that while none of the West German political parties felt strong enough to oppose the expellees, neither did they believe any longer that border changes were possible.[130] Kohler told Spasowski that he thought the story in the *Times* was "probably premature" but added that the State Department had encouraged West Germany to "seek better relations" with Poland.

Spasowski then referred to his earlier conversation with Robert Murphy, who had told him that the State Department was actively pursuing the matter. Kohler affirmed this and pointed to the many declarations from Bonn denouncing the use of force to change the border. He read to Spasowski the 3 October 1954 declaration when West Germany entered NATO and disclaimed the "'recourse to force to achieve the reunification of Germany or the modification of the present boundaries'" of West Germany. When Spasowski pointed out that German officials had made several statements "contrary to the spirit" of this declaration, Kohler contended that such statements were made unofficially and should not be considered to have the same force as the 1954 declaration. Kohler closed the discussion by affirming that the United States considered official West German declarations to be "absolutely binding" and added the United States would demand the "complete observance" of the 1954 declaration. He assured Spasowski of the State Department's conviction that the Federal Republic would not use force to change the border.[131] During this discussion Kohler seemed to be assuring the ambassador that both Bonn and Washington were aware of the problem but was also indicating that Bonn had to take the peaceful initiative.

The Polish Council of National Unity also notified the State Department of its views regarding the Geneva Conference. In a letter of 11 June 1959 Jan Starzewski expressed the "disappointment and anxiety in Polish public opinion" with respect to the Herter Plan because it did not address the problems of divided Europe and failed to confirm the Oder–Neisse Line, which left the Soviet Union in control of the situation as the sole guarantor of the line. The council seemed to be lessening its demand for formal U.S. recognition of the line when it called for a "special guarantee" by the West of West Germany's "pledge to respect" the line and for the military withdrawal of Soviet forces from East Central Europe. In this letter the council made no distinction between exiled Poles and Poles living in the area of Poland; Starzewski spoke for all Poles. Valdemar Johnson noncommittally acknowledged the letter.[132]

The next month the Polish Council of National Unity sent to Herter a copy of an appeal prepared by the London-based Polish Western Association, an organization formed by Polish exiles born in the Oder–Neisse lands. The group maintained that the Potsdam Agreement had intended the Oder–Neisse Line to be final and called for Western recognition of the border in order to weaken Soviet control of Poland. The appeal dismissed the "no force" pledge of West Germany as having an "ominous ring" since it was similar to Hitler's pledges in the interwar period and condemned the "revisionist slogans" of Germany that the West German government had not repudiated. The authors argued that since a peace treaty with Germany might be delayed "almost indefinitely," the Western states should follow DeGaulle's lead and issue a "clear and unequivocal statement" on the border. This letter was also simply acknowledged by the State Department's Office of Eastern European Affairs.[133]

About the same time that the State Department was reviewing these letters, Ambassador Bruce in Bonn notified the secretary of an article that appeared in *Die Welt* claiming that Germany was considering an offer to Poland and Czechoslovakia leading toward normalized relations. Bruce informed the secretary that the rationale for the move was said to be based on the assumption that the Poles would not make recognition of the border a precondition and that the offer would contribute to an improved "climate" at the Geneva Conference.[134] Hopes for reduced tensions were not high, however. The Polish press noted that West German governmental spokesmen quickly denied these rumors and questioned the worth of such renouncements of the use of force while West Germany continued to rearm.[135]

Relations between the United States and Poland, on the other hand, were extremely good, especially between American representatives and the Polish people, as shown by Vice President Nixon's visit to Warsaw on his return from Moscow. Although the vice president's trip to Moscow was planned well in advance, his stopover in Warsaw was a last-minute decision and reflects the perceived importance of U.S. ethnic politics. Just prior to Nixon's departure, Alvin Bentley, a Republican congressman from southeast Michigan, informed him that "several leading members" of the Detroit Polonia favored such a visit to show the "'pro-western orientation'" of Poland and that he had discussed it with the State Department. Although Nixon informed Bentley in June that his full schedule would make such a visit impossible, the White House announced on 25 July 1959 that the vice president would visit Warsaw at the invitation of the chairman of the Council of State of Poland.[136]

The news that Vice President Nixon was to travel to the Soviet Union and Poland was well covered in the Polish press, although editorials pointed out that the United States still did not recognize the Oder–Neisse Line.[137] One Polish daily bluntly claimed that improved U.S. relations with the East were directly related to the death of Secretary Dulles and his replacement by Christian Herter, who was much more willing to perceive the peaceful intentions of the Soviets and was unwilling to subordinate American policy to West German goals.[138] Ambassador Beam, Milton Eisenhower, and Foy Kohler accompanied Vice President Nixon, whose visit to Warsaw turned out to be personally rewarding. He sent Eisenhower a long telegram informing him that his warm reception in Warsaw was a "most moving experience" and highlighting the points of his talks with Polish leaders including Gomułka, Cyrankiewicz, and Rapacki. He claimed that the discussion was "frank and free" and noted that while Gomułka was as much a "'true believer'" as Khrushchev, he was more Western-oriented and better-mannered. Nixon reported that Gomułka raised the issue of U.S. policy regarding West German rearmament and claimed that U.S. silence on the border issue "encouraged German militarists." He urged that the United States confirm the border as DeGaulle had and warned that the Oder–Neisse Line would be changed only by war. Nixon responded by pointing to the changes in Germany that had resulted largely from the integration of Germany into the European community; he asked Kohler to address the border question.

Kohler fell back on the typical State Department response that the United States favored a complete solution to the German problem and therefore was unwilling to "engage in piecemeal settlements of separate aspects." He gave no hint that the Department of State was urging Bonn to find a solution to the border problem, but both he and Nixon "assured" Gomułka that the United States "would give sympathetic consideration" to the Polish view of the matter. Gomułka then brought up the legal aspects of the border issue and urged recognition of the border on "political grounds." Nixon assured Gomułka that he would bring the matter to the president's attention. When Nixon raised the issue of a divided Germany, Rapacki referred to a January 1958 statement by the West German minister of all German affairs to the effect that the reunification of Germany would be shortly followed by the raising of territorial claims. This, Rapacki said, was one reason that Poland did not favor a reunited Germany. The conversation then turned to other matters, including economic aid and the changes in the Soviet Union under Khrushchev.[139]

Kohler returned to Washington and reported on his trip to the heads of mission of NATO members and also met with Franz Krapf, a minister of the

German Federal Republic, who wished to be more fully briefed on Kohler's visit. Krapf told Kohler that he was responsible for preparing Chancellor Adenauer for President Eisenhower's visit to Germany during August 1959 and wanted specifically to ensure that Bonn and Washington had a "clear understanding" of American policy for Poland. Krapf assured Kohler that he was among the great majority of members of the Federal Government and the Bundestag who favored closer German relations with Eastern Europe; he claimed that the expected opposition from refugee groups and representatives "was not likely to be crucial." Kohler informed Krapf point-blank that the Polish delegates with whom he had spoken had been "emotionally aroused" when Germany was discussed, claiming that the West German government favored aggression and militarist solutions. This, Kohler explained, was the main difference of opinion between the United States and Poland. He told Krapf that he had responded to Gomułka's request for U.S. recognition of the Oder-Neisse border by stating that it was a matter that could be settled only as part of the total solution to the German question. He also noted that while Gomułka was less inclined to favor a divided Germany, the other Polish delegates emphatically held to the idea that two German states existed. He added that when Nixon had asked Gomułka about his lack of fear of East Germans in light of the Polish fear of West Germany, Gomułka replied that East Germany had recognized the Oder–Neisse Line and had undertaken an education campaign among the population to emphasize the permanence of the border.[140]

The day following that interview Acting Secretary Dillon sent more information about the interview to the American Embassies in Bonn, Warsaw, Prague, and Moscow and the Mission in Berlin. Dillon explained that Krapf had asked Kohler directly whether a West German approach to better relations with Poland would conform to U.S. policy in Eastern Europe. Kohler, Dillon wrote, had agreed that it was in accordance with U.S. policy but stated that the "methods and channels" were up to the Germans. Dillon added that the State Department had been "long interested" in using the "unexploited German potential" to further Western aims in Eastern Europe in order to undermine Moscow's attempts to use the German "bogey" to keep the Soviet satellites in line while boosting "morale" in Germany through hints about the possibility of reunification. Dillon listed three difficulties with this course: German expellee groups, the Oder–Neisse question, and the recognition of East Germany by Soviet satellite states. He concluded with his assessment that the first two obstacles "do not appear insuperable" and that the third "may be possible" to address.[141] The acting secretary assured the Bonn Embassy that the State Department did not anticipate any "precipitous or rash" actions on the part of West Germans that might interfere or conflict with "international negotiations" regarding the German question. On the contrary, Dillon wrote, the West German government appeared to favor a slow and cautious approach in negotiating with Poland and Czechoslovakia.[142]

President Eisenhower's visit with Chancellor Adenauer led the Office of German Political Affairs to issue a memorandum regarding these talks. The memorandum pointed out that Adenauer's main concern was not that the United States fully supported German reunification but that Washington had lost faith in him personally as part of the "Western team." The memorandum encouraged Eisenhower to reassure Adenauer and pointed to the "intensive" campaign in the Soviet Union and its satellites to portray Adenauer and West Germany as "disturbers of international peace." To counter this, the authors of the memo stated that the president had to push "energetic German involvement" in NATO to show its peaceful intentions, another portrayal of "double containment." This would also foster the West's efforts to promote "political evolution" in Eastern Europe by drawing the satellite states into closer association with the European community and thereby undermine the East German government.[143]

In spite of Dillon's optimistic assessment, the State Department remained reluctant to proclaim publicly that a policy change on the border might be possible. When asked at a meeting of the Operation Control Board on 26 August 1959 about the status of any contingency plans for the border issue, Albert Sherer explained that the State Department was not developing such alternative plans since this would "contravene" the "current policy" of dealing with the German problem as a whole rather than "'piecemeal.'" The issue was not dormant, however. Robert Murphy stated that while he generally agreed with Sherer about further actions on the part of the United States, he did not want to exclude the "likelihood of some initiative" by East Germany, pointing out the "possibility of a relationship between the Polish and Berlin problems."[144] This rather cryptic remark, which was not followed up, would be clarified later in the year.

The meeting between Eisenhower and Adenauer was uneventful; they discussed the Geneva Conference and various aspects of the German question, reaffirming the Federal Republic's participation in the Atlantic Alliance.[145] However, Eisenhower's press conference in Bonn following the meeting captured some attention. When a reporter for *Time Magazine* asked Eisenhower about his refusal the previous day to support demonstrators calling for a return of the Oder–Neisse lands, the president explained that in discussions with Khrushchev he was trying to "melt a little of the ice" and did not want to complicate matters by dealing with specific issues such as the border question.[146] Although Eisenhower did not indicate any policy change, his refusal to openly support the revisionists was widely hailed in Poland. *Trybuna Ludu* ran a front-page story expressing its "'satisfaction'" with Eisenhower's statement.[147]

The Polish press also hailed Senator Hubert Humphrey's speech in the Senate on the twentieth anniversary of the Nazi attack on Poland in which he supported the Oder–Neisse Line and continued to condemn West German militarism. Humphrey urged increased economic aid and the realization that

"Poland's western border—on the Oder–Niesse [*sic*] River—is a historical and traditional boundary." His statement that the United States should "take steps" to recognize the line was reported in the Polish press.[148] The following week Frank Siscoe, the chargè at the American Embassy, reported that the Polish press continued its anti-German campaign, summarizing articles in the West European press urging West Germany to recognize the Oder–Neisse Line.[149] Siscoe commented that the Poles' reaction indicated that they were unable to respond favorably to any overtures from West Germany at that time since Warsaw had to demonstrate unity with Moscow.[150]

The Warsaw government's suspicions of Bonn were clearly revealed when Polish officials traveled to the United States in October 1959. In every recorded conversation with State Department representatives they condemned West German revanchism. Edward Ochab, minister of agriculture, complained to Robert Murphy and Foy Kohler about revisionist statements in the German press and about Chancellor Adenauer's being photographed in the costume of a medieval Teutonic Knight. Murphy did not directly address that complaint but simply stated that he believed that the situation was changing. Ochab maintained that West German policies encouraged revanchism in spite of the fact that the border issue could be reopened only by war. He blamed Adenauer for not being clearer with the German people about this matter; he suggested that the the West German government emulate the "frankness" of the Polish government that had helped the Polish people overcome the disturbing loss of Lwow and Wilno. Murphy contended that the Polish government had "more powerful means of political persuasion" available than did the West German government. The reception ended inconclusively at this point, with Ochab simply reiterating the Polish position on the Oder–Neisse Line and on the existence of East Germany.[151]

A more open dialogue was held at a meeting between Secretary Herter and Foreign Minister Rapacki on the same day. In preparation for the visit, Ivan White of the Bureau of European Affairs prepared a memorandum for the secretary outlining the topics that Rapacki might raise. White suggested that the foreign minister might refer to West Germany's "designs on Poland" Western Territories" as an example of Bonn's revisionism and might suggest that the United States recognize "at least informally" the Oder–Neisse Line and perhaps the existence of two Germanys. White also recommended that the secretary express understanding of Poland's concern regarding West German rearmament but contrast the policies of Nazi Germany with those of the Federal Republic and cite the controls imposed on Bonn by international organizations. Again echoing the State Department's official position on the border, White recommended that the secretary "state that we are not challenging Poland's right to administer the Western Territories but we regard Poland's western border as provisional pending a final decision on a peace settlement, and are opposed to piecemeal settlement of separate aspects of the German problem."[152]

When Rapacki met with Secretary Herter the next day, he indeed raised the issue of "revisionist propaganda" in light of West German nuclear rearmament. He continued to maintain that most Poles realized that while "revisionist tendencies" were not "deep rooted" in the German people, as most of the refugees had been assimilated into West Germany, a few small vocal groups wanted to turn the refugees into a "revisionist force." He cited as evidence the West German government's promotion of such statements as Minister for All German Affairs Ernst Lemmer's that assimilation should be discouraged so a dissatisfied element would continue to work for the return of the eastern lands. Herter refused to address Lemmer's statement; he simply asked Rapacki for specific quotations that the foreign minister promised to supply.

Rapacki repeated a similar refrain when he added that another component that served to support revanchism was the United States and United Kingdom's refusal to recognize the border. He seemed to be backing away from Poland's previous "all or nothing" position, however, when he stated the hope that the United States "would not regard the frontier problem in a legalistic manner but rather from a moral and political point of view." Herter assured him that the United States was "giving careful consideration" to the border question and to other matters of concern to the two states.[153]

A few days after Herter's meeting with Rapacki, Foy Kohler helped the secretary prepare for his meeting with Agriculture Minister Ochab, who had been touring the United States as part of an International Education Exchange Service program. Kohler prepared a list of possible points that Ochab might raise, including a call for U.S. support on the Oder–Neisse Line "from a 'moral and political' (if not 'legal') standpoint." This was, of course, the same point that Rapacki had made in his discussion with the secretary and again perhaps reflected a softening in the Polish approach to the problem. The State Department was not then willing to go that far, however. Kohler recommended that Secretary Herter acknowledge the fact that Poland had suffered extensively during the war but reiterate that West Germany was curtailed from action by international controls. Kohler advised the secretary to emphasize that while the United States was not "challenging Poland's right to administer" the lands, the U.S. government opposed "piecemeal settlement" of the German issue and continued to consider the border provisional.[154]

Although Secretary Herter and his assistants continued to oppose publicly a settlement of the Oder–Neisse issue prior to a peace conference, evidence reveals that the State Department was considering a new proposal in light of the summit scheduled for 1960. In October 1959 Martin Hillenbrand of the Office of German Affairs sent Foy Kohler a memorandum for discussion regarding the possibility of West Germany's taking the initiative to connect the border issue with the Berlin question. Hillenbrand reported that, as he understood the matter, Robert Murphy had "expressed the wish that this possibility be considered."[155] This apparently was the proposal to which

Murphy had briefly referred in the Operations Coordinating Board (OCB) meeting in August 1959. The proposal explained that "in the past" the possibility had been discussed of West Germany's offering to recognize the Oder–Neisse Line if it was linked with a Western proposal for German reunification. "A watered-down version" of this idea, the report noted, was a suggestion that was to have been made at the 1959 Geneva Conference. This idea, which was not used, was that the government of the Federal Republic offer to Poland and Czechoslovakia the assurance that it would never use force to change the border in connection with a reunification proposal.

The authors of this new proposal to link the Oder–Neisse and Berlin questions noted that it was a new departure and "might provide a means of increasing the attractiveness to the USSR of a western offer on Berlin." They pointed out that this option "could be added to any of a number of proposals." They warned, however, that Adenauer showed "little disposition" to make offers regarding the border or to establish diplomatic recognition and contended that Adenauer had "apparently been convinced" by his political advisers that the refugee vote in the 1961 elections was crucial for CDU control of the government. This, they thought, was why Adenauer had rejected the idea of diplomatic relations with Poland and would probably "strongly resist" any proposals offering the Oder–Neisse Line as a "quid pro quo for a Berlin settlement."[156]

A sample proposal was attached that declared that the Four Powers agreed that atomic weapons would not be located in Berlin, that activities that might interfere with the Berlin situation would be avoided, that access to West Berlin would continue as at present, that armed forces in Berlin would be limited, and that disputes would be settled among the Four Powers for three years. Regarding the border, the sample proposal suggested that the Four Powers approve a West Germany declaration that either:

> it has renounced the use of force in the settlement of international disputes and is prepared to conclude bilateral treaties of non-aggression with the Governments of Poland and Czechoslovakia pursuant to this renunciation.
>
> Or
>
> it recognizes as the permanent frontier of Germany the line [specified in the Potsdam Accord] running from the Baltic Sea immediately west of Swinamunde, and thence along the Oder River to the confluence of the western Neisse River and along the western Neisse to the Czechoslovak frontier and renounces all right, title and claim to the former German territories east of this line.[157]

Shortly after this memorandum was sent to Kohler, State Department Legal Adviser Eric Hager, sent the undersecretary for political affairs a memorandum explaining the potential ramifications of a proposal for West Germany to recognize the Oder–Neisse Line. Hager explained that any such proposal would erode somewhat or "obliterate" the principle maintained thus far by the West that the question of Germany's frontiers was a matter to be decided by an all-German government. Damage could be limited to some extent by placing the Federal Republic's acceptance of the line within the "context of a German peace settlement," but he pointed out that any statement would be considered a commitment that West Germans acting in an all-German government would be obligated to accept. The Soviets might, he said, use such a declaration to support their view of the existence of two Germanys, which the West could refute. He closed by pointing out that his office was not authorized to determine whether the disadvantages of such a proposal outweighed the advantages, but the general tenor of the memorandum suggested such an assessment.[158]

The potential legal ramification of a statement on the border was only one of many considerations for the State Department. Also at issue was the problem of getting Bonn to agree to negotiate the matter; the closing months of 1959 were not promising. DeGaulle's press conference reiterating his 25 March 1959 statement supporting the Oder–Neisse Line and the French prime minister's statement on 13 October openly supporting the border stirred further controversy in the Federal Republic.[159] The Bonn Embassy reported that the opposition parties in West Germany had used the French president's statements for political gain by refuting the Adenauer government's contention that DeGaulle's statement was not an attempt to "undercut" Bonn's position. The embassy reported that President DeGaulle's remarks led the West German political parties to "forge [a] display of identity" on views of the border regardless of their position on establishing relations with the East bloc and stimulated discussion about the "wisdom" of keeping ties with France.[160]

An 11 November 1959 telegram from Bonn informed the State Department that Foreign Minister von Brentano, "under prodding" from the expellee groups that had been upset by DeGaulle's "seeming acquiescence" in the border, had been forced to "justify and restate" the government's firm position on the boundary. Von Brentano seemed to walk a diplomatic tightrope when he affirmed that the Allies continued loyally to accept Bonn's position and stated his belief that the only danger to Bonn's position came from Germans who accepted Poland's assertions that the French had "betrayed" Bonn on the issue. Von Brentano also explained that: "the Federal Government protests against any attempt to interpret as revanchism or revisionism this adherence to an undeniably rightful claim put forward in a spirit of sincere reconciliation." The embassy officer who reported this exchange told the secretary of state that a member of the West German Foreign Office believed that it had been prompted by two factors: expellees who feared that Western Allies would force Bonn to accept the Oder–Neisse Line and accusations that the Foreign Office was willing to exchange the eastern territories for "some vague indefinable understanding" with the satellite states.[161]

Shortly following this report, Bonn also notified the Department of State that State Secretary Thedieck of the Ministry for All-German Affairs at a meeting of the Landsmannschaft der Oberschlesier had insisted that Bonn continue to maintain that the border could be handled only by a freely elected, all-German government. He added that this position was supported by the three major Western Allies, which was "more important" than DeGaulle's statements at a press conference. He denied the Polish claim that the area represented "recovered" land for Poland since "'at no time did the German Eastern territory in its entirety ever belong'" to Poland, nor was it settled by Poles. He added that "few other boundaries in Europe" have been recognized as long as the one separating Silesia and East Prussia from their "Eastern neighbors."[162] A few days later, the consulate general in Frankfurt reported that Bundestag Deputy and Hessian DP Chairman Ludwig Schneider had stated that prior to his visit to Warsaw he had favored diplomatic recognition between Bonn and Warsaw. While in Poland, however, the head of the German Division in the Polish Foreign Office told him that Poland would never enter negotiations if Germany maintained that such recognition did not affect the status of the border and that diplomatic recognition would constitute de jure acceptance of the line. In January 1960, the German Embassy in Washington reported that Ernst Lemmer, federal minister for all-German affairs, and State Secretary Franz Thedieck spoke of the border issue as a "European problem" to be settled by major European powers. Lemmer stated that it was not in Europe's interest to make permanent the "injustice" of the Oder–Neisse Line. Thedieck maintained the German legal claims to the land but added that Germany must take account of the "rights and claims" of its neighbors, which included renouncing the use of force.[163]

The Polish press kept close track of these statements and events, and the American Embassy in Warsaw monitored the press reports. An officer at the Warsaw Embassy reported to Washington that a meeting of the Society for the Development of the Western Territories noted that "the idea is taking root" in capitalist states that world peace was "unbreakably linked" with recognition of Poland's border at the Oder–Neisse Line, but a resolution adopted at the meeting claimed that West German revisionists were "'feverish[ly]'" working to stop such moves. The society called on its members to "draw the Polish emigration" into its work and "'to take the offensive against West German revisionism abroad as well as against its infiltration into some milieus in Poland.'" The embassy officer contended that such statements reflected the "uncertainty and suspicion" in Poland about the future of the western border.[164]

The *Christian Science Monitor's* correspondent in Bonn, J. Emlyn Williams, confirmed this contention on the occasion of Khrushchev's planned trip to Poland in July 1959. According to Williams, Poles looked eagerly for a definite statement about the future of the Oder–Neisse territories since the Polish government wanted to concentrate on improving the economy of the western lands, but settlers there wanted assurances of security. Williams reported the persistence of rumors that the city of Szczecin would be given to East Germany but noted that Khrushchev's planned visit to that city made such an action highly doubtful. The correspondent closed by pointing out that reports continued to surface in Bonn that West Germany would recognize the border, but he added that such talk was always followed by the statement that the border issue would be settled at a peace conference.[165]

The increased tension between Bonn and Warsaw continued to be an obstacle to closer ties between Warsaw and Washington, according to the secretary of commerce. Secretary Mueller traveled to Poland along with government and business leaders to reciprocate the October 1958 visit of Polish delegates to the United States. In his report of the visit, the secretary noted that "perhaps the most important factor" affecting Poland's relations with the West was Poland's traditional hatred and suspicion of Germany. Concomitantly, many Poles could not understand the U.S. position on Germany that "has been interpreted by the Poles as a barrier to better political relations." He offered little hope that the Poles would compromise on the issue since "the passage of time" had led Poles to accept the border as an "established fact." He warned that any softening of the U.S. position in favor of Bonn would be a "serious blow" to the Poles and would devastate the friendship already existing between Poland and the United States.[166]

The Polish American Congress and Polish émigré organizations continued to pressure the U.S. government to issue a statement favoring recognition of the border. When Congressman Frank Karsten (D) of Missouri received a letter from the Polish American Congress in St. Louis proposing U.S. recognition of the Oder–Neisse Line, he asked for information from the State Department. Assistant Secretary of State for Congressional Relations William Macomber informed the congressman of the official U.S. position that Poland would administer the area pending a peace conference. He assured Karsten that America's position had not been altered and that the United States was not "challenging" Poland's right to administer the lands. Macomber used the typical response that while the State Department recognized the importance of settling the question, the department believed that the issue should be placed within its European context and not handled in a "partial" settlement.[167]

Stefan Korbonski of the Polish Council of National Unity and the Polish Delegation to the Assembly of Captive European Nations (ACEN) spoke with Richard Johnson of the Office of Eastern European Affairs on 16 November 1959 to discuss his organizations' proposals favoring U.S. recognition of the border. Korbonski affirmed in this interview that his proposals represented the views of the Polish delegation of the ACEN as well as of the Polish Council.[168] He bemoaned the increased pressure placed on Gomułka's government by the Soviet Union and contended that Moscow continued to control Warsaw with the threat that it would give East Germany the Oder–Neisse lands. Korbonski suggested that the United States could do much to discredit this Soviet threat by "echoing" DeGaulle's statements about the permanence of the Oder–Neisse Line.[169]

The Brookings Institute prepared a report for the U.S. Senate Foreign Relations Committee on U.S. policy toward Poland that agreed with Korbonski's assessment of the Central European situation. This report maintained that Gomułka was restrained from making "striking assertions of domestic autonomy," largely because of Poland's geographic position. The western border, the authors argued, led "even anti-Communist Poles" to feel that "Soviet support for the Oder–Neisse frontier necessitates close Polish–Soviet ties, in the name of Polish national (not Communist) self-interest."[170] Also, the ACEN and the Polish American Congress prepared statements prior to the 1960 summit calling on West Germany and the United States to dispel Polish fears of West German remilitarization by declaring "unequivocally" that Poland is considered a state within its western boundary on the Oder–Neisse Line. The U-2 crisis immediately prior to the 1960 summit, however, meant that any proposals for American prodding of West Germany to act on the border came to nothing.[171]

Some U.S. agencies, however, continued to reflect a softer approach to the issue. The guidelines of Radio Free Europe (RFE) broadcasts to Poland were updated and revised in January 1960, superseding earlier guidelines that had censored references to the border on RFE broadcasts.[172] The new policy contended that RFE should not "speak as an émigré radio station, . . . or as the purported voice of an 'opposition' party within Poland" but should seek to influence communist opinion leaders in Poland with accurate information. The policy statement pointed out the Polish audience's antipathy for propaganda and advocated accurate broadcasts of information about the "Free World," the Sino–Soviet bloc, and areas "where the regime attempts to withhold or distort the facts in Poland." Specific guidelines were laid out for broadcasts about the Polish–German border. The issue would be announced only "as news, without comment," in press surveys, or as part of a pronouncement by recognized organizations. All such reports needed advanced approval of the Office of the European Director.[173]

A review of U.S. policy toward Poland by the Operations Coordinating Board in the spring of 1960 concluded that NSC 5801/1 regarding U.S. policy in Poland did not need to be reviewed, although note was taken that U.S. policy toward Poland often required a different treatment than U.S. policy in other satellite states because of the Polish regime's "significant deviations" from bloc policies and Poland's "relatively friendly" relations with the United States. However, "peaceful evolution" was still advocated over any policies "likely to provoke retrogression . . . or the use of force by the USSR." The report took note of the improved U.S.–Polish and NATO–Polish relations, with the exception of Polish–West German relations that had worsened since the April 1958 policy was formulated. The authors pointed to the Polish government's propaganda campaign against West German remilitarization as a threat to the Oder–Neisse territories and confirmed that the lack of improvement in FRG–Polish relations "directly" affected U.S.–Polish relations because Polish officials isolated the United States as the leading proponent of West German rearmament. They noted that although U.S. representatives continued to point out to Polish officials that West Germany was limited in its actions by its NATO partners, they admitted that such arguments had little effect, and they held out "little likelihood" of improved relations between West Germany and Poland as long as the questions of the Oder–Neisse border and West German rearmament remained unanswered. The report favored a continuation of the American policy that refused to act on the border issue prior to an all-German peace conference unless other developments occurred.[174]

Polish suspicions of West German intentions continued to be noted by newspaper reporters who verified the secret State Department assessments of conditions. In June Ernest Pisko, *Christian Science Monitor* correspondent in Warsaw, reported that in "all conversations" with Poles lasting more than ten minutes, the issue of West German revanchism arose. Most Poles, he stated, considered the Oder–Neisse question closed, in light of the Potsdam Agreement and of Soviet, East German, and French recognition of the border. What frightened Poles most, Pisko contended, was a West German invasion of Poland; Poles also resented the perceived pro-Bonn policy in Washington. His attempts to correct these "misapprehensions," he wrote, were useless.[175]

The *New York Times* reported that when the Polish government sent a note to Washington and other NATO capitals asking for clarification of NATO's commitment to West Germany in light of Adenauer's recent statement to a refugee organization in Düsseldorf that East Prussia would be returned to Germany "'if we stand firmly with our allies,'" the State Department reassured Poland that a "careful reading of the entire speech" revealed Adenauer's peaceful intentions. The State Department confirmed that West Germany had never sought NATO's assistance to "press claim" to the territories and maintained that U.S. policy was still based on the Potsdam Agreement, even though it recognized that the division of Germany hindered possibilities for a peace settlement.[176]

Gomułka traveled to the United States in September 1960 to attend the UN session and was received by Secretary Herter, "the only Communist visitor to be so honored." Gomulka issued a speech reiterating the threat of German revanchism and claiming the inviolability of the Oder–Neisse Line.[177] The ongoing antagonism between Polish émigrés and representatives of the Polish government was shown, however, when Adam Niebieszczanski, a member of the Polish delegation to the ACEN, spoke at the eightieth meeting of the Plenary Assembly held in New York, prior to Gomulka's visit to the UN. Niebieszczanski stated that Gomułka's presence at the UN showed simply that he had "joined the chorus of puppets." He contended that Gomułka would advocate the affirmation of the Oder–Neisse Line as all Poles wanted and would warn against German revanchism, even though Gomulka was not the "best man" to call for Western recognition since he had agreed to the Soviet landgrab in the East. He favored Western recognition because the line represented "justice, peace and political wisdom" and because recognition would correct the "present paradoxical situation" where the USSR was the only guarantor of the line, which provided the Soviets "with the potent weapon of blackmail."[178]

The Polish Council of National Unity also declared on 14 September 1960 that in foreign policy matters Gomulka continued to be Moscow's "docile tool." The council also believed that Gomulka would call for Western recognition of the Oder–Neisse Line "as a condition indispensable to the existence of a free and independent Polish state." Like the ACEN the council bemoaned the present situation where the Soviets guaranteed the border while West German politicians led by Adenauer issued "revisionist declarations," and the rest of the world simply listened.[179] After Gomułka's speech Korbonski wrote a letter to the *Washington Evening Star* stating that his only points of agreement were in Gomułka's statement that Poles fear German militarism and that recognition by the United States of the line might dispel this fear.[180]

Gomułka's visit to the United States was not the only occasion in which the Oder–Neisse Line issue received press attention. The presidential election of 1960 offered the candidates the opportunity to discuss the issue, even though they had reportedly agreed with West German officials that discussion of the "controversial issue" would not help relations between Bonn and Washington.[181] When Senator John Kennedy spoke at the Chicago office of the Polish American Congress on 1 October 1960, he argued that Poland's fear of the West, especially of Germany, had to be eliminated. He contended that disputes would have to be settled peacefully and that Eastern European nations must never again be "violently stripped of their territories. . . . We cannot impose a boundary settlement on other nations," he said, "but we can encourage peaceful and mutual accommodation in the spirit of free Europe."[182] Although Kennedy added nothing new to West Germany's pledge that borders would not be changed by force, Polish Americans widely hailed his speech at that time and during the coming months.[183]

When Vice President Nixon spoke at the Polish Union Hall in Buffalo, New York, in late October 1960, he stated that all Poles were united in support of the Oder–Neisse Line, which he referred to as a postwar fact.[184] His statements, according to the *New York Times*, seemed to "suggest that he favored going beyond Administration policy" and urged that the next administration formulate policies to strengthen the "morale and vitality of the Polish people." Correspondent Sydney Gruson reported from Bonn that the Adenauer administration faced criticism of Nixon's statement with "equanimity." Although some West German officials interpreted Nixon's remark as an indication that as president he would "forego the West's long-held stand" that the border awaited settlement at a peace conference, others maintained that such election-time statements held no commitment.[185] While the Polish American newspaper *Dziennik Związkowy* praised Nixon's statement, the German-language newspaper *Abendpost* of Chicago warned that Nixon would lose the votes of many German Americans because of the statement.[186] The editor of the paper, Richard Sperbe, said that if Nixon's statement was interpreted to mean that he favored recognition of the line, it would "violate every principle this country has stood for since its origin."[187]

Polish speculation about possible actions by a new Republican administration headed by Nixon proved at this point to be moot. An overall evaluation of the second Eisenhower administration, however, shows that the State Department was more actively involved in finding a solution to the Oder–Neisse problem than any time since 1947; yet such activity was not made public, and it eventually came to nothing. Indeed, it seems that the reactive position taken by the State Department resulted in increased rumors and speculation about the future of the border rather than putting to rest the fears of Poles, Polish Americans, or West Germans. For Washington to make a clear-cut statement that it supported the existing border, the State Department had to be sure of at least two things: that the expellees in West Germany were not strong enough to force the Bonn government into negotiating some type of deal with Moscow that would weaken the Western Alliance and that U.S. recognition would indeed loosen Moscow's hold on Warsaw as Polish Americans repeatedly and Polish officials sometimes suggested. Washington did not feel confident enough on either point to support a change in its border policy, and a policy statement on Poland prepared in January 1961 suggested that this confidence would continue to be absent in the upcoming Kennedy administration.

The 1961 policy statement reiterated that NSC 5808/1 was still in effect, although it noted that Gomulka followed Moscow's lead more closely than in previous years. It outlined the limits of Polish independence, including Poland's geographical position, the Poles' perceptions of West German resurgency, and their perceived need for Soviet support to counter it and defend the border. In light of all this, the policy statement advocated that the United States should continue to support "peaceful evolution" and greater Polish orientation toward the West, with a long-range goal of seeing the fulfillment of the Polish people's right for self-determination.[188] Thus, Washington officials continued to maintain the legalistic position that finalization of the border awaited a peace conference in spite of Senator Kennedy's suggestions to the contrary. This position would come under increasing scrutiny in the 1960s as alternative policies were suggested to match the changing geopolitical situation.

NOTES

1. Piotr Wandycz, *The United States and Poland* (Cambridge: Harvard University Press, 1980), 359–360.

2. Memorandum of Conversation, Winiewicz, Spasowski, and Murphy, 23 January 1957, RG59, 611.48/1-2357.

3. Ibid.

4. Ibid.

5. Ibid.

6. *News from the German Embassy*, No. 1 (4 February 1957), 2–3.

7. Despatch 1319, O'Shaughnessy to Department of State, 6 February 1957, RG59, 762C.022/2-657. The Bonn Embassy also informed the State Department that the West German government had adopted official phrases signifying the Oder–Neisse territories. They would be described either as the "'*Deutsche Reichsgebiete in den Grenzen vom 31. Dezember 1937 unter vorlaeufiger polnischer, bezw. sowjetischer Verwaltung*,'" or the abbreviated form of "'*Ostgebiete des Deutschen Reiches (Stand 31. Dez. 1937) zur Zeit unter fremder Verwaltung*.'" Despatch 1104, Hodgson to Department of State, 8 January 1957, RG59, 762.022/1-857.

8. For more, see also Memorandum of Conversation, Herter, Stone, and Stimpson, 13 March 1957, Christian Herter Papers, Chronological File, Box 9, Dwight D. Eisenhower Library, herafter cited as DDE/L. See also Wandycz, *The United States*,366; Wladyslaw W. Kulski, *Germany and Poland: From War to Peaceful Relations* (Syracuse, NY: Syracuse University Press, 1976), 112.

9. Wolfram F. Hanrieder, *Germany, American, Europe: Forty Years of German Foreign Policy* (New Haven, CT: Yale University Press, 1989), 165.

10. Despatch 139, Meney to Department of State, 1 February 1957, RG59, 648.62A/2-157.

11. Ibid.

12. Ibid. See Telegamm 793, Guffler to Secretary of State, 6 February 1957, RG59, 762C.022/2-657.

13. Rapacki also expressed interest in establishing closer ties with Polish émigrés rather than viewing them as reactionaries. Despatch 445, Johnson to Department, 9 April 1957, RG59, 748.13/4-957.

14. Alvin Bentley reported on his visit to Poland and favored some economic aid. See *Congressional Record*, 85th Cong., 1st sess., 103, pt. 6 (20 May 1957): 7292–7294; Wandycz, *The United States*, 364–368.

15. *Congressional Record*, 85th Cong., 1st sess., 103, pt. 15 (5 February 1957): A 788.

16. *Congressional Record*, 85th Cong., 1st sess., 103, pt. 6 (16 May 1957): 7117-7132; Hanrieder, *Germany, America, Europe,* 435, n14. See also Wolfram F. Hanrieder, *West German Foreign Policy 1949–1963: International Pressures and Domestic Response* (Stanford, CA: Stanford University Press, 1967), passim.

17. *Congressional Record*, 85th Cong., 1st sess., 103, pt. 11 (15 August 1957): 14972–14978. In the 1950s West German agriculture indeed represented a problem for the Bonn government with small farms and obsolete machinery predominant. In addition, many farmers voted CDU, and their union was "one of the most effective pressure groups in Europe," with many products subsidized and protected. Some of these problems were ironed out by the European Economic Community (EEC). See F. Roy Willis, *France, Germany and the New Europe 1945–1967* (Stanford, CA: Stanford University Press, 1965; reprint ed., London: Oxford University Press, 1968), 288–292.

18. Machrowicz continued to advocate Western recognition; Reece continued to read into the *Congressional Record* reports and articles by German expellees. *Congressional Record*, 86th Cong., 1st sess., 105, pt. 14 (1 September 1959): 17633-

17634.

19. Walter Drzewieniecki, "The American Poles and the Odra-Nysa Frontier," *Polish Western Affairs* 9, no. 1 (1968): 168. See also Marek Swiecicki and Roza Nowotarska, *Gentleman from Michigan*, trans. Edward Cynarski (London: Polish Cultural Foundation, 1974), 276–279; Wienczylaw Wagner, *The Gentleman from Tennessee Is Wrong: The Truth about the Odra–Nysa Border* (New York: Balticum Mid-European Studies Center, n.d.); Jedrzej Giertych, *Poland and Germany: A Reply to Congressman B. Carrol Reece of Tennessee* (London 1958).

20. Letter, Gordon to Secretary, 17 May 1957, RG59, 611.48/5-1757.

21. Letter, Hill to Gordon, 20 May 1957, RG59, 611.48/5-1757.

22. Ibid.

23. *Congressional Record*, 85th, 1st. sess., 103, pt. 8, 11011–11012.

24. *Congressional Record Appendix*, 85th Cong., 1st sess., 103, pt. 20 (13 June 1957): A5356.

25. *Congressional Record Appendix*, 85th Cong., 1st sess., 103, pt. 20 (13 June 1957): A5207–A5208.

26. Ibid., A5208.

27. *Congressional Record Appendix*, 85th Cong., 1st sess., 103, pt. 20 (18 June 1957): A5127.

28. *Congressional Record*, 85th Cong., 1st sess., 103, pt. 11 (21 August 1957): 15446–15454.

29. Letter, Kennedy to Oberndorf, 8 June 1957, Pre-Presidential Papers, Box 676, Legislation File, JFK/L.

30. Letter, Polish Western Association to Kennedy, 10 October 1957, Pre-Presidential Papers, Box 676, Senate File, JFK/L. Kennedy was apparently in contact with this association. The letter just cited referred to an earlier request from Kennedy for a list of persons interested in his remarks.

31. Telegram 250, Beam to Secretary of State, 23 August 1957, RG59, 611.48/8-2357.

32. Letter, Lewandowski to Kennedy, 8 July 1957, Pre-Presidential Papers, Box 676, Legislation File, JFK/L.

33. Letter, Bates to Secretary of State, 21 August 1957, and Letter, Hoghland to Bates, 28 August 1957, RG59, 648.623/8-2157.

34. "Relations with Poland—Talking Points" for Adenauer visit on 26–29 May 1957, n.d. Department of State Briefing Book [May 1957], White House Central Files, Confidential File, 1953-61, Box 74, DDE/L.

35. The "anti-Gomulka-Stalinist" designation was apparently open to question. One of the Polish Embassy staff reportedly removed was viewed by State Department officers as having been glad of some of the post-October reforms. See Memorandum of Conversation, Kmiecik and Johnson, 3 June 1957, RG59, 611.48/6-357. See also Memorandum of Conversation, Kmiecik, Walaszek, and Lister, 15 July 1957, RG59, 611.48/7-1557.

36. Wandycz, *The United States*, 372.

37. Letter, Beam to Murphy, 3 September 1957, RG59, 611.48/9-357.

38. Telegram 317, Beam to Secretary of State, 6 September 1957, RG59 611.48/9-557.

39. Ibid.

40. Richard Hiscocks, *Poland: Bridge for the Abyss: An Interpretation of Developments in Post-War Poland* (London: Oxford University Press, 1963), 260. See also Telegram POLTO 596, Perkins to Secretary of State, 13 September 1957, RG59, 762C.022/9-1357.

41. Despatch 155, Marcy to Department of State, 2 October 1957, RG59, 762C.022/10-257.

42. Tito recognized East Germany in October, probably at Khrushchev's urging and in an attempt to support Khrushchev as a "'progressive force.'" Zbigniew Brzezinski, *The Soviet Bloc, Unity and Conflict* (Cambridge: Harvard University Press, 1967 rev.), 316.

43. Kulski, *Germany and Poland*, 112 cites Jerzy Sulek, *Stanowisko Rzadu NRF wobec Granicy na Odrze i Nysie Luzyckiej: 1949–1966* (Poznan: Instytut Zachodni, 1969), 171, which refers to one of Gomulka's speeches in the fall of 1957 as evidence of Warsaw's firm committment to the establishment of border recognition as a precondition to negotiations with Bonn, but failure to address subsequent announcements by Warsaw suggesting that that position was not definite. See also Otto Stenzl, "Germany's Eastern Frontier," *Survey: A Journal of Soviet and East European Studies* no. 51 (April 1964): 124; "Gomulka Firm on Border," *Christian Science Monitor*, 25 September 1957, 10.

44. Memo, Elbrick to Secretary, 25 May 1957, 611.62A/5-2557; Memorandum of Conversation, Dulles and Adenauer, 28 May 1957, General Correspondence and Memorandum Series, John Foster Dulles Papers, Box 1, DDE/L.

45. Ibid.

46. Senate, *Documents on Germay, 1944–1970*, 319–320.

47. Memorandum of Conversation, Jaenicke and Linebaugh, 1 October 1957, RG59, 648.62a/10-257.

48. Ibid.

49. Ibid.

50. Hanrieder, *Germany, America, Europe*, 144–151.

51. Despatch 588 with enclosure of interview, O'Shaughnessy to Department of State, 2 October 1957, RG59, 648.62A/10-257.

52. Ibid.

53. Ibid.

54. Beam reported that Rapacki said he "winces" whenever he heard that U.S. aid would sever Warsaw's ties to Moscow.

55. Letter, Beam to Dulles, 17 September 1957, RG59, 748.13/9-2657.

56. Ibid.

57. Ibid.

58. Letter, Dulles to Beam, 1 October 1957, RG59, 748.13/9-2757.

59. Memo, Elbrick to Secretary of State, 8 October 1957, RG59, 748.13/10-857.

60. Prior to this meeting Rapacki had delivered a speech at the United Nations on 2 October 1957 dealing with disarmament, stating that Poland was vitally interested in disarmament and arms limitations because of the German–Polish border question. He claimed that the "militarist and 'revanchist trends" were still powerful in West Germany, and he concluded by reiterating the finality and inviolability of Poland's western border.

He cryptically suggested that "it would be a good thing for the diplomats of countries which wish to maintain friendly relations with Poland to draw the proper conclusions." *Documents on Germany*, Address by Rapacki, 2 October 1957, 214–217.

61. Memo, Elbrick to Secretary of State, 14 October 1957, RG59, 748.13/10-1457.

62. Memorandum of Conversation, Dulles, Rapacki, Spasowski, et al., 16 October 1957, RG59, 611.48/10-1657.

63. Memorandum of Conversation., Dulles, Rapacki, Spasowski, et al., 16 October 1957, RG59, 611.48/10-1657.

64. Ibid.

65. Memo, Larson to Johnson, 7 November 1957, RG59, 611.48/11-157.

66. Despatch 203, Beam to Department, 12 November 1957, RG59, 762C.022/11-1257.

67. Ibid.

68. Ibid.

69. White House Office-Office of SA for NSA: Records, 1955-61, NSC Series, Policy Papers Subseries, Box 23, DDE/L.

70. Ibid.

71. Ibid.

72. Despatch 311, Beam to Department of State, 14 February 1958, RG59, 748.13/2-1458.

73. Ibid.

74. Telegram 4367, Houghton to Secretary of State, 21 March 1958, RG59, 762C.022/3-2158.

75. Ibid.

76. Memorandum of Conversation, Dobrosielski and Ramsaur, 16 May 1958, RG59, 648.62A/5-1658.

77. Ibid.

78. Memorandum of Conversation, Dulles, von Brentano, Bruce, et al., 6 June 1958, RG59, 648.62A/6-558.

79. Ibid.

80. Despatch 2290, Bonn to Department of State, 25 June 1958, RG59, 648.62A/6-2558.

81. Ibid.

82. Memorandum of Conversation, Osmanczyk and Johnson, 27 June 1958, RG59, 611.48/6-2758.

83. Memorandum of Conversation, Sherer and Spasowski, Kmiecik, and Dobrosielski, 28 June 1958, RG59, 611.48/6-2858.

84. Memorandum, Dulles to Goodpaster and White House, 3 August 1958, Whitman File, DDE Diary Series, Box 35, August 1958 Staff Notes, DDE/L.

85. Ibid. See also Memorandum of Conversation, Dobrosielski and Sherer, 3 June 1958, RG59, 611.48/6-358.

86. Memo, Dulles to Goodpaster, 3 August 1958.

87. Kennan obviously considered himself one of "those people" who had predicted disaster in 1945. See George F. Kennan, *Russia and the West under Lenin and Stalin* (Boston: Little, Brown, 1960), 361; George F. Kennan, *Memoirs, 1950–1963*

(Boston: Little, Brown, 1972), 213–215.

88. Memo, Dulles to Goodpaster, 3 August 1958.

89. Airgram G-176, Bruce to Secretary of State, 5 September 1958, RG59, 762C.022/9-558.

90. Airgram G-140, Beam to Secretary of State, 15 September 1958, RG59, 762C.022/9-1558. Otto Stenzl cites two West German newspapers *Die Welt*, 3 September 1958, and *Stuttgarter Nachrichten*, 22 November 1958, which carried stores about the Polish Foreign Office's rejection of Zarzycki's statement. See Stenzl, "Germany's Eastern Frontier," 124.

91. Telegram G-193, Bruce to Secretary of State, 11 September 1958, RG59, 762C.022/9-1158.

92. Despatch 202, Trivers to Department of State, 16 September 1958, RG59, 762C.022/9-1658.

93. White House Office: Office of the Special Assistant for National Security Affairs: Records 1952-1961, NSC Series, Policy Paper Subseries, Box 23, DDE/L.

94. Memorandum of Conversation, von Baudissin and Allen, 10 September 1958, RG59, 648.62A/9-1058.

95. Memorandum of Conversation, Pauls and Freers, 26 September 1958, RG59, 648.62A/9-2658

96. Despatch 163, Siscoe to Department of State, 14 November 1958, RG59, 748.13/11-1458. Frank Siscoe, the chargè d'affaires ad interim, reported that he had received the record of the conversation from a reliable source who did not reveal the name of Gomułka's friend. Siscoe confirmed that the statements appeared to be true in light of other information obtained by the embassy.

97. Ibid.

98. Senate, *Documents on Germany, 1944–1970*, 350–355.

99. "Gomulka's Words Said to Deter U.S.," *New York Times*, 5 December 1958, 6; Jack Raymond, "U.S. to Aid Poles with New Credit Despite Attacks," *New York Times*, 13 December 1958, 6.

100. Senate, *Documents on Germany 1944–1970*, 358.

101. Ibid., 350–361, 375.

102. Ibid., 411–412, 420; Frank Ninkovich, *Germany and the United States: The Transformation of the German Question Since 1945* (Boston: Twayne, 1988), 124-125.

103. Despatch 753, Tyler to Department of State, 12 November 1958, RG59, 648.62A/11-1258. On 10 November 1958 at a meeting with Polish representatives, Khrushchev accused the West of violating the Potsdam Accord by supporting "militarist revenge seekers" in West Germany who wanted to take over East Germany and the Oder–Neisse lands. He warned that the West was "playing with fire" since the line was the "frontier of peace," and he assured the Poles of Soviet friendship against any encroachment on their frontier. See *Documents on Germany*, Address by Premier Khrushchev, 10 November 1958, 308–312.

104. Memorandum of Conversation, Winiewicz, Spasowski, Herter, et al., 14 November 1958, RG59, 748.13/11-1458.

105. Memorandum of Conversation, Spasowski, Kohler, and Sherer, 19 November 1958, RG59, 611.48/11-1958.

106. Telegram 807, Beam to Secretary of State, 8 December 1958, RG59,

611.48/12-858.

107. Telegram 809, Beam to Secretary of State, 9 December 1958, RG59, 648.00/12-958.

108. Despatch 482, Henderson to Department of State, 16 January 1959, RG59, 611.48/1-1659. The State Department deleted the name of the Polish official in the declassified copy of the despatch.

109. Ibid.

110. NSC 5808, U.S. Policy toward Poland, 11 February 1959, RG273, Records of the National Security Council, National Archives.

111. Airgram G-469, Tyler to Secretary of State, 18 February 1959, RG59, 762C.022/2-1959.

112. Despatch 329, Siscoe to Department of State, 6 March 1959, RG59, 748.00(W)/3-659.

113. A. M. Rosenthal, "Poles Encourage Settlers in West," *New York Times*, 4 March 1959, 5.

114. Despatch 329, Siscoe to Department of State, 6 March 1959, RG59, 748.00(W)/3-659.

115. Henry Kissinger, "'As Urgent as the Moscow Threat,'" *New York Times Magazine*, 8 March 1959, 19, 76–79.

116. Memorandum of Conversation, Rozmarek, Lagodzinski, Kohler, et al., 16 March 1959, RG59, 611.48/3-1659.

117. See *Dziennik Związkowy*, 16, 17 March 1959, and *Dziennik Polski*, 23 March 1959.

118. *Congressional Record*, 86th Cong., 1st sess., 105, pt. 5 (20 April 1959): 6251.

119. Memorandum of Conversation, Mossin and Johnson, 7 April 1959, RG59, 762C.022/4-759.

120. Memorandum of Conversation, Kmiecik and Johnson, 7 April 1959, RG59, 762C.022/4-759.

121. Memorandum of Conversation, Burke and Johnson, 7 April 1959, RG59, 762C.022/4-759. In addition to this difficulty for the State Department, President Eisenhower delivered a television address concerning the Berlin situation, standing in front of a map of Europe with the area east of the Oder–Neisse Line labeled "Poland." When a German exchange student living in New York wrote asking for clarification, the White House forwarded the letter to John A. Calhoun, director of the Executive Secretariat, asking for advice on a reply. On 19 April Press Secretary Hagery responded in a letter to the German student that the map used by the president was intended to show Berlin and its supply routes and had oversimplified its illustration of the East Central European situation. He reiterated that the map reflected no indication of American policy regarding other problems; the United States maintained that Germany's eastern border awaited a final peace settlement. See Letter, Zirkel to Hagerty, 21 March 1959, DDE Central Files, Official File, Box 865, File 182, DDE/L.

122. Wandycz, *The United States*, 372; Brzezinski, *The Soviet Bloc*, 364.

123. Memorandum of Conversation, Spasowski, Murphy, and Johnson, 10 April 1959, RG59, 611.48/4-1059.

124. Ibid.

125. Kulski, *Germany and Poland*, 93. See also Wladyslaw W. Kulski, *DeGaulle and the World: The Foreign Policy of the fifth French Republic* (Syracuse, NY: Syracuse University Press, 1966), 289. The Warsaw Embassy had reported to Washington on the satisfaction of the Polish press with DeGaulle's suggestion and gave "prominence" to Bonn's "dismay" at his statement. See Despatch 362, Donovan to Department of State, 3 April 1959, RG59, 748.00(W)/4-359.

126. Memorandum of Conversation, Spasowski and Kohler, 10 April 1959, RG59, 611.48/4-1059.

127. Intelligence Report 8015, Declassified Documents Catalog, 1981 (Woodbridge, CT Research Publications, 1981), Fiche No. 81, 19.

128. Hanrieder, *Germany, America, Europe*, 164–165; Gatzke, *Germany and the United States*, 189–190, and Ninkovich, *Germany and the United States*, 126.

129. Memorandum of Conversation, Spasowski and Kohler, 22 May 1959, RG59, 648.62A/5-2259.

130. Sydney Gruson, "Bonn to Reaffirm Views on Borders," *New York Times*, 17 May 1959, 18.

131. Memorandum of Conversation, Spasowski and Kohler, 22 May 1959, RG59, 648.62A/5-2259.

132. Letter, Starzewski to Herter, 11 June 1959, RG59, 762C.022/6-1159.

133. Letter, Starzewski to Herter, 22 July 1959, RG59, 762C.022/7-2259.

134. Telegram 193, Bruce to Secretary of State, 27 July 1959, RG59, 648.62A/7-2759.

135. Despatch 53, Donovan to Secretary of State, 31 July 1959, RG59, 748.00(W)/7-3159; Despatch 468, AmEmbassy Warsaw to Department of State, 5 June 1959, RG59, 748.00(W)/6-559.

136. Letters, Gasowski to Bentley, 19 May 1959, Bentley to Nixon, 22 May 1959, Nixon to Bentley, 6 June 1959, Bentley correspondence, Alvin Bentley Collection, Box 30 Bentley Library; *Department of State Bulletin* (17 August 1959), Vol. 41, No. 1051, 236.

137. Despatch 62, Siscoe to Department of State, 7 August 1959, RG59, 748.00(W)/8-759.

138. Despatch 53, Donovan to Secretary of State, 31 July 1959, RG59, 748.00(W)/7-3159.

139. Telegram 209, Beam (for Nixon) to Secretary of State (for Eisenhower), 4 August 1959, White House Office of Staff Secretary, International Trips and Meetings, Box 7, Vice-President's Trip to Russia and Poland, DDE/L. When President Zawadzki invited the vice president to stay at the president's lake house in the area of Mazury, the recording officer noted parenthetically: "Although I am not entirely certain of it, I believe that the land and the house described by President Zawadzki are on former East Prussian territory." See Memo, Glenn to Sherrer, 17 August 1959, RG59, 611.48/8-1759.

140. Memorandum of Conversation, Krapf, Kohler, and Dean; 12 August 1959, RG59, 648.62A/8-1259.

141. Telegram 361, Dillon to Amembassy Bonn, 15 August 1959, RG59, 648.62A/8-1359.

142. Ibid.

143. Memo, Williams, 22 August 1959, Ann Whitman File, International

Meeting Series, Box 3, DDE/L.

144. Memo, O'Connor to Merchant, 26 August 1959, RG59, 611.48/8-2659.

145. Senate, *Documents on Germany, 1944–1970*, 481–482.

146. *Public Papers of the President-Eisenhower*, 1959, Section 191.

147. A. M. Rosenthal, "Eisenhower a Hero to Warsaw as a Result of His Stand in Bonn," *New York Times*, 29 August 1959, 4.

148. *Congressional Record*, 86th Cong., 1st sess., 105, pt. 14: 17491.

149. Despatch 106, Siscoe to Department of State, 18 September 1959, RG59, 748.00(W)/9-1859.

150. Ibid.

151. Memorandum of Conversation, Murphy, Kohler, Ochab, et al., 6 October 1959, RG59, 748.13/10-659.

152. Memo, White to Secretary, 5 October 1959, RG59, 611.48/10-559.

153. Memorandum of Conversation, Herter and Rapacki, et al., 6 October 1959, RG59, 748.13/10-659.

154. Memo, Kohler to Secretary, 13 October 1959, RG59, 748.13/10-1359.

155. Memo, Hillenbrand to Kohler, 19 October 1959, White House Office, Office of Staff Secretary: Records of Paul T. Carroll, Andrew J. Goodpaster, L. Arthur Minnich, and Christopher H. Russell, 1952–1961, International Series, Box 6, DDE/L. This memorandum was an addendum to a memo of 16 October 1959 regarding proposals for the upcoming summit.

156. Ibid.

157. Ibid.

158. Memo, Hager to Undersecretary for Political Affairs, 28 October 1959, RG59, 762C.022/10-2859.

159. Kulski, *DeGaulle and the World*, 289–290.

160. Telegram 934, Timberlake to Secretary of State, 13 November 1959, RG59, 762C.022/11-1359; Telegram 922, Timberlake to Secretary of State, 11 November 1959, RG59, 762C.022/11-1159.

161. Telegram 922, Timberlake to Secretary; *News from the German Embassy* 3, no. 15 (7 November 1959): 4.

162. Airgram G-245, Timberlake to Secretary of State, 25 November 1959, RG59, 762C.022/11-2559.

163. Despatch 190, Consulate General in Frankfurt to Department of State, 1 December 1959, RG59, 648.62A/12-159; *News from the German Embassy* 4, no. 1 (6 January 1960): 3–4.

164. Despatch 163, Warsaw Embassy to Department of State, 30 October 1959, RG59, 748.00(W)/10-3059. Another report in *Trybuna Ludu* on 29 December 1959 cited a statement by University of Bonn professor Jan A. Iwand, who favored recognition of the Oder–Neisse and who called attention to DeGaulle's statement and to Nixon's "'eloquent silence'" on the issue when he was in Warsaw. See Despatch 262, Magistretti to Department of State, 30 December 1959, RG59, 748.00(W)/12-3059.

165. J. Emlyn Williams, "Bonn Focuses on Poland," *Christian Science Monitor*, 14 July 1959, 4.

166. Memo, Mueller to Paarlberg, 3 December 1959, DDE Central Files, Official File, Box 886, DDE/L.

167. Letter, Macomber to Karsten, 4 November 1959, RG59, 762C.022/10-2759.

168. In a 2 April 1957 letter to the chairman of the ACEN, the Polish Delegation under Korbonski complained that the assembly had "avoided taking a positive stand on the question . . . despite the fact that such a recognition is not in conflict with the territorial interests of any members of the Assembly." The letter stated the Polish delegation viewed the assembly as a "certain hinderance in defense of these interests." ACEN Papers, 4.402 Polish Delegation to ACEN file, IHRC. In Korbonski's memoirs he notes that in 1958 the Romanian delegate opposed having a Pole as chairman of the ACEN partly because of the "hostile" attitude toward West Germany over the border issue displayed by the Polish representatives. See Stafan Korbonski, *Warsaw in Exile*, trans. David J. Welch (New York: Frederick Praeger, 1966), 164.

169. Korbonski also left with Johnson a copy of a "circular letter" that had appeared in the Paris émigré journal *Kultura* on 22 August 1959 that also favored U.S. recognition of the line in order to lessen the Soviet hold on Poland. Memorandum of Conversation, Korbonski and Johnson, 16 November 1959, RG59, 611.48/11-1659.

170. The report also contended that ideology also restricted Gomulka, in spite of the Poles' expression of nationalism. U.S. Congress, Senate, "United States Foreign Policy: The Formulation and Administration of United States Foreign Policy," 86th Cong., 2nd sess. (13 January 1960), no. 9.

171. "Memo on Forthcoming Summit Conference Paris 1960 to Herter—Submitted by Polish American Congress 14 March 1960," ACEN General Committee, 16 March 1960, ACEN, 7.264 PAC, Inc. File, IHRC. Congressman Machrowicz (D-MI) read the text of this PAC memorandum into the *Congressional Record. Congressional Record Appendix*, 86th Cong., 2nd sess., 106, pt. 18 (17 March 1960): A2413–A2414.

172. Wandycz, *The United States*, 352.

173. "RFE Broadcasting Policy toward Poland," DDE/L in Declassified Documents, 1989, Fiche 166.

174. Gomułka's isolation after the support that he expressed for Yugoslavia and his objection to the Nagy execution was noted in the report. "Report by Operations Coordinating Board—Approved by President: 16 April 1959, Covers 11 February 1959–30 March 1960," White House Office—Office of Special Assistant for National Security Affairs Records, 1952–1961, NSC Series, Policy Paper Subseries, Box 24, DDE/L.

175. Ernest Pisko, "Warsaw Eyes Bonn Darkly," *Christian Science Monitor*, 14 June 1960, 12.

176. "Polish Note Studied," *New York Times*, 28 July 1960, 2; "U.S. Explains to Poland," *New York Times*, 12 August 1960, 5; "Poland Quizzes NATO on East Prussia's Future," *Christian Science Monitor*, 27 July 1960, 4; "U.S. Reassures Poland in Border Dispute," *Christian Science Monitor*, 3.

177. Wandycz, *The United States*, 370.

178. ACEN Papers. 4.433 Mr. Adam Niebieszczanski file, IHRC.

179. Presidium of Polish Council of National Unity in U.S., ACEN Papers, 4.400 Polish Council of National Unity File, IHRC.

180. Korbonski, *Warsaw in Exile*, 289.

181. "U.S. Stands Firm on Poland's Line," *New York Times*, 25 October 1960, 23.

182. ACEN, 6.686 John F. Kennedy Folder, IHRC.

183. Telegram, Polish Home Army Association to Kennedy, 2 November 1960, Pre-Presidential Papers, Box 738, JFK/L.

184. Korbonski, *Warsaw in Exile*, 285.

185. Sydney Gruson, "Adenauer Taking Buffeting Calmly," *New York Times*, 24 October 1960, 10.

186. "*Nixon o Odrze i Nysie,*" *Dziennik Zwiazkowy*, 25 October 1960, 6.

187. "*Nixon und die Oder-Neisse-Linie,*" *Abendpost*, 25 October 1960, 2; "Editor Scores Nixon," *New York Times*, 27 October 1960, 29.

188. "Statement of U.S. Policy toward Poland," NSC 6103, White House Office: Office of the Special Assistant for National Security Affairs: Records 1952–1961, Papers Received since 10 January 1961 Series, Box 1, DDE/L.

7 The Kennedy and Johnson Administrations

The administrations succeeding Eisenhower continued to grapple with the Oder–Neisse issue as it gained increasing prominence as "'one of the most pressing issues of concern'" in Washington, according to a State Department official in 1967.[1] The Kennedy and Johnson administrations sustained the momentum begun during the Eisenhower administration, pushing the initiative for action on the border issue from Washington to Bonn as changes in the leadership and outlook of West Germany's government led to increased contact with the Soviet satellite states of East Central Europe.

Kennedy's election as president was warmly hailed by Polish Americans and by the Polish people who generally viewed him as an advocate of Polish causes and of working-class concerns. His Catholicism was probably an added advantage in the eyes of most Polish Americans.[2] The young president's dynamic personality and his talk of a "New Frontier" in American foreign policy seemed to offer hope for change from the perceived passivity of the aging Eisenhower administration. Kennedy's January 1961 State of the Union message included an expression of friendship and an interest in offering aid to Poland. More than simple rhetoric was needed in dealing with the Polish situation, however. Gomułka's closer alliance with Moscow resulted in the Warsaw government's open condemnation of the Bay of Pigs incident and the development of a "united front" of East Germany and Poland against West Germany.[3] This lessened Washington's chances for successfully pressuring Bonn into adopting a more open attitude toward East Central Europe, chances already complicated by the clash of personalities and style of Kennedy and Adenauer. Kennedy's youthfulness made him suspect by Adenauer; in turn Kennedy viewed *der Alte* as one of the "inflexible remnants of the Cold War."[4]

In addition to handling these diplomatic tensions arising from the European situation, the Kennedy administration faced increasing pressure from members of Congress, Polish American organizations, and foreign policy scholars to recognize the Oder–Neisse Line. In spite of this pressure and "New

Frontier" rhetoric, President Kennedy and the State Department continued the approach begun during the second Eisenhower administration of publicly maintaining that the final solution to the border problem awaited a peace conference, while confidentially discussing the possibility of pressuring Bonn to recognize the Oder–Neisse in order to foster closer Bonn–Warsaw relations.[5] Much of Kennedy's attention to Poland centered on the question of economic assistance and trade, with the president eventually winning from Congress limited discretionary power to apply most-favored-nation status through legislative loopholes.[6] While this economic assistance was vitally important to Poland, Polish representatives also looked for a positive U.S. statement on the Oder–Neisse Line, especially in light of the continuing tension between Bonn and Warsaw.

Secretary of State Dean Rusk outlined the status of these relations between West Germany and Poland as a possible discussion item when Kennedy met with West German Foreign Minister Heinrich von Brentano in February 1961. Rusk predicted that von Brentano would express an interest in improving relations with Warsaw in spite of such obstacles as the border question, Poland's recognition of the East German regime, and the Polish government's condemnation of the expellees' activities. Rusk encouraged Kennedy to express appreciation for the expanded contact between the former enemies and to convey the hope that Bonn would take "every suitable opportunity" to continue such contacts.[7] A subtle, but noticeable, softening of dialogue is evident in the secretary's recommendations to the president concerning West German matters, perhaps reflecting the Kennedy State Department's need for time to establish its own diplomatic tone following eight years of Eisenhower rhetoric.

When Rusk met with outgoing Polish Ambassador Spasowski on 10 April 1961, the ambassador stated pessimistically that the Adenauer government seemed to be playing into the hands of the pressure groups in West Germany that demanded territorial revision and an aggressive military stance.[8] At a news conference a few days later Kennedy was asked about a statement that Gomułka had made claiming that during the presidential campaign someone high in the Kennedy administration had given assurances (with Adenauer's knowledge) that if Kennedy were elected, he would perceive the border as final. Kennedy replied that he had read the story but was unaware of Gomułka's contact. He reverted to the standard diplomatic response by stating, "In any case, I was not informed of any conversation then or since then. . . . I think that the satisfactory solution on the line should be part of a general solution of the problem of Germany, involving the peace treaty with Germany and all the rest."[9]

The State Department continued its tone of caution in recommending points of discussion for the president when he received Polish Ambassador-designate Edward Drozniak in June 1961.[10] The State Department sent a memorandum to the White House warning that Drozniak might raise "matters of substance," even though the Polish government had assured Washington that he would not. The memo, listing some of these points, recommended that the president not address them if Drozniak initiated a discussion about them. One of those points was the claim that West German rearmament and "alleged German 'revisionism'" threatened Poland's western border. The State Department thought Drozniak might take the opportunity to urge Kennedy to issue a statement that the United States viewed the line as permanent. The authors recommended that the president give a noncommittal reply that the U.S. accepted Bonn's announcements renouncing the use of force and that West Germany's participation in NATO made German aggression unlikely. Kennedy was urged to highlight the point that the United States favored settlement of all the German issues, including "the now vital problem of Berlin," as a whole rather than in a "piecemeal fashion."[11]

Although President Kennedy had to fulfill these diplomatic functions, his primary interest continued to be strategic foreign policy. Like the Bay of Pigs, the 1962 missile crisis had a negative impact on U.S.–Polish relations as Polish officials denounced American recklessness as a threat to peace.[12] The resolution of the crisis, however, resulted in increased communication between the superpowers as they "eased into a period of coexistence."[13] The growing suspicion in Bonn that Washington was satisfied with the status quo in Germany led the West German government to recognize the need to formulate a policy toward the East bloc to keep up with the shifting geopolitical situation. Because the West German government continued to oppose the Oder–Neisse border and persisted in calling for *Heimatrecht*, however, Bonn's contacts with Poland were limited to commercial missions.[14] In March 1962 Premier Cyrankiewicz reinforced Poland's earlier requirement that Bonn accept the Oder–Neisse border before diplomatic relations could be established.[15] In the same month, Poland's Foreign Minister Adam Rapacki bluntly told Secretary of State Rusk that Poland did not favor German unification "under contemporary circumstances" and that Poland still feared "West German designs." Rapacki seemed unmoved by Rusk's attempt to justify German reunification as the "best long-term guarantee against future recrudescence of expansionist nationalism."[16]

Kennedy refused to alter the U.S. position on the Oder–Neisse border issue, but with his continued expressions of support for freedom for Poland, his standing in the Polish American community remained high. The Polish Institute of Arts and Sciences in America published a collection of documents and statements recording Kennedy's expressions of support for Poland.[17] Nevertheless, the problems of Berlin and Germany, not Poland, became for Kennedy the focus of the Cold War in Central Europe. His summit meeting with Khrushchev in Vienna in June 1961 ended with the Soviet premier's threat of a December 1961 deadline when he would sign a peace treaty with East Germany. Kennedy delivered a televised address announcing that Berlin had become "'the great testing place of Western courage and will.'"[18] The Soviets and East Germans moved on 13 August to enclose the city. In Adenauer's eyes, Kennedy's response to the building of the wall was insufficient and indicated Washington's lack of real interest in settling the German problem to Bonn's satisfaction. Some high-ranking West Germans had expressed such misgivings during the Eisenhower administration, but suspicions were further heightened by the tensions between Adenauer and Kennedy.

Adenauer's fears were justified; State Department and White House memoranda showed that some American officials were willing to compromise on the two issues that Bonn considered nonnegotiable: East Germany and the Oder–Neisse Line. A member of the NSC staff proposed in a memorandum that the United States negotiate a deal with the Soviets and East Germans offering recognition of East Germany and acceptance of the Oder–Neisse Line in return for guarantees of Berlin and "mutual security."[19] In an April 1963 airgram from Warsaw, Ambassador John Cabot referred to the possibility of U.S. recognition of the Oder–Neisse Line in order to gain concessions from the Polish government. He advised against such a move, however, since "Germany is an ally and Poland is a member of a hostile bloc." Although the ambassador disapproved of such a move, his reference to U.S. recognition provides evidence that the border issue continued to be discussed and debated in high diplomatic circles.[20] McGeorge Bundy, Kennedy's security adviser, reported to the president the "growing belief among those at work on our negotiating position" that the United States should change its position to accept the East German regime, recognize the Oder–Neisse Line, and accept two peace treaties and a nonaggression pact with the Soviets. No movement was made in this direction, however. In an analysis of this situation published in 1988, Bundy placed the onus on Khrushchev for not initiating any such proposals that "would have . . . [been] powerful reasons to press Bonn for concessions."[21] The 1961 Berlin crisis revealed the differences between Bonn and Washington more openly; Bonn began seriously to reflect on its involvement with the Eastern satellites in the face of its disappointments with the West.[22]

Although the White House refused to upset the uneasy equilibrium in Germany, the Berlin crisis offered congressmen the opportunity to express their views and urge action in Germany and Poland. A lengthy memorandum from Senator Claiborne Pell (D-RI) analyzed various solutions to the German problem. Pell contended that it was vitally important to deal with the German problem as a whole rather than settle the Berlin situation separately since, he said, neither the United States nor the USSR could retreat on Berlin. Thus any attempt to reach agreement solely on that issue would fail. He offered three possible courses of action for the United States, "any one of which we could accept." The first was that the United States could foster stability in East Central Europe by accepting the Oder–Neisse Line as President DeGaulle had done. He pointed out that 2.5 million Poles had been born in the territories and he contended that "the average German is not losing sleep over it." The second was a temporary recognition of East Germany with provisions for Berlin, and the third was a commitment by Washington never to provide nuclear weapons to West Germany if the Soviets did the same for East Germany.[23]

Senator Pell reiterated this position in the Senate in September 1961, where he was "congratulated" by senators, according to the *New York Times*.[24] Pell's recommendations took on increased urgency after he spent three weeks in East Central Europe, including the area along the Oder and Neisse Rivers. He sent the president a letter from the NATO Conference in Paris on 15 November 1961 urging him to read the letter before his meeting with Adenauer, forcefully telling Kennedy that U.S. recognition of the Oder–Neisse Line would do more than anything else to "wean Poland from the Soviets." He wrote that the Poles whom he met were much more afraid of a German invasion than of negative actions by the Soviets and reiterated the claim that Adenauer was more upset with the idea of two Germanys than were most Germans. He encouraged the president to persuade Adenauer that recognition of the Oder–Neisse and acceptance of the "loss of Prussia" would be the greatest contribution to Western integration that he could make.[25] Other members of Congress also took up the Oder–Neisse issue by reading into the *Congressional Record* resolutions or correspondence from Polish American organizations echoing traditional Polish American views that the land belonged to Poland and that West Germany was a revanchist power.[26]

In addition to having congressmen present the views of Polish American organizations, the Polish American Congress and the Polish Western Association of America (PWA) continued to champion their cause directly with the Executive Branch. The PWA sent to the president and the State Department a letter in April 1961 prior to Kennedy's Vienna meeting with Khrushchev. The letter reviewed the issue of the Oder–Neisse Line and called for West German recognition of the line as a way to normalize and to confirm peaceful relations between Bonn and Warsaw.[27] In June 1961 the PWA sent a memorandum on the border to Edward Derwinski (R-IL) that he forwarded to Dean Rusk with the note that it was a "calm and pertinent analysis, which discusses a subject of major importance with vast political repercussions in the sphere of European affairs."[28] Assistant Secretary Brook Hays' response to the memorandum must have discouraged the Polish American organizations. He outlined the U.S. position by citing the Yalta and Potsdam provisions and told Derwinski that since the Potsdam Conference, the United States had maintained, in spite of Soviet obstruction, that a total, rather than piecemeal, settlement of the issue was needed. He encouraged Polish Americans to acknowledge the West German renunciation of force and view the situation in the light of an overall European peace settlement.[29]

In spite of such dissuasion, Polish American spokesmen continued to press their point. The Polish American Congress issued a memorandum in August 1961 addressing the German problem. Like the State Department, the PAC opposed dealing separately with the Berlin crisis. Unlike Washington, however, the Polish American organization wanted an "intensified diplomatic, economic, political propaganda and cultural offensive against the Soviet empire," since, the authors of the memorandum stated, "the road of European unity in freedom . . . does not end in Berlin." The focus of this campaign, they argued, should be Poland, and one of the primary actions in the campaign would be American recognition of the Oder–Neisse Line. The memorandum contended that West German revisionists were "perhaps unwittingly" strengthening Moscow's hold over Warsaw with their "unrealistic demands and turmoils" by weakening the pro-Western orientation of the Polish people. The PAC cited as "a matter of record" appropriations by the government in Bonn for increased propaganda in the United States and Great Britain favoring revision of the border. The authors claimed that Poland had resettled the western lands without outside help and pointed out that over half of the 8 million Poles in the territories were born there. From a logistical point, they argued that if Germany were reunified, it would have great difficulty repopulating the "eastern half now occupied by the Soviets" and contended with emotion that if the western lands were given to a reunited Germany, Polish slave labor would again be used.[30] John Kluczynski (D-IL) read this memorandum to the House of Representatives in September 1961 and noted that Rozmarek had presented it in person to Kennedy and Rusk.[31]

While this correspondence about the Oder–Neisse Line from Polish American organizations reflected a dogged determination that Poland hold onto the western territories, much of it began to present practical considerations and justification for retention of the line rather than reiterations of the argument that the Potsdam Agreement had definitively returned historically Polish lands to Poland. By the early 1960s Polish Americans and some members of Congress began arguing that the Polish settlement of the region and the high birthrate of the settlers made German demands for *Heimatrecht* less persuasive since the generation of Poles born in the territories had a right to their birthplace. Advocates of the Oder–Neisse Line also presented arguments about the German problem that Washington found difficult to refute without revealing confidential information about the Washington–Bonn alliance.

On 28 May 1962 Roman Pucinski noted a series of articles by the bureau chief of the Chicago Daily News Service that argued that Warsaw was "nourish[ing] the suspicion" that Bonn would try to recover the Oder–Neisse territories.[32] Pucinski also read into the *Congressional Record* the statement adopted by the Polish American Congress at the Sixth National meeting in Washington, D.C., in June. The PAC contended that the U.S. position in Berlin was nonnegotiable and that the issue could be solved only within a large European framework. The first step in achieving this "grand strategy of peace" was recognition of the Oder–Neisse Line as outlined by Senator Kennedy in 1960.[33] The Polish American group also reiterated that the Poles had recovered the land to make its industrial and agricultural output higher than it had been under the Germans.

The statement that Pucinski read claimed further that the United States had three options. The first was to support Bonn's revisionism, which the Soviets wanted in order to strengthen their ties to Poland. The second was to continue its middle-of-the-road policy, thereby making the United States unpopular with both the Poles and revanchist Germans. The third was to recognize the Oder–Neisse Line in order to convince East Central Europeans that Germany's drive to the east would be halted. Germany's nonforce pledge, the statement continued, was meaningless, as were calls for a NATO guarantee of this pledge since they left open the possibility of border revision. The policy statement emphasized that the land was vital to Poland and that its transfer was not negotiable.[34]

In issuing such warnings of potential German actions, Polish American organizations continued to differentiate between a revanchist German minority and a majority which accepted the loss of the eastern territories. The Committee for the Affairs of Polish Western Territories, part of the California-Arizona Division of the Polish American Congress, argued this point in its July 1962 publication "Polish Western Territories." The editor, Joseph Sanocki, quoted statements from a number of prominent West German politicians supporting the Oder–Neisse Line and rebuking the expellee organizations' propaganda campaign. Sanocki's claim that the West German majority was ready to accept the line in opposition to a small, but vocal, minority supporting revision echoed the stance taken by communist officials of the Polish government. This shows again the ironic and certainly unacknowledged partnerships created by the Oder–Neisse issue since the Polish American Congress maintained a staunch anticommunist stance that opposed most of Warsaw's other views and activities.[35]

In addition to these voices from the U.S. Congress and Polish American organizations, respected members of the foreign policy community outside the administration urged action by the United States on the Oder–Neisse border issue. Zbigniew Brzezinski, associate professor of law and government at Columbia, published a number of articles favoring some type of government declaration on the line. In a 1961 article in *Foreign Affairs* Brzezinski claimed that the time was right for U.S. initiatives to encourage diversity in Eastern Europe. He pointed especially to the situation in Poland, where the communists exploited the West's "lack of clarity" on the border issue to further their position, and to the expellee pressures in West Germany that made it impossible for Bonn to recognize the border. He did not consider formal recognition by the United States possible under international law since a unified Germany did not exist but he urged instead that the United States and NATO endorse Bonn's no-force pledge and make a commitment to having the pledge put in a peace treaty. Brzezinski also wanted the United States to press the point in West Germany that reunification was impossible without major changes in relations with Poland and the Soviet Union. This, he wrote, would reduce Poland's fear of

German revanchism and would show West Germany and Poland that the U.S. position on the border was in the long-term interest of Germany. Brzezinski also urged that the U.S. open consulates in either Szczecin or Wroclow as a symbol of the American commitment to maintenance of the Oder–Neisse border.[36] Although his suggestions were not immediately followed, Brzezinski's opinions carried some weight in the White House.

In a letter to "Mac" (McGeorge Bundy), Brzezinski informed him of conversations that he had held with Polish Embassy officials at their request. In a conversation on 22 August 1961 the Polish officials had told him that they perceived "no problem" with the Oder–Neisse Line and considered talk of Western recognition of the border in connection with the Berlin crisis "unrealistic." The Polish ambassador told Brzezinski that the only way to secure peace in East Central Europe was to eliminate the German "threat," especially the "diversionary activity" in West Berlin and the claims on Poland's western lands. He added that since world opinion was turning against the West on these issues, he believed that Khrushchev's terms would be met.[37] Bundy thanked Brzezinski for the information and stated that while he saw no reason for Brzezinski not to participate in such talks with Polish officials, the White House had "more channels" than it could use when it came to more "serious two-way communication."[38]

Another scholar of international relations who, like Brzezinski, would later serve the White House also supported some type of U.S. acknowledgment of the Oder–Neisse Line. In his 1962 publication, *The Necessity for Choice: Prospects of American Foreign Policy,* Henry Kissinger criticized the lack of initiative shown by Washington regarding the German problem in the late 1950s and questioned the wisdom and morality of the initial decision to move the border and expel the population. He also advocated a realistic assessment of the situation by West Germany, because, he said "the mistakes of the past should not be compounded by new errors." Kissinger claimed that the Federal Republic should be willing to "pay for unification" by recognizing the Oder–Neisse Line and that the West should formally renounce the use of force to change the line. Kissinger, again like Brzezinski, believed that the United States and NATO should give a military guarantee of the line pending unification. He differed from Brzezinski in his contention that while this would not dramatically change the situation, it would "define the issue" and separate the territorial question from the problem of reunification.[39]

Finally, Hans Morgenthau, another respected authority on international politics, called for a more realistic assessment of U.S. border policy. In his 1962 *The Restoration of American Politics*, Morgenthau openly urged the West to recognize the Oder–Neisse border as DeGaulle had done in 1959, rather than continue to foster the belief in Bonn that Germany would recover its eastern lands, a position that Morgenthau termed "an illusion in the trappings of a policy."[40] His article in the *New York Times* entitled "Germany Gives Rise to Vast Uncertainties" reiterated this position in September 1963 after Kennedy's trip to Berlin. Morgenthau baldly outlined the realities of the situation in which Bonn held a veto over U.S. action in Europe with the unspoken "nightmare" of an eastern-oriented Germany since there was still doubt about Adenauer's successors and about German "tendencies." An "unhealthy state of affairs" existed, Morgenthau claimed, when West German politicians privately admitted that the means to achieve reunification and recovery of the eastern areas were limited but publicly committed themselves to attaining these unachievable goals through the medium of Western integration. U.S. policy, he argued, should seek to lessen the gap between illusion and reality by "toning down the verbal commitments" and helping to establish relations between West and East Germany. The dangers facing the United States if it did not adjust to the realities, Morgenthau claimed, were twofold. The lesser danger was of another Rapallo; the greater was of losing the impetus in a newly realigned Europe, ironically at the hands of the new West German leaders.[41]

Internal governmental sources confirmed the assessments made by these foreign policy scholars. An analysis of West Germany's political and economic situation by the State Department's Intelligence Bureau predicted that while West Germany would continue to hope for improved relations with the satellite states, an active policy was considered almost impossible in light of the unresolved question of reunification. Like Morgenthau, the intelligence officers believed that West German leaders had a realistic assessment of East Central Europe, which meant that they knew that the recovery of the Oder–Neisse lands was not a "vital irredentist issue" even among the expellees. "West Germans on the whole have little expectation that the German border will be moved east of the Oder–Neisse Line except in the context of a larger German settlement," they stated. They believed also that the Hallstein Doctrine was negotiable if it proved to be an obstacle to better relations with Poland.[42]

These evaluations by Polish American organizations, scholars, and State Department officials that the majority of West Germans were willing to compromise on the border issue were accurate. West Germans in the 1960s increasingly expressed interest in "Poland and things Polish."[43] A growing number of prominent voices in West Germany favored settlement of the issue in order to foster improved relations with the East bloc. The historian Golo Mann published articles advocating acceptance of the line.[44] Hansjakob Stehle, a Warsaw-based correspondent for the West German newspaper *Frankfurter Allgemeine Zeitung*, promoted a German guarantee of the Oder–Neisse Line prior to the required peace treaty in a popular book published in 1963.[45] Adding to the list of prominent Germans who supported the line was Klaus von Bismarck, great nephew of the former chancellor, who along with other members of the Protestant Church issued a memorandum in November 1961 to all Protestant members of the Bundestag. The memo accused the government of hiding the truth about the need to abandon German claims to the eastern territories and favored recognition of the border within "the framework of a broadly conceived understanding" in order to foster better relations with the East bloc.[46]

The West German government responded to such calls by working toward improved trade relations with Warsaw.[47] Washington continued to favor Bonn's openings to the East but made a point of publicly supporting the Bonn–Washington alliance, thereby showing, according to Wolfram Hanrieder, that "Bonn and Washington did not fully trust one another, but neither side felt free to bring out in the open the underlying conflict of interests and intensions."[48] Kennedy traveled to Berlin in June 1963 to meet with West German leaders and in a speech at the Berlin Wall to show U.S. solidarity with the aspirations of the German people for freedom. For the United States, France, and Great Britain Berlin had symbolic importance; it became the "residue of their interest in the German question" that kept in the forefront the rights of the Allied powers.[49] Bonn recognized this growing rift with its powerful allies, but the government's tenacious hold on its demands for territorial revision in the east and its rejection of the two Germanys idea limited its flexibility. Even after administrative changes in 1963, when Ludwig Erhard became chancellor, Bonn would not move beyond this position.[50] The changes in Bonn were matched by dramatic changes in Washington and Moscow after Kennedy's assassination and Khrushchev's October 1964 fall from power. Nevertheless, it was not until the mid-1960s when the CDU lost its twenty-year hold on the government that real changes in Bonn's *Ostpolitik* could be made.

Kennedy's assassination provoked shock and mourning not only in the United States but also in Poland.[51] Johnson vowed to continue his predecessor's foreign policy and kept many of Kennedy's advisers. The new president's attention was focused, however, much more on Asia than Europe. America's involvement in Vietnam made the United States increasingly unpopular in Europe and coincided with DeGaulle's efforts to formulate a "Europe from the Atlantic to the Urals" without American involvement.[52] The French president's efforts were suspect in Bonn, however, and were a prime motivating factor for Bonn's determination to mend fences with Washington. While Erhard developed a close personal friendship with Johnson, these personal ties could not mask the diverging foreign policy goals of these Cold War allies.[53] The Johnson administration was determined not to abandon East Central Europe, advocating a policy of "bridge building" that was intended to promote contact with Eastern Europe through cultural exchanges, trade, and emergency aid.[54] The president wanted especially to maintain good relations with Warsaw, but Gomulka's support of the Vietcong and his efforts to stay in the good graces of Moscow strained these relations.[55]

In July 1964 Ambassador John Cabot in Warsaw sent a telegram to the secretary of state informing him of the content of speeches by Gomułka and Khrushchev at a rally in Warsaw, reported by the Polish Press Agency. The Polish leader's comments were very anti-German and anti-American, claiming that German imperialism was being revived with U.S. aid as seen in Bonn's desire to "'swallow'" East Germany and in its territorial demands and calls for atomic capability. Gomułka claimed that Bonn would not try to attack the east without its NATO allies. "At this point," Cabot informed Rusk, "I walked out." The Polish leader continued his diatribe against the United States, especially Washington's alleged attempt to place nuclear weapons in West Germany.[56] This warlike direction, he claimed, was furthered by the nomination of Barry Goldwater as the Republican presidential candidate. He noted that Goldwater's chances were "doubtful" but argued that his nomination showed the threat to world peace by advocates of "aggressive imperialist circles" who would not hesitate to "put their finger to [the] safety catch of joint nuclear force . . . [and] let it off . . . to unleash war." Gomułka continued in this vein; Cabot reported that the British Ambassador left after Gomułka finished speaking and did not wait for Khrushchev's speech.[57]

When Khrushchev was removed from power a few months later, American representatives closely monitored the situation for its potential impact on East bloc relations. In a memorandum Thomas Hughes of the Intelligence and Research Office of the State Department informed the secretary of a TASS announcement that Brezhnev, Kosygin, and Andropov had met with Gomułka, Cyrankiewicz, and Politburo member Kliszko on the Polish–Soviet frontier. Hughes stated that the timing of the meeting suggested the extent of the concern that the Soviets felt about East Europe, especially Poland's "self-assertive reaction to Khrushchev's fall." Hughes stated that the Soviet leaders had reassured Gomulka "on matters of vital interest to him," which probably included an explanation of Khrushchev's removal, a reassurance of their commitment to the Oder–Neisse, recognition of Poland's interest in negotiations between the Soviets and Germans, and recognition of Poland's concern about Soviet economic relations with Poland.[58]

Later in the year, Secretary Rusk heard firsthand about Poland's views of its neighbors when he met with Foreign Minister Adam Rapacki at the United Nations. Rapacki expressed concern about the potential instability that the proposed Multi Lateral Force (MLF) would bring to Central Europe, a region where tensions remained high in spite of increased economic and cultural contacts. He made reference to the Oder–Neisse Line by pointing out that only France recognized the border and expressed doubt that the Bonn government had any intention of seeking to reduce tensions with Warsaw. When Secretary Rusk reiterated that Poland's safety would be better secured by resolution of the "German problem" with a U.S. guarantee, Foreign Minster Rapacki expressed scepticism, noting that Poland had "had the strongest of guaranties in 1939 and then lost six million people." In response Rusk reminded Rapacki somewhat bluntly that the United States had fought "in two world wars in which it did not find itself on the same side as Germany."[59]

Economic contacts with the United States suffered as Congress continued to debate and set limits on aid to Poland and other communist countries, but cultural contacts with Poland improved during Johnson's presidency.[60] Also, President Johnson was determined that U.S. involvement in Vietnam would not preclude improved East–West relations; the State Department tried to improve diplomatic relations by using the Polish government's ties to the North Vietnamese to establish Warsaw as the site for secret meetings with North Vietnamese leaders.[61] Thus, like the Kennedy administration, the Johnson administration recognized the importance of the Oder–Neisse issue and continued to pressure Bonn to act. Also like Kennedy, Johnson found powerful obstacles to better Bonn–Warsaw relations, especially West Germany's growing military strength. It is also evident that Johnson, again like Kennedy, was pressured for settlement of the border issue from members of the foreign policy establishment, Congress, and Polish American organizations. Added to this pressure, frequent coverage of the issue in the mainstream press in the 1960s demanded the attention of the government and public.

Although Johnson did not have Kennedy's personal appeal in the Polish American community, his "bridge- building" program had the support of the Polish American Congress.[62] His reappointment of Kennedy's Postmaster General John Gronouski in 1963, the first Polish American to hold a cabinet post, was also popular with American Polonia. Gronouski provided information to the White House about the views of Polish Americans on a number of issues, including the Oder–Neisse Line. In a 21 July 1964 memorandum to McGeorge Bundy, the president's special assistant for national security affairs, Gronouski reported that the Polish American press constantly analyzed the Oder–Neisse issue and noted that it constituted part of every resolution adopted by Polish American organizations. He further explained that Polish Americans viewed the territories as historically Polish, as partial compensation for destruction caused by the Germans, and as "just compensation" for the lands given to the Soviets in the east. He predicted that the issue would "become quite prominent" in the election campaign, especially in light of Barry Goldwater's interview in *Der Spiegel* in which he said that he would be willing to go to the brink of war in Europe, an interview illreceived by Polish Americans.[63]

Gronouski informed Bundy that in future speeches to Polish Americans he would state that the United States recognizes the importance of the Oder–Neisse issue to Polish Americans and acknowledges the fact that almost 10 million Poles had settled the area since 1945. He would also promise that the United States would "do everything in its power," along with its Allies, to find a "speedy solution" to this vitally important issue, in accordance with the "spirit and the letter of the Potsdam agreement which made the Order–Niesse [*sic*] line a de facto western frontier of Poland." No response from Bundy was attached to Gronouski's proposal, so it is unknown whether his statement about the de facto establishment of the Oder–Neisse Line at Potsdam had administrative approval.[64] Gronouski implemented some well-received changes in the postal service and was used by the administration to court the Democratic vote among

Polish Americans in the 1964 election.[65] In 1965 he experienced a major career change, however.

President Johnson removed him as postmaster general to name him ambassador to Poland, a position that he retained until 1968. Johnson wrote in his memoirs that he made the appointment "as a symbol" of America's desire to improve relations with Eastern Europe, but the appointment was not unanimously praised.[66] Although Democratic congressmen applauded the appointment and the Senate quickly approved the nomination, Republican Congressman Melvin Laird of Wisconsin reported in the *Congressional Record* that many of his constituents viewed the appointment as a demotion since an ambassadorship did not carry cabinet-level rank, and it removed the only Polish American from a high-ranking administrative position.[67] In addition, John Cabot wrote bitterly in his memoirs that Johnson had wanted to remove Gronouski as postmaster general but without upsetting the Polish American community, so he offered the ambassadorship without a "word of thanks" for Cabot's many years of service.[68]

After the new ambassador had been intensely briefed about the situation in Poland prior to his departure for Warsaw, he sent the president an evaluation of U.S. policy in Poland that reiterated his prior positions. He contended that Eastern Europeans were more interested in improving their own situation than in automatically supporting Moscow's goals in spite of the Polish government's support for the Vietcong. "Failure to fully exploit this tendency," he told Johnson, "would be a major, and tragic, omission in our foreign policy." The ambassador went on to suggest specific ways that this could be accomplished, one of which was U.S. recognition of the Oder–Neisse Line in order to destroy the solidarity of the communist bloc and gain concessions for the United States.[69]

In a more detailed evaluation of the issue, Gronouski claimed that the border issue was an "anchor" that kept Poland and most other East European countries except East Germany in line with the Soviet Union's foreign policy goals. He stated that a U.S. policy focusing on "West German sensitivities" and viewing the issue as an "additional bargaining point" at a future peace conference was of dubious value as a negotiating tool, especially in light of the favorable climate in West Germany for finding a solution. In effect, Gronouski told President Johnson that U.S. policy was out of step with the general trend of the situation. He wanted to implement a reexamination of U.S. border policy and recommended that "some modified form of recognition" or a declaration such as DeGaulle's would loosen the Soviet ties in East Central Europe without, he believed, "seriously impair[ing]" the U.S. position in West Germany or hindering chances for German reunification. Gronouski's statements show that he recognized the importance of the U.S.–West German alliance but did not want that alliance to control U.S. foreign policy. "We should use our good offices with the Federal Republic of Germany to explore this matter now," he urged. In concluding his letter, Gronouski claimed that his suggestions for improving relations with Poland would "in time" help to force the communist governments to reform internally and favor closer contact with the West, one of the major objectives of Johnson's bridge-building program toward Eastern Europe.[70] Overall, Gronouski's recommendations outlined a program very similar to the Eisenhower administration's policy promoting "evolutionary rather than revolutionary" changes in Eastern Europe.

Ambassador Gronouski's proposals suggest that he was unaware of the activity in the State Department's Office of German Affairs and of the increasing pressure that Washington was placing on Bonn to strengthen ties with the eastern bloc concerning the Oder–Neisse Line. When the West German Foreign Office submitted a draft initiative on Berlin and Germany to the United States, France, and Britain in January 1964, American officials met to analyze and discuss the proposal, which stated: "A peace conference, at which the problem of the German–Polish border will have to be clarified and a just decision on the German regions on the other side of the Oder and Neisse freely agreed upon, should be preceded by an improvement of the human, economic and political relations between the German people and its neighbouring nations in the East."[71] The American officials' consensus was that this statement was unacceptable; Secretary Rusk expressed his concern with this proposal at various meetings, focusing on its potential as a Pandora's box of unanswered questions.[72]

When Mayor Brandt called on Secretary Rusk in May 1964 in Washington to discuss questions relating to Berlin and Germany, one of the issues that he raised was the Oder–Neisse border. Brandt pointed out the "incongruous situation" that Poland faced in wanting to recognize West Germany as well as East Germany, "but asking the one with which they did not have a common border to guarantee the border with the other state." Brandt presented as a point of discussion the idea of "some kind of qualified nonaggression arrangement" between Bonn and Warsaw to try to reassure Poland that West Germany had no violent intentions.[73]

Attorney General Robert Kennedy's visit to Bonn and Poland in late June 1964 stimulated increased discussion about the Oder–Neisse issue among State Department officials in Bonn. U.S. Ambassador to Germany George McGhee corresponded with Secretary Rusk about some ideas that might assist in the establishment of more open relations between Bonn and Warsaw. Both Chancellor Erhard and Foreign Minister Schroeder spoke with Robert Kennedy about whether he could "put in a [good] word for the Federal Republic while in Warsaw." According to McGhee, these German leaders acknowledged that the Oder–Neisse issue represented an obstacle but seemed optimistic that it could be overcome. According to the ambassador, however, their view of the situation represented a very traditional point of view: "The Chancellor said that the Germans could not hand over to the Poles the Oder-Neisse territory on a golden tray, since according to the Potsdam Agreement the 1937 frontiers were valid until the peace treaty was signed. The Chancellor added, however, that it was implicit that the new frontiers would not be the old frontiers."[74]

McGhee reported that the German leaders were very appreciative of Kennedy's expressions of optimism in Poland that a solution to the apparent border impasse could be found. His idea was to coordinate something with Foy Kohler, U.S. Ambassador in Moscow, "by quite private talks, more or less directed towards planting a seed" among that leadership in Moscow that would allow them "to take a more friendly attitude toward Bonn." McGhee expressed full awareness of the many obstacles in Germany's making progress on the issue such as "a relinquishment of the hypothetical legal claim to the Oder–Neisse territories which is still stubbornly maintained by all elements in Germany." The ambassador contended that the German people were "still victims of a false perspective . . . [that] with each passing year becomes more unrealistic" and expressed optimism that over time the Germans would come to see reality.[75]

This optimism was echoed in an August 1964 telegram from McGhee to the State Department after the American Embassy in Bonn reviewed a research memorandum prepared by the Historical Office concerning the Oder–Neisse issue. McGhee noted two developments in West Germany regarding the border issue. The first was increased discussion in "intellectual and student circles" of the "probability" that Germany would not recover the "former eastern territories." While the drawback of such discussion, McGhee noted, was a "harsh and loud" backlash from expellee groups, he did not believe that such a reaction indicated any kind of general trend among the German population as a whole. McGhee did not favor a change in the United States' "formal position" on the border but did propose to implement a subtle "moratorium" on discussion of the issue for the year preceding the German elections in an attempt not to sway the estimated 5–10 percent of the vote for which the SPD and the CDU competed. McGhee proposed that the United States avoid "public restatements" of its position on the border issue and respond to questions in public statements "in minimum terms and low key." In private, McGhee proposed, American representatives should point out that the U.S. position on the border issue is "procedural . . . rather than substantive" in that the United States was responsible for negotiating a peace settlement and was "committed to support some 'accession (to Poland) of territory in the north and west.'" He also urged that U.S. officials privately discourage German thinking that Germany will "realistically gain territory" and emphasize instead that no countries would ever support an attempt to recover these lands by force.[76]

Despite this apparent progress, however, McGhee reported to Rusk in January 1965 on another "major period of upset" occurring in Germany stemming from an ongoing feeling of insecurity about Germany's future. McGhee reported that Fritz Erler, chairman of the SPD Bundestag Faction, allegedly supported a West German dialogue with Poland about the border. McGhee bluntly, almost militantly, told the secretary his concern about this: "I myself have long been concerned at the German attitude toward borders, which I think is the one most disturbing subject of discussion here. I agree that the time may very easily come when we should speak out. I would not be willing, for example, to continue supporting an irredentist Germany. . . . I think we might first threaten and then, if it continues, later publicly disassociate ourselves from any German hope of territorial gain."[77]

Other voices continued to favor a policy change in East Central Europe. Zbigniew Brzezinski, who became a member of the Policy Planning Staff in 1966, wrote to Bundy in April 1965 suggesting that the president issue a 3 May celebration statement calling for a Polish–West German rapprochement "instead of the usual slogans."[78] This, he argued, would reiterate U.S. interest in the European situation, undermine DeGaulle's overtures in Eastern Europe, and be well received in Germany as a "constructive" effort on the part of the United States. "Neither the Poles nor the Germans," Brzezinski believed, "would object if the President made the point that it is high time to put to rest the old hostilities which benefit neither Poland nor Germany, but which are kept alive by those who see a benefit to themselves in the Polish–German feud." He promoted an active part for the United States in initiating a move that could lead to the reunification of Germany in contrast to the Soviet Union's policies that perpetuated the division of Germany. Brzezinski's letter was sent to David Klein, a member of the National Security Council, for comment prior to a scheduled luncheon between Brzezinski and Bundy. Klein stated that although the Polish government had halted the 3 May celebrations, Brzezinski's point was similar to those that he and his colleagues had been discussing in relation to Johnson's anticipated speech commemorating VE Day.[79]

Brzezinski also argued in his 1965 *Alternative to Partition* that the Communist Party in Warsaw used nationalism to promote its interests at the expense of better German–Polish relations.[80] He contended that on the Oder–Neisse issue, American policy had followed when it should have led but pointed out that this position did not stem from any wide-spread administrative support for the return of the land to Germany. Instead, it sprang partially from the "inherent difficulty" of trying to change a long-established position, but more importantly, he wrote, the "American immobilise" was due to the misplaced fear that West Germany would consider itself betrayed by its ally if the United States took any initiative on the border issue and would turn to the Soviets for a new Rapallo-type agreement. This inactivity, Brzezinski continued, created a kind of cycle where German politicians, even those who realistically accepted the loss of the territories, could not appear "more yielding" on such an emotional issue than was a foreign government like the United States.[81]

To deal with such a situation, Brzezinski argued that as one of its major policy goals the United States should promote a German–Polish rapprochement that contrasts the Soviet goal of keeping alive the tension between these states. He realized that the United States would have to move carefully in order to maintain close ties with Bonn and that the Federal Republic had to play a prominent role in this situation by developing a bipartisan acceptance of the loss of the Oder–Neisse lands. As in his journal articles, Brzezinski recommended a step-by-step approach that would convince the Poles that the West did not want a revision of Poland's western border, thus undercutting one of the major holds that the unpopular Polish government had on the Polish people. The first step, he argued, would be to open consulates in Wrocław or Szczecin in the western territories. Then, NATO should commit itself to "oppose the use of force" in border changes, and the president should publicly reiterate such a declaration, specifically pointing to the need to end the tension between Poland and West Germany. His final recommendation was for the Western states to commit themselves formally to recognize the border immediately after Germany was reunified. This, Brzezinski claimed, would foster Poland's interest in German reunification and concomitantly lessen Poland's insecurity and desire to maintain a divided Germany. These changes, he argued, could be fostered by increased German–Polish American meetings and activities that focused especially on youth activities.[82]

An August 1965 Policy Planning Council paper expressed doubt about the efficacy of Bonn's eastern policy but encouraged U.S. support for it, claiming that it provided the West Germans a sense of involvement in their own affairs that might provide them insight into the "obstacles to a German settlement." The paper stated: "The sense of being active in their own interest will assuage their chronic distemper over being merely the 'object' of the policies of others." The authors forthrightly stated that for West Germany to make any progress with Poland, Bonn needed "at some point . . . to make a cleancut statement recognizing Poland's present Western frontier. . . . It is fantasy to pretend that this 'concession' can be held out as a bargaining counter in some eventual negotiation on a final settlement."[83]

In a candid letter from Ambassador McGhee to Secretary Rusk a year later, however, McGhee warned that the German government was feeling "inordinate pressure" from Washington. He suggested that it would be prudent to wait for a better time to push Germany to act to improve relations with its Eastern neighbors and recommended that the United States take time to formulate "an approach" to be ready when the time offered. The issues that "create[d] problems," McGhee continued, were the Oder–Neisse border, the concomitant issue of German claims to *Heimatrecht*, and Bonn's "reluctance to declare the Munich Agreement void ab initio." In all these cases McGhee saw no actual bargaining tool held by the Germans, even though politicians maintained that they could not "'give up something for nothing.'" He called the tendency to "fall back" on the Potsdam Agreement a "sterile position" and told the secretary that he saw the Germans losing nothing by declaring that they would accept the Oder–Neisse "with minor modifications, . . . if and when reunification comes about." Such an offer, McGhee contended, should be accompanied by a reiteration of Bonn's March 1966 declaration against the use of force as well as a possible initiation of diplomatic relations since the path that the West Germans followed had only bound the East Central European states more closely to the Soviet Union against a "'revanchist and militaristic'" Germany.

Ambassador McGhee continued this critical tone: "There are no Germans east of the Oder–Neisse line. Germany does not need Lebensraum—it has a deficit in workers. There is no ally of Germany who would back her in obtaining territory beyond the Oder–Neisse line through threats or use of force. . . . A renunciation by Germany would produce an immediate improvement in . . . relations with Poland, which because of this issue are worse than those with any other Eastern European country." He went on to denounce *Heimatrecht* and its associate self-determination as "creeping aggression" that was impossible for Germans to achieve. Secretary of State Rusk agreed with McGhee that the time was not right to pressure the West Germans to take action toward reunification "if they are not inclined to move on their own."[84] In another telegram to the secretary of state in July 1966, Ambassador McGhee proposed that Rusk urge the West German officials in upcoming meetings with Secretary McNamara and President Johnson to "soften their present façade" on the Oder–Neisse and *Heimatrecht* issues.[85]

There was, however, no evidence of such a "softening" in a September 1966 conversation that Chancellor Erhard held with Secretary Rusk. The chancellor reported that West Germany heard only negative language from Poland when Bonn made overtures to Warsaw. He expressed disappointment with this situation since, he claimed, "the matter of borders would certainly present no problems in the event of German reunification." He also added that "there was hardly a German left to whom the revision of the Oder–Neisse Line was sacred." He noted that arguments about the border sprang from political motives rather than from conviction.[86]

In a speech before the National Conference of Editorial Writers in New York in 1966 President Johnson affirmed that one of the "bedrocks" of U.S. foreign policy toward Europe was "opposition to the use of force to change existing frontiers." In his memoirs Johnson claimed that he specifically meant the Polish–German border, "the most important unresolved border problem in Europe." His aim in the speech, he claimed, was to avoid offending America's German ally while assuring Poland and the Soviet Union that borders would not be changed forcefully.[87] In response to this speech, the West German Minister to the United States Georg von Lillenfeld expressed to Secretary Rusk some concern that it had not contained an expression of the traditional U.S. position that a final determination of Germany's borders had to await a peace conference. Secretary Rusk replied noncommittally that the president had delivered a short speech that did not cover all aspects of U.S. position and that as secretary of state he would present a more detailed reply to the West Germans soon.[88]

The State Department continued to monitor the situation in Central

Europe. In November 1966 Henry Owen, chairman of the State Department's Policy Planning Council, reported his favorable impressions of the situation after a visit to Poland. Owen asserted that the Poles' primary concern for security was understandable in light of Poland's history and geographic situation. He referred to President Johnson's October speech as conveying a vision of Europe built on the concept of communities "rather than merely national states rolling around loosely." Owen contended that a West German renunciation of the Oder-Neisse lands could be the catalyst for "deep changes in the Polish view of the kind of world they are living in [and] might over the long run gradually make still further changes possible."[89]

The next month Ambassador McGhee reported on a meeting that he had had with newly appointed Foreign Minister Willy Brandt at which Brandt informed him that while the new government's policy toward Eastern Europe was not yet clarified, Bonn had as a goal the normalization of diplomatic relations if a "formula" could be found. Brandt added that the chancellor's speech to the Bundestag would include "something special" regarding Poland and Czechoslovakia; he would also "make a gesture to the expellees" such as a clear statement that the government did not approve of their expulsion but would also warn that Germany was "prepared for solutions" that would not "be easy" for the Germans to accept. A memo from Walt Rostow to President Johnson accompanying the McGhee memo noted that Brandt's statements seemed to acknowledge that "the Germans need to be talked to as if they were grown up." Rostow added that the United States would have to see if the West Germans really were "responsible partners."[90]

Ambassador McGhee also sent to the State Department an assessment of Polish–West German relations that he had composed in consultation with Ambassador Gronouski when McGhee visited Warsaw. The first of many steps that he recommended was for Bonn to announce its intention to accept the Oder–Neisse Line when reunification was attained by the Potsdam-prescribed final peace settlement in order to eliminate Warsaw's dependence on Moscow and serve as a precursor to Polish–German diplomatic relations. McGhee contended that evidence suggested that Poland would be open to establishing diplomatic relations with West Germany on the one condition that Bonn accept the Oder–Neisse. He stated clearly, though, that Washington was not in the position to propose officially such a course of action since it "would represent an assumption of responsibility for Germany's future which we are in no position to take." The ambassador, however, wanted to have a private conversation with Chancellor Kiesinger and Foreign Minster Brandt in which he would praise West Germany's *Ostpolitik* and would urge continued dialogue with Poland about the Oder–Neisse Line.[91]

Almost a year later, Ambassador McGhee reported to Washington a private conversation that he had had with Chancellor Kiesinger in which the chancellor expressed satisfaction with the "well-balanced Eastern policy" that

Bonn had developed. "He saw," McGhee reported, "no advantage in Germany's giving up anything on the Oder–Neisse at this time merely to assuage the Poles. It would only result in a stabilization of the status quo." McGhee included no personal comments about his own view of this conversation, which certainly outlined little progress on the status of the Oder–Neisse border issue.[92] McGhee noted a somewhat softer tone just a few months later when he met again with Chancellor Kiesinger in November 1967 to ask about the accuracy of a press statement on the government's position on the Polish border issue. Kiesinger told McGhee that while Bonn still held that no final decision on the Oder–Neisse Line could be made until a peace treaty was negotiated, joint discussions could be held if the Poles were willing. The chancellor hoped that such discussions might "'build up a little more trust'" but he noted his awareness of the Poles' skepticism about German assurances based on their "unhappy contacts with the Prussians" in the past.[93] West Germany's *Ostpolitik* continued, in spite of such obstacles.

When West Germany established diplomatic relations with Romania in 1967, Ambassador Gronouski met in Warsaw with Vice Minister of Foreign Affairs H. E. Jozef Winiewicz to discuss the possible impact of such an opening on Polish–West German relations. The vice minister conveyed his lack of surprise at this diplomatic opening since the countries of Central Europe that had not had Poland's "bad experience" with Germany had a "different attitude" toward such relationships, and he predicted that Bulgaria and Hungary were "the next likely candidate[s]" to negotiate with West Germany. He then traced the contemporary history of Poland's relationship with the Federal Republic, pointing to 1959 as the pivotal year when West Germany "started showing an interest in atomic weapons" and Poland upped the ante by requiring recognition of the Oder–Neisse Line as a precondition for establishing formal diplomatic relations. When Winiewicz chastised the Western nations (excluding France) for failing to grant de facto recognition to the border as a way for the "German authorities to sell it to the German people," Gronouski outlined the diplomatic tightrope that the United States walked with its West German ally: "I pointed out that sometimes it is very costly for a country's friends to attempt to take the lead in matters of this sort; that in terms of internal politics it could create a situation where the opposition to the German leadership could argue that Germans were not running their own foreign policy but were being forced into an action by their allies. I said he ought to consider the possibility that it is better in the long run to have Germany take its own initiatives in these matters."[94] In spite of this apparent obstacle to the establishment of formal diplomatic relations between Warsaw and Bonn, Winiewicz made it clear that Poland would continue to strive for a normalization of relations with West Germany through cultural contacts as a necessary preliminary step toward formal diplomatic relations.[95]

Months later in December 1967, the Polish ambassador in Washington, Jerzy Michalowski, told Walter Stoessel Jr., acting assistant secretary for

European affairs, that Warsaw found Bonn's claim to speak for all the German people as more objectionable than the Oder–Neisse problem since Poland had relations with the German Democratic Republic. When Stoessel suggested that Romania seemed not to have such "preoccupations," the ambassador "acknowledged, somewhat ruefully, that Romania's views on the subject differed from those of Poland." In the same conversation, Zdzislaw Szewczyk, the Polish Embassy counsellor, stated that he did not see any great urgency for Poland to establish diplomatic relations with the Federal Republic since Poland already enjoyed some advantages of closer ties with West Germany in such areas as trade, cultural contacts, and tourism.[96]

Americans continued to probe West German officials about Bonn's *Ostpolitik*. Ambassador McGhee in February 1968 reported to Washington of a meeting that he had had with Foreign Minister Brandt in which Brandt told McGhee that he was optimistic that Bonn's relations with Moscow were progressing and that it seemed possible to "reduce the potential danger of existing differences." When Brandt gave as an example the possibility that Bonn could tell Warsaw that West Germany could accept the Oder–Neisse Line "until the matter could be considered in connection with a peace treaty," McGhee expressed approval of this approach.[97]

Poland's participation in the Soviet invasion of Prague in 1968, however, had a chilling effect on Poland's relations with the United States and with the countries of Western Europe, including France. The new U.S. ambassador in Warsaw, Walter Stoessel, noted this in a September telegram, contending that Poland's "careful efforts" to generate sympathy in Western Europe for its views on Germany, European security, and European border problems seemed to have "suffered [a] severe setback." The Poles, Stoessel predicted, "will no longer enjoy [the] psychological advantage as [the] leading victims of Nazi wartime brutality and as [the] first East European country to liberalize its internal structure in 1956."[98]

By December 1968, Ambassador Stoessel, as part of a policy review "during [the] transition period," sent a long telegram to the State Department offering recommendations for U.S. policy toward Poland that urged progressive steps toward strengthening U.S.–Polish ties. One of those suggestions was that the United States consult with West Germany on taking a "public position recognizing [the] de facto permanency" of Poland's western border. He expressed an awareness of the "difficult and complicated nature" of the issue, especially as it concerned U.S.–FRG relations. Stoessel was also "under no illusions" that recognition of the Oder–Neisse Line by the United States and/or West Germany would "result in [an] immediate improvement" of relations or end the security and political problems resulting from the Cold War. "However," Stoessel's telegram continued, "I am impressed with insistence and effectiveness of Polish propaganda re impermanent nature of western frontiers, and I am also impressed with fact that no responsible Western official seems to believe that significant alteration in Oder–Neisse boundary will be feasible or that FRG recognition at some later date can be traded for anything worthwhile." The ambassador urged that Washington prepare a statement expressing "confidence that delimitation of [the] boundaries of [a] reunified Germany in a peace treaty would reflect [the] factual situation east of the Oder–Neisse." He recognized the need for careful diplomacy with West Germany and other U.S. allies regarding the wording and timing of such a statement but thought that the long-range impact of "injecting realism" into East–West relations would somewhat offset any negative repercussions.[99]

Voices outside the Johnson administration continued to call for action on the Oder–Neisse issue. In 1967 the Thirty-first American Assembly under Eisenhower's chairmanship met at Columbia University to discuss issues vitally important to America. The final report of the assembly followed the lead of Robert Byrnes, a scholar at Indiana University who had provided an information essay favoring acceptance of the Oder–Neisse Line but with Europe playing the leading role in initiating such recognition. Also, former Kennedy adviser Theodore Sorenson, speaking in Berlin, Hamburg, and Munich, warned Germans that they faced isolation if they did not give up calls for nuclear arms and did not accept the loss of the Oder–Neisse lands.[100]

The border issue was also one of the issues discussed in Senate Foreign Relations Committee hearings in the summer of 1966 that were called to provide information about U.S. policy in Europe after DeGaulle began questioning NATO's role. In his testimony McGeorge Bundy, then president of the Ford Foundation, speaking before the committee as a private citizen, reiterated the position that he had promoted while national security adviser, that the German public needed to accept the reality of the Oder–Neisse Line as an important step toward an eventual peace settlement. He rejected the claim that denying recognition of the line provided a "bargaining advantage" to the West; on the contrary, he said, it helped "those in the East" who played on fears of Germany.[101] Bundy concluded this portion of his testimony with the point that while the border "possibilities" were more for German than American decisionmakers, he believed that the United States could "suggest at least that the opening of doors" to Eastern Europe was a vital part of a final peace settlement.[102] The senators reportedly praised Bundy's recommendation, and as the hearings continued, other witnesses and senators joined in the call for action on the border. Norman Cousins, editor of the *Saturday Review* and an expert on disarmament and international affairs, agreed that the Oder–Neisse issue strengthened the Soviet hold on Poland and contended that recognition of the border constituted a "vital part of any effective stabilization in Europe."[103]

In spite of these well-received recommendations, the testimony by Undersecretary George Ball suggested that the administration would not push the border issue for settlement.[104] While he agreed with Bundy's statement that the issue was a matter for German settlement, he disagreed with the suggestion that the United States was in a position to "express a view" on the matter. He emphasized this point when he stated that it would be "inappropriate" for the United States to follow the French lead by making a statement on the border and held out little hope that the border issue would even be discussed in U.S. talks with West Germany: "We discuss a great many matters with the Government of the Federal Republic covering a wide range of things, but we also observe a good deal of reticence about matters which seem to be primarily for them to decide."[105]

In addition to special congressional hearings, the border issue continued to be part of some congressmen's day-to-day activities as they showed support for U.S. recognition of the line by reading into the *Congressional Record* extensive correspondence from Polish American individuals and organizations. In December 1963 Congressman Bernard Grabowski (D-CT) read an appeal by the Polish Western Association for the United States to recognize the border in order to promote peace and justice. Such a move, the organization argued, would be in line with the French and British position supporting recognition. The appeal contended that the settlement and revitalization of the lands by the 8 million Polish inhabitants proved false the German propaganda claim that the Poles were unable to settle the area completely. It also noted the crucial situation for the German expellee propagandists since a new generation of Poles born in the western territories would be ready to vote soon whereas many of the original German expellees were dying.[106]

The Polish American Congress also assessed the East Central European situation in a memorandum hand-delivered to President Johnson and John Gronouski on 11 May 1964 and read to the House by John Kluczynski (D-IL) on 1 July 1964. The PAC argued that although the possibility of restoring full freedom in Poland seemed slight, the United States should keep demanding it as vocally as it demanded a solution to the German problem—another seemingly impossible task. The PAC contended further that "no other single act" on the part of the United States could strengthen Poland and the peoples of East Central Europe more than recognition of the Oder–Neisse Line, and that the "policy of postponement" thus far had forced Poland into allegiance with the Soviet Union. Recognition, the authors of the memo argued, would have many positive results affecting Poland, Germany, and the Western Alliance. It would provide the groundwork for the establishment of diplomatic relations between Warsaw and Bonn; it would "form a realistic condition for future reunification of Germany"; it would strengthen the West's position in relation to the Soviet Union; and it would enable the Poles to identify with the United States in their call for justice. They stated that the time was ready for "bold and imaginative" moves on the part of the West since the Soviet "predicament" offered opportunities to the West.[107]

In March 1966 Clement Zablocki (D-WI) read into the *Record* an analysis of the border situation by Dr. Stanley Stein, a respected scholar who traced the history of the border and referred to the many favorable remarks by prominent American, British, and French officials concerning recognition of the border. He claimed that West German renunciation of force was meaningless when "at the same time hopes [of a border revision] are nourished . . . by West German politicians." He castigated those politicians for their lack of "civil courage" in not being realistic with their constituents.[108] The substance of Stein's accusation was confirmed by a Warsaw-based staff correspondent for the *Christian Science Monitor* who contended that "Bonn politicians . . . simply genuflect before a presumably powerful bloc of voters, who look longingly over their shoulders at the homelands they lost."[109]

Leaders of the Polish American community tried to make the Oder–Neisse Line a political issue. The Polish Western Association of America used the occasion of the Democratic and Republican Party conventions in the summer of 1964 to urge that U.S. recognition of the Oder–Neisse Line be made part of both parties' platforms. Congressman Edward Derwinski (R-IL) was to present the view to the Republicans; Congressman Zablocki (D-WI), to the Democrats. The group sent hundreds of letters supporting this ultimately unsuccessful move. In a letter to the Polish Western Association, Zablocki offered some reasons that the move had failed. He explained that since the Democratic Party was in office, putting such a statement in the party platform "'would seem to the rest of the world to be semi-official in nature.'" In addition, he wrote that while the State Department was "sympathetic to this proposal," officials feared that making it part of a party platform would "jeopardize" future negotiations. Stefan Marcinkowski, the president of the Polish Western Association, thanked the congressman for his help, asked and received permission to quote Zablocki, and predicted that 1965 or 1966 would be "the year of decision" regarding the German situation.[110]

Although this attempt to make the issue part of the party platforms failed, it resulted in a number of prominent politicians responding to the letters with positive statements of support for U.S. recognition. Vice President Humphrey promised to raise the issue with platform committee members; Senator Paul Douglas (D-IL) informed the group of his support for the move; Senator Claiborne Pell (D-RI) reiterated his support and reminded the group of his speeches favoring recognition; and Roman Pucinski (D-IL) claimed that he was "in the forefront in this battle here in Congress" and promised to do "everything possible" to make it part of the Democratic Party platform.[111]

In September 1964 the Polish American Congress held its Sixth National Convention in Chicago, where the main topic of discussion was U.S. recognition of the Oder–Neisse Line. "Almost every delegate," an observer and member of the Polish Western Association of America noted, "pointed out that this problem is the key one for all Americans of Polish descent." The upcoming presidential and congressional elections lent added importance to the PAC convention. Prominent guests and speakers at the convention included the Republican Vice Presidential nominee and his wife, who delivered a "few words in Polish"; Congressmen Edward Derwinski (R-IL), Roman Pucinski (D-IL), and Clement Zablocki (D-WI); the governor of Illinois; Mayor Daley of Chicago; Postmaster General Gronouski; and Vice President-Elect Humphrey. President Johnson prompted a "very pleasant surprise" by delivering a speech over the telephone commending the courage of the Polish people and referring to the U.S. "bridge building" policy that would encourage peaceful change in Poland. The convention also approved a resolution sent to the State Department pointing to the upcoming millennial celebration in Poland and calling for "bold and imaginative moves" by the United States, such as recognition of the Oder–Neisse border in order to strengthen the Polish nation and weaken Moscow's control in Eastern Europe.[112]

The conference delegates adopted a policy statement that included the border issue, noting "with growing apprehension" that the Federal Republic of Germany had increased its contributions to revisionist organizations in West Germany and calling on the West to recognize the line in order to show the futility of such propaganda. The authors contended that no Germans existed in the western territories and pointed out that one-third of the 8 million Poles who lived there had been born there. The policy statement continued: "All that is needed is an acknowledgment de jure of the situation which has already been in existence de facto for the past sixteen years."[113]

In July 1965 the Wisconsin Division of the Polish Western Association prepared a memorandum on the border situation that was read into the *Congressional Record* and given by Congressman Zablocki to Johnson, Humphrey, all cabinet members, and many members of Congress. The memorandum warned of the growing communist strength in all parts of the world and pointed especially to Soviet propaganda claiming to be Poland's only protector of the borders as an example of how the Soviets were building up the image that the United States supported German militarism. The memorandum also noted the situation in the territories where of the 8 million Poles living there, 3 million were born there. It claimed that in spite of the French government's recognition of the border, French–German relations "still remain quite friendly" and contended that U.S. refusal to do the same marked the "only shadow on the traditional" friendship between the United States and Poland and hindered closer ties between the United States and other states of East Central Europe that were also suspicious of Germany.[114]

The memorandum stimulated a mixed response from the State Department and Congress. Douglas MacArthur II, assistant secretary of state, wrote noncommittally that the State Department considered the border issue a "matter of continuing concern" with "international importance." He promised to bring the views of the Polish American organization to the attention of other officers in the State Department.[115] Senator Thomas Dodd (D-CT), a member of the Foreign Relations Committee, wrote that while he believed that "most thinking Germans" viewed the border as final, "political, diplomatic and legal difficulties" stood in the way of formal recognition. Senator Pell (D-RI) confirmed that he was the only senator publicly to support recognition and expressed the wish that more senators would do so.[116]

In addition to corresponding with members of the administration and Congress, the Polish American Congress played a more direct political role in promoting U.S. recognition of the line. In July Charles Rozmarek testified to the Republican Platform Committee about the Oder–Neisse line and other issues of concern, stating that the United States "should assume the initiative" by recognizing the line in order to "stabilize the situation" in East Central Europe. He noted that France had already publicly supported the border and claimed that British "public opinion is overwhelmingly in favor" of the line. He added that American postponement until "some indefinite day of a General Peace Treaty" served the Soviet interest in the area. Recognition, Rozmarek claimed, would also "open a new era" in relations between Poland and Germany and "could prove to be a powerful factor in eventual German reunification" by eliminating the Poles' fear of German revisionism.[117]

Other voices echoed this potential for optimism regarding the changing situation in Central Europe. Harry Rosenthal, a scholar at Columbia University, argued in *The Polish Review* that largely because of West Germany's economic recovery, the majority of the expellees had been integrated into West Germany's social and economic system, in spite of provisions in West German law that included the children of expellees as part of the total expellee population.[118] He also, however, warned that the idea of *Heimatrecht* carried a great deal of emotional appeal that could be exploited when discontent arose.[119] Another official report of the expellees' situation edited by two prominent expellees confirmed that the leaders of the expellee organizations who demanded the right to return to the Oder–Neisse lands rarely spoke for the rank and file; West German media confirmed that expellees were generally uninterested in returning to the lands east of the Oder and Neisse Rivers.[120] Polls showed that increasing numbers of West Germans, including expellees, were no longer interested in returning to the Oder–Neisse lands. Whereas 11 percent of those polled in 1953 said they were no longer interested, by 1968 the number had reached more than half: 56 percent. Concomitantly, the number who opposed recognition of the border dropped. In 1951, 80 percent opposed it; by 1967 only 33 percent opposed it.[121]

In addition, church groups in West Germany and Poland initiated a peace offensive in 1965 that brought the border issue into the press when the Evangelical Church in West Germany issued a memorandum promoting reconciliation based on humanitarian grounds.[122] The Roman Catholic Church in Poland sent a letter to German bishops explaining Poland's position and granting "forgiveness" to the West Germans after acknowledging Polish responsibility regarding the expulsion of Germans from Poland.[123] The West German bishops responded in a similar vein but did not commit the church to a specific position on the border.[124] These initiatives were well received by the

U.S. press, with the editor of the *New York Times* calling the Evangelical Church memorandum a "faint beginning toward realism" that might lead to recognition of the Oder–Neisse Line and thereby speed the normalization of relations.[125] The *Christian Century*, an ecumenical magazine, said much the same.[126]

The difference between what Bonn knew to be possible and what politicians could acknowledge was openly evaluated in the American press as the momentum increased in West Germany for action on the border. In a major reversal, the *New York Times* began to reflect a more favorable attitude toward U.S. and West German recognition of the line. An editorial in the *Times* on 26 July 1964 argued that "Stalin's" solution of a united western Poland and eastern Germany led to the continual Polish fear of German revanchism. The editor called for a "clear statement by the Germans that they accept the Oder–Neisse line" in order to "alter the entire political picture in Eastern Europe, improving it immeasurably." A brief letter to the editor by Stefan Korbonski supported this idea but contended that U.S. recognition of the line prior to West German acceptance would "speed up" the process.[127]

The *New York Times* also reported on the "squabbling" between the SPD and CDU politicians, even though "few, if any, informed West Germans have any illusions about the possibility of recovering the area east of the Oder–Neisse Line." The editor contended that the danger of such quarreling was in the illusions that it encouraged among nationalists and neo-Nazis in West Germany and in providing "fodder" for Soviet and East European propagandists.[128] A few days later C. L. Sulzberger, Bonn reporter for the *Times*, summarized the postwar history of the line and warned that the issue was still a political tool in West Germany even among Germans who would not return to the area if given the chance since they might "vote from the heart."[129] Correspondents for the *Christian Science Monitor* also noted the West German politicians' lack of openness on the border issue.[130]

The border issue received increased attention in 1967, when DeGaulle publicly reinforced his support for the Oder–Neisse Line.[131] Pressure for Bonn to act intensified since the issue "strained the Grand Coalition from the beginning," according to Wolfram Hanrieder.[132] In the spring of 1968 Brandt, speaking as a leader of the Social Democrats rather than as foreign minister, called for recognition of the border until a peace conference definitely settled the issue.[133] In the Senate in April 1968, Claiborne Pell praised the "signs of realism and commonsense" on the part of some West Germans. He pointed specifically to the statement by prominent Catholic laymen urging recognition of the border and to Brandt's announcement in March urging the SPD to support "in principle the idea of recognizing" the border. Both moves, Pell claimed, would be useful and realistic steps toward eliminating one of Moscow's holds on the states of East Central Europe. He then read into the record two editorials from newspapers in Rhode Island supporting the West German actions.[134]

The Polish American Congress also continued its call for U.S. recognition of the border. Charles Rozmarek spoke before both party platform committees in 1968 about the situation in East Central Europe. Although basically the same, Rozmarek's statement to the Democrats contained a paragraph lacking in his address to the Republicans that supported Secretary Rusk's statement regarding American anticommunist objectives and expressed appreciation for the "bridge-building" policy, even though it "fell short of its goals." Regarding the Oder–Neisse Line, Rozmarek's statements to the party committees were basically the same call for U.S. recognition in order to foster stability in East Central Europe and the "liberation of Poland" and to remove the "main obstacle" to Polish–German rapprochement. He claimed that the present "policy of procrastination" served to encourage the "ultra-nationalistic circles" in West Germany that held hope that the Oder–Neisse lands would be recovered. Rozmarek included another paragraph about the Potsdam Agreement that was also missing in his statement to the Republicans. He revealed his political astuteness by invoking the name of the Democratic president who had signed the original agreements involving the German–Polish border. He told the Democrats that the signers of the Potsdam Agreement intended the line to be permanent as seen by their approval of the transfer of Germans from the area. "It is obvious," Rozmarek told the Democratic Platform Committee members, "that President Truman and Prime Minister Attlee would not have agreed to the transfer of millions of human beings, if this transfer was to have only temporary character. No responsible statesman could have affixed his signature to a document providing for a temporary transfer of millions of people to Germany from the territories East of the Oder–Neisse Line." He went on to review the favorable comments and actions of prominent West Germans and urged further activity before revisionist propaganda took effect.[135]

The California-Arizona Division of the Polish American Congress adopted a political platform in 1968, outlining its assessment of the situation in East Central Europe.[136] The PAC Platform, read on the floor of the House by Henry Helstoski (D-NJ), emphasized both the American and ethnic nature of its members when it stated that "as American voters" their backing for candidates would be affected by the candidate's position "on the expectations of one hundred million Europeans behind the Iron Curtain who are supported by some twenty million kinsmen proud of their American citizenship." The platform sought a united Europe with "just ethnic boundaries" and called on the United States to recognize the Oder–Neisse border in order to remove one of the major obstacles to unity. The platform also reiterated the PAC stance that the Oder–Neisse Line was confirmed by the Potsdam Accord as partial compensation from Germany and argued that U.S. recognition would loosen Moscow's hold on Poland and would "secure the existence" of the 10 million Poles in the territories. "Consequently," the platform declared, "American Polonia will actively support those candidates who commit themselves to the task of obtaining an unequivocal declaration that the Polish–German frontier has been unconditionally determined in Potsdam regardless of any eventual peace conference."[137]

The 1968 elections offered Rozmarek his last opportunity to address party platform committees in an official capacity. Due largely to internal difficulties and disaffection with the organization's perceived lack of attention to domestic issues, membership of the PAC declined in the 1960s, and alternative organizations appeared, none of which gained the prominence of the PAC. After a "major shake-up" when Aloysius Mazewski was elected president in 1968, the PAC refocused its attention on domestic issues such as antidefamation, teaching of the Polish language, and promoting the appointment of Polish Americans to governmental positions.[138] In spite of this refocusing, the PAC never lessened its call for action on the German–Polish border issue.

In October the Polish American Congress held its Seventh National Convention and adopted resolutions that addressed both domestic and foreign policy concerns of American Polonia. Lucien Nedzi (D-MI) presented the resolutions to the House of Representatives. After pledging support for American efforts to bring "peace, order and stability" in Vietnam and efforts to restore law and order in the United States, the PAC expressed concern and sympathy for Czechoslovakia and the other states of Central Europe. Regarding Poland's western lands, the congress continued its call for U.S. recognition of this "integral part" of Poland in order to strengthen the "psychological resistance" of Poles against Soviet "imperialism" and as a contribution toward peace and security in both Europe and America; the congress continued to reject the Yalta provision giving eastern Polish lands to the Soviet Union. The final points of the resolution pledged to promote the status of American Poles in all aspects of American society.[139]

The changes in leadership and focus of the Polish American Congress matched changes in U.S. politics as Richard Nixon gained the presidency. A summary of Johnson's foreign policy was provided in an Administrative History of the State Department from November 1963 to January 1969. The evaluation noted that the Polish retreat from its October 1956 freedoms and the support given to the Vietcong by Warsaw made Johnson's bridge-building program "increasingly difficult," especially in light of congressional and public reaction, which further hindered negotiations between the two states.[140] In spite of these major setbacks the Johnson administration scored a few points in its program, most notably by increased contact with Hungary and Bulgaria and through participation at commercial fairs in various East European cities. The report noted that while the Soviet invasion of Czechoslovakia made continued Western contact with Eastern Europe uncertain, "there was no ground for questioning the validity of the . . . policy over the long run."[141] In short, the State Department under Johnson justified its policies in Eastern Europe as promoting evolutionary rather than revolutionary changes and thus echoed the Eisenhower administration.

NOTES

1. Michel Cieplinski, Deputy Assistant Secretary of State for Administrative Affairs, supplied this quote in an interview on 13 June 1967. See Charles A. Baretski, "A Content Analysis of the *Polish American Journal* Newspaper in Reflecting the Political Attitudes, Issues and Perspectives of the Polish-American Group during the Period, 1950–1966" (Ph.D. diss., New York University, 1969), 284.

2. Wandycz estimates that Kennedy received 78 percent of the Polish American vote. Piotr Wandycz, *The United States and Poland* (Cambridge: Harvard University Press, 1980), 374; Stanley Wagner, "The Polish-American Vote in 1960," *Polish American Studies* 31, no. 1 (January–June 1964): 3, 8. Wagner considers domestic issues to have been more important than foreign policy in explaining Kennedy's appeal among Polish Americans.

3. Arthur Rachwald, *Poland between the Superpowers: Security vs. Economic Recovery* (Boulder, CO: Westview Press, 1983), 62.

4. Wolfram F. Hanrieder, *Germany, America, Europe: Forty Years of German Foreign Policy* (New Haven, CT: Yale University Press, 1989), 14; Frank Ninkovich, *Germany and the United States: The Transformation of the German Question since 1945* (Boston: Twayne, 1988), 141.

5. Alexander Bregman, "Polish–German Relations: A New Phase," *East Europe* 12, no. 11 (November 1963): 4.

6. Wandycz, *The United States*, 376.

7. Memo for President, 15 February 1961, Rusk to Kennedy, cited in *Declassified Documents Reference System: Cumulative Subject Index*, Pt. 2, microfiche 477A, John F. Kennedy Library; hereafter cited as JFK/L.

8. Memo of Conversation, Spasowski, Rusk, et al. 10 April 1961, FRUS, 1961–1963, 16: 72.

9. Jan Wszelaki, ed., *John F. Kennedy and Poland: Selection of Documents, 1948–63 with 8 Illustrations*, (New York: Polish Institute of Arts and Sciences in America, 1964), 110; "Gomulka Ties U.S. to Oder Line Issue," *Christian Science Monitor*, 12 April 1961, 12; "Test of President Kennedy's News Conference on World and Domestic Affairs," *New York Times*, 13 April 1961, 18. The *Christian Science Monitor* article stated that Reuters had claimed that Walter Rostow in January had recommended that Kennedy recognize the line in exchange for guaranteed access to Berlin, but sources close to the administration denied that the president had given any "detailed consideration" to the issue.

10. Memo of Conversation, Kennedy, Spasowski, et al., 15 June 1961, FRUS, 1961–1963, 16: 75.

11. Memo from Department of State, 18 July 1961, Press Office Files-Countries, Box 123b, Poland 1961–1963 File, JFK/L.

12. Wandycz, *The United States*, 377.

13. Hanrieder, *Germany, America, and Europe*, 47.

14. Wladyslaw W. Kulski, *Germany and Poland: From War to Peaceful Relations* (Syracuse, NY: Syracuse University Press, 1976), 118.; see also Otto Stenzl, "Germany's Eastern Frontier," *Survey: A Journal of Soviet and East European Studies*, no. 51 (April 1964): 123–125.

15. "Warsaw: Door Closed to West Germany?" *Christian Science Monitor*, 12

March 1962, 6.

16. Memo of Conversation, Rusk, Rapacki, et al., 16 March 1962, FRUS, 1961–1963, 16, 112–113. The secretary of state and foreign minister were attending the Geneva disarmament talks when this conversation took place at the Polish Mission in Geneva.

17. Wszelaki, *John F. Kennedy.*

18. Ninkovich, *Germany and the United States*, 128.

19. Cited in ibid., 132, from a memorandum by Carl Kaysen, 22 August 1962, in the Arthur Schlesinger Jr. Papers, JFK/L.

20. Airgram 873, Embassy in Poland to Department of State, 25 April 1963, in FRUS, 1961–1963, 16: 168.

21. McGeorge Bundy, *Danger and Survival: Choices about the Bomb in the First Fifty Years* (New York: Random House, 1988), 385.

22. Hanrieder, *Germany, America, Europe*, 171.

23. Memo from Claiborne Pell, Press Office File-Countries, Box 116A Germany (General 7/61) File; also found in Letter to McGeorge Bundy, 1 August 1961, White House Central Subject File Box 55, CO92, JFK/L.

24. "In the Nation," *New York Times*, 21 September 1961, 34. Pell's proposal stimulated correspondence from Oliver Radkey, professor of Russian and German history at the University of Texas, opposing Pell's views, and from Adam Bromke of Cambridge. See "Berlin Proposal Attacked," *New York Times*, 21 September 1961, 34, and "Berlin Proposal Upheld," *New York Times*, 7 October 1961, 22.

25. Letter, Pell to Kennedy, 15 November 1961, Press Office Files—Countries—Germany General File, Box 116A, JFK/L.

26. Samuel Stratton (D-NY) read a resolution by the New York Chapter of the PAC; see *Congressional Record Appendix*, 87th Cong., 1st sess., 107, pt. 25 (14 September 1961): A7284; Harris McDowell Jr. (D-DE) read a resolution of the Delaware Chapter of the PAC; see *Congressional Record Appendix*, 87th Cong., 1st sess., 107, pt. 25 (14 September 1961): A7258-A7259; Kenneth Keating (R-NY) read a resolution of the Downstate New York Division of the PAC; see *Congressional Record*, 87th Cong., 2nd sess., 108, pt. 8 (6 May 1962): 10198–10899.

27. Letter to State Department in author's possession.

28. *Quarterly of the Polish Western Association of America*, July 1961, no. 2/3, 5.

29. Ibid.

30. Memo of PAC, 17 August 1961, Press Office Files-Countries, Box 123b Poland 1961–1963 File, JFK/L. The memorandum referred to *Advertiser's Weekly* of London, which stated that the West German Embassy in the United States spent $820,000 for publicity.

31. *Congressional Record Appendix*, 87th Cong., 1st sess., 107, pt. 24 (7 September 1961): A7071–A7072.

32. *Congressional Record Appendix*, 87th Cong., 2nd sess. 108, pt. 22 (28 May 1962): A4170.

33. Ibid., A4624. The statement also was the focus of a banner headline in the "Polish American Congress News Letter," August 1962, 9, no. 1, Immigration History

Research Center, St. Paul, MN; hereafter cited as IHRC.

34. *Congressional Record Appendix*, 87th Cong., 2nd sess. (18 June 1962): A4623–A4624.

35. Joseph Sanocki, "West Germans and the Oder–Neisse Boundary," Polish Western Territories, July 1962, 6, no. 12, Wilhelm Wolny Papers, Folder 6, IHRC.

36. Zbigniew Brzezinski and William Griffith, "Peaceful Engagement in Eastern Europe," *Foreign Affairs*, 39, no. 4 (July 1961): 642–665. See also Zbigniew Brzezinski, "United States Foreign Policy in East Central Europe—A Study in Contradictions," *Journal of International Affairs* 11, no. 1 (1957): 60–71.

37. Letter, Brzezinski to "Mac," 25 August 1961, White House Central Subject Files, Box 68, CO236, JFK/L.

38. Ibid., Letter to "Zbig," 4 September 1961.

39. Henry Kissinger, *The Necessity for Choice: Prospects of American Foreign Policy* (Garden City, NY: Anchor Books, Doubleday, 1962), 151–152. The editor of the *Quarterly of the Polish Western Association of America* later disagreed with Kissinger's proposition and expressed hope that Kissinger would reiterate his position more strongly and bring it to the president's attention for immediate action. See "German Chronicle," *Quarterly* 11, no. 3 (1970): 17.

40. Hans J. Morgenthau, *The Restoration of American Politics*, vol. 3: *Politics in the Twentieth Century* (Chicago: University of Chicago Press, 1962), 223, 331.

41. Hans Morgenthau, "Germany Gives Rise to Vast Uncertainties," *New York Times*, 8 September 1963, 6: 21.

42. Memo, Hilsman to Secretary of State, 3 August 1962, Papers of President Kennedy, National Security Files, Countries—Germany File, Box 75, JFK/L.

43. Alexander Bregman, review of *Nachbar Polen*, by Hansjakob Stehle, *East Europe*, 12, no. 11 (November 1963): 51. Bregman was chief editorial writer for the London-based newspaper *Dziennik Polski*.

44. Stenzl, "Germany's Eastern Frontier," 129.

45. Bregman, review of *Nachbar Polen*, 51.

46. Stenzl, "Germany's Eastern Frontier," 129. The report was applauded by Stefan Korbonski in a letter to the editor, 12 March 1962, *Christian Science Monitor*, 5; the memorandum was also acknowledged as significant by Alexander Bregman in "Polish–German Relations: A New Phase," *East Europe* 12, no. 11 (November 1963), 7.

47. Bregman, review of *Nachbar Polen*, 4.

48. Hanrieder, *Germany, America, Europe*, 173.

49. Ibid., 176–177.

50. Ibid., 178.

51. Wandycz, *The United States*, 377.

52. Hanrieder, *Germany, America, Europe*, 183.

53. A more complete analysis of the strains between Washington and Bonn appears in Ninkovich, *Germany and the United States*, Chapter 6; Hanrieder, *Germany, America, Europe*, Chapter 6.

54. Lyndon B. Johnson, *The Vantage Point: Perspectives of the Presidency, 1963–1969* (New York: Popular Library, 1971), 471.

55. Wandycz, *The United States*, 379–382.

56. For an analysis of this MLF idea see Ninkovich, *Germany and the United States*, passim; Hanrieder, *Germany, America, Europe*, passim.

57. Telegram, Cabot to Secretary of State, 22 July [c.] 1964, National Security File, Country File, Container 200, Title #68, Lyndon B. Johnson Library; hereafter cited as LBJ/L.

58. Memo, Hughes to Secretary of State, 26 October 1964, National Security File, Country File, Container 200, Poland, Vol. 1, Correspondence 196, LBJ/L.

59. Memo of Conversation, 10 December 1964, in FRUS, 1964–1968, 17: 334–335.

60. Wandycz, *The United States*, 378, 382; Johnson, *Vantage Point*, 471–473.

61. Wandycz, *The United States*, 384.

62. Donald Pienkos, "The Polish American Congress—An Appraisal," *Polish American Studies*, 36, no. 2 (Autumn 1979): 25.

63. "*Deutschland Haette Beide Kriege Gewinnen Koennen,*" *Der Spiegel*, 18, no. 28 (8 July 1964): 56–58; "The GOP in San Francisco," *Newsweek,* 20 July 1964, 17, claimed that some of Goldwater's quotations "came back to haunt him." Gronouski's contention that Polish Americans viewed the Oder–Neisse Line as compensation for lands lost in the east was not totally correct since the idea of compensation was not universally acknowledged by Polish Americans as it would recognize the permanent annexation by the Soviets of that land.

64. Memo, Gronouski to Bundy, 21 July 1964, National Security Files, Country File, Poland Vol. I, Correspondence #160, LBJ/L.

65. See Tad Szulz, "Gronouski Scores Talk of Backlash," *New York Times*, 7 September 1964, 7.

66. Johnson, *Vantage Point*, 473. The Polish government quickly approved Gronouski's appointment. See *New York Times*, 30 August 1965, 14.

67. Although Zablocki of Wisconsin hailed the appointment, Laird read some newspaper clippings from the Buffalo and Detroit Polish American newspapers claiming that Johnson could have appointed any number of other qualified Polish Americans to the ambassador position. The Detroit newspaper quoted Edward Derwinski's warning that Polish Americans might view this move negatively and vote Republican in the 1964 and 1968 elections. See *Congressional Record Appendix*, 89th Cong., 1st sess., 111, no. 168: A5123; *Congressional Record*, 89th Cong., 1st sess., 111, pt. 16, :22199-22200; *Congressional Record*, 89th Cong., 1st sess., 111, pt. 17: 22450–22451; *Congressional Record Appendix*, 89th Cong., 1st sess., 111, no. 187: A5679; *Congressional Record Appendix*, 89th Cong., 1st sess., 111, no. 163: A5012. A story in the *New York Times* claimed that although Gronouski seemed pleased when Johnson made the announcement at the press conference, an administrative source stated that Gronouski had not asked for the appointment, "which amounts to a step down in the administration," but he was interested in getting involved in foreign affairs. See "O'Brien Is Named New Postal Head; Gronouski Envoy," *New York Times*, 30 August 1965, 1, 14; "Senate Unit Backs Gronouski as Envoy," *New York Times*, 9 September 1965, 15.

68. Cabot accepted the administration's offer to become Deputy Commandant of the National War College. John M. Cabot, *First Line of Defense: Forty Years' Experiences of a Career Diplomat* (Washington, DC: Georgetown University, School of Foreign Service, n.d.), 131.

69. Letter, Gronouski to Johnson, 2 November 1965, White House Central File, CF [Confidential File] FO [Foreign Affairs] 1964-1965, Box 44, LBJ/L.

70. Ibid.

71. Paper, 15 January 1964, in FRUS, 1964–1968, 15: 2–3.

72. Memo of Conversation, Rusk, Tyler, et al., 9 March 1964, in FRUS, 1964–1968, 15: 35–37; Memo for the Files, Washington, 21 April 1964, in FRUS, 1964–1968, 15: 60.

73 Memo of Conversation, 18 May 1964, FRUS, 1964–1968, 15: 891–892.

74. Letter, McGhee to Secretary, 21 July 1964, FRUS, 1964–1968, 15: 142.

75. Ibid.

76. Telegram, McGhee to Department of State, 14 August 1964, FRUS, 1964–1968, 15: 148–151.

77 Telegram, McGhee to Sec. of State, 15 January 1965, FRUS, 1964–1968, 15: 211.

78. In a policy paper outlining German issues drafted by Brzezinski in November 1966, the author outlined the "basic ingredients" needed for improved relations between East and West Germany, one of which was a "formal commitment" by both Germanys that a reunited Germany would "not seek to alter existing external German frontiers" in order to lessen Poland's fears. See Policy Planning Council Paper, 6 November 1967, in FRUS, 1964–1968, 15: 605.

79. Letter, Brzezinski to Bundy, 9 April 1965, National Security File, Country File, Container 200, Poland, Vol. I, Correspondence #145, LBJ/L.

80. Zbigniew Brzezinski, *Alternative to Partition: For a Broader Conception of America's Role in Europe* (New York: McGraw-Hill, 1965), passim.

81. Ibid., 124–125.

82. Ibid., 143–144.

83 Policy Planning Council Paper, 10 August 1965, FRUS, 1964–1968, 15: 321.

84. Letter, McGhee to Rusk, 25 August 1966, in FRUS, 1964–1968, 15: 394–396. Rusk's response is in footnote on page 396.

85. Telegram, McGhee to Department of State, 7 July 1966, in FRUS, 15: 380.

86. Memo of Conversation, Rusk and Erhard, 26 September 1966, FRUS, 1964–1968, 15: 432.

87. Johnson, *Vantage Point*, 474–475. In a footnote Johnson wrote that he was "pleased" at the December 1970 treaty between Warsaw and Bonn affirming the Oder–Neisse border.

88. Memo of Conversation, Rusk, Lillenfeld, et al., 13 October 1966, FRUS, 1964–1968, 15: 443.

89. Memo, Owen to Rusk, 1 November 1966, FRUS, 17: 343–346.

90. Memo, 8 December 1966 in NSF Country, Europe, and USSR, Box 182, Germany, Memos 12/66–3/67, 12, LBJ/L.

91. Telegram, McGhee to Department of State, 14 December 1966, FRUS, 1964–1968, 15: 462–465.

92. Telegram, Bonn to Dept of State, 22 September 1967, FRUS, 1964–1968, 15: 589.

93. Telegram, McGhee to Department of State, 15 November 1967, FRUS, 1964–1968, 15: 609.

94. Memo of Conversation, Winiewicz and Gronouski, 9 February 1967, FRUS, 1964–1968, 17: 350–351.

95. Ibid.

96. Memo of Conversation, Michalowski, Szewczyk, et al., 13–14 December 1967, FRUS, 1964–1968, 17: 360.

97. Telegram, McGhee to Sec. of State, 20 February 1968, FRUS 1964–1968, 15: 626–630.

98. Telegram, Warsaw to Washington, 17 September 1968, FRUS, 1964–1968, 17: 373–374. American officials noted other "illiberal" actions such as a rise in anti-Semitic rhetoric and a shakeup in the Polish government.

99. Telegram, Stoessel to Dept. of State, 11 December 1968, FRUS, 1964–1968, 17: 378–380.

100. Wandycz, *The United States*, 385; Robert F. Byrnes, "American Opportunities and Dilemmas," in Robert F. Byrnes, ed., *The United States and Eastern Europe* (Englewood Cliffs, N.J.: Prentice Hall, 1967), 167. The American Assembly was organized to discuss issues of concern to the American government; "Sorenson Warns Bonn on Arms," *New York Times*, 9 May 1966, 7.

101. U.S. Congress, Senate, 89th Cong., 2nd sess., *United States Policy toward Europe (And Related Matters)* (Washington, DC: U.S. Government Printing Office, 1966), 9. Hereafter cited as Senate, *United States Policy.*

102. Ibid., 10.

103. Ibid., 382–383.

104. The *New York Times* reported that Bundy's comments were praised by the senators, and Ball was criticized by Senate liberals. See Benjamin Welles, "Bundy Asks Bonn Accept Oder Line," 21 June 1966, 1, and Max Frankel, "Senate Liberals Criticize Ball as He Defends U.S. Policy on Europe and Atlantic Alliance," 14 July 1966, 15.

105. U.S. Senate, *United States Policy*, 342.

106. *Congressional Record Appendix*, 88th Cong., 1st. sess., 109, no. 200 (4 December 1963): A7498-A7499.

107. Although the memorandum did not elaborate on the "Soviet predicament," the timing suggests that the authors referred to the changes in Soviet leadership, the explosion by the Peoples' Republic of China of an atomic device, and the growing Sino–Soviet rift. *Congressional Record*, 88th Cong., 2nd sess., 110, pt. 12 (1 July 1964): 15603–15604.

108. *Congressional Record Appendix*, 89th Cong., 2nd sess., 112, no. 36 (1 March 1966): A1074–A1075.

109. Harry Ellis, "Poles Remain Cool to Both Germanys," *Christian Science Monitor*, 20 June 1966.

110. Letter, Marcinkowski to Zablocki, 25 January 1965, Zablocki Papers, Marquette University.

111. "Draft Statement for Representative Zablocki on the Question of Poland's Western Frontier," "circa September 1964" [handwritten], Zablocki Papers, Box 169, Marquette University; Stefan Marcinkowski, "The Oder-Neisse Frontier," *Quarterly of the Polish Western Association of America*, 6, no. 1/4, January 1965, 16–19.

112. L. Poray, "Pac. Convention," *Quarterly of the Polish Western Association of America*, 6, no. 1/4, January 1965, 1–4.

113. "Sprawozdanie Prezesa Kongresu Polonii Amerykanskiej," 18, 19, 20

September 1964, Wilhelm Wolny Papers, Box 1, Folder 7, IHRC.

114. L. Poray, "The Problem of Central Europe," *Quarterly of the Polish Western Association of America,* 6, no. 3/4 (1965): 13–16; *Congressional Record Appendix*, 89th Cong., 1st sess., 111, no. 119 (1 July 1965): A3502.

115. Poray, "The Problem."

116. Ibid.

117. Rozmarek statement before Republican Platform Committee, 7 July 1964, National Security File, Poland, Correspondence #160, LBJ/L.

118. Harry Rosenthal, "The Assimilation and Integration of the German Expellees," *The Polish Review*, 8, no. 1 (Winter 1963): 108.

119. Ibid., 78–111.

120. Stenzl, "Germany's Eastern Frontier," 128.

121. Rachwald, *Poland between the Superpowers*, 62; Kulski, *Germany and Poland*, 136–138.

122. The *Christian Science Monitor* reported that expellee groups in the Federal Republic mounted a campaign in response to this memorandum, which apparently shows that, even though fewer and fewer expellees wanted or expected to return to the Oder–Neisse region, they were not yet ready to publicly admit it. See Harry Ellis, "Oder–Neisse Issue Stirs," *Christian Science Monitor*, 21 November 1965, 1.

123. Kulski, *Germany and Poland*, 135; "West Germany: Of Hopes and Heimatsrecht," *Time*, 3 December 1965, 33; "Poland: Beginning of A Dialogue?" *Time*, 24 December 1965, 18–19. The Vatican's view of the border is presented in Edmund F. Konczakowski, "Vatican Policy toward the German–Polish Oder–Neisse Line, 1945–1972" (Ph.D. diss., University of Pennsylvania, 1976).

124. Rachwald, *Poland between the Superpowers*, 63.

125. "Recognizing the Oder-Neisse," *New York Times*, 19 November 1966, 38.

126. The editors of *Christian Century* also hailed the correspondence. See "West Germany," 83 (9 February 1966): 188–90 and "Testimony pro the German Church on Oder–Neisse," 83 (6 April 1965): 442–445.

127. "Communist Poland's 20 Years," *New York Times*, 26 July 1964, IV, 8; Stefan Korbonski, "Poland's Boundaries," *New York Times*, 5 August 1964, 32. In the 1940s and 1950s, *New York Times* editorials reflected the official governmental position that finalization of the border awaited a peace conference.

128. "Border Politics in Bonn," *New York Times*, 19 January 1965, 32. A letter to the editor the next week objected to the editorial, pointing out that in 1947 and 1950 *New York Times* editorials questioned Poland's claims to the land. See "German–Polish Boundary," *New York Times*, 26 January 1965, 36. The next week a letter to the editor from John T. Kazmierski objected to the previous letter and called for a peaceful resolution of the problem within the context of the United Nations. See "Oder–Neisse Line Upheld," 1 February 1965, 22.

129. C. L. Sulzberger, "Foreign Affairs: How Germany's Frontier Was Drawn," *New York Times*, 12 February 1965, 28.

130. See Harry B. Ellis, "Oder-Neisse Issue Stirs," *Christian Science Monitor*, 21 November 1965, 1; Ellis, "Poles Offer Feelers on German Issue," *Christian Science Monitor*, 24 January 1966.

131. "What Poland Got from a DeGaulle Visit," *U.S. News and World Report*, 18 September 1967, 13.

132. Hanrieder, *Germany, America, Europe*, 190.

133. Ibid.

134. *Congressional Record*, 90th Cong., 2nd sess., 114, pt. 8 (18 April 1968): 10004–10005.

135. "Statement of Charles Rozmarek, President of the Polish American Congress, before the Republican Platform Committee in Miami Beach, July 29, 1968," Mazewski Papers, Box 18, Republican Convention Folder, IHRC; "Statement of Charles Rozmarek, President of the Polish American Congress, before the Democratic Platform Committee in Chicago, Illinois—August 22, 1968," Mazewski Papers, Box 18, Democratic Convention Folder, IHRC.

136. *Congressional Record*, 90th Cong., 2nd sess., 114, pt. 9 (30 April 1968): 11071–11072.

137. Ibid.

138. Pienkos discusses the difficulties of the PAC in "The Polish American Congress," 35–43. A Polish American leader in Wisconsin, Dr. Edward Tomasik, urged Polish Americans to follow his "Wisconsin Plan" in the upcoming presidential and congressional elections, claiming: "All that is needed are 250 Pol-Ams in 250 U.S. Congressional districts." See Pienkos article and "Dr. Tomasik Says Wisconsin Plan Can Affect Destiny of Pol-Ams," *Polish American Journal*, 16 September 1967, in Wilhelm Wolny Papers, Folder 9, IHRC.

139. *Congressional Record*, 90th Cong., 2nd sess., 114, pt. 24 (12 October 1968): 31203–31204.

140. Department of State, Administrative History, Chapter 3, Section F, Eastern Europe—Poland File, January 1969, LBJ/L. The report briefly detailed the various economic agreements.

141. Ibid.

8 Nixon to Bush

The presidential administrations following Johnson held to the formulas specified in Allied agreements while some State Department officers, members of Congress, Polish American organizations, and foreign policy scholars continued to urge recognition of the Oder–Neisse Line. A thorough, critical analysis of the border issue during these years awaits the release of classified materials from the State Department. A narrative of events from the Nixon to Bush administrations, including President Bush's participation in the settlement of the border conflict in 1990, however, can be pieced together from various sources such as memoirs, public documents, correspondence, and newspapers and journals.

Initially, Nixon's main foreign policy focus was on the Vietnam War, but he, like his predecessor, could not ignore the European situation. Also like Johnson, Nixon faced continued pressure from Polish American organizations and members of Congress urging U.S. recognition of the Oder–Neisse Line.[1] By the time that Nixon took office, West German officials had assumed responsibility for some type of preliminary action on the border issue, always with the limitations prescribed at Potsdam in mind. The Soviet invasion of Czechoslovakia and the West German election had led to increased debate and discussion about the proper course of Bonn's eastern policy.[2] While the CDU continued to speak for the expellees, SPD politicians publicly called for a new *Ostpolitik,* and when the Free Democrats joined in this, a new coalition in the Federal Republic appeared possible. This coalition government took office in October 1969 and broke the deadlock on the question of establishing relations with the states of East Central Europe.[3]

WEST GERMANY'S INITIATIVES

In a series of "little steps" Willy Brandt changed West Germany's foreign policy priorities. Whereas Adenauer had planned for reunification to be followed by elections and territorial negotiations, Brandt placed recognition of the status quo as the first step toward negotiations for reunification, and he began a dialogue with Moscow and Warsaw.[4] The Soviets took the initiative from Gomułka after he hesitated about adhering to East Germany's demand that Bonn recognize the East German government as a precondition to finalizing diplomatic relations. Brandt's *Ostpolitik* resulted in West Germany and the Soviet Union's signing a treaty on 12 August 1970 after intense negotiations. The intention of this Moscow Treaty was to strengthen relations between the two states and to foster peace in Europe. Article Three of the treaty dealt with border issues, and the two sides agreed to "respect without restriction" the integrity of European states as they then existed; they denied any territorial aspirations, with special note taken of the inviolability of the Oder–Neisse Line.[5] The Federal Republic sent notes to the United States, France, and Great Britain informing them of this treaty and acknowledging Allied "rights and responsibilities" in Germany and Berlin prior to a peace conference. In its reply, the United States affirmed that it maintained those rights, but Secretary of State Rogers declared U.S. "satisfaction" with the signing of the bilateral treaty.[6]

U.S. RESPONSE

Polish Americans and some members of Congress urged the Nixon administration to go beyond mere expressions of satisfaction in order to foster this closer relationship between Bonn and Moscow for the benefit of Poland. A 15 August 1970 letter from the Polish American Congress notified the White House that the Eighth National Convention of the Polish American Congress requested the president's "approval of this boundary on behalf of the United States" as an indication that the United States supported peace. In a meeting with President Nixon in October 1970, leaders of the Polish American community presented a memorandum criticizing the "stock answers" that they had received from the State Department declaring that a border solution awaited a peace treaty. The memorandum stated that this attempt to use international law as a screen for inactivity did not take into account the realities of the situation in the territories that the Poles had securely settled. The Polish American leaders appealed again for U.S. recognition of the border in order to aid the states suffering under Soviet oppression and in order to "substitute the ambiguity of the Bonn–Moscow Pact with a clear cut declaration." President Nixon noncommittally promised to consider all the points of their discussion and affirmed that one of the principal goals of the United States was national self-determination.[7]

In the Senate Claiborne Pell (D-RI) spoke approvingly of the West German–Soviet treaty as opening a "path forward to peace" and pointed to his ten-year-long drive to have the West accept the Oder–Neisse Line. He also expressed his approval of West Germany's demand that a satisfactory solution to the Berlin problem be found prior to ratification of the treaties. The senator called for the Executive Branch to keep the Committee on Foreign Relations apprised of progress in the resumption of negotiations on the Berlin situation.[8]

WARSAW TREATY

The treaty had more symbolic than actual impact, since it simply "acknowledged the territorial and political consequences" of World War II, but it paved the way for Bonn's participation in detente with Soviet satellite states.[9] In the months following the Moscow Treaty signing, negotiations between Warsaw and Bonn bore fruit. In December 1970 West Germany and Poland signed a treaty in Warsaw normalizing relations, renouncing the use of force, and recognizing the "inviolability" of the existing borders with special note taken of the Oder–Neisse Line as laid out at Potsdam.[10] A note accompanying the treaty addressed the issue of repatriating Germans who remained in Poland. West Germany refused to submit to Poland's demands that the words "final" and "recognition" be part of the clause concerning the border because, the Germans pointed out, the Four Power Allies still had responsibility for treaty agreements. The Poles accepted a less definite agreement that the Oder–Neisse Line as described in the Potsdam Agreement constituted Poland's western frontier and that the border was inviolable. In effect, West Germany still only recognized the border de facto, but it gave up claim to the area. Finalization awaited a peace treaty, and Bonn sent the Western Allies assurances that their rights had not been violated.[11] Poland had won a victory by gaining Western recognition of its position that Potsdam had established Poland's western border, and Warsaw viewed the problem as settled.

The Bundestag had a different interpretation of the treaty than did the Polish Sejm, however, with Bonn continuing to assert that the Germany of 1937 was the ultimate goal of unification. After the Allies signed a Four Power treaty in September 1971 affirming their jurisdiction over Berlin, the Bundestag, after a fierce debate, ratified the Moscow and Warsaw treaties in 1972.[12] The deputies passed the Moscow Treaty with 248 votes approving, 10 against, and 238 abstaining. The Warsaw Treaty received 248 favorable votes, 17 votes against, and 230 abstentions. The Christian Democrats abstained as a party.[13] In Warsaw the Polish Sejm approved the treaty after some discussion of West Germany's intentions.[14]

The State Department issued a press release noting U.S. "satisfaction" with the Bonn–Warsaw treaty and expressing confidence that it would lead to improved relations between Poland and West Germany and would "eliminate sources of tension in Europe." Nevertheless, President Nixon did not grant official U.S. recognition of the Oder–Neisse Line as requested in a memorandum from the Polish American Congress.[15] Some members of the administration and of Congress were concerned about the possibility of *Ostpolitik* resulting in "a free-wheeling German nationalism that might demoralize Europe" or in an acquiescence of the status quo with the Soviets in control of Eastern Europe.[16]

The mainstream press and Polish American organizations reflected a generally favorable, but cautious, attitude toward the Moscow and Warsaw treaties. A *New York Times* editorial summarized the impact of the treaties by pointing out that while they would not usher in the "millennium," they would open the way for increased East–West contact. "At any rate," the editor noted, the West Germans gave up only the "illusion" of recovering the lost lands rather than any practical goals.[17] The *Christian Science Monitor* called the agreement between Bonn and Warsaw a "wise treaty" that satisfied justice by compensating Poland for the suffering inflicted by Germany. Like the *Times*, the *Monitor* expected that the treaties would improve contact between East and West and would eventually open the way for German reunification.[18]

Although Polish Americans did not express great trust in West Germany, they supported the Warsaw Treaty and contended that it offered the opportunity for the United States to grant recognition of the border. Roman Pucinski (D-IL), an officer in the PAC, expressed grave concern about America's lack of recognition, which he blamed on "those in the State Department who are unable to comprehend the geopolitics of Europe."[19] The editor of the *Quarterly of the Polish Western Association of America* also expressed doubt about the sincerity of Washington's statement and accused the administration not only of "shying away from a positive statement regarding recognition [of the borders]" but also of "undermining" Chancellor Brandt's work by "spreading doubt as to the wisdom of the treaty." The organization based this accusation on a letter from William Macomber Jr., assistant secretary for congressional relations, to Congressman Pucinski which stated that the United States maintained that Germany's borders awaited settlement at a final peace treaty. The editor of the *Quarterly* contended that Macomber's reply was "unconvincing and unsatisfactory" since the intention of Potsdam was to mark the finality of the borders. He also argued that since a peace treaty had not been signed in the last twenty-six years, there appeared little hope that one would be signed. He stated further that West Germany had recognized this and had decided to act without the "questionable sanction of a Peace Treaty."[20] Throughout the Nixon presidency, these Polish American organizations continued to call for U.S. recognition of the Oder–Neisse Line, and continued to monitor activities of West German revisionists as well as statements by German American groups opposed to the treaty.[21] At the Ninth National convention of the Polish American Congress in Detroit, the delegates reiterated the call for U.S. recognition of the line.[22]

In Poland, celebration of the treaty signings quickly gave way to domestic unrest. The treaties represented Gomułka's last hurrah since he had been facing increasing internal trouble, indirectly the result of the 1967 Arab–Israeli conflict. While popular opinion in Poland favored Israel, Soviet support of the Arabs led Gomułka to accuse some Polish Jews of being a "fifth column," using anti-Semitism to forward his position, even though he had avoided the tactic in the past. Polish participation in the Czechoslovak invasion in the spring of 1968 negatively affected Gomułka's popularity both in Poland and in the West.[23] In December 1970 drastic price hikes in food resulted in violent riots in Gdynia, where workers fought government troops. Gomułka lost the support of his party and was replaced by Edward Gierek, initially viewed as the "least parochial and most Western of the Communist leaders" in Poland.[24]

U.S.–POLISH RELATIONS IN THE 1970S

Gierek tried to solve the difficult economic problems that he had inherited by opening trade with the United States and making more concessions to the Soviets. Relations between Washington and Warsaw improved, and Gierek received a great boost by President Nixon's one-day stop in Warsaw in May 1972. The Polish people warmly received President Nixon, and he found the talks with governmental representatives fruitful. He and Gierek issued a communiqué on 1 June affirming the need for increased East–West contacts and welcoming the border provisions in the Warsaw–Bonn Treaty as an important step toward European cooperation.[25] After this visit Nixon announced that the United States opposed interfering in East European relationships, and a new consulate was established. Contrary to earlier suggestions, however, it was set up in Krakow rather than a city in the western territories, probably indicating U.S. reluctance to commit an action that could be interpreted as formal recognition of Poland's control of the area.[26] Nixon also appointed Richard Davies, an experienced Eastern European diplomat, as ambassador to Poland in December 1972.

The improved relations between Washington and Warsaw continued under President Ford.[27] One of Ford's first forays into diplomacy involved a reception for Gierek, the first non-Soviet Communist Party chief to be honored at the White House as a head of state. In public speeches the two men affirmed traditional ties of friendship between the United States and Poland and in a joint statement affirmed that relations were founded on principles of the United Nations Charter and international law, including the inviolability of frontiers and the nonuse of force.[28]

Although Poles considered the visit as signifying a "new phase" in relations, and the Ford administration and mainstream press welcomed these contacts with representatives of the Polish government, Polish Americans were not convinced of the wisdom of such a move that seemed a mark of approval of the communist regime.[29] The president of the PAC, Aloysius Mazewski, declined the White House invitation for a dinner with Gierek.[30] A proposed meeting between Ford and PAC representatives was delayed until after Gierek's visit on the advice of the National Security Council "because of possible international ramifications."[31]

HELSINKI ACCORD

Another especially divisive issue between Polish Americans and the Ford administration was the Helsinki Final Act, signed by the U.S. president and thirty-four other leaders on 1 August 1975. The Helsinki meeting was part of the Conference on Security and Cooperation in Europe (CSCE), formally organized as a result of the 1972 Strategic Arms Limitation Talks (SALT).[32] On his way to Helsinki in July 1975 President Ford returned Gierek's visit by stopping in Warsaw, where the Polish people received him unenthusiastically. Polish American scholar Piotr Wandycz suggests that this lack of enthusiasm sprang from President Ford's inability to project a strong, statesmanlike image and from his intended purpose in Helsinki.[33]

The Helsinki Accord was a nonbinding agreement that recognized the post–World War II boundaries in exchange for Soviet promises of a "'positive and humanitarian attitude'" on human rights issues and scientific and cultural exchanges.[34] After extensive negotiations, the West German delegates successfully pushed through a clause that left open the possibility of the peaceful change of frontiers—including the reunification of Germany.[35] Thus, territorially, the Helsinki Agreement was to Poland's advantage by granting de facto recognition of the Oder–Neisse Line in the West, as already acknowledged in the Moscow and Warsaw Treaties. At the same time, however, the Helsinki Agreement also approved the Soviet acquisition of Poland's eastern lands.

Overall, American response to the Helsinki Accord was generally negative. According to John Maresca, one of the U.S. delegates to the CSCE, the responsibility for this reaction lay partly with the Ford administration's downplaying of the "potential political importance" of the negotiations. Thus, when Americans learned of the Final Act, they tended to perceive it as another Western concession to Moscow rather than as an agreement promoting human rights issues.[36] Conservative Republicans opposed the accord as acceptance of the Soviet domination of Eastern Europe and were upset by the administration's poor handling of the issue.[37] Congresswoman Millicent Fenwick (R-NJ), on the other hand, saw the potential usefulness of the Final Act to promote human rights activities in the Soviet Union and pushed for a bill establishing a joint "watch committee" to monitor CSCE successes.[38]

Much of the mainstream press objected to U.S. participation in the negotiations, focusing on the gains made by the USSR. Flora Lewis of the *New York Times* called the Final Act a "tedious" document that recognized the status quo while blurring the tensions remaining between East and West. She noted that the accord was unofficially called an "ersatz peace treaty" that for the Soviets contained the "key phrase" regarding the inviolability of borders.[39] In a commentary for the *Christian Science Monitor,* Roscoe Drummond called Helsinki an "Unmitigated Mistake" that ratified Moscow's permanent control over Eastern Europe without leaving room for future change in political alignments.[40]

Americans of East European heritage strongly opposed the Helsinki Final Act for its alleged legitimization of a Soviet sphere of influence in Eastern Europe, even though the Ford administration tried to counter this view. Spokesmen tried to explain that the conference represented a real contribution to reduced East–West tensions and increased cooperation and to point out that the Helsinki Agreement was nonbinding and would not affect the legal status of any European territorial questions.[41] The Polish American Congress sent Ford a letter in July expressing opposition to U.S. signing of the agreement "without reservation" because it granted the Soviet Union "what it has been seeking" since World War II—the "guarantee of the inviolability" of postwar borders—and because the Soviets rarely honored the spirit and letter of such agreements. PAC President Mazewski called for an unequivocal policy statement that the

Helsinki meeting was to promote favorable conditions for the realization of self-determination for all peoples and that signing of the Final Act did not signify final recognition of the borders.[42]

The negative reaction of Polish Americans to the Helsinki Accord reveals another irony of the Oder–Neisse issue: American participation in the Final Act meant that the United States indirectly granted de facto recognition of Poland's western border on the Oder and Neisse Rivers, a move that Polish Americans had urged for thirty years. In their rejection of the Helsinki Accord, which accepted post–World War II borders, Polish Americans did not mention the Oder–Neisse Line. Instead, Mazewski's letter opposed in general terms Soviet "domination of East-Central Europe," specifically the Baltic states. Subsequent letters, however, show that these Polish Americans understood that neither the Warsaw Treaty nor the Final Act signified U.S. recognition of Poland's border, so their omission of the issue in the 1975 protest letter cannot be explained that easily. Possibly, Mazewski did not want to qualify and possibly weaken his organization's general opposition to the Helsinki Agreement that gave a stamp of approval to Soviet territorial acquisitions by pointing to this specific element that would benefit Poland.

In any case, the Helsinki Agreement was not the last point of contention between Polish Americans and the Ford administration. Difficulties resulting from the casual announcement of the so-called Sonnenfeldt Doctrine, which some interpreted as U.S. acceptance of Soviet control of Eastern Europe, as well as the president's gaffe during a debate with Jimmy Carter when he denied that the Soviets dominated Eastern Europe seemed to confirm the suspicion among American ethnic groups that Ford lacked the necessary presidential qualifications. An unofficial and small political sampling suggests that Ford lost to Carter in Polish American votes by 41 to 59 percent.[43] Ford's defeat, according to political scientist Donald Pienkos, represented a real "blow" to the "prestige" that Polish Americans enjoyed during the Nixon–Ford presidencies, but many Polish Americans soon found the Carter administration appealing.[44]

THE CARTER PRESIDENCY

The Carter presidency set a new "style to East–West relations," and his focus on human rights as well as his appointment of Zbigniew Brzezinski as national security advisor signaled to the Poles and Polish Americans new possibilities. In his memoirs Brzezinski confirmed that the Carter administration's human rights focus led to a reevaluation of U.S. policy in Eastern Europe. This resulted in Presidential Directive 21, which promoted a policy giving preference to those states with more liberal domestic policies or those more independent of Soviet foreign policy. The president's subsequent visit to Poland also stemmed from his desire to emphasize this policy change.[45] The convening of a Polish–American Day Conference by the Department of State on 5 October 1978 is another example of this focus. At the conference, Stefan Marcinkowski of the PWA stimulated a discussion about de jure recognition of the Oder–Neisse border by the United States.[46] The chairman of the conference, Assistant Secretary of State for European Affairs George Vest, requested former Ambassador Richard Davies to reply to Marcinkowski's inquiry. Davies stated that although the United States accepted the Bonn and Warsaw Treaty provisions regarding the border, such acceptance did not constitute de jure recognition because the United States held to the position that the border would be finalized at a peace conference. He admitted his skepticism about such a peace conference ever being held, but he firmly declared that "we have come as close as we can in accordance with our obligations under international law, to recognizing the Oder–Neisse boundary."[47] In letters to Marcinkowski on 31 October 1978 and 3 May 1979, Jack Seymour Jr. of the Polish Office in the State Department followed up on Davies' verbal reply by stating that since the Allies collectively retained obligations in Germany, the United States could not act alone on the matter at the risk of undermining its position on "certain issues stemming from World War II." Such reasoning did not satisfy the leaders of the PWA, who remained firm in their determination to see formal U.S. recognition of the border.[48]

U.S.–POLISH RELATIONS UNDER GENERAL JARUZELSKI

Although the rise of the Solidarity trade union movement, General Jaruzelski's appointment as prime minister in February 1981, and the imposition of martial law in December 1981 captured much of the attention of Polish Americans in subsequent years, they did not ignore the border issue.[49] The Polish American Congress and the Polish Western Association continued to monitor words and actions of American and West German politicians regarding the border. In March 1983 Aloysius Mazewski protested to the State Department the speech by Friedrich Zimmermann, West German minister of interior, that West Germany "'would not limit the question of German unity to the regions now under [its] control . . . but rather would also include former German territories east of the Oder and Neisse rivers.'"[50] The PAC sent similar protests to the German ambassador in Washington; the Polish Western Association of America sent protest letters to Chairman Charles Percy of the Senate Foreign Relations Committee and Clement Zablocki of the House Foreign Affairs Committee. The replies to these protests could not have been very comforting to the Polish American organizations. Thomas Niles, deputy assistant secretary for European affairs, wrote that, "strictly speaking," Zimmermann's statement was correct since the Allies had not yet signed a postwar peace treaty. He quoted, however, from the 1970 Polish–West German Treaty and the 1975 Helsinki Final Act regarding the inviolability and integrity of borders, assuring Mazewski that the United States "has not retreated from its pledges and has no intention of doing so." He stated his belief that the Bonn government would accept similar commitments.[51] The West German ambassador responded by quoting from the 1972 Bundestag resolution: "'By demanding that the right to self determination be realized, the Federal Republic of Germany does not claim any changes concerning territories or borders.'" He added that West Germany wanted to foster a Europe without divisions and favored good relations with Eastern Europe.[52] Even Zablocki, who had continually supported U.S. recognition of the Oder–Neisse Line, wrote Marcinkowski of the Polish Western Association that "any future agreement on the border between Germany and Poland must be the subject of negotiation between the parties involved." The congressman was very pessimistic about the prospects for such an agreement in the near future. The editor of the PAC Newsletter pointed out that Zimmermann's statement contradicted the West German–Polish Treaty agreement that neither country had territorial claims against the other. "One cannot have it both ways," the editor of the newsletter announced.[53]

U.S.–Polish relations reached a "postwar nadir" in 1983, and the United States left vacant the ambassador post in Warsaw to protest Jaruzelski's actions concerning the imposition of martial law and the repression of Solidarity.[54] Within the next decade, however, Gorbachev's "revolution" in openness led the Soviet satellites to begin the process of liberalization, and relations between Poland and the United States began to improve. The dramatic events of 1989 resulted in the collapse of the communist regimes in Poland and Germany and opened new doors for American diplomacy in Europe. The American government cautiously supported German reunification.[55]

This caution was echoed in a statement issued by the Executive Committee of the Polish American Congress, noting that while the PAC applauded the right to self-determination and unification called for by Germans, the eventual "implementation must be based on recognition of territorial integrity and security of other nations." The committee gained encouragement from President Bush's statement that German unification had to occur within the context of its NATO commitment and his reiteration of U.S. support for the Helsinki Final Act concerning the inviolability of borders. The letter closed with a statement indicating that the Polish American Congress would closely monitor events in East Central Europe.[56]

As if in an attempt to caution its readers not to expect immediate settlement of outstanding matters, the May and December 1989 issues of the *Quarterly of the Polish Western Association of America* focused on past and present relations between Poland and Germany. The December issue contained a copy of the 1939 Nazi–Soviet Pact, an evaluation by Stanley Stein of the consequences of World War II, an article entitled "Poland and the Problem of German Unification," and a report on West German Chancellor Kohl's trip to Warsaw fostering full reconciliation.[57]

NEGOTIATING THE FINAL TREATY

The PWA's caution seemed justified in light of Chancellor Kohl's reticence on the border issue in the months immediately following the collapse of the Berlin Wall. Kohl was concerned about the estimated 15 percent of the German voters in the upcoming elections who favored the right-wing Republican Party that opposed the loss of land.[58] He continued to state that neither West nor East Germany had a legal right to settle the border issue since the Four Powers maintained ultimate authority on that issue.

Concern among Polish Americans increased when the State Department announced in February 1990 that Poland would not be one of the participants in Allied negotiations scheduled to deal with a reunified Germany. President Edward Moskal of the Polish American Congress immediately wrote Secretary of State James Baker asking him to reconsider. "We do not want a Yalta II," Moskal wrote. He also urged that the United States issue a reiteration of its "long standing" position on the inviolability of borders and argued that Washington had to "do everything in its power to ensure that the security interests of Poland are fully protected as the two Germanies re-unify." Moskal contended that the present border had to be recognized on a "legal basis" before or during the negotiations.[59]

Philip Zelikow and Condoleezza Rice, two members of President Bush's National Security Council who participated in the German reunification talks, assess Kohl's political Scylla and Charybdis in the reunification process in *Germany Unified and Europe Transformed.* They state that the chancellor faced pressure from West German politicians to accept the border while having to "pander to a few voters" who might go with the far right if they perceived too much "German territory" being sacrificed.[60] The Poles found Kohl's position "unsettling."[61]

In *A World Transformed* President George Bush writes of his February 1990 meeting at Camp David with Helmut Kohl, where the chancellor gave a more realistic assessment of the border issue than he presented to the public:

> Kohl downplayed the problem of the Polish border. "The border question is not serious," he declared with a confident smile. "Among friends I can be honest. In the FRG today eighty-five to ninety percent of the population are in favor of the Oder–Neisse border. The vast majority knows that this will be the border. The man who built Camp David, Mr. Roosevelt, will never be popular in Germany. The Poles were pushed west and the Germans were expelled. This was a reaction to Nazi crimes, but the Germans who were affected were innocent—this was twelve to fourteen million people. One third of the 1937 Reich was cut off. In 1945, two million German civilians were killed fleeing from Eastern Europe.[62]

Kohl contended that the struggle was to reassure the Poles about the 1,000-kilometer border, while making them understand that the decision had to come from a treaty ratified by an all-German parliament. "'The problem,' he stated, 'is that the Poles may demand reparations, . . . I would find that unacceptable. We have already paid one hundred and fifty billion deutsche marks to Poland, Israel, and individuals. We won't pay more, fifty years after the war.'"[63] Another potentially contentious issue that Kohl told Bush about at Camp David was that he supported a "consultative" rather than participant role for Poland at the treaty talks.[64]

National Security Adviser Brent Scowcroft, who coauthored *A World Transformed,* writes of his disappointment at Kohl's "more than a little disingenuous" position on the Oder–Neisse border issue. Scowcroft labels as "coy" the chancellor's response to a question at a press conference that the "legal situation" in Germany made the German people responsible for deciding such matters as the border issue. Scowcroft contends that the chancellor was playing politics by "angling" for votes on the border from the West German right wing. He felt that Kohl could have been more diplomatic than political by expressing Bonn's support for the Oder–Neisse border while holding to the position that "only a united Germany could act de jure on the border.[65] Zelikow and Rice echo Scowcroft's reading of Kohl's press statement: "Kohl again got in trouble over the border issue by repeating the formal legal position that the FRG lacked the capacity to settle the matter definitively on its own." President Bush stated clearly that the United States recognized the Oder–Neisse Line as part of the Helsinki Final Act.[66]

The situation remained relatively tense as Polish Prime Minister Mazowiecki responded to Kohl's hesitancy by calling for a German–Polish treaty settling the border issue before German unification. This treaty, Mazowiecki contended, was to be written and initialed by all parties *before* unification and then signed by an all-German government when one came into being.[67] Kohl's reticence on the border issue became the focus of anxiety among government leaders who worried about German unification.[68] President Bush conducted a "secret mediation" between the German chancellor and the Polish prime minister to establish a basic agreement on the border issue before Bush and Mazowiecki met in Washington, with Bush securing Kohl's reassurance in a telephone conversation "about his determination to accept the existing border."[69]

After equivocating for weeks, Kohl on 2 March 1990 stated that Germany would issue a firm guarantee of Poland's western border in return for Poland's reaffirmation of a 1953 promise not to seek reparations from Germany. The statement "touched off cries of alarm," raised European-wide questions about Kohl's leadership abilities and intentions, and led to a "stormy" cabinet meeting in Bonn on 6 March. Following that long meeting, Kohl withdrew the conditional requirement and agreed that both German parliaments would renounce any claims to Polish lands prior to reunification.[70] After further conversations, Kohl told Bush that he could agree to the wording of a common declaration about the border issue that would be issued by the two German governments.[71]

When Mazowiecki met with Bush at Camp David on 21 March 1990, he expressed appreciation for Bush's position that Poles be brought into the "Two-plus Four" discussions on matters regarding Poland since, he told the president, "'The Polish people are paranoid about agreements being made over their heads.'" Mazowiecki wanted full assurance that Poland's western territories were guaranteed to Poland by all the Allies and not just viewed as "'a gift from Stalin.'" The prime minister assured Bush that while he fully trusted Helmut Kohl, Poles still maintained concerns about the position that a strong, united Germany might take on the border issue.[72]

The Polish Western Association of America sent to Polish American newspapers a copy of its telegram to Bush supporting Prime Minister

Mazowiecki's request that Poland be included in the German reunification negotiations since such talks would deal with the Polish border issue.[73] A response by Acting Director of the Office of Eastern European and Yugoslav Affairs Michael Hornblow was printed in Detroit's *Polish Daily News* on 18 April 1990. Hornblow stated firmly that the United States "recognizes the current border . . . as constituting the permanent German–Polish border" and assured the readers that President Bush would "make sure that decisions that affect Poland's interests will not be made without Poland's involvement."[74]

A report by the executive director of the Polish American Congress claimed victory on this issue as gauged by "a series of positive editorials and op-ed columns" that appeared in the *Chicago Tribune, New York Times*, and *Washington Post*. The PAC had sent a memorandum to President Bush before his February meeting with Kohl that enabled him to "point out to the German leader the importance of the border issue to Polish Americans and resulted in the President making strong public statements on the subject." The president of the PAC met with Bush on 14 March 1990, and eventually both the U.S. and West German governments "issued strong statements" on the permanence of the border. Poland was invited to participate in the "Two plus Four" talks when border and security issues were discussed. "Our lobbying efforts were paid the ultimate compliment when an assistant to President Bush stated that the PAC lobbying campaign on these two issues was one of the best and most effective that Washington had seen in years," the report stated.[75]

In addition to dealing with West Germans, Poles, and Polish Americans concerned with the Oder–Neisse issue, President Bush had to mediate with America's Allies regarding Chancellor Kohl's approach to the border issue and to reunification in general. Bush relates his telephone conversations with Prime Minister Thatcher and President Mitterrand, conveying their suspicion of, and irritation, with Kohl. Mitterrand was furious with Kohl and insisted that the peace talks should be "Four-plus-Two" when the participants discussed border issues rather than the "Two-plus-Four" that would be in place when the issue of German reunification was on the table. Thatcher also expressed irritation at Kohl's handling of the border issue. President Bush, however, thought that the British prime minister's real fear centered on "the notion of a giant Germany in the middle of Europe" and that she was using the border issue as an example of Germany's dangerous potential.[76] President Bush expressed his trust that Kohl would recognize the Oder–Neisse Line.

Throughout the summer and fall of 1990 representatives from the United States, Soviet Union, Great Britain, France, West and East Germany, and Poland negotiated the border issue as one of the many issues to be resolved before a peace treaty with Germany could be signed. At a Harvard commencement address in June 1990, Chancellor Kohl pledged that the border would remain "inviolable" after German reunification.[77] In July 1990 the foreign ministers meeting in Paris announced that a border treaty retaining the Oder–Neisse Line would be signed by Poland and Germany as soon as possible after German reunification.[78] On 12 September 1990 in Moscow the foreign ministers of the four leading World War II Allies signed away their rights and responsibilities for Germany and Berlin in the presence of the foreign ministers of West and East Germany, clearing the way for German unification. Regarding united Germany's border, Article One of this nine-part treaty establishes that:

> 1. The united Germany shall comprise the territory of the Federal Republic of Germany, the German Democratic Republic and the whole of Berlin. Its external borders shall be the borders of the Federal Republic of Germany and the German Democratic Republic and shall be definitive from the date on which the present Treaty comes into forces. The confirmation of the definitive nature of the borders of the united Germany is an essential element of the peaceful order in Europe.
> 2. The united Germany and the Republic of Poland shall confirm the existing border between them in a treaty that is binding under international law.
> 3. The united Germany has no territorial claims whatsoever against other states and shall not assert any in the future. [79]

When President Bush sent the treaty to the Senate on 25 September 1990, he included a letter briefly tracing the history and provisions of the treaty, stating in part: "The Treaty makes clear that the current borders of the Federal Republic of Germany and German Democratic Republic shall be the final and definitive borders of a united Germany. All the provisions relating to Germany's border with Poland were worked out with the participation and approval of the government of Poland."[80] The Senate ratified the treaty on 10 October 1990 with two negative votes.[81] On 14 November 1990, after intense negotiations between Chancellor Kohl and Prime Minister Mazowiecki, both of whom faced elections, the foreign ministers of Poland and Germany signed a three-page treaty confirming the Oder–Neisse border and committing the countries to building a "'peaceful European order.'"[82] Poland and Germany then signed a treaty of friendship in June 1991.[83]

The relative lack of ceremony surrounding the foreign ministers' signing of the Treaty on the Final Settlement with Respect to Germany in 1990 provides a clear counterpoise to the confusion and tension stemming from the Potsdam Accord. Although the Oder–Neisse border issue was only one of many points addressed in these treaties, it serves as an example of America's handling of one of the crucial European Cold War issues that sprang from World War II. The State Department chose to maintain the posture adopted at Potsdam, refusing to grant formal recognition to the provisionally established border until a peace treaty with Germany was approved. Policymakers determined that the danger of not doing so was to open a Pandora's box of potential power struggles and realignments that would threaten the fragile stability of the European continent. If this danger was not always conveyed clearly to America's Cold War friends like West Germany and opponents like Poland and the Soviet Union or to American constituents who advocated a change in the U.S. policy, it was an ever-present threat in the minds and actions of U.S. policymakers who did not and perhaps could not let it be known that the Oder–Neisse Line issue was often under review and discussion at many different levels of the foreign policy bureaucracy. At times, the State Department's announcements about the border issue sounded more like posturing and cliché than a well-considered policy. Perhaps that is simply one of the paradoxes of diplomacy in a democracy.

NOTES

1. Senator Thomas Dodd spoke on the floor of the Senate in March 1970 referring to a *Newsweek* article that stated that Poland's claim to the Oder–Neisse lands was the one issue on which all Poles agreed. Dodd reiterated his position that Western nonrecognition of the line was a "meaningless irritant" that could be removed. See *Congressional Record*, 91st Cong., 2nd sess., 116, pt. 7 (23 March 1970): 8680-8681.

2. Wladyslaw W. Kulski, *Germany and Poland: From War to Peaceful Relations*, (Syracuse, NY: Syracuse University Press, 1966), 158

3. Kulski analyzes these steps and negotiations thoroughly in ibid., Chapter 8.

4. C. L. Sulzberger, "Foreign Affairs: Fading Lines," *New York Times*, 31 October 1969, 44.

5. Stefan Marcinkowski, "German Chronicle," *Quarterly of the Polish Western Association of America* 11, pt. 3 (1970): 14.

6. *Documents on Germany 1944–1970*, 861–862, 866.

7. White House Referral Slip to Thaddeus Adexko, 18 August 1970, CO [Country File] 121 Pol[and] (1969–1970) File, Nixon Materials, National Archives, Alexandria, Virginia. Hereafter cited as NA/A. Marcinkowski, "German Chronicle," 15. "*Sprawozdanie Prezesa Kongresu Polonii Amerykanskiej: Na Dziewiata Krajowa Konwencje w Detroit, Michigan, w dniach 6, 7 i 8 pazdziernika 1972 r,*" Zablocki Papers, Box 169, Marquette University.

8. *Congressional Record*, 91st Cong., 2nd sess., 116, pt. 27 (12 October 1970): 36319–36320.

9. Wolfram F. Hanrieder, *Germany, America, Europe: Forty Years of German Foreign Policy* (New Haven, CT: Yale University Press, 1989), 203.

10. Mieczyslaw F. Rakowski, *The Foreign Policy of the Polish People's Republic: Sketches from Thirty Years of History* (Warsaw: Interpress, 1975), 162–163.

11. For an analysis of the treaty, see Jerzy Sulek, "The Normalization Agreements of 1970–1972 and European Security," *Polish Western Affairs* 13, no. 2 (1972): 219–244. The *New York Times* reported in 1971 that after 400,000 ethnic Germans were permitted to travel to West Germany, the Polish government began refusing permission for more to leave. See James Feron, "Poles Said to Curb German Expellees," *New York Times*, 19 November, 1971, 2.

12. Kulski, *Germany and Poland*, Chapter 10.

13. Arthur Rachwald, *Poland between the Superpowers: Security vs. Economic Recovery* (Boulder, CO: Westview Press, 1983), 70; Kulski, *Germany and Poland*, 256.

14. Kulski, *Germany and Poland*, 269–271.

15. Stephen Wozniak, "The Polish-German Treaty and U.S. State Department Views," *Quarterly of the Polish Western Association of America* 12, pt. 2 (1971): 6.

16. Henry Kissinger, *Years of Upheaval* (Boston: Little, Brown, 1982), 57; Senator Allott spoke in the Senate in 1970 reflecting concern about the future of NATO and European stability because of Brandt's policies. See *Congressional Record*, 91st Cong., 2nd sess. (21 December 1970): 43064–43065.

17. "After Bonn's Treaties," *New York Times*, 21 May 1972, IV, 14.

18. "A Wise Treaty," *Christian Science Monitor*, 8 December 1970, 24.

19. See *Congressional Record*, 91st, 2nd, 116, pt. 30 (10 December 1970): 41097–41098.

20. The concern sprang partly from some German-language textbooks at the

University of Illinois that contained maps showing Germany's 1937 borders. In his response to Pucinski's request for information, Macomber stated that the United States maintained that Germany's borders awaited settlement through a peace treaty; he denied any knowledge or control over the publication of maps in textbooks. See Wozniak, "The Polish German Treaty," 6–8.

21. "Revisionism," *Quarterly of the Polish Western Association of America*, 13, pt. 3 (1972): 14. Edward Rozanski, president of the Illinois Division of the PAC, sent a letter to Nixon asking for U.S. recognition since England and France had already given their "seal of approval." See *Zgoda* 90 (1–15 January 1971), cited in Rozanski Papers, Box 1, Folder 24, IHRC. PAC President Aloysius Mazewski spoke before Congress in Washington on 4 February 1971 calling for increased cultural and educational contacts with Poland and for U.S. recognition of the line. See Zablocki Papers, Box 568, Subject Reference File, Poland, Marquette University.

22. "*Sprawozdanie Prezesa Kongresu Polonii Amerykanskiej*," 6–7, Zablocki Papers, Box 169, Marquette University.

23. Wandycz, *The United States*, 389.

24. Ibid., 393.

25. *Department of State Bulletin* 66 (26 June 1972): 914; James Feron, "Nixon Visit Brings Pride in Poland," *New York Times*, 5 June 1972, 7.

26. Piotr Wandycz, *The United States and Poland* (Cambridge: Harvard University Press, 1980), 402.

27. Leo Ribuffo traces the rocky road of relations between the Ford administration and the Polish American community in "Is Poland a Soviet Satellite? Gerald Ford, the Sonnenfeldt Doctrine, and the Election of 1976," *Diplomatic History* 14, no. 3 (Summer 1990): 385–403.

28. *Department of State Bulletin*, 71, no. 1845 (4 November 1974): 603; Memo, Kissinger to Ford, 9 October 1974, CO[untry File] 121, Gerald R. Ford Library and Museum. Hereafter cited as GRF/L.

29. Rakowski, *The Foreign Policy*, 197–199.

30. Memo, Niemczyk to O'Donnell, 9 October 1974, CO 121, GRF/L

31. Memo, Rustand to Baroody, 8 October 1974, CO 121, GRF/L.

32. See Arie Bloed, ed., *From Helsinki to Vienna: Basic Documents of the Helsinki Process* (Dordrecht, Netherlands: Martinus Nijhoff, 1990), 1–2; John J. Maresca, *To Helsinki: The Conference on Security and Cooperation in Europe 1973–1975* (Durham, NC: Duke University Press, 1985).

33. Wandycz, *The United States*, 405.

34. Robert F. Byrnes, "United States Policy toward Eastern Europe: Before and after Helsinki," *Review of Politics*, 37, no. 4 (October 1975): 435. A thorough analysis of the documents, negotiations, and results of the Helsinki Conference is presented in Vojtech Mastny, *Helsinki, Human Rights, and European Security: Analysis and Documentation* (Durham, NC: Duke University Press, 1986); Maresca, *To Helsinki;* Bloed, *From Helsinki to Vienna*.

35. Maresca, *To Helsinki*, 88–94. See Wladyslaw W. Kulski, "German–Polish Relations since World War II," *Polish Review* 24, no. 1 (1979): 66–67.

36. Maresca, *To Helsinki*, 159.

37. Aleksandr Solzhenitsyn in mid-1975 opposed the CSCE as a sellout to the Kremlin. Conservative Republicans urged Ford to meet Solzhenitsyn at the White House, but on Kissinger's and Scowcroft's warning that such a meeting would "offend the Kremlin," the White House announced that the president was "too busy" to meet with the Soviet dissident. When the press leaked the real reason that the meeting was not held, conservatives

claimed that Moscow "held 'veto power'" over Ford's schedule. See Ribuffo, "Is Poland," 390; IT [International Organizations Collection] 104 CSCE, GRF/L contains a number of letters from congressional constituents forwarded to Ford reflecting concern about CSCE.

38. Congress generally approved the bill, and Ford signed it, even though some members of the administration believed it unconstitutionally mixed legislative and executive powers. Maresca, *To Helsinki,* 160, 207.

39. Flora Lewis, "'The Document in Helsinki' Confirming 1945 Realities," *New York Times*, 27 July 1975, Sec. IV, 1; "Ford vs Solzhenitsyn II," *New York Times*, 20 July 1975, 28.

40. Roscoe Drummond, "Helsinki: Unmitigated Mistake," *Christian Science Monitor*, 6 August 1975, 27. Drummond points out that even the *New York Times* and *Washington Post,* which had supported past efforts at détente, rejected the Final Act as something that "'should not have happened.'"

41. Meeting Agenda, 25 July 1975, IT 104 CSCE 8/9/74 - 7/31/75, GRF/L; Mailgram, Nationalities Council of Michigan to Ford, 27 July 1975, ibid.; Letter Kendall to Percy, 30 May 1975, ibid.; Telegram, Polish Cavalry and Horse Artillery Veterans Association in North America to Ford, 24 July 1975, CO 121, Poland, GRF/L; Letter, Olech to Ford, 23 July 1975; ibid.; Letter, Backaitis to Ford, IT CSCE 8/1/75 - 8/31/75, GRF/L; Ribuffo, "Is Poland," 390–391.

42. Letter, Mazewski to The President, 24 July 1975, Mazewski Papers, Box 44, Helsinki Folder, IHRC.

43. Ribuffo, "Is Poland," 403; Maresca, *To Helsinki*, 159-160.

44. Donald E. Pienkos, "Polish American Congress—An Appraisal," *Polish American Studies* 36, no. 2 (Autumn 1979), 23.

45. Zbigniew Brzezinski, *Power and Principle: Memoirs of the National Security Adviser 1977–1981* (New York: Farrar, Straus, and Giroux, 1983), 296–297.

46. Stefan Marcinkowski, "German Chronicle," *Quarterly of the Polish Western Association of America* 19, no. 3/4 (1978): 14–16.

47. Ibid.

48. Stefan Marcinkowski, "German Chronicle," *Quarterly of the Polish Western Association of America* 20, no. 1/2 (1979): 1–6.

49. Bennett Kovrig, *Of Walls and Bridges: The United States & Eastern Europe* (New York: New York University Press, 1991).

50. Letter, Mazewski to Schultz, 7 March 1983, in author's possession.

51. Stefan Marcinkowski, "German Chronicle," *Quarterly of the Polish Western Association of America* 25, no. 1 (June 1983): 12.

52. Ibid.

53. Ibid., 13, 15.

54. Kovrig, *Of Walls and Bridges*, 140.

55. The journalist Elizabeth Pond traces these events in Germany in *After the Wall: American Policy toward Germany* (New York: Priority Press, 1990).

56. Statement by Polish American Congress, 15 December 1989, in author's possession.

57. See *Quarterly of the Western Association of America*, 29, no. 3/4, (December 1989).

58. James P. Gannon, "Poland Fears Reunited Germany May Make Grab for Land," *Detroit News*, 24 December 1989, 9; William Pfaff, "Kohl's Evasion of a Higher Responsibility," *Chicago Tribune*, 14 January 1990, 4, 3.

59. Letter, Moskal to Baker, 22 February 1990, in author's possession.

60. Philip Zelikow and Condoleezza Rice, *Germany Unified and Europe*

Transformed: A Study in Statecraft (Cambridge: Harvard University Press, 1995), 153.

61. Ibid., 207.

62. George Bush and Brent Scowcroft, *A World Transformed* (New York: Alfred A. Knopf, 1998), 251.

63. Ibid., 251–252; Zelikow and Rice, *Germany Unified,* 213.

64. Kohl contended that Gorbachev was not interested in the border issue; his big concern was that the issue of Poland's eastern border not be raised since "there are old Polish cities in the USSR." Bush and Scowcroft, *A World Transformed*, 252.

65. Ibid., 249–250, 255–256.

66. Zelikow and Rice, *Germany Unified*, 216.

67. Mazowecki, according to Rice and Zelikow, "launched a major diplomatic initiative" in February 1990 by sending letters to Bush, Gorbachev, Thatcher, and Mitterrand proposing his idea that the two German states initial a treaty on the border. Zelikow and Rice, *Germany Unified*, 208.

68. Ibid., 217; Joseph Bierman, "The Neo-Nazi Factor," *Macleans* 103 (19 March 1990): 31.

69. Zelikow and Rice, *Germany Unified,* 219–220.

70. Bierman, "The Neo-Nazi Factor," 31.

71. According to Scowcroft, they "had lost the forest for the trees" since this breakthrough became moot when German reunification occurred according to Article 23 since that approach made the Federal Republic bound by its former "legal commitment to the Oder–Neisse line. See Bush and Scowcroft, *A World Transformed*, 262; Zelikow and Rice, *Germany Unified*, 220, 222.

72. Bush and Scowcroft, *A World Transformed,* 261.

73. Letter, Marcinkowski to Bush, 21 February 1990, in author's possession.

74. "'Poland Has a Right to Secure Borders,'" Letters to the Editor, *Polish Daily News (Dziennik Polski*), 18 April 1990, 8.

75. "Report of the PAC National Executive Director: For the Period from January 1 through June 25, 1990," in author's possession; Zelikow and Rice write that in the PAC meeting with Bush, the representatives "urged him to join Mazowiecki in issuing just the kind of joint statement Kohl feared." Zelikow and Rice, *Germany Unified*, 434, 48n.

76. Bush and Scowcroft, *A World Transformed*, 248–249, 256–257.

77. Craig Whitney, "Kohl, At Harvard, Reaffirms Border," *New York Times,* 8 June 1990, A7.

78. Susan Bennett, "German Unity Advances with Deal to Keep Polish Border," *Detroit Free Press*, 18 July 1990, 1; George de Lama, "Border Deal Opens Way to One Germany," *Chicago Tribune*, 18 July 1990, 1; *Foreign Policy Bulletin* 1 (September/October 1990): 74–81; Bush and Scowcroft, *World Transformed*, 298.

79. U.S. Department of State Dispatch, 8 October 1990, 1, no. 6, 164.

80 Ibid.

81. "Message to the Senate Transmitting Treaty," *Compilation of Presidential Documents* 26 (1 October 1990): 1443–1444. Bush sent the treaty to the Senate on 25 September; it was ratified with only two negative votes on 10 October 1990. See *Congressional Record*, 136, no. 134, S14863-S14874.

82. Thomas Friedman, "Four Allies Give Up Rights in Germany," *New York Times*, 13 September 1990, 1; George de Lama, "Allies Relinquish Hold on Germany," *Chicago Tribune*, 13 September 1990, 1; George de Lama, "Allies to OK Key German Unity Pact," *Chicago Tribune*, 12 September 1990, 4; Joseph A. Reeves, "Poland, Germany Sign Border Treaty," *Chicago Tribune*, 15 November 1990, 10.

83. Zelikow and Rice, *Germany Unified*, 364.

Selected Bibliography

PRIMARY SOURCES

National Archives, Washington, DC
- Record Group 43, Records of World War II Conferences and Records of the Control Commission
- Record Group 59, Records of the Department of State Decimal Files
- Record Group 218, Records of the Joint Chiefs of Staff

National Records Center, Suitland, MD
- Record Group 84, Foreign Service Posts of the Department of State, Poland, Warsaw Embassy, General Records, 1945–1949
- Record Group 335, Records of the Secretary of the Army
- Record Group 319, Records of the Army Staff

National Records Center, Alexandria, VA
- Nixon Presidential Materials Project

Presidential Libraries—Various Collections
- Harry S. Truman Library, Independence, MO
- Dwight D. Eisenhower Library, Abilene, KS
- John F. Kennedy Library, Boston, MA
- Lyndon B. Johnson Library, Austin, TX
- Gerald R. Ford Library and Museum, Ann Arbor, MI

Immigration History Research Center, St. Paul, MN
- Assembly of Captive European Nations Papers
- Walter Drzewieniecki Papers
- Polish American Congress (Chicago) Records
- Polish American Congress (Illinois Division) Records
- Edward C. and Loda Rozanski Papers
- Aloysius Mazewski Papers
- Newspaper and Serials Collection
- Wilhelm A. Wolny Papers

Polish Museum of America, Chicago
- Newspaper and Serials Collection

Marquette University Library, Milwaukee, WI
- Clement Zablocki Papers
- Charles Kersten Papers

Bentley Library, University of Michigan, Ann Arbor
Alvin Bentley Collection

Published Documents

Embassy of Poland. *Poland, Germany and European Peace: Official Documents,1944–1948.* London: Embassy of Poland, 1948.

Ministry for Foreign Affairs of the Polish People's Republic. *Documents on the Hostile Policy of the United States Government toward People's Poland.* Warsaw: Polish Institute of International Affairs, 1953.

Polish American Congress. *Polish American Congress, Inc., 1944–1948: Selected Documents.* Chicago: Polish American Congress, 1948.

Public Papers of the Presidents, Truman–Bush. Washington, DC: U.S. Government Printing Office.

Research Publications. *The Declassified Documents Catalog, 1975–1990.* Woodbridge, CT: Research Publications.

Ruhm von Oppen, Beate, ed. *Documents on Germany under Occupation, 1945–1954.* London: Oxford University Press, 1955.

U.S. Congress. Senate. Committee on Foreign Relations. *Documents on Germany,1944–1970.* 92nd Cong., 1st sess., 1971.

U.S. Department of State. *Germany 1947–1949: The Story in Documents.* Washington, DC: U.S. Government Printing Office, 1950.

U.S. Department of State. *Foreign Relations of the United States*, 1943–1968. Washington, DC: U.S. Government Printing Office, 1967–1999.

U.S. Department of State. *Policy Planning Staff Papers 1947–1949.* New York: Garland, 1983.

Wszelaki, Jan, ed. *John F. Kennedy and Poland: Selection of Documents, 1948–1963 with 8Illustrations.* New York: Polish Institute of Arts and Sciences in America, 1964.

Congressional Documents

U.S. Congress. *Congressional Record.* 80th–92nd Congress. Washington, DC: U.S. Government Printing Office.

U.S. Congress. House. Committee on International Relations Selected Executive Session Hearings of the Committee, 1943-1950, (Historical Series).

U.S. Congress. Senate. Committee on Foreign Relations. *Executive Sessions of the Senate Foreign Relations Committee.* 80th Cong., 1st and 2nd sess., vol. 1, 1976.

———. *Review of the World Situation, 1949–1950: Hearings Held in Executive Session before the Committee on Foreign Relations.* 81st Cong., 1st and 2nd sess., 1974. *On the World Situation.*

U.S. Congress. Senate. Committee on the Judiciary *Hearing before the Subcommittee on Amendments to the Displaced Persons Act of the*

Committee on the Judiciary to Amend the Displaced Persons Act of 1948. 81st Cong. 1st and 2nd sess., 1950.
U.S. Congress. Senate. *United States Policy toward Europe (And Related Matters).* 89th Cong., 2nd sess, 1966.

Newspapers and Periodicals

Chicago Tribune
Christian Science Monitor
Department of State Bulletin
Department of State Dispatch
Dziennik Polski
Dziennik Związkowy
Głos Ludowy
New York Times
News from the German Embassy
Polish American Studies
Polish Review
Quarterly of the Polish Western Association of America

Published Memoirs, Diaries, and Speeches

Acheson, Dean G. *Present at the Creation: My Years in the State Department.* New York: W. W. Norton, 1969.
Adenauer, Konrad. *Memoirs, 1945–1953.* Chicago: Henry Regnery, 1966.
Beam, Jacob D. *Multiple Exposure: An American Ambassador's Unique Perspective on East–West Issues.* New York: W. W. Norton, 1978.
Bohlen, Charles E. *Witness to History, 1929–1969.* New York: W. W. Norton, 1973.
Brzezinski, Zbigniew. *Power and Principle: Memoirs of the National Security Adviser1977–1981.* New York: Farrar, Straus, and Giroux, 1983.
Bush, George, and Scowcroft, Brent. *A World Transformed.* New York: Alfred A. Knopf, 1998.
Byrnes, James F. *All in One Lifetime.* New York: Harper and Brothers, 1958.
———. *Speaking Frankly.* New York: Harper and Brothers, 1947.
Cabot, John M. *First Line of Defense: Forty Years' Experiences of a Career Diplomat.* Washington, DC: Georgetown University Press, School of Foreign Service, n.d.
Churchill, Winston S. *Triumph and Tragedy.* Boston: Houghton Mifflin, 1953.
Clay, Lucius. *Decision in Germany.* Garden City, NY: Doubleday & Co., 1950.
Conant, James B. *My Several Lives: Memoirs of a Social Inventor.* New York: Harper and Row, 1970.
Dulles, John Foster. *War or Peace.* Rev. ed. New York: Macmillan, 1957.
Eisenhower, Dwight D. *Crusade in Europe.* Garden City, NY: Doubleday, 1948.

Gomułka, Wladyslaw. *On the German Problem: Articles and Speeches.* Warsaw: Ksiazka i Wiedza, 1969.

Griffis, Stanton. *Lying in State.* Garden City, NY: Doubleday, 1952.

Hull, Cordell. *The Memoirs of Cordell Hull.* Vols. 1 and 2. New York: Macmillan, 1948.

Johnson, Lyndon B. *The Vantage Point: Perspectives of the Presidency, 1963–1969.* New York: Popular Library, 1971.

Kennan, George F. *Memoirs: 1925–1950.* Boston: Little, Brown, 1967.

———. *Memoirs, 1950–1963.* Boston. Little, Brown, 1972.

Kissinger, Henry. *Years of Upheaval.* Boston: Little, Brown, 1982.

Korbonski, Stefan. *Warsaw in Chains.* New York: Macmillan, 1959.

———. *Warsaw in Exile.* Translated by David J. Welch. New York: Frederick Praeger, 1966.

Lane, Arthur Bliss. *I Saw Poland Betrayed: An American Ambassador Reports to the American People.* Indianapolis: Bobbs-Merrill, 1948.

Leahy, William D. *I Was There: The Personal Story of the Chief of Staff to Presidents Roosevelt and Truman Based on His Notes and Diaries Made at the Time.* New York: Whittlesey House, McGraw-Hill, 1950.

McGhee, George. *At the Creation of a New Germany: From Adenauer to Brandt: An Ambassador's Account.* New Haven, CT: Yale University Press, 1989.

Mikolajczyk, Stanislaw. *The Rape of Poland: Pattern of Soviet Aggression.* New York: McGraw-Hill, 1948.

Murphy, Robert D. *Diplomat among Warriors.* New York: Doubleday, 1964.

Smith, Jean Edward, ed. *The Papers of General Lucius D. Clay: Germany, 1945–1949.* 2 vols. Bloomington: Indiana University Press, 1974.

Smith, Walter Bedell. *My Three Years in Moscow.* Philadelphia: J. B. Lippincott, 1950.

Stettinius, Edward R. *Roosevelt and the Russians: The Yalta Conference.* Edited by Walter Johnson. New York: Doubleday, 1949.

Truman, Harry S. *Memoirs.* 2 vols. Garden City, NY: Doubleday, 1955–1956.

von Brentano, Heinrich. *Germany and Europe: Reflections on German Foreign Policy.* Translated by Edward Fitzgerald. New York: Frederick A. Praeger, 1962.

Zelikow, Philip, and Rice, Condoleezza. *Germany Unified and Europe Transformed: A Study in Statecraft.* Cambridge: Harvard University Press, 1995.

UNPUBLISHED STUDIES

Baretski, Charles Allan. "A Content Analysis of the *Polish American Journal* Newspaper in Reflecting the Political Attitudes, Issues and Perspectives of the Polish-American Group during the Period, 1950–1966." Ph.D. diss., New York University, 1969.

Cable, John N. "The United States and the Polish Question, 1939–1948." Ph.D. diss., Vanderbilt University, 1972.

Conover, Denise O'Neal. "James F. Byrnes, Germany and the Cold War, 1946." Ph.D. diss.,Washington State University, 1978.

Glinka-Janczewski, George H. "American Policy toward Poland under the Truman Administration." Ph.D. diss., Georgetown University, 1965.

Irons, Peter. "America's Cold War Crusade: Politics and Foreign Policy, 1942–1948." Ph.D. diss., Boston University, 1973.

Konczakowski, Edmund F. "Vatican Policy toward the German–Polish Oder–Neisse Line, 1945–1972." Ph.D. diss., University of Pennsylvania, 1976.

Linnes, Erhard. "Antecedents of the Oder–Neisse Frontier and Present Day Attitudes of the Two Germanies and Poland." Master's thesis, American University, 1966.

Polson, Janet F. "Oder–Neisse Line: The Question of Poland's Western Frontier after World War II." Master's thesis, Northeast Missouri State University, 1983.

Rachwald, Arthur Richard. "Foreign Policy of Poland, 1939–1974." Ph.D. diss., University of California at Santa Barbara, 1975.

Sadler, Charles G. "The Expendable Frontier: United States Policy on the Polish–German Frontier during the Second World War." Ph.D. diss., Northwestern University, 1971.

Stein, Barry N. "The Boundaries of Eastern Europe with Emphasis on the Oder–Neisse Boundary." Ph.D. diss., New York University, 1969.

SECONDARY SOURCES

Books

Arski, Stefan. *The New Polish–German Border: Safeguard of Peace.* Washington, DC: Polish Embassy, 1947.

Barber, Joseph, ed. *American Policy toward Germany: A Report on the Views of Community Leaders in Twenty-Two Cities.* New York: Council on Foreign Relations, 1947.

Bloed, Arie, ed. *From Helsinki to Vienna: Basic Documents of the Helsinki Process.* Dordrecht, Netherlands: Martinus Nijhoff, 1990.

Bogacki, Anatole C. J. *A Polish Paradox: International and the National Interest in Polish Communist Foreign Policy1918–1948.* Boulder, CO: East European Monographs, 1991.

Bromke, Adam. *Poland's Politics: Idealism vs. Realism.* Cambridge: Harvard University Press, 1967.

Brzezinski, Zbigniew. *Alternative to Partition: For a Broader Conception of America's Role in Europe.* New York: McGraw-Hill, 1965.

Buehler, Phillip A. *The Oder–Neisse Line: A Reappraisal under International Law*. East European Monographs, no. 277. New York: Columbia University Press, 1990.

Bukowczyk, John. *And My Children Did Not Know Me: A History of the Polish-Americans*. Bloomington: Indiana University Press, 1987.

Bundy, McGeorge. *Danger and Survival: Choices about the Bomb in the First Fifty Years*. New York: Random House, 1988.

Byrnes, Robert F. *The United States and Eastern Europe*. Englewood Cliffs, NJ: Prentice-Hall, 1967.

———. *U.S. Policy toward Eastern Europe and the Soviet Union*. Boulder, CO: Westview Press, 1989.

deZayas, Alfred M. *Nemesis at Potsdam: The Anglo-Americans and the Expulsion of the Germans: Background, Execution, Consequences*. London: Routledge and Kegan Paul, 1977.

Divine, Robert A. *Roosevelt and World War II*. Baltimore: Johns Hopkins University Press, 1969.

Drzewieniecki, Walter M. *The German–Polish Frontier*. Chicago: Polish Western Association of America, 1959.

Feis, Herbert. *Between War And Peace: The Potsdam Conference*. Princeton, NJ: Princeton University Press, 1960.

———. *Churchill, Roosevelt, Stalin: The War They Waged and the Peace They Sought*. Princeton, NJ: Princeton University Press, 1967.

Garrett, Stephen A. *From Potsdam to Poland: American Policy toward Eastern Europe*. New York: Praeger, 1986.

Gatzke, Hans W. *Germany and the United States: A "Special Relationship"?* Cambridge: Harvard University Press, 1980.

Gerson, Louis L. *The Hyphenate in Recent American Politics and Diplomacy*. Lawrence: University of Kansas Press, 1964.

Giertych, Jedrzej. *Poland and Germany: A Reply to Congressman B. Carol Reece of Tennessee*. Southend-on-Sea, England: Nore Press, 1958.

Halecki, Oscar. *A History of Poland*. New York: Barnes and Noble, 1993.

Hanrieder, Wolfram F. *Germany, America, Europe: Forty Years of German Foreign Policy*. New Haven, CT: Yale University Press, 1989.

———. *West German Foreign Policy 1949–1963: International Pressure and Domestic Response*. Stanford, CA: Stanford University Press, 1967.

Hiscocks, Richard. *Poland: Bridge for the Abyss?: An Interpretation of Developments in Post-War Poland*. London: Oxford University Press, 1963.

Hughes, Barry B. *The Domestic Context of American Foreign Policy*. San Francisco: W. H. Freeman, 1978.

Isaacson, Walter, and Thomas, Evan. *The Wise Men: Six Friends and the World They Made: Acheson, Bohlen, Harriman, Kennan, Lovett, McCloy*. New York: Simon and Schuster, 1986.

Johnson, Donald B., comp. *National Party Platforms*. Vol. 1. Urbana: University of Illinois Press, 1978.

Jonas, Manfred. *The United States and Germany: A Diplomatic History*. Ithaca, NY: Cornell University Press, 1987.

Jordan, Zbigniew. *Oder–Neisse Line: A Study of the Political, Economic and European Significance of Poland's Western Frontier*. London: Polish Freedom Movement, 1952.

Keesing's Research Report. *Germany and Eastern Europe since 1945: From the Potsdam Agreement to Chancellor Brandt's "Ostpolitik."* New York: Scribners, 1973.

Kennan, George. *Russia and the West under Lenin and Stalin*. Boston: Little, Brown, 1960.

Kissinger, Henry A. *The Necessity for Choice: Prospects of American Foreign Policy*. Garden City, NY: Anchor Books, Doubleday, 1962.

Klafkowski, Alfons. *The Polish–German Frontier after World War II.*. Translated by Edward Rothert. Poznan: Wydawnictwo Poznanskie, 1972.

———. *The Potsdam Agreement*. Translated by Aleksander Trop-Krynski. Warsaw: Polish Scientific, 1963.

Kokot, Jozef. *The Logic of the Oder–Neisse Frontier*. Translated by Andrzej Potocki. Poznan: Wydawnictwo Zachodnie, 1959.

Korbel, Josef. *Poland between East and West*. Princeton, NJ: Princeton University Press, 1963.

Kovrig, Bennett. *The Myth of Liberation: East-Central Europe in U.S. Diplomacy and Politics since 1941*. Baltimore: Johns Hopkins University Press, 1973.

———. *Of Walls & Bridges: The United States & Eastern Europe*. New York: New York University Press, 1991.

Kruszewski, Z. Anthony. *The Oder–Neisse Boundary and Poland's Modernization: The Socioeconomic and Political Impact*. New York: Praeger, 1972.

Kulski, Wladyslaw W. *DeGaulle and the World: The Foreign Policy of the Fifth French Republic*. Syracuse, NY: Syracuse University Press, 1966.

———. *Germany and Poland: From War to Peaceful Relations*. Syracuse, NY: Syracuse University Press, 1976.

Lachs, Manfred. *The Polish–German Frontier*. 2nd ed. Warsaw: Polish Scientific, 1965.

Levering, Ralph B. *The Public and American Foreign Policy, 1918-1978*. New York: William Morrow, 1978.

Lukas, Richard. *Bitter Legacy: Polish–American Relations in the Wake of World War II*. Lexington: University of Kentucky Press, 1982.

———. *The Strange Allies: The United States and Poland, 1941-1945*. Knoxville: University of Tennessee Press, 1978.

Maresca, John J. *To Helsinki: The Conference on Security and Cooperation in Europe 1973–1975*. Durham, NC: Duke University Press, 1985.

Mastny, Vojtech, ed. *Helsinki, Human Rights, and European Security: Analysis and Documentation.* Durham, NC: Duke University Press, 1986.

———. *Russia's Road to the Cold War: Diplomacy, Warfare, and the Politics of Communism, 1941–1945.* New York: Columbia University Press, 1979.

Morgenthau, Hans J. *The Restoration of American Politics.* Vol 3: *Politics in the Twentieth Century.* Chicago: University of Chicago Press, 1962.

Ninkovich, Frank. *Germany and the United States: The Transformation of the German Question since 1945.* Boston: Twayne, 1988.

Nowak, Margaret Collingwood. *Two Who Were There: A Biography of Stanley Nowak.* Detroit: Wayne State University Press, 1989.

Pogue, Forrest. *George C. Marshall: Statesman 1945–1949.* New York: Penguin Books, 1989.

Pond, Elizabeth. *After the Wall: American Policy toward Germany.* New York: Priority Press, 1990.

Rachwald, Arthur. *Poland Between the Superpowers: Security vs. Economic Recovery.* Boulder, CO: Westview Press, 1983.

Rhode, Gotthold, and Wagner, Wolfgang, eds. and comps. *The Genesis of the Oder–Neisse Line: In the Diplomatic Negotiations during World War II: Sources and Documents.* Stuttgart: Brentano Verlag, 1959.

Roberts, Henry. *Russia and America: Dangers and Prospects.* Foreword by John McCloy. New York: Mentor Books, 1956.

Rozek, Edward J. *Allied Wartime Diplomacy: A Pattern in Poland.* New York: John Wiley and Sons, 1958.

Schwartz, Thomas A. *America's Germany: John J. McCloy and the Federal Republic of Germany.* Cambridge: Harvard University Press, 1991.

Stuart, Graham H. *American Diplomatic and Consular Practice.* 2nd ed. New York: Appleton-Century-Crofts, 1952.

Swiecicki, Marek, and Nowotarska, Rosa. *Gentleman from Michigan.* Translated by Edward Cynarski. London: Polish Cultural Foundation, 1974.

Szaz, Zoltan M. *Germany's Eastern Frontiers: The Problem of the Oder–Neisse Line.* Chicago: Henry Regnery, 1960.

Vitas, Robert A. *The United States and Lithuania: The Stimson Doctrine of Nonrecognition.* New York: Praeger, 1990.

von Wilpert, Friedrich. *The Oder–Neisse Problem: Towards Fair Play in Central Europe.* Bonn: Atlantic Forum, 1964.

Wandycz, Piotr. *The United States and Poland.* Cambridge: Harvard University Press, 1980.

Warburg, James P. *The United States in the Post War World: What We Have Done, What We Have Left Undone, and What We Can and Must Do.* New York: Atheneum, 1966.

Wasserman, Charles. *Europe's Forgotten Territories.* Copenhagen: R. Roussell, 1960.

Watt, Richard M. *Bitter Glory: Poland and its Fate 1918–1939.* New York: Simon and Schuster, 1982.

Wiskemann, Elizabeth. *Germany's Eastern Neighbours: Problems Relating to the Oder–Neisse Line and the Czech Frontier Regions*. London: Oxford University Press, 1956.

Zink, Harold. *The United States in Germany, 1944–1955*. Englewood Cliffs, NJ: Van Nostrand, 1957.

Articles

Bierman, Joseph. "The Neo-Nazi Factor." *Macleans* 103 (19 March 1990): 31–34.

Bregman, Alexander. "Polish–German Relations: A New Phase." *East Europe* 12, no. 11(November 1963): 2–7.

———. Review of *Nachbar Polen* by Hansjakob Stehle. *East Europe* 12, no. 11 (November 1963): 51–52.

Brzezinski, Zbigniew. "United States Foreign Policy in East Central Europe—A Study in Contradictions." *Journal of International Affairs* 11, no. 2 (1957): 60–71.

Brzezinski, Zbigniew and Griffith, William E. "Peaceful Engagement in Eastern Europe." *Foreign Affairs* 39 (July 1961): 642–654.

Byrnes, Robert F. "United States Policy toward Eastern Europe: Before and after Helsinki." *The Review of Politics* 37, no. 4 (October 1975): 435–463.

Drzewieniecki, Walter M. "The American Poles and the Odra–Nysa Frontier." *Polish Western Affairs* 9, no. 1 (1968): 167–175.

Irons, Peter H. "'The Test is Poland:' Polish Americans and the Origins of the Cold War." Polish *American Studies* 30 (Autumn 1973): 5–63.

Kaplan, Stephen S. "United States Aid to Poland, 1957-1964: Concerns, Objectives and Obstacles." *Western Political Quarterly* 28 (March 1975): 147–166.

Kissinger, Henry. "As Urgent as the Moscow Threat." *New York Times Magazine*, 8 March 1959, pp. 19–79.

Pickett, Ralph H. "Germany and the Oder–Neisse Line." *Peace Research Reviews* 2 (1968): 1–109.

Pienkos, Donald E. "The Polish American Congress—An Appraisal." *Polish American Studies* 36, no. 2 (Autumn 1979): 5–43.

Ribuffo, Leo. "Is Poland a Soviet Satellite?" *Diplomatic History* 14, no. 3 (Summer 1990): 385–403.

Rosenthal, Harry K. "The Assimilation and Integration of the German Expellees." *Polish Review* 8 (Winter 1963): 78–111.

St. Mary's College Symposium. "Polish-American Congressmen in Review." *Polish American Studies* 11 (January–June 1964): 23–42.

Stenzl, Otto. "Germany's Eastern Frontiers." *Survey: A Journal of Soviet and East European Studies*, no. 51 (April 1964): 118–130.

Sulek, Jerzy. "The Normalization Agreements of 1970-1972 and European Security." *Polish Western Affairs* 13, no. 2 (1972): 219–244.

Wagner, Stanley P. "The Polish-American Vote in 1960." *Polish American Studies* 11 (January–June 1964): 1–9.

Index

About the Author

DEBRA J. ALLEN is Associate Professor of History at Concordia University, Austin. She has received a Fulbright Scholarship to teach foreign policy in Poland.